*For Les Carlyon: mentor and mate, master of writing
horses and people, man of true grit and grace*

*And in memory of my uncle E.J. 'Squib' Rule,
who ran his hands over the young Phar Lap*

WINX

THE
AUTHORISED BIOGRAPHY

ABOUT ANDREW RULE

Andrew Rule has been a feature writer, investigative journalist and columnist for three daily newspapers, deputy editor of a Melbourne Sunday newspaper and roving correspondent for a national magazine. He is the author of the definitive biography of businessman Kerry Stokes, *The Boy From Nowhere*, and of *Cuckoo*, a non-fiction bestseller about murder and its detection. He is also co-author of the *Underbelly* book series behind the hit television drama. He has won the Gold Walkley, two Graham Perkin Australian Journalist of the Year Awards and the Gold Quill. He is currently an associate editor of Australia's biggest daily, the *Herald Sun*. He grew up around horses in country Victoria and claims to be the only Journalist of the Year to have ridden in a horse race.

WINX

THE
AUTHORISED BIOGRAPHY

ANDREW RULE

ALLEN&UNWIN
SYDNEY•MELBOURNE•AUCKLAND•LONDON

First published in 2018

Copyright © Andrew Rule 2018

Allen & Unwin
83 Alexander Street
Crows Nest NSW 2065
Australia
Phone: (61 2) 8425 0100
Email: info@allenandunwin.com
Web: www.allenandunwin.com

 A catalogue record for this book is available from the National Library of Australia

ISBN 978 1 76063 108 6

Statistics section compiled by Susan Keogh
Index by Puddingburn Publishing Services
Set in 12.75/18.5 pt Adobe Garamond Pro by Midland Typesetters, Australia
Printed and bound in Australia by Griffin Press

10 9 8 7 6 5 4 3 2 1

The paper in this book is FSC® certified. FSC® promotes environmentally responsible, socially beneficial and economically viable management of the world's forests.

Mr Riddle was far prouder of Man o' War than you are of your children, and probably with more reason. But he didn't spend his time feeding sugar to the horse, or drooling over him. He remembered that even if Man o' War was the most magnificent horse ever, he was still a horse, and that his interests lay in hard oats and clean hay and good grooming and a comfortable stall, and that is what he got.

Joe Palmer, *This Was Racing*

Contents

Foreword

It was early Sunday morning, the last day of the Commonwealth Games. I was walking through Broadbeach at about 4.30 am on my way to call the marathon.

Before too long, I encountered a couple of blokes slightly the worse for wear. My first instincts were to cross the road and avoid them—but they were in a jovial, talkative mood.

'Hey, loved your call on Winx yesterday,' said one of them. I was taken aback. I hadn't called the race. I'd been at the Gold Coast stadium between athletics events. On the way to the stadium I'd driven the other commentators mad in the back of the car, worrying about Winx and her performance and imagining I would not be able to see it.

But someone arranged for me to watch the race through a monitor and, as it turned out, my reaction had been recorded on a phone and then posted through social media.

I'd felt that day that something momentous was about to unfold, something historic and life-changing. A mighty mare facing a mighty challenge. It was a stunning field and I had this feeling Winx's long winning streak could come to an end.

It's a feeling I rarely get. I'd felt it with Ali before a couple of his fights—and with Bolt, when he lined up for that third 100 metres in Rio.

It's the best and the worst. The consequences of a win or a loss are significant. They change so much.

Watching that Queen Elizabeth Stakes was both thrilling and frightening. As in so many of Winx's races, there was a furlong where you thought she couldn't win. And then, when she did, everything in the world felt right.

Her rise through the ranks has been one of the most remarkable and enjoyable sporting stories in my lifetime. That first Cox Plate in record time against a star-studded line-up proved that she was top class.

The following autumn, her win in the Doncaster established her as the number-one horse in the country.

Winx became a champion when she won her second Cox Plate. And she was something even greater when she pulverised a champion in her second George Ryder victory. And then, a legend, with that unforgettable, fighting win over Humidor to join Kingston Town as a three-time winner of the championship race of Australia.

We've felt part of her story, learned about her connections: her laidback jockey, her emotional trainer, her thoughtful and excitable owners. The team around Winx has engaged all of us and, as a nation, we've shared a wild ride.

FOREWORD

Comparisons in sport are always subjective. It's an inexact science but I do think she's as good as any horse that has raced in this country. The facts are insurmountable:

Three consecutive springs and three consecutive autumns without a defeat. Twelve out of twelve in the spring and eleven of eleven in the autumn, when the best horses compete and the greatest races are run.

In so many of Winx's now-famous victories, defeat has seemed almost certain at the top of the straight and yet, in others—like that Ryder and the Turnbull and that second Cox Plate—she has just romped away.

As I write this, over a streak of twenty-six wins, she's beaten 153 different horses—53 of them Group One winners. Since the very first of her Group One wins—the Queensland Oaks in May 2015—150 horses have fulfilled every owner's dream by winning at least one Group One race in this country. Of that elite group, a handful have won two or more Group Ones but none has won more than five. Whereas Winx has won *nineteen*, and counting. As we go to print, she seems destined to win more than twenty.

I reckon there are half a dozen landmarks in the history of Australian racing: Phar Lap's fabulous four at Flemington in 1930, Rising Fast's triple crown in 1954, the King's three Cox Plates, the Diva's three Cups, Black Caviar's perfect twenty-five— and now Winx and her collection.

We sit at the start of spring 2018 not knowing whether the unbeaten run will continue and if a fourth Cox Plate is achievable.

Nothing that happens from this moment on will diminish this mare's place in Australian sport. But if there could be one wish for all of those who love racing and this mighty mare, it would be that, like the Diva, the King, Big Red, Tulloch and Black Caviar, her last race is a victory.

Bruce McAvaney

1

2015: THE HINT OF GREATNESS

Late that Saturday, Hugh Bowman vaults onto the patent-leather wafer that passes for a saddle as casually as most of us step into a car. Handles the white reins the way Eddie Charlton chalked a cue. Slides paper-thin boots into alloy stirrup 'irons' that have all the heft of a wedding ring.

Bowman's cool, always is. Looks as if he was born with a slow heartbeat and just enough nerves to stay awake. Doesn't even blink much. Could ride before he could read, a sixth-generation horseman from cattle country. It still shows in little ways: feet full in the irons, hands light and casual, reins long.

He's walking the mare around the yard at Moonee Valley, wondering if he can break into racing history against the best Cox Plate field in years. If you could ask him this minute if he's as confident as the punters lining up to back her, he'd shrug. He knows how much can go wrong.

He has ridden in a Cox Plate before but never got near winning. He's steered this lean young mare he still calls 'the filly' to three wins up north, so he knows she's no pretender. Still, he's been around the track too long to let the buzz about her inflate his opinions or his ego.

Yeah, you can hear him saying in his dry way, she obviously likes Melbourne and she worked a treat here at the Valley on Tuesday. That's why he's on her today, not the Derby winner. But who knows if she can step up again after winning four straight?

He doesn't have to point out that the odds against preserving a winning streak lengthen with every race. That's why the thing punters call a picket fence, a '1' for every win, is so rare in form guides. She's been a gun filly against her own age—but she ran into stronger ones a couple of times.

Horses that keep winning are like gamblers who always throw heads or land on black: about as common as the Tasmanian tiger.

Besides, even the best three-year-old fillies rarely bridge the gulf between beating their own age group and beating open company at weight for age. She won the Theo Marks and the Epsom but they're handicaps, not championships.

Glen Boss, the acrobat who rode Makybe Diva to win three Melbourne Cups, might be getting past his best in the saddle but his judgement is sharp. Boss has told reporters the field is four lengths better than the one the Irish horse Adelaide beat the previous season.

'And not just one horse is four lengths better—there are about eight of them,' says Boss. The winner has to be something special.

None of this stops a trickle of money turning into a stream that makes Bowman's mare favourite by race time. One of her owners doesn't mind a bet. Some punters might be following his lead; others must have been dazzled by the way she galloped on Tuesday morning.

Chris Waller's stable isn't known as a betting outfit and the trainer's growing confidence in their lightly built mare's ability hasn't been trumpeted. Then again, it hasn't been hidden to protect the odds, either. Her form is as transparent as anything is in racing. It's excellent as far as it goes, but is it enough to take on this lot?

Now the clock's ticking past 5.30 pm and the time for talking is gone. The horses stalk and fidget around the mounting yard, waiting for the call to go out on the track. Nothing else matters except what's going to happen in ten minutes.

The Valley has been called a velodrome, a cauldron and a cockpit and you see why on Cox Plate day, when the stands are full of people and pent-up expectation. There are no gentle curves and generous straights in the glorified paddock that William Cox gave to the club in 1883: it's the blunt shape of a boxing ring, a square with rounded corners, and the crowd has a ringside seat right down one side, from the 2040-metre start past the post to the first turn. The straight is 100 metres shorter than the picnic racetrack at Hanging Rock and is surely the shortest in top-class racing anywhere.

Once horses and riders file down the tunnel under the grandstand to face the crowd and their destiny, there is nowhere to hide. There's a gladiatorial atmosphere, a whiff of the bullring.

The mare's star is rising after her four straight wins. But the experts, number crunchers who weigh facts and figures, dismiss hopeful talk as wishful thinking. She's in with the big boys today: the only mare in a field of the dominant males of their generation, mostly older and heavier and stronger than she is. Under the weight-for-age scale, age and gender are theoretically allowed for. But she still looks like a kid playing in the firsts.

Except for a trio of other four-year-olds, the field is aged five or older, some future stallions among them, with a sprinkling of tough old geldings. The other four-year-old that's heavily fancied, Highland Reel, is a last-start Group One winner in the United States. His Irish owners have flown him across the world for this, plotting back-to-back wins for their Coolmore racing empire.

These are the Irish hardheads who have matched wits and wallets with the Arab sheikhs who breed or buy the most expensive horseflesh in the world. In a game that runs on compulsive loss making, the Irish horse traders are mostly winners.

As the runners peel off in racebook order out of the tiny yard tucked beside the stand, the scion of the Magnier family, Tom, strides around the committee room upstairs with pockets full of banknotes and a heart full of hope, shoulders squared and eyes gleaming. He's eager for battle and no wonder.

It was Magnier's crew that landed the previous Cox Plate with Adelaide, sired by the same world-beating stallion as Highland Reel, ridden by the same world-beating jockey in Ryan Moore, trained by the same world-beating trainer, Aidan O'Brien. Despite the name, Adelaide was neither South Australian nor a mare.

He was the first European horse to win this great southern race, and his owners are thinking Highland Reel is better still.

Francesca Cumani, playing the English rose for Network Seven's wall-to-wall coverage, is doing a piece to camera that disarmingly dismisses the colonials. The European horses are the ones to beat 'because dare I say it, they could be just a bit better than the locals,' she says with a dazzling princess smile.

Not that Cumani thinks it's a laydown misère for Highland Reel.

'My head says Arod,' she gushes, talking up the Qatari royal family's entry trained by Englishman Peter Chapple-Hyam. 'But my heart says Gailo Chop.' This is a reference to the fact she has a share in the long-striding campaigner from France, sought out and brought over by staying stalwarts Terry Henderson and Simon O'Donnell and friends.

For Bowman, Highland Reel is the one to beat but not the only one to worry about. As he canters the mare down the sawn-off straight to the start of the weight-for-age championship of the southern hemisphere, he isn't planning any victory speeches. Just 'minding my own business', he drily recalls much later. He's hoping the mare isn't spooked by the crowd, which is fired up by five hours of drinking and five minutes of bellowing the Cox Plate anthem 'The Horses' along with hardy annual Daryl Braithwaite. She's as sensible as anything he's ever ridden but liquored-up Cox Plate crowds would try the patience of a plodding police horse.

Bowman is wondering who and what he's going to have to watch in the run. Highland Reel is a freewheeling 'on-pacer' who will sit on the leaders' heels then let rip when Ryan Moore pulls the trigger. He might be as good on turf as any young horse in the world. Moore is a fly-in, fly-out specialist and consistently brilliant on any course in any country, unlike the luckless and sometimes feckless Frankie Dettori, whose Australian form is erratic.

There's the pair of bright chestnuts: not just Francesca's favourite Frenchman Gailo Chop, under local rider Brad Rawiller, but also the smashing Criterion, trained by the resurgent Hayes stable at its huge new base at Euroa. Criterion's pilot is Michael Walker, a pig-shooting tattoo enthusiast once hailed as the best Kiwi apprentice since the child prodigy Brent 'The Babe' Thomson, the cherub who won a Cox Plate before he could vote and three more by his twenty-first birthday.

Bowman can't dismiss the mare's stablemates, Preferment and Kermadec, stallions-in-the-making being moulded by master-trainer-in-the-making Chris Waller. Neither would be here if they had no chance. Especially Preferment, something Bowman knows only too well. It's in the back of his mind.

No one outside the stable knows how much Bowman has tossed up whether to choose Preferment, winning Derby colt and last-start Turnbull Stakes winner, ahead of the improving but enigmatic mare. It was a dilemma because Preferment had won narrowly against the best around while the mare had been lethal against weaker company.

Bowman guessed that Preferment the stayer 'would just get there or just miss', whereas the mare 'if she's up to that level she could win by four'.

Two days before, Bowman told a reporter that Preferment could win if the race was run to suit him but that he chose the mare because 'she's got a really electric turn of foot and Preferment doesn't'.

And he added a description with a catchy ring to it: 'She's going to have that X factor—that if she needs a bit of speed at some stage, she's got it.'

If Preferment wins, the connections have a ready-made stallion, a money tree to underwrite their racing interests for years. But if the mare wins, they have one of the best young females on the planet, no argument. No wonder the extended Tighe and Kepitis families have gathered in a knot at the centre of the mounting yard to savour having two runners. The Treweekes are content with an interest in the mare only.

Bowman is happy he's drawn the inside alley, next to the old Tasmanian galloper The Cleaner, a cult horse because he was cheap and he's tough, a headstrong 'miler' with battler owners and a battler trainer, Mick Burles. Mick and his horse are blue-collar heroes among the toffs and multimillionaires, not least because Mick has only half a lung and survives a hard life mostly on a mixture of cigarettes and bottled oxygen.

The Cleaner is the Happy Gilmore of Group racing: what he lacks in pedigree, stamina and tactical finesse, he makes up for with speed and attitude. He hits the ground running, rushes to the front and keeps going as long as he can, like a show-off kid swimming underwater holding his breath. He doesn't know much else. Riding him is journeyman jockey Noel 'King' Callow, a hard case who might have followed the rodeo circuit or wrestled crocodiles if he'd been too heavy for the jockey business.

Every betting outlet in Tasmania is fielding sentimental bets from twice-a-year punters praying the old tearaway will pull off a miracle and pinch the race from the mainlanders and foreigners. They're punting on Steven Bradbury luck. If six better horses get in a scrimmage, The Cleaner just might polish them off. Such things have happened at the velodrome.

The odd couple from Tassie might be racing's best battler yarn since a taxi-driver named Joe Janiak and a $1250 reject named Takeover Target took their double act around the world a decade earlier. Bowman doesn't care about that. He just knows the old horse is fast and bold and will blister the paint on the rails until he hits the wall somewhere in the straight. The trick is to guess when and where and dodge the backwash when the brake lights go on.

One thing Bowman has up his sleeve is how well the mare has settled into Melbourne: the wide, open spaces of Flemington seem to suit her loner personality better than the ants' nest of her home track at Rosehill.

The other good thing is that she likes leading on her 'Melbourne leg'. A lot of horses don't mind which direction they gallop—clockwise in New South Wales, anti-clockwise in Victoria—but Bowman reckons those that *do* show a preference tend to favour the Melbourne way. The gun filly from the north might go even better south of the Murray.

As long as she jumps 'almost on terms' he'll be happy. Missing 'the kick' by half a length doesn't matter much to her, because she settles off the pace. Any further back than that could be bad news. Bowman wants to be forward enough to keep an eye on Highland Reel. He can't be giving world-class gallopers too much start.

Thirteen horses are drawn outside the mare. Among them will be the dominant male of the 'herd'. Dominance is not always obvious to humans but it is to horses, which can be intimidated by it. But the male pecking order is of little consequence to a mare not in season and this mare isn't. Besides, she is an independent and aloof animal not afraid to leave the herd behind, a useful mental quality in a racehorse already blessed with rare physical attributes.

The line-up is orderly, even if the crowd isn't after a long afternoon at the bar. She stands quietly in her stall, the deep blue colours with the white M, epaulettes and pompom easy to see. The white bridle Waller always uses on race days stands out against her dark bay hide.

Highland Reel is three stalls over, drawn perfectly in number four. Criterion is in barrier seven. He looks the dominant male here.

The gates crash open, the crowd roars, and the mare jumps maybe as well as she ever has, before or since.

Bowman, automatically on the rail, lets her drop back a little as Highland Reel slots behind The Cleaner in the fast lane. The Irish horse comes on smoothly, perfectly placed by the imperturbable Englishman, Ryan Moore. But Criterion misses the start just enough that Walker has to settle him behind the mare. Walker, like Bowman this day, is not afraid of the rails.

The mare's galloping action is as effortlessly efficient as it looked at trackwork the previous Tuesday, the beat of her hoofs and the bob of her head as even as a pendulum as she skims the turf with nose tucked down, not flailing at the ground or reefing at the bit. She ignores other horses, which means Bowman can place her exactly where he wants to, fifth on the rails.

A race can turn into a chess game in a split-second, with jockeys switching moves instinctively to counter changing tactics around them. But, for Bowman, this one turns out as simple as a game of dominoes.

As the field streams past the mile crossing down the Dean Street side, Bowman watches Moore ease Highland Reel away from the rails. It's a reflex move ingrained in European jockeys for fear of being trapped on the fence behind tired horses.

But Bowman sees opportunity in Moore's caution. Highland Reel's move gives Bowman five lengths of clear air on the rail behind The Cleaner. He knows the pride of Tasmania can't keep up this pace indefinitely but still has petrol in the tank for a while yet. Besides, Australian jockeys tend to ride 'tighter' than their overseas counterparts and are often willing to back themselves to thread their way through a field or along the rail to save ground.

'At about the 800 metres I was just minding my own business when Ryan moved out again,' Bowman will recall. 'I wasn't in a position to follow him. I had to go inside or wait. She was a pretty small filly at that stage; I expected her to go well but not to explode the way she did.'

He is reluctant to use up his 'filly' by going wide enough to get around the Irish horse as Moore takes aim at the leaders. That's starting to look like the only option when the unexpected happens.

Bowman is waiting for The Cleaner to hit the wall but the old-timer doesn't hit it—he runs away from it, swerving from the fence as if he's seen a tiger snake.

Whatever the reason, The Cleaner's exit to the right leaves a gap on the fence just as Bowman starts angling out ready to chase Highland Reel.

It all happens faster than it takes to read these words. Bowman knows the gap is a gift from the gods and instantly switches back towards the fence just as Walker on Criterion, trailing him, starts his run on the rail. In diving back towards the gap, Bowman jams Criterion, perhaps the only horse in the field capable of making a race of it. Criterion is the dominant male all right: he dominates every male horse in the finish as they chase the dominant female.

Conventional racetrack wisdom says Bowman should wait longer but instinct trumps wisdom. Instinct says steal the gap before it closes—then keep going. So he pulls the pin from the grenade with the little signals she knows well: shakes the reins, clicks, squeezes her with his heels. What happens next surprises even him.

'When The Cleaner rolled off the fence she just exploded,' he recalls of that moment, the wonder not dimmed by more than two years and much retelling. 'She put the race to sleep in three strides. It was like a fairy tale. A star was born that day.'

She wins the 2015 Cox Plate by nearly five lengths, running away. The performance makes her name.

Winx: a win with X factor.

•

Three years and twenty-one more straight wins and $15 million in stakes later, ask Bowman which of her races stand out for him and he still looks back to that first Cox Plate.

He sensed before she passed the post that no matter how many years he rides, how many hundreds more wins he tallies, he'll ride only one winner as great as Winx. Her subsequent wins prove to the world what was already revealed to him halfway down the Moonee Valley straight.

No secret is as close as that between rider and horse, the saying goes. Any casual watcher can tell she has won by nearly five lengths and broken Might And Power's seventeen-year-old race and track record. But only Bowman knows how nonchalantly she does it.

Stopwatches tell time but they don't tell the story. The story is that this good filly of the previous season has turned into something else, like bronze into platinum.

She jogs back to scale as calmly as a drover's horse, showing little sign of exertion, let alone exhaustion. Stopwatches can't tell you that, either.

Bowman, the horseman's horseman, normally as dry as a drought, fights tears when Seven's mounted reporter Sam Hyland sidles up waving a radio microphone for the obligatory interview. Winx is as unfussed as Hyland's hack but the emotion of it mugs Bowman in a way it rarely does again.

'All I wanted to be when I was a little boy was to be a jockey,' he begins, voice quavering. 'To be here riding on this stage is one thing. But to win a race like this, I can't tell you how much it means.'

A touching moment, the more so looking back, because in the next three years and all those wins, he doesn't lower his guard so much again. One reason for his later composure, maybe, is that nothing Winx does afterwards actually surprises him as much as this has.

Watching the scene then and reflecting on it later, you might be struck by how much taller Winx is than Hyland's porky pony shuffling beside her—but also how much narrower.

Bowman jogs her down the grandstand side to salute the ecstatic crowd. Crowds know things. This one knows it's not one of those Cox Plates where a horse got lucky on the day.

Winx is escorted by a clerk of the course, Shane Patterson, the man in red on his regulation grey. He is a saddler and horse breaker of note and possibly the most pokerfaced person on a racecourse since his father John, known throughout racing simply as 'Patto', not long retired as Melbourne's senior clerk of the course. Shane's face suggests something special has happened. Freeze frame the scene and you can see it: he nearly smiles.

Waiting back at the winner's stall, Peter Tighe looks mighty pleased and slightly dazed to see his Magic Bloodstock colours sail past the post. The laconic Queenslander is happy to back his trainer's judgement in the sales ring and his own in the betting ring. But he's not one to make a fuss.

Debbie Kepitis, suddenly the most public face of Sydney's Ingham dynasty, bubbles with quotable quotes—the start of a lasting relationship with the media, eager for a new star to replace Black Caviar's football team of connections and, before that, Makybe Diva's mulleted fishing millionaire Tony Santic. Debbie is wearing the black and blue silk outfit with a dash of 'good luck' purple in her hair that is to become the signature look of Winx's winning streak.

The owner who named Winx, Richard Treweeke, in his eighties, has watched the race on television in Sydney but his family and various relatives and friends are there, the nucleus of a clan gathering that gets so much bigger that by 2017 they virtually have their own marquee.

Waller, known for showing emotion at big moments, this time almost holds it in check. Asked the compulsory question— 'What makes Winx so special?'—he answers with a grin: 'She's fast. She just won a Cox Plate.' Then he takes pity on the questioner, puts on his game face and serves a version of the all-purpose answer to any question about any winner: 'She's just a superior athlete.'

Sports writers from around the nation look for angles to tell the story of the new heroine to the vast but temporary audience outside racing's bubble of insiders.

The Australian's magisterial columnist Patrick Smith, sportsman turned horse owner, makes his finding: technically, Bowman went too early but thank God for that.

'If Bowman had a doubt about Winx it was the distance of the Cox Plate,' Smith writes. 'Well, not so much the distance as the speed at which his mare would be asked to run it. Winx had already run the Queensland Oaks over 2200 metres. But this Cox Plate was being run at record speed. Nonetheless, Bowman's instincts take over.'

Elsewhere in the elbow-to-elbow Press Room, Richard Hinds is tapping out a story that compares Bowman with David Copperfield—the magician, not the Dickens character.

'She appeared in a puff of smoke suddenly, incredibly, lengths clear and bursting unchallenged to the line,' Hinds writes for the *Daily Telegraph*.

'Now you don't see her, now you can't catch her. The field was not only left beaten 500 metres from home but left wondering if Bowman also had their wallets and Rolexes in his saddle bags, too.'

A great trick, Hinds writes, but Hughie Copperfield couldn't do it without a magical horse beneath him: 'A horse that can make a field disappear.'

Losing jockeys usually just mumble a cliché to state the obvious but, after unsaddling the outclassed Fawkner, the battle-hardened Damien Oliver nailed the day's main event in seven crisp words.

'The winner was in a different hemisphere.'

•

Once the presentations end, the new princess of racing goes back to being just another horse. Race gear and trophy rug off, head collar and lead on, hosed down and dried off the way racehorses are everywhere, the only difference now being that some awed onlookers gather to watch.

For the staff, having an audience for mundane race-day chores is the beginning of things to come.

She's led back to stall forty-six to wait for the float to take her back to Waller's Flemington stables and the comfortable routine of feeding and grooming.

Stripped and standing still, she doesn't radiate the charisma or physique the public might associate with a 'champion'. This is not So You Think, Hollywood handsome with foppish forelock and dished face, as well as a wonderful galloper. It's not the intimidating Octagonal, the warhorse who won the Cox Plate for Debbie Kepitis's father Bob and uncle Jack, the famous Ingham brothers, exactly twenty years earlier. Not Saintly, imposing example of a thoroughbred powerhouse and instantly recognisable even years after retirement.

Winx at four years old is well disguised as just another leggy mare, unfinished and unfurnished, a plain bay that wouldn't stand out in a mob of breedy horses in any paddock anywhere. Which is nothing against her. The extraordinary Northerly looked so ordinary that his trainer Fred Kersley got 'stuck' with him when he lost the toss for the choice between two untried youngsters. Kersley tells the story of how the 'good sort' he wanted was flat out trying to win a maiden.

Stall forty-six faces west, into the afternoon sun, unlike the shady corner facing east that she gets as a celebrity drawcard on subsequent Cox Plate appearances. She is next to a big gelding, Strawberry Boy, which Waller trains for John Singleton.

Winx is maybe only half a hand shorter than Strawberry Boy but could fit inside him. Her belly runs up sharply to slender flanks tucked in front of deep but still lightly muscled hindquarters. She looks like a greyhound next to a mastiff.

Something about her seems familiar—not as a horse but as an athlete, to use Waller's description of her down at the winner's stall a little earlier.

Back in 1991, I'd gone to the launch of a book about the world champion fighter Lionel Rose at his trainer Jack Rennie's old boxing gym in Essendon. A girl turned up there, shy and quiet, with her three-in-one boyfriend, coach and manager, a sometime athletics writer who knew more about athletes than about writing. She was from country Queensland and the boyfriend of many parts was confident she was a very promising runner. It wasn't easy to see the reason for his confidence as she mooched around. She was shy and diffident and whippet thin, almost scrawny.

What you couldn't see in that lean, immature body hidden inside the loose tracksuit were qualities that were invisible anyway: the balance, the reflexes, the muscle twitch, the unique geometry of bone and sinew and the heart and lung capacity that makes one athlete faster than another over a set distance. And the capacity to endure pain, of course: the thing we call bravery. It was all in there but you didn't know that until you saw her run.

The boyfriend-coach-manager had seen her run. He knew.

The skinny kid's name was Cathy Freeman, just turned eighteen. That's who Winx reminds me of the day she wins her first Cox Plate.

I look at her after the race and wonder: how good will you be when you grow up?

A question her trainer had asked himself for months. And he wasn't the only one.

That evening Hugh Bowman sent a message to an older jockey in Brisbane, one who'd helped him when he was an apprentice kid from the bush.

You were right, he texted. *Winx is a freak.*

2

THE STAND-IN

The man who got the text from Hugh Bowman is one of professional sport's great survivors. His name is Larry Cassidy. Everyone in racing knows Cassidy in his own right as a top-class jockey. To the wider sporting world he is the younger brother of Jimmy 'The Pumper' Cassidy, who first tasted fame by winning the 1983 Melbourne Cup with a last-to-first ride on Kiwi.

If the Cassidy brothers had been policemen instead of jockeys, extremely unlikely given their size, Larry could easily have played good cop to Jimmy's bad. Whereas J. Cassidy veered from highs—he won more than 100 Group One races—to extreme lows, such as being banned for three years, L. Cassidy was by comparison a model of decorum. Not for him brazenly running around with scallywags the stewards did not approve of. Jimmy won more headlines, more Group One races and more prize money, but Larry won more races overall.

His evergreen career in New Zealand and Australia, with seasons in Singapore and Macau, has seen off most jockeys of his era.

Larry won his first race in 1986 as a teenager in New Zealand and since then has landed more than 2000 winners in about 15,000 races over three decades. He has ridden generations of horses for two generations of trainers. At the time of writing, he still is. His age is still a smaller number than his riding weight in kilograms, but the gap is closing.

In Australia, people in racing's closed society are often connected. In New Zealand, especially when the Cassidy brothers were growing up in the 1970s, the local racing scene was more like an extended family than an industry. Nearly everyone in it was tied by blood or marriage or deep neighbourhood loyalties, a clannishness that survived time and distance.

Larry, the conscientious Cassidy, was apprenticed at Awapuni in Chris Waller's home district—and served the last year of his apprenticeship with Bruce Marsh, who had been apprenticed to Chris's great-uncle J.J. Waller.

Jimmy, the colourful Cassidy, rode for Noel Eales, the revered horseman who trained for Chris Waller's grandfather and so gave young Waller his first exposure to a professional racing stable.

So both Cassidy brothers, older than Waller, were admired as local gun jockeys when he was growing up in the 1980s. He saw them reach the top of their profession, first at home then across the Tasman, and when he followed them to Australia he never forgot the hometown link.

Even before Waller moved to Sydney permanently, when he campaigned a horse in Australia he often called on one Cassidy or the other, especially on Larry; he attracted less heat from stewards who frowned on Jimmy's choice of associates, riding tactics and anti-authority streak.

The connection dimmed a little when Larry rode overseas, first in Singapore, then in Macau, and Waller used more of Darren Beadman and other leading riders. But even after Larry moved to Brisbane, where he has held his own for the last two decades, the rising trainer would book him when he could.

Waller would also sometimes call on Jimmy's experience in Sydney. One morning in May 2014, he got the veteran to ride a green two-year-old filly in a barrier trial at Warwick Farm. Waller horses are not pushed out in barrier trials. Jimmy let this one finish fifth of nine. He liked the way the tall bay filly went but didn't get the ride when she started the following month.

Jason Collett, Waller's former apprentice, got the first two race rides on Winx, for two wins, before he 'got off' her in favour of another two-year-old. That's why Hugh Bowman took the next ride, her first win in a busy three-year-old year. She would have ten starts as a three-year-old for four wins, and be ridden by five jockeys. Larry Cassidy got his turn in May 2015.

Waller called to ask Larry to ride the filly after she was beaten in the Australian Oaks with the Brazilian whiz Joao Moreira in the saddle. Whether Waller blamed the distance of the Oaks (the classic 2400 metres) or the Brazilian's bravura is something he kept to himself, although he never publicly laid any blame on a ride that riled punters.

He was never afraid to travel a horse to where he thought it could win, and he was heading north looking for an easy kill for Winx in the Sunshine Coast Guineas on 16 May. But Hugh Bowman wouldn't be riding her because Waller had several horses running in Sydney and wanted his regular number-one rider on them.

Would Larry stand in?

Of course he would. It was like old times back when Waller had called him first most weeks. Later, Cassidy realised there were other old connections linking him and his 'pick-up ride'.

The astonishing thing is not what jockeys forget but how much they remember about the thousands of horses they see and ride.

One of Cassidy's 2000-odd winners was a horse named Al Akbar he'd ridden in the mid-1990s. He recalls 'quite a nice, big, strong horse', a handsome, well-muscled sprinting type. He remembers riding him 'two or three times' and winning 'a Canterbury Stakes against Big Dreams'.

That was on 5 March 1994. Al Akbar beat Big Dreams for the then sizeable stake of $80,000, highlight of a middling career for an honest horse with an unfashionable pedigree. But for horses as well as people, it pays to be nice.

Because Al Akbar was a 'genuine' racehorse and tried bravely in every race, and a good type with a lovely nature, he got lucky. When he finished his career on the track—with eight wins but rarely further back than fifth—he was still an 'entire', the formal term for an ungelded horse.

Instead of being sold off cheaply to face (at best) being gelded as a hack, he went to stud back in New Zealand. He was what racing people call a 'bread and butter' stallion, first with one stud then another, at a modest fee. He ended up in relative obscurity but it was a good life while it lasted—which, as we shall see, is a story in itself.

The best filly Al Akbar sired (there weren't many) ended her racing days with a win in Australia after early success in New Zealand. This move was a shrewd gambit by her owners because it set her up to be sold very profitably as a broodmare. Her second foal was the leggy filly that went to Chris Waller to train and was later named Winx. Which meant that when Waller booked Larry Cassidy to ride her on the Sunshine Coast, it had gone full circle: the veteran jockey would be riding the granddaughter of the handy sprinter he had ridden in Sydney twenty-one years earlier.

There was, Cassidy says, 'no real resemblance' between the middle-distance filly and her forebear Al Akbar. 'She was tall and gangly,' he recalls. She was also in a different class, until then something not totally obvious to those who'd seen her beaten the previous month in the Oaks by a filly that hadn't set the world on fire.

Waller might well have concluded that the 'classic' distance (2400 metres being the metric version of the traditional mile-and-a-half) suited dyed-in-the-wool stayers better than it suited Winx. The Sunshine Coast Guineas was Group Three and worth a relatively humble $125,000. It was run over 1600 metres, a specialist distance demanding too much brilliance for dour stayers but still at least 200 or 300 metres too far for pure sprinters. Like elite human 400-metre runners, thoroughbred 'milers' have to be able to sustain high speed then quicken at the line.

It is more conventional in a horse's preparation to step up in distance with each race than to drop back so far—from 2400 to 1600 metres—but clearly enough punters thought she'd adjust to the faster tempo because she started favourite despite a wide barrier draw.

Cassidy does his homework and studies replays of her previous runs to know what to expect. But when he sees the filly in the flesh at the track at Caloundra, his first thought is, 'You're going to be nice in twelve months.'

He is prepared for her to drop back after starting from 'the car park'—but not quite as far as she does. At the 800-metre mark he is one horse width off the fence and giving the leaders fifteen lengths start. At the 600 metres, he recalls, 'horses were pulling out in front of me and taking off four or five wide'.

He is worried she won't handle a 'gut-buster' because it has been five weeks since her last run, and resigns himself to nursing her into a place, at best.

'I thought I'd wait as long as I could and then she'll probably run home and run a nice third or fourth or fifth. I angled her to the outside as we straightened [for the run home] and within four or five strides it was like she changed gear. They were probably twelve lengths in front but I knew I had them beaten.'

At that moment, of course, no one else knows. The caller has made a pointed reference to her—dutifully informing punters how badly the favourite is placed—before concentrating on calling the business end of the race, a long way ahead of the white bridle and blue colours.

'Winx is last—she'll have to come past the seventeen of them,' he says in the tone of a man who has done his money, then sweeps his binoculars forward to the leaders on the rails. He's so engrossed in the unfolding battle for the lead he loses sight of Winx as she rounds the field and comes down the middle of the track.

The crowd—and television viewers elsewhere—are like the audience at a pantomime: they can see the 'villain' coming before the other players can. The ones who helped make her favourite must have been yelling by then, before the call catches up with what they're watching.

For a few long seconds, the caller is calling one race, between horses in the leading bunch, while another unfolds just outside the crosshairs of his binoculars. Out there, very wide and still well back, Winx has settled into that deadly efficient stride that will become her trademark, and is forging past horse after horse.

The caller doesn't glimpse her until the field passes the 100-metre mark. At the fifty-metre mark she still has horses ahead of her but now she has his absolute attention. He knows she is going to get there because she is running past them so swiftly. She looks not so much a different class as a different species, like a kelpie heading a mob of sheep.

His voice leaps, finds an even more urgent pitch.

Winx! he yells as she flashes over the line almost two lengths in front.

She's come from last. She's stormed down the outside. Oh, what a win!

It is, in its way, as stirring as when Larry's brother Jimmy stormed down the Flemington straight and into history on Kiwi thirty-two years earlier. The Melbourne Cup was on a much bigger stage with much more at stake and witnessed by a huge audience, but a winner can only beat the horses it's racing on the day: Winx's superiority at Caloundra is as breathtaking as Kiwi's at Flemington.

Doubters could say it's only the Sunshine Coast and only three-year-olds and only Group Three. But the man on her back is in no doubt about what has just happened.

Cassidy won six races on Sunline in 1998 and 1999, including the Doncaster, the Flight Stakes and the Warwick Stakes, before Greg Childs took over as her regular rider. Sunline was a champion, a freakish mare who dominated her era. For the next seventeen years, Cassidy had happily declared Sunline the best horse he'd ridden and no one argued. In fact, he retired the saddle he'd used on Sunline and had it mounted and framed, the only time he'd done that in his career.

But now Cassidy had the unsettling feeling that lightning had struck twice: he'd ridden one even better. He had felt an extra dimension to Winx, he said later. He had known, even as she was picking up the stragglers after the turn, a dozen horses strung out in front, that she would accelerate and keep accelerating and make the almost impossible look almost easy.

It has become a signature story and he tells it well. On the way home, as he does after every race meeting, he called his wife Michelle to run through the day's events, a reassuring routine in a profession that requires an ambulance to follow its practitioners.

'I rang my wife and said: "She could be the best horse I have ever ridden."

'She said "Really?" and we started rattling off horses like Sunline, Golden Sword, Secret Savings and Not A Single Doubt, which went through my mind. But I said I had never had a horse accelerate like that . . . ever.

'It is an incredible feeling, one every jockey craves for. To put it into perspective, I was probably fifteen lengths off them when I came to the outside. I thought, "I'm in trouble here . . . I probably can't win but I won't panic."

'Yet when I pushed the button, still ten to twelve lengths off them, I knew I was going to win.

'It was like being in a Ferrari in third gear, just idling, then pumping it. The thing that struck me was the acceleration.'

The Sunshine Coast Guineas was a lead-up to the Queensland Oaks. Because Eagle Farm racecourse was under repair, the Oaks was switched to Doomben that season, and pared back to 2200 metres due to the shape of the track. Shortening the race made it just that bit more suitable for the filly, Waller calculated. In any event, she would never start over 2400 metres again.

Cassidy knew his was a once-only guest appearance. Hugh Bowman would be back in the saddle for the Queensland Oaks. Cassidy spoke to Bowman by telephone and said, 'She could be the best horse I have ridden.'

Bowman couldn't help being surprised. 'What about Sunline?' he asked.

Cassidy said, 'I know, but horses just can't win like that.'

He started off her remarkable winning streak and predicted great things, but Cassidy is the first to admit he couldn't have imagined she'd never be beaten again.

No one could. Not the owners. Not Hugh Bowman. And not even Chris Waller.

3

THE FARM BOYS

When the phone wakes you at 2.58 am, usually it's not good news. Unless you're in Wallerland. Then it's normal.

Chris Waller sets his phone alarm to wake him at precisely that time six days a week. Those two minutes before the hour matter. They mean he can be at his stables at Rosehill racecourse no later than 3.30 am, maybe a minute earlier if every traffic light from Baulkham Hills is green so the Benz can purr through the intersections bang on the speed limit. That way he is there when his staff is due to start work.

If anyone arrives early, he knows. If anyone is running late, he knows. If any horses seem out of sorts, he knows.

Most of all, perhaps, the boss's punctuality sends a consistent message to his staff: *I start when you do and don't expect any of you to work harder than I do.* It's as much about mutual respect and a shared approach to the enterprise as about supervision and management. Waller says 'we' and 'our' more often than he says 'I' and 'my'.

He strides around block after stable block, not looking for anything in particular until he sees it. Some detail left undone, or that has come undone overnight, he makes sure to have fixed right away. A horse leaving a little feed uneaten or with its rug askew or a fresh scratch. Even a horse looking 'unhappy'. Does it need more hay because a particular high-protein feed isn't suiting it? Is it sore or jaded from galloping? Is it a sign it needs time in the paddock away from the pressure so it can mature a little more?

Hospitals should be run this well. Not many are.

On the walls of the office are lists to show new staff exactly how to groom a horse. Meaning how Waller wants his horses groomed, all worked out to give the animal the maximum benefit in the time available.

Taped to the door of this or that loosebox is a piece of paper printed clearly in large type with a can't-be-missed message about some gear or feed requirement: BELL BOOTS EVERY DAY or HEAT PACK BEFORE WORK or HAY X 2.

Posting bold notes to doors to make sure things are done right the first time won't surprise those who have watched Waller's rise and rise to the top of Australasian racing. He has form. He was the earnest teenager who produced a notebook and pen and took notes on his first week in a professional racing stable.

Waller believes there is a right way and a wrong way to do everything and is more determined than most of us to do something about it. Whether this unswerving belief in a systematic approach is a product of nature or nurture is an even-money proposition. On his own evidence, he's like the horses he prepares: both bred and trained for the job.

Chris's father, John Waller, was a dairy farmer (now retired) who did things his own way and did them well. On the farm, his son says, John was a good all-round stockman and strict about hygiene in the milking shed and keeping his herd disease-free. So were his father Colin Waller and Colin's father before that: they were farmers and horsemen rather than gamblers looking for winners.

Waller combines a capacity for work with a propensity to think up ways of doing it more efficiently. If he hadn't gone in for racehorses, he would have made an excellent time and motion expert. In a sense, of course, that's what he is, but his factories are full of horses, not machines.

So after the Cox Plate, when he was asked by one of the chorus line of interviewers to describe Winx's future, Waller didn't need think music.

'A pretty good one,' he said instantly. He was smiling but it wasn't exactly a wisecrack. Winx's future was something Waller had started to ponder and plan since her winning streak had begun five months before.

Winning the Cox Plate meant she would be aimed at elite races, but nothing else about her program would change much because things are done in accordance with the Waller system. He would rarely drop everything and scramble to draw up new plans overnight because a horse turns out better than expected or not as good as hoped. Whether it is Winx or any of the other

200 on the books, every horse has to have its basic needs met in the most efficient and effective way.

It's what he does best, manipulating the endless moving parts of a three-state enterprise, a giant Rubik's cube in which any wrong move can be costly if not a calamity.

For a young man in a hurry to fill the unforgiving minute, Waller makes time so the horses are *not* hurried. He's a perfectionist who does everything to a tight timetable but the young horses in his care get all the time they need. Like all serious trainers, he is constantly sorting swans from geese, but if it takes two years and several patient preparations to do that, so be it. He treats his staff well, too. The ones who last at Waller's are fond of him and tell stories of his thoughtfulness. But it would be a rash strapper who turned up late for work twice.

On the subject of patience, Waller apparently agrees with the philosophy of the late Bart Cummings, who said you should give horses time 'because it's one thing you have plenty of'.

So where some other trainers—and some other owners— might have been eager to see the new star rushed back into work ready for another kill, something like an improving football team being given a tough pre-season, Waller was not. He never has been. And in the three key people who own Winx he has supporters, not critics or wannabe trainers or chancers who need the stakes money more than they love the horse.

It doesn't always happen like this. Racing has always had some owners and trainers who push horses too hard too often. Not to mention owners who push trainers because they are giddy with adrenalin, applause and avarice.

Waller is far too polite to be caught saying the sort of withering things Cummings did on the subject of 'hands-on' owners, but you suspect he might agree with 'the Master' on some things.

Bart once told a prospective owner it would cost a set amount per day to train their horse 'unless you want to help me train it, in which case it will cost double that'.

Waller trains for longevity. Doesn't care about scorching track gallops and trying to impress new owners and old track watchers by 'winning' barrier trials. Doesn't want a stable full of precocious two-year-olds pumped up and pushed to their limit—or beyond it—to try to win a couple of races before they break down physically or mentally.

On the Wednesday after the Cox Plate he puts Winx on the truck back up the Hume Highway and turns her out for twelve weeks.

By the time Michelle Payne wins the Melbourne Cup on Prince Of Penzance on the first Tuesday in November, racing's other new princess, the four-legged one, is in a paddock at a unique property west of Camden, an hour's drive and a world away from Sydney.

•

The great sports writer Red Smith once gave directions for the annual racegoers' pilgrimage to Saratoga, the venerable racecourse founded in upstate New York in 1863, the year after Archer won his second Melbourne Cup.

It's simple, Smith said: drive 175 miles north from New York City, turn left and go back a century.

Smith's line comes to mind as you drive into the country to see Winx.

To reach the place where she and a handful of others are given a break from the routine of the racing stable, you head west of Sydney to a sleepy little town west of the Nepean River, turn left and drive back a century.

It's easy to miss the turn-off. It has been there since drays and bullock wagons used it but there is no need to signpost it too much. The few horse-float drivers who go there know where it is. Not many others need to.

The access road runs straight through the front gate and becomes a long driveway up a gentle rise towards the original house. It is called the Hermitage and is one of the oldest colonial homesteads still standing so close to the city. From the front door, on a good day, you can see the skyscrapers poking through the haze. Turn around and you see the house's original chapel, all restored and painted.

A little further away is a different sort of temple, bigger than the chapel. It's a stable block built recently to blend in with the original outbuildings. Near it is a 'tie-up shed' for stripping and saddling horses before exercise, and for washing them and grooming them afterwards. It has been converted from a hayshed in the way that a Tribeca apartment is converted from an old warehouse: you can guess what it used to be, but only just.

The front paddocks are dotted with wagyu cattle. The wagyus, the 'thoroughbreds' of beef breeds, are notionally a business sideline on the farm but the truth is they help make it the perfect horse property.

In Ireland, home of perhaps the world's craftiest horse handlers, elite studs like Coolmore run cattle in the paddocks alongside fabulously valuable thoroughbreds. The cattle keep down the coarse pasture that horses dislike and help control the parasites that can damage a horse's gut. Besides, calm cattle give nervy horses the benefit of benign company, an animal their own size that's no threat and will not gallop wildly around the paddock.

It makes sense that horses are soothed by having other grazing animals around them, a leftover from the ancient past when different herbivores shared the steppes and savannahs and plains, the way zebras and antelope still do in Africa, providing a sort of mutual warning system against predators. Paying attention to those instincts gives a thoughtful trainer another tiny psychological edge in the endless quest to keep horses not just healthy but also happy.

When Peter Moody used to send the world's greatest sprinter Black Caviar to spell at Murchison in Central Victoria, she had a goat as a paddock mate, much to the delight of photographers. But using Billy the goat was not a Disney-ish prop to 'cutify' the remarkable Black Caviar story. It was horse sense, something trainers like Moody and Waller have plenty of.

Trainers often have little ponies to keep nervy racehorses company in their yards. They can help relieve boredom and fretting and also encourage neurotic horses to eat better. Winx has never required that sort of close-up company. She 'eats up' well, doesn't like being fussed over and thrives perfectly if she has one stablemate she has 'palled up' with in the loosebox next to her corner stall at Waller's Rosehill stables. The stable staff make sure she gets friendly with another horse that requires spelling at the same time, cutting any risk that she will fret in the paddock.

Her earliest pal was her contemporary Amicus, the expensive blue-blood filly who became so valuable she was sold to Europe to be mated with thoroughbred royalty, Galileo.

Winx's next pal for a long time was the feisty little grey Foxplay, a firecracker that might have been a multiple Group One winner herself if she hadn't been overshadowed on the track by her champion stablemate. Then came Shillelagh and Unforgotten. The funny thing is, Waller points out, each of them became Group One winners *after* a stint as Winx's stable buddy. As if class rubs off.

Waller horses are treated equally but some are more equal than others and, even before her Cox Plate win, Winx was rising fast on a very short list. Usually only the stable's 'Group' horses spell at the Hermitage. It makes absolute sense. The farm doesn't need to be run on a strict commercial footing so the manager can give his undivided attention to Winx and a few other VIP guests. The horses that make the cut are like film stars on retreat at a private chalet, resting before going back to the gym to tone up for the next role.

For the man who runs the place, it's a joy to see the new star arrive—and a relief to see her go back to Wallerland. Three months is a long time to babysit an animal suddenly worth millions, with the potential to win many millions more. But someone has to do it.

•

Olly Koolman is by nature a happy man. He sees the world in a rosy light. He is happy to be in charge of Winx's day-to-day handling when she arrives at the property. He is even happier, many weeks later, when the truck with *Waller Racing* livery eases its priceless load away from the loading ramp and down past the cattle paddocks, back to the twenty-first century.

For a start, it means he can relax enough to drive to the nearest town for a counter meal or a beer after work. While Winx is in residence he doesn't do that, any more than Nicole Kidman's bodyguard goes swimming when she's relaxing by the pool. The job isn't hard while nothing goes wrong: the hard bit is making sure nothing *does* go wrong. Still, working with the rich and famous beats digging ditches. Or milking cows, which he has done.

Koolman and Chris Waller go back a way, to when they were unknown stablehands working for New Zealand trainers. It says a lot that when their bosses wanted to send horses to Australia or Hong Kong, each of them was trusted to do it at a young age.

It is not quite true there is a 'Kiwi mafia' in horse racing but anyone wanting to make the case might point to Koolman and Waller.

They are similar in their get-on-with-it attitude to work and share a similar background, but are different in other ways.

Waller is lean and dark and on the quiet side of friendly. Koolman is fair, thickset and on for a chat. He's an enthusiast, naturally gregarious, laughs easily. Like Waller, he's a farm boy. He grew up at Otaki—just down the road from the Waller farm at Foxton—surrounded by many dairy cows and a few thoroughbred horses. Like Waller, he chose the horses and hasn't regretted it.

His father Anton Koolman was a dairy farmer who trained horses, much like Waller's forebears. But Koolman senior became a niche bloodstock agent, using his knowledge of New Zealand and Australian breeders and bloodlines to find horses for the Hong Kong market.

Olly absorbed the basics of handling horses as a child and it never left him. He worked for good trainers, and was good enough to follow the work overseas. At twenty-two he went to Ireland to work with horses. He was there six months, long enough to meet and marry Irish horsewoman Karen Russell before returning as Dermot Weld's assistant when the Irish wizard made history by bringing Vintage Crop to win the 1993 Melbourne Cup.

Vintage Crop was the first European horse to win the Cup. After playing his part in that win, Koolman went to work for Gai Waterhouse. There he met a quiet young track rider named Ben Cadden, who rode work on Gai's top horse Juggler and strapped him at the races. Their paths would cross later, with an even better horse and the trainer who would take over from Waterhouse as the best in Sydney.

While Olly's father, Anton, looked for prospective gallopers for Hong Kong, he got to know some owners there. One of them was a hard businessman with a soft spot for horses. He wanted to find a retirement home for a favourite racehorse, a stallion with nowhere to go. This was Cheval De Troy, which once upon a time won a listed race in New Zealand before going to Hong Kong to race under a different name.

'Cheval' got lucky. His owner, as sentimental about horses as he is wealthy, asked Anton Koolman to find the old galloper not only a home but also a harem. Cheval De Troy had survived his career intact and the man paying the bills thought it only reasonable he should get to breed. Not every breeding expert would agree that the horse's future was at stud, but his owner didn't care. He can afford to indulge his whims, even when the whim is a 600-kilogram stallion.

Finding a stud home for the horse was a tall order, and many racing people might have ducked the request, but Anton Koolman took it seriously. He made a lot of telephone calls around his network of contacts and eventually found a Queensland hobby breeder willing to lease Cheval De Troy *and* find him some mares to serve. The horse repaid this touching faith in him by throwing a few winners to moderate mares.

Then he got even luckier: his owner decided to buy his own property near Sydney as a permanent home for Cheval De Troy and any other superannuated horses he wanted to keep. Naturally, the obliging Anton Koolman was commissioned to find the right property.

Koolman knew just the place, a historic farm owned by a Sydney family who had tired of ponies and peace and quiet on weekend visits. It had an early nineteenth century homestead, a chapel, a hayshed, spacious paddocks and endless room for improvement. The buyer had the means to transform it but he was flat out doing business in Hong Kong. He needed someone to make his plan a reality.

Enter Olly Koolman. By this time he had trained winners on his own account but when offered the challenge of transforming the old property into a horse resort, he couldn't resist. He was given a budget that might not have been bottomless but was certainly elastic, an excellent start to any venture at the high end of the horse business.

After seven years and many millions of dollars, the original house and chapel have been restored 'for visitors' and two new staff houses and the boss's stone mansion built.

Then there's the stabling and post-and-rail paddocks and the exercise track which is needed on the ideal spelling and pre-training property. The result is a showpiece that attracts some of the best racehorses in Sydney—and the best mare in the world.

'It was clear she was more than the average Joe,' says Koolman about the first time Winx arrived. 'We look after Chris's five-star horses. She was paddocked next to Amicus.' This was the $500,000 filly Debbie Kepitis bought in partnership at the same sale as Winx was sold.

Low numbers of horses on the place cut the risk of infectious diseases as well as injury through misadventure. But Waller's philosophy is simple: in the end, champions have to be treated like horses or they can't thrive.

Up the back of the farm, in stallion yards well out of sight or smell of Winx's quarters, the luckiest old horse in Australia,

Cheval De Troy, is still looked after as if he is the champion that his sire Zabeel was. He is even visited by the occasional brood-mare owned by optimists who reckon his aristocratic bloodlines are a bargain at a grand a throw.

The farm has everything that opens and shuts—except an automatic water trough plumbed into the strong timber-railed day paddock built especially for Winx. This is not an oversight. There are no hard edges in the paddock at all, not even water troughs or feed bins. When Winx is in residence, Olly and his helpers fill a water bucket by hand. It's a little more work but that's fine by them. The simplest way is the safest.

If she's there for more than a few weeks, they take her shoes off and let her go barefoot in the paddock so there is less chance of hurting herself when she kicks and plays. It also gives her feet a chance to grow out naturally.

There is an identical paddock next to Winx's for her 'mate' of the season, close enough to sniff each other but with a fence to block the sort of horseplay that can break the skin, or even bones. When Winx leaves, no other horse is allowed into her paddock; the staff mow it so the grass doesn't grow long and rank. The paddock is effectively a quarantine station, kept as close to sterile as possible in terms of horse diseases. They don't take chances with the champ.

Koolman has built a private track to make sure the world's best racehorse on turf has something like the world's best turf to canter on in her pre-training exercise. This is a light regimen to keep her limber for the painstaking fitness program mapped out for her back at Rosehill. When a horse spells, it needs a mental break from the rigours of the full-time racing stable; what it doesn't need is to get fat and lazy.

Of every improvement he's made on the place, the turf track might be Koolman's favourite. It's a straight 1600 metres up a gentle slope, sheltered by bush along its entire length, rising a few degrees before cresting the slope and flattening out at the top.

Koolman brought in a road contractor with heavy machinery to lay it out like a road base, with a subtle crown in the middle to shed water. Then he ordered in dozens of truckloads of kikuyu turf to be rolled out and watered in with a sprinkler system. It cost north of $200,000 but the result is a flawless and forgiving 'gallop' to rival the best of the English downs where thoroughbreds have trained since the reign of Charles II. No matter how much it rains, the cushion of kikuyu is never boggy.

It's at least as good as the prized 1400-metre straight track at the Ballarat training centre, where Darren Weir and other trainers prepare dozens of winners.

Horses have to work harder to gallop up a slope, which is good, but with minimal strain on their vulnerable front legs, which is even better. The fact the track has no turns also prevents lateral strain on joints and tendons. Every tiny advantage reduces the chance of the wear and tear that shortens a racehorse's career.

'I've never had to replace a divot,' says Koolman. Which is hardly surprising, given that, for weeks at a time, maybe the best private track in New South Wales is used by only two horses: Winx and a training mate.

There are sixteen generous looseboxes in the simple timber stable, its lines as uncluttered as a Shaker table, its roomy central aisle swept cleaner than most houses. Step inside at sunset six weeks after the 2017 Cox Plate and only two looseboxes are occupied. In the box second from the door is a bay mare. This is the excellent racehorse Shillelagh, a Group One winner with more than $800,000 in stakes in New Zealand and Australia.

Next to her, closest to the door, is another bay mare: Winx. The Queen and her lady-in-waiting.

The behaviour of 'the Queen' is, in fact, a little regal. She is well-behaved but aloof—at least, with adults. Lean over her stall door and she shows no reaction. Those who know her best notice she sometimes walks to the back of her stall rather than socialise. Except when children visit.

Koolman reckons she loves kids. His theory is she is intelligent enough to sense that children have never saddled her, or nailed on her shoes, or filed her teeth, or any of the other chores and minor annoyances and major physical efforts that are a working racehorse's lot.

Others wonder if it is just that children are a novelty to a racehorse in training. They are different from the workaday adults, smaller and with higher voices. Many animals seem to tolerate young members of their own or other species.

When Olly Koolman's pair of primary-schoolers Riaan and Kian pick handfuls of clover and take it to Winx, she whinnies and nuzzles them when they come into the stable. Koolman has never seen her do that for an adult, even the ones who feed her.

The Koolman children return the favour. They have been told that Winx's whereabouts is best kept quiet when she's on the farm, and their father swears they have never let it slip at school, tempting as it must be.

He recalls Chris and Stephanie Waller bringing their children Nikita and Tyler up to the farm one Sunday. Tyler jumped out of the car and announced, 'My dad works where Winx lives.'

For a horse, that's fame.

For Tyler's dad, working where Winx lives is the highest point so far of a remarkable rise. The chain of chance events that brought man and horse together goes back a long way.

4

THE WRONG O'BRIEN

Peter O'Brien shares one of the most famous surnames in the thoroughbred world. But he doesn't belong to either of the Ballydoyle O'Brien dynasties of Vincent O'Brien or his unrelated successor Aidan O'Brien, trainers who between them have dominated elite racing in England and Ireland for the last half century. The surname didn't help Peter at the start, back home in Ireland where O'Briens are as common as potatoes.

In semi-suburban Dalkey, on the outskirts of Dublin, Peter O'Brien was just another schoolboy and not an overly keen one. He had never been closer to large animals than helping his cousins and uncles to milk cows on their farm during summer holidays. His father Patrick was a hard-working builder. His mother Noreen was a hard-working mother of five, not a rare occupation in Ireland in the 1960s.

The youngster might have been expected to choose between

his father's trade and studying enough to land a white-collar job of the sort becoming available in the changing Irish economy. And he might have taken either of those options, had it not been for the first and most important turning point in his life. At an early age, while still at his Dalkey primary school, he was infected with a contagion for which death is the only cure. Whether this was inevitable or random is hard to say.

The O'Brien family's neighbour was a well-known Irish racing journalist, Tom McCormack, whose son John McCormack was Peter's best friend. In Ireland, ancestral home of the horse and horsemen, racing writers enjoy more respect than in many places, where they might be slandered as touts with typewriters. McCormack senior was respected in his own field—Irish newspapers and racing—and in the Dalkey community.

When McCormack took his son John to the races, John's friend Peter O'Brien often tagged along. For Peter, it was eye-opening and then life-changing. It could have been football or stamps or bird watching or any other decent obsession, but for the O'Brien boy it was horses—more particularly the thoroughbred horse.

Tom McCormack knew the truth of the Jesuit axiom 'Give me a child until he is seven and I will give you the man'. He gave his young disciple books that whetted his appetite: nearly fifty years later O'Brien still dreamily recites titles like *Unbroken Line*, memories that take him back to the childish infatuation he never shook off. As the lad became more fascinated, Tom McCormack lent him catalogues and pedigree charts. In those pre-internet days when facts and knowledge were laboriously shared via ink on paper, these documents and artefacts were a sort of Holy Writ to the boy.

•

On a recent Christmas back in Ireland, the now middle-aged O'Brien sifted through a box of things he'd saved as a boy and that his mother had put away for him. Tucked away among scrapbooks and newspaper cuttings and photographs was a primitive career guidance brochure he had been asked to fill in when he was twelve, ready for secondary school. In the space where the pupil was asked to fill in their career preference, two words are written firmly in his schoolboy hand: STUD MANAGER.

To his elders this ambition must have seemed scarcely more realistic than the boy imagining he would coach the Irish football team. At least he could play football; O'Brien had hardly put his hand on a horse. But a little thing like ignorance and lack of experience or the right background didn't deter the budding stud manager. One thing he knew for certain: he wasn't academic in other disciplines. His future would be with the breeding of racehorses if he could only crack the entry code to that exotic world and apprentice himself to its masters.

The Irish have looked to America since the Potato Famine, at least, and the boy knew very young that the powerhouse of thoroughbred breeding in the English-speaking world was Kentucky, where rich buyers and breeders had been plundering the best Irish and English bloodlines for most of the twentieth century. Two world wars had weakened the financial state of the great thoroughbred nurseries of the Old World and the Americans had plucked the best available from straitened breeders there.

So the kid hand-wrote earnest letters to 138 stud farms in Kentucky: a huge investment in time, paper and writer's cramp. He received only one reply, and that was from Michael Osborne, one of the many Irish abroad. Osborne was managing North Ridge Stud in Kentucky. But he had an ulterior motive in answering young O'Brien's appeal for help—Osborne also managed the Lexington Irish soccer team and was always looking for players. O'Brien was playing for a Dublin club that had fielded a good team back in Osborne's era but had faded badly since. That obscure connection was enough. So one day in 1984, aged just eighteen, O'Brien took a plane to New York and then a Greyhound bus to Kentucky. The combined trip took two days.

Michael Osborne's son John picked him up from the Greyhound depot in Lexington. His first words to the exhausted immigrant and would-be stud groom were 'Have ya got your football boots?' It turned out John was driving him straight to a game—to play.

How did he go?

'I was shite,' recalls O'Brien agreeably. Then again, so was the job Osborne had lined up for him, in the sense that he was put to work with another recruit doing the shittiest shift in the stables. Literally. The Kentucky summer was so hot and steamy that the yearlings were turned out in paddocks overnight to cool down. While they were outside, O'Brien and his co-worker spent all night mucking out seventy-six stalls between them. That's a lot of shite, all of it mixed with bedding reeking with the pungent ammonia smell of horse urine. As long as they were finished by dawn, they kept their job as the basest labourers in the factory of dreams.

It was, O'Brien worked out much later, 'a test of our mettle' to see who would stick at it. He didn't have a lot of options. At that stage, he recalls, grinning at his own childish confidence, 'I'd never physically touched a horse', and if he wanted to change that he just had to keep swinging his pitchfork and lugging his dung bag.

The job was at Taylor-Made Farm. The manager was a horseman named Mike Helmbrecht, who taught the green Irish kid who knew nothing about horses (apart from their pedigrees) how to handle the actual animal, literally from the ground up. Cleaning and greasing horses' feet is one daily chore of many in a stable.

'He saw how keen I was, and he kept me back [after work] for extra tuition,' says O'Brien. Three months after picking up a pitchfork to muck out stalls, he got to lead a million-dollar yearling in the sales ring. He was away.

For the dreamy boy from Dalkey, it was like breaking into Hollywood. He went to Windfields Stud in Canada, where the greatest living thoroughbred stallion Northern Dancer had been bred. Bernard McCormack, son of his Irish mentor Tom McCormack, managed the farm, which was handy. Northern Dancer had long before been moved south of the border to Maryland—even Mohammed has to come to the mountain—and the highlight of O'Brien's time at Windfields was taking mares into the United States to be served by the already legendary stallion.

'Northern Dancer was at his zenith by that stage,' O'Brien says. 'Each mare service was a million dollars and no return if she didn't get in foal.'

He got to pat Northern Dancer—and learned *not* to pat his cranky chestnut son The Minstrel, who was notoriously temperamental and tough, and had half-killed a careless groom or two.

Being at Windfields was almost a religious experience for O'Brien the pedigree student. In winter, it was also astonishingly cold: sometimes thirty degrees below freezing. O'Brien's morning and afternoon chore on the farm was to break the ice on the water troughs with a pick-axe so the horses could drink. It amazed him to see that the animal with its origins in the desert had adapted so well to the frozen north that Canada had become the source of the world's finest racehorse strains.

From Windfields, O'Brien returned to Ireland but not to the Dublin suburbs. He had a job at Coolmore, the thoroughbred world's version of Camelot. He got to work with well-known people and horses—notably Sadler's Wells, who would take over from his sire Northern Dancer as the world's leading stallion. But O'Brien had the wanderlust. He loved the job but not the miserly money so he went to London to labour on a building site for twenty times as much. In a week he had earned £600— the price of an air ticket to the other side of the world.

O'Brien had applied to work at Gooree Stud in New South Wales, run at the time by Irishman Martin Byrne. There was one hitch: the job was for someone who could ride a horse, and he had not mentioned in his application that he could not actually do that. His intentions were honourable, or so he says: he rushed back to Ireland and spent a week at Brendanstown Riding Stables doing a crash course in the saddle. It seemed a good plan at the time.

It wasn't. On the first day at Gooree, the boss asked him to jump on a stock horse and run some mares into the yard.

'The horse bolted and I fell on my arse and they realised I couldn't ride as well as I'd suggested.'

The boss was understanding. But after one breeding season at Gooree, O'Brien was restless again. He wanted to experience more. He surprised himself when Neville Begg's renowned racing stable in Sydney hired him as soon as he made a tentative inquiry.

It was astonishing to the poor youngster that racing royalty like the Beggs would treat him so well. At first, he wondered why stable staff ushered him to the trainers' hut in the middle of the track at Randwick and handed him the work sheets for each horse. The penny dropped later, when he was invited to dinner with the family. Part way through the meal, one of the Begg women leaned over and smiled at the Irish lad, saying she had seen a picture of 'your father' in the newspapers and had noticed how well the old chap looked and how remarkable he was.

O'Brien grinned and replied that unless it was a picture of a man working on a building site, it wouldn't have been his father in the paper. His hosts had mistaken him for a son of the world's then most eminent trainer, Vincent O'Brien.

To be fair, he says, the Beggs treated him surprisingly well after that revelation, even if his opinion of the work sheets no longer seemed so keenly sought.

After two months he left the stable and went back to Ireland to work for Coolmore again for six months. He was then entrusted with travelling the shuttle stallions to Australia and New Zealand. He took horses to Ra Ora Stud in New Zealand, and escorted Alzao, Bluebird and Persian Heights to Lindsay Park in South Australia, the world-renowned training and breeding estate Colin Hayes had created on rolling farmland.

Next he went to Woodlands, at that time the Ingham brothers' showpiece breeding property in the Hunter Valley. O'Brien, grateful for every opportunity to learn from every employer, was extra grateful to the 'chicken kings'. They saw in him someone who could sell nominations to their stallions. The perceived value of horses, far more so than that of boats or cars or houses, is tied to the story attached to them, and O'Brien could tell that story nicely indeed, to be sure. A lilting Irish accent is no disadvantage in the horse business or the comedy circuit the world over. The Inghams knew a natural when they saw one.

'Jack and Bob were pivotal to me in many ways,' says O'Brien. 'They gave me a breeding right in Night Shift for one season. I sold it and got ten grand and bought my first mare, Mrs Clayton.' He bred from the mare to sell yearlings on his own account, which gave him a financial start.

The breeding right and the mare he bought with it weren't all he got from Woodlands: he says the manager Peter Flynn 'showed me how to judge mares and foals—and how to behave'.

The Inghams' offer for him to stay at Woodlands gave O'Brien confidence that he could succeed at the highest level of the business. One day Bob Ingham took him aside and said, 'You can do anything if you work hard enough at it.' The advice wasn't novel but it was sincere and it was timely: the young Irishman needed to hear it from someone he admired who would not bother with false reassurances or empty promises and platitudes.

One thing led to another. Staying at Woodlands led to a meeting that would resonate later. It was with Bob's daughter Debbie Kepitis, then a young mother bringing her daughters and her husband to the property for family outings. O'Brien was struck by her 'intense interest' in the horses. It was a pleasure to look after her mares 'because she adored them', he says. 'She has empathy.'

It planted a seed. Years later, after Winx had become a household word, he would say to Debbie Kepitis, 'I don't know anybody in the horse world who deserves Winx more than you do.'

O'Brien would leave Woodlands and go to Arrowfield for two seasons, which meant minding the world's greatest shuttle stallion Danehill and others as they commuted from Ireland to Australia. But in 1996 his old bosses at Coolmore bought the original Arrowfield property at Jerrys Plains in the Hunter Valley and O'Brien stayed on as manager.

Since being settled by the pioneer George Bowman, ancestor of Hugh, in 1824, the Arrowfield property had produced outstanding horses, among them the 1920 Melbourne Cup winner Poitrel, champion racehorse and sire Heroic, and the marvellous Manfred.

When Coolmore took over, there was one mare and one weanling left on the farm. The mare was Shantha's Choice— and her weanling was Redoute's Choice, whose rise from top racehorse to stellar stallion would make him heir-apparent in Australia to the international breeding juggernaut Danehill.

This time, by way of a change from his nomad days, O'Brien would settle in for what would become a long stay at Coolmore Australia, with its thousands of acres and its hundreds of horses.

Early in that time, on a Sunday just before Christmas in 2000, a car came up the long driveway from the highway that winds through the vineyards and horse studs. It was a silver BMW sedan, dusty and insect-spattered after the long drive from Sydney. In it were a couple and three children. The driver was a tall, dark-haired man with a friendly face. He got out as O'Brien stepped out of the house to meet and greet.

'John Camilleri,' he said, putting out his hand. That was the start of the friendship that produced Winx.

5

THE RIGHT CAMILLERI

The Camilleris of Malta and the O'Briens of Ireland have something in common: there are plenty of them, and each clan originates in an island nation with a love of racing horses that infects every level of society.

John Camilleri, second-generation Maltese-Australian, was brought up in a family of harness-racing enthusiasts but lost his connection with standardbreds as a young man, whereas Peter O'Brien toiled and talked his way into thoroughbred breeding in his late teens and came to Australia as an adult.

O'Brien could just as easily have ended up in North America or back in Ireland or England. The odds were well against the Sydney poultry and real estate tycoon meeting the Dublin builder's son.

There are thousands of Camilleris in Australia. Hundreds of them are called John. Not all have distinguished themselves the way this John Camilleri has.

Good John Camilleri is a tough businessman but has done nothing but the right thing for racing and racehorses. Bad John Camilleri, a self-described 'grub', was disqualified from racing for four years and six months in 2015 for his involvement in the cobalt doping scandal. The unfortunate coincidence led racing authorities to issue a statement stressing there was no connection between the two, unrelated except that they shared a common pair of names.

'John Camilleri of Fairway Thoroughbreds is a person of good standing in thoroughbred racing, such that he was appointed to the inaugural ATC Board,' said the chief of Racing NSW, Peter V'landys, in the year the cobalt scandal tarnished the sport with the sort of headlines that give racing administrators a headache.

'As an owner and breeder, he has made, and continues to make, a valuable contribution to the thoroughbred industry in Australia, including breeding the most recent Golden Slipper winner Vancouver.'

It's not easy to get Good John Camilleri to talk about himself and his remarkable success as a boutique breeder. Apart from the fact he is frantically busy as chair of the Baiada Group, you suspect he doesn't want to big-note just because his hobby has thrown up spectacular results in a relatively short time. He knows racing is fickle, luck fades, and no good comes of going the early crow.

Still, he can't help wanting to pay tribute to his late grandfather, Celestino 'Charlie' Baiada. Charlie arrived from Malta aged fourteen in 1916. That he worked so hard did not make him unusual in the tough years between the wars. What made him unusual was his instinct for turning his capacity for work into business opportunities.

As Australia recovered from the Great Depression and geared up for war, Charlie took on government contracts to supply potatoes and cabbages and the like. Meanwhile, he grew poultry to sell at the Sydney markets, starting out with a horse and cart.

Charlie and his wife Giovanna—teenage bride, mother of seven, grandmother at thirty-five—plucked and dressed thirty chickens a day on the five-acre market garden at Pendle Hill that was the springboard for a Rich List family fortune. Starting with a few dozen hens, a vegetable patch and a couple of house cows, they laid the foundations for the family's poultry and real estate empire. The gleaming new headquarters of the Baiada Group are built on the original market garden, a site choice as pragmatic as it is poetic.

The new corporate offices actually incorporate the double-storey brick house where the Baiadas lived until Charlie died in 1983. When John Camilleri and his brother Simon (now managing director) sit at the boardroom table and look down the hall, they can see what used to be their grandparents' bedroom. That splicing of old and new says something about a family enterprise, still thrifty despite success and proud of its humble origins, proof that not all family businesses lose their way in the third generation.

Camilleri muses how much has changed since he was a kid in the 1960s, helping his grandparents pluck chickens. First they plunged the freshly slaughtered birds in scalding water, putting up with the strong smell of wet feathers as they held the legs and pushed the carcasses into the spinning drum of the primitive plucking machine with its rubber fingers whirring. If John and the other grandkids weren't plucking chickens, they were pulling out weeds or picking tomatoes. His early childhood memories are mostly of work and he's proud of that. The sense of shared enterprise welded the family together. Still does.

How Charlie and Giovanna built the business is quite a story, which is why the family recently commissioned a detailed history so the migrant couple's many fortunate descendants will know it all started with hard manual work and risk-taking.

Their story has many parts that weave into the story of twentieth century Australia and the expansion of its capital cities since World War II. But one linking thread is Charlie Baiada's love of horses, which he transmitted to his grandson. John Camilleri explains it this way: that in the Malta his grandfather left in 1916, most people either owned a trotter or knew someone who did.

Camilleri describes rural Malta as a place where, behind each spotlessly clean stone house, there's a 'mini farm' with a trotter, a couple of pigs, rabbits and chickens. The Maltese brought their love of racing harness horses when they migrated. Among Camilleri's earliest memories is his grandfather taking him to watch his trotters. The best of them was Michael Bruce, a durable performer who had 'maybe nine' trainers in a long career competing with champions of his era. Charlie wasn't shy about sacking trainers, which might have been a wise precaution. But he loved his horses and his grandchildren and that left its mark.

John hardly missed a harness meeting from the age of five until he was twenty-two. He went with his grandfather and father Frank Camilleri to Harold Park 'headquarters' and to harness tracks at Penrith, Fairfield, Menangle and the old Parramatta track.

Instead of maths and English homework, he says, 'I would do the trots form.' He bought the form guide and read every line. Despite (or because of) this, he graduated in accountancy at the University of New South Wales and landed a job at what was Coopers & Lybrand, where he worked for four years.

By the time Charlie Baiada died in 1983, the business had grown from hand-plucking thirty birds a day in the backyard to processing tens of thousands a week in purpose-built plants. It is now in the millions, and poultry is not the group's only enterprise.

Five months after his grandfather's death, the bright young accountant walked away from the safety of a big city firm to join the family business as one of the youngest chief executives in the land. It was, and is, a cut-throat competitive game but Baiada enjoyed the same advantage the other big producers did: a growing appetite for chicken in a growing population. As the occasional Sunday roast chook gave way to fast-food franchises from coast to coast, a big small business became a seriously big business.

Eventually, the Baiada Group would take over the Steggles and Lilydale brands and broaden its interests into stockfeeds, other forms of agriculture and the booming real estate market that underpinned many a 1970s fortune.

The paddocks Charlie Baiada had bought to run cows, raise chickens and grow vegetables and fodder turned into residential subdivisions, as the old man had foreshadowed. When Baulkham Hills council paid him £360,000 for a paddock, it was Charlie's big break, the one that set the family up. Forty years later, Chris Waller and his wife Stephanie bought a house at Baulkham Hills close by the old Baiada paddocks. One way or another, everything is connected.

The rise of Charlie Baiada and his heirs roughly paralleled that of the Inghams, whose father Walter started the family's first poultry farm close by in Sydney's market garden belt. The Inghams, too, had been involved in harness racing before Debbie Kepitis's father Bob quit that code to join his brother Jack in breeding and racing thoroughbreds.

Trotting's loss was galloping's gain. The Inghams took the view that if they had to pay massive amounts of tax on business turnover, they might as well get enjoyment from it. They invested heavily in breeding and racing gallopers—hundreds of them. Even if it wasn't profitable, it was pleasurable.

John Camilleri was a generation younger than Jack and Bob Ingham. For twenty years he had no time to think of anything beyond the business and his young family. But inside the high-flying executive and fond husband and father was still the kid who'd loved going to the trots with his father and grandfather. So when a bloodstock agent put a proposition to him and a group of lunch mates one day, he agreed to pay up for a share in a horse he'd never seen.

It's the sort of thing that happens every week, especially around racing carnivals and the big yearling sales. The difference is that this group of mates got extremely lucky, which is why the story gets an airing every time John Camilleri is involved with a winner. It goes like this.

In 1998 Camilleri agreed to lunch with the firm's long-time insurance broker Anthony Gow-Gates and three other friends at Kingsley's Steakhouse in Sydney. It was a friendly ambush. The late Harry Lawton turned up to show them photographs of two yearlings he'd bought at the Karaka sales in New Zealand.

Lawton, one of the first full-time syndicators, was liked for his honesty. He had an agile mind hidden behind a knockabout persona. The poet laureate of Australian racing, Les Carlyon, once affectionately described Lawton in his best suit at the spring carnival races having the unpretentious but slightly uncomfortable look of 'a wharfie at his daughter's wedding'.

People trusted Harry, partly because he was mostly willing to keep a share in the horses he'd bought. The photographs he dropped on the lunch table at the steakhouse were of two colts that were similarly priced but contrasting in colour. Lawton, a practical student of human nature, might have reckoned this made it easy for potential syndicate members to choose one over another. If so, it was the same practical logic that motivated him to give well-bred colts strong, memorable names in case they were good enough to be sold as stallions.

Of the two colts he presented to the lunchers—Camilleri, Anthony Gow-Gates and their friends—one was an almost black colt by Danzero, the other a chestnut by the old champion stallion, Sir Tristram.

The novices went for the black Danzero colt. Lawton syndicated the chestnut elsewhere; named Noble House, it would start twice and ran nowhere.

The $40,000 Danzero colt, named Fairway and gelded, would go on to win ten of twenty-three starts, three of them Group One races, and $2.6 million in prize money. He beat Sunline in the Turnbull Stakes, won the AJC Derby and ran third in a Caulfield Cup, and was probably Danzero's finest progeny, close to the best horse of hundreds Lawton syndicated in thirty-five years.

To get Fairway was like winning TattsLotto with your first ticket. Camilleri was hooked. The subsequent bloodstock investments of those who took the chestnut colt are unknown, although it is interesting that Harry Lawton kept a share in the 'dud', proof of the proposition that selecting horses is a raffle and an expert is someone who was right once.

It was hardly a surprise that Fairway's early success on the track would spur someone with Camilleri's analytical instincts to move to the next level: a mare to breed with. He called his new venture Fairway Thoroughbreds in honour of their Danzero hero.

Horse dealers have much in common with Jane Austen, she who noted the 'truth universally acknowledged'—that a man in possession of a good fortune must be in want of a wife.

As an Irish horse trader, Michael Kirwan, of the Australian arm of Coolmore's international operation, was probably no student of genteel English literature but he instinctively applied a version of Austen's theory: he knew that men of good fortune must be in want of a broodmare.

The mare was La Lucre.

Kirwan was the salesman, one of the Irish *craic*-dealers who had descended on Australia in the 1990s to exploit the market created by the generous stakes money here. He was running Coolmore's property at Jerrys Plains. The place was new to the Irish bloodstock barons but not to breeding good horseflesh. Under its original name, Arrowfield, it was one of the most venerable thoroughbred nurseries in Australia, all the way back to when Hugh Bowman's ancestor George Bowman settled there in the 1820s.

The Irishman had a walk-up start to selling the mare to Camilleri, who had bought a black Woodman colt out of La Lucre at the yearling sales in 2000 and so obviously approved of her pedigree. He'd named him Bentham after his first house at Hunters Hill, and also because the name has seven letters, a favourite superstition among some people with racehorses.

Fairway was almost black, so it's easy to see why La Lucre's colt had caught Camilleri's eye at the sales. Bentham showed enough early promise at Ron Quinton's stables for Camilleri to like the idea of buying his mother when Michael Kirwan mentioned he knew the 'Irish fellas' who owned her and would part with her for a modest $75,000. All the better, she was in foal to the Irish stallion King Of Kings.

It turned out, Camilleri says with good humour, that the likeable Kirwan knew La Lucre's Irish owners very well indeed because he was one of them.

La Lucre was 'nothing too pretty' and none too young, Camilleri recalls, but she was well bred, by Widden Stud's evergreen stallion Bletchingly, sire of the champion Kingston Town and dozens more top gallopers. Despite his strong name, strong colour (black like Kingston Town and Fairway) and his strong pedigree, Bentham was like most young racehorses: he did not live up to the hopes placed in him.

But by then Camilleri was already enmeshed in the secret men's business of memorising and analysing pedigrees, looking for patterns in the past to plot success in the future. La Lucre would have her foal by King Of Kings. Then he would embark on breeding the next of a series of foals from her.

The King Of Kings foal was born on Remembrance Day, 11 November 2000, but Camilleri didn't call him Remembrance or Armistice or Eleventh Hour. He called him San Simeon in homage to the iron horse of harness racing, the West Australian pacer who'd won twenty-nine races straight from 1978 to 1981. He loved the idea that you could breed a horse that might do that.

It was a desire to look at La Lucre's foal that prompted Camilleri to take the family on the drive up to the Hunter Valley to Coolmore late in the breeding season of 2000. They arrived mid-morning on a perfect early summer day at some of the world's finest grazing and viticultural land. Mare owners come and go at the big horse studs and many are 'tourists', wealthy enough to buy horses they would be hard put to recognise. But O'Brien recalls that the Camilleris impressed him from their first meeting. He chooses almost the same words as John Camilleri does to describe him: 'affection for the animal'. They were sympatico.

O'Brien soon saw something else, too. Camilleri had an intuitive feel for breeding, pedigrees and genetics—a practical edge that came from being raised around trotters and dairy cattle and, of course, from breeding millions of chickens. The difference between the many failed poultry businesses and Camilleri's massively successful one (and Inghams', too) had to do with mastering genetic advances as well as scientific feeding. Camilleri's brain was tuned to the practical science of breeding animals successfully, not to abstract notions.

Says O'Brien: 'He was the first person I'd met who wasn't already engrossed in the industry that understood it in a heartbeat. He picked up thirty years of experience in six months, gave me windburn as he went past.'

Camilleri admits this but is a little harder on himself: 'I started reading pedigree books cover to cover—a lot of pedigrees I memorised. It's probably a sickness.'

But on that Sunday before Christmas at the turn of the century, to be looking over your first thoroughbred mare and foal at one of the oldest and best pieces of horse country in the southern hemisphere didn't feel like a sickness. More like the start of an adventure.

O'Brien jumped in the farm ute and led the way to the mares in the big paddocks 'down the back' where the Hunter winds through its broad valley. The Camilleris and their children followed in their car.

By the time the visitors had looked over La Lucre and her foal, the right Camilleri and the wrong O'Brien were chatting like old friends. It is something each of them looks back on with pleasure. O'Brien calls John and Deborah Camilleri 'my Australian family' and the Camilleris have visited his family in Ireland.

Nearly two decades after that first meeting, sitting outside his company's suite high in the new Randwick stand before the running of the 2018 Queen Elizabeth Stakes and Sydney Cup, Camilleri is in an expansive mood.

Winx's imminent appearance in the feature race, gunning for her twenty-fifth straight win, is the high point of the Sydney Championships and the sense of anticipation is palpable. Besides, Camilleri has just watched a horse he bred win the South Pacific Classic, a Listed race. Things are good.

He jumps up to have a bet or watch a race or fetch a drink or to talk to any one of the half dozen serious racing people who stop on the way past. He offers to call a friendly milliner for an elderly lady in a wheelchair whose hat has come adrift. In between, he fills gaps in the story of how he came to fall in love with thoroughbred racing.

He talks about two people who have influenced him most: his grandfather, Charlie Baiada, and his Irish friend Peter O'Brien.

Winners are grinners. Camilleri is all smiles and jokes but when he sums up his relationship with O'Brien, he leans forward, suddenly serious, to emphasise that he's speaking from the heart.

'What I saw in Peter was a guy in love with the animal, incredibly affectionate and very passionate about the work he was doing—and it's about more than financial gain. That's what sets Peter apart from many others in the industry. Quote me on that.'

6

THE BEST MARE THERE

Racing and breeding has its own language. On horse studs, groups of broodmares are called bands. Like a rock band, a broodmare band will often have a star, a mare with quality that can be polished but not fabricated.

A potential star broodmare is auditioned on pedigree, forces her way into the line-up on looks and charisma but is retained only if she produces results. There is no more ruthless meritocracy than racing apart from the professional prize-fighting ring.

John Camilleri started his breeding hobby with La Lucre, a well-bred mare a little past her prime who did not live up to her purchase price. Her indifferent record at producing winners did not faze him. He's a realist from a harder place and had seen enough of harness horses with his grandfather to know that whether you're buying or breeding, the odds of racetrack success are always slim.

For someone with fewer resources and less resolve, sacking a $75,000 mare might be enough to encourage a new enthusiasm for golf or yachting. But Camilleri's deep interest was matched by deep pockets and patience, a formidable combination, though never a guarantee of success, because there isn't one.

The experience with La Lucre might have made him more determined to consider the subject from every angle and allow that pedigree charts alone do not a racehorse make. It's a concession that pedigree purists have to make if they want to lead in winners more than they want to pore over fine print.

Black Caviar's breeder Rick Jamieson and his bloodstock agent Peter Ford make a useful parallel with Camilleri and O'Brien. Jamieson, like Camilleri, is a fiercely competitive and independent entrepreneur who studies pedigrees as keenly as he does most things. He hit the jackpot when Ford selected an unraced filly, Helsinge, that not only matched Jamieson's pedigree markers but was also a superior physical specimen, albeit one that had broken down in her first preparation and was available for less than half her considerable yearling price.

No one knows which bit was more 'right'—the pedigree or the animal. The truth is, both were right or there would have been no Black Caviar. That's the beauty of racing.

But the bloodstock experts, professional horse watchers, need patrons to back their judgement. With Peter O'Brien as a second set of eyes, Camilleri put together a broodmare band he could be proud of.

He did this partly by applying the unsentimental logic of the commercial breeder in other fields, from beef cattle to wool sheep to poultry to cabbages: cull heavily to isolate and propagate desirable traits and reduce undesirable ones.

But even in the Space Age, the science of horse breeding still clings to a measure of intuition, not to mention superstition. It's about aesthetics as well as genetics, belief as much as biomechanics. Leonardo da Vinci might have made a terrific horse breeder, something like his countryman Federico Tesio, the cavalryman who became known as a genius horseman in the first half of the last century. But for anyone who is not a once-in-a-millennium polymath, it is handy to enlist specialist advisers.

By instinct and training, Camilleri analyses data then makes decisions, whereas O'Brien brings something else, the things born of experience that horse people call 'eye' and 'feel' and 'touch'. These are intangible qualities that humans use to recognise and label intangible qualities in a horse, such as 'presence' and 'character', as well as the rather more measurable aspects of conformation—its shape, size and physique.

Using the 'two heads are better than one' principle, the odd couple draws up lists of potential broodmare purchases, then compares notes. In the end, because Camilleri bankrolls the enterprise, he has the final say. They do not argue but they do have animated discussions.

In 2008, they went to the Gold Coast Magic Millions broodmare sale to look over prospective buys. Camilleri was firm about what he wanted—depth of pedigree and good conformation above individual racetrack performance. In fact, Camilleri doesn't mind an unraced mare if the rest of her credentials stack up, given that many successful broodmares were not great gallopers. It is almost axiomatic that champion race mares produce nothing remotely as good as themselves. Some horse people wonder if a mare races too hard and too often, does she 'leave it on the track' and so not produce top-class foals.

Camilleri had marked up a list of mares for O'Brien to look over at the sale: it was his choice of pedigree but he wanted the Irishman to check mares in the flesh for 'type' and also their suitability to deliver and mother foals, the way a farmer might judge a breeding cow. This thoroughly rational plan, combining theory and practical knowledge, was fine right up until the moment they threw it out the window.

•

O'Brien is walking around the barns at the sale, working his way through the mares on his list, when he glimpses something that turns his head across the busy yard. It's like falling in love at first sight.

'She was about four boxes away,' he recalls. 'She got pulled out', meaning the mare had been led from her loosebox for someone to look at her walk up and down.

O'Brien can't take his eyes off her. She is a big bay with a beautiful head and haunches to match: a New Zealand mare with an eye-catching frame to go with her ear-catching name, Vegas Showgirl.

Peter O'Brien has seen plenty of broodmares: many of them aristocrats who have won classics or were bred from classic winners.

He's seen more regally bred mares than this one but none that strike him as more beautiful.

She is a film star among duchesses: athletic, gorgeous and maternal all at once. Which is why she is at the sale. Desirability brings a premium.

She has racecourse performance as well as looks. She was one of the better two-year-olds of her year in New Zealand and went on to win races at three and four. But she 'didn't have a pedigree', says O'Brien, meaning she's not fashionably bred.

'She was an Al Akbar,' he says. This is shorthand, meaning her sire is Al Akbar, a tough but moderate Australian-bred racehorse regarded as a 'bread and butter' stallion at best. He stood at a down-country stud where farmers and other small breeders sent mares to produce cheap homebred gallopers to race for sport, or to sell on as a tried horse, as opposed to breeding sought-after commercial yearlings to sell at auction to international buyers.

O'Brien, like his countryman Oscar Wilde, can resist anything but temptation. He gives in without a struggle. The surprising thing is that there is no resistance from the man who has to foot the bill for this infatuation.

'It was so overpowering. I told John [Camilleri], hoping he would agree. He, too, fell for the mare when he saw her, and promised me, "We are buying her."'

So they do—but not without having to outbid several others who have also fallen under the Showgirl's spell.

Camilleri bids far past his intended limit to pay $455,000 for her. It's twice what she earned on the track, and twice the figure they estimated would buy her.

She is big and well-fleshed but not coarse or gross or raw-boned. O'Brien says he's never seen a mare with better hips, meaning wider hips. The old-time axiom that a mare should have 'a head like a lady's maid and a bottom like a cook's' applies perfectly.

Vegas Showgirl walks with the lithe and nonchalant ease the horse watchers look out for: long and low and swinging, stepping through with no mincing or jigging. Part athlete, part burlesque.

Gerry Harvey is the underbidder, proof that the Harvey Norman and Magic Millions entrepreneur and his formidable wife and business partner Katie Page are often on the money.

But it is Camilleri's day.

Buying Vegas Showgirl comes at a cost, however—it holes the budget so much he decides not to buy another mare on their list. Her name is Regard, and she goes on to produce the multiple Group winner Atlantic Jewel.

To have earmarked both Vegas Showgirl and Regard at the same sale shows that the cheerful Irishman and the tycoon are in top form. They've chosen the right one. As good as Regard is, their Showgirl is better.

So is the story that comes with her.

7

THE WRONG STALLION

Every birth is a lottery because random chance conspires against predictable outcome. But the odds against the birth of Winx's mother happening at all were outrageously long, like fluking one ace after another from a deck of cards. Proof there is no bigger gamble than breeding racehorses.

The man who tells the story behind the story has ended up well north of his birthplace of Gore, deep in the remote Southland grazing country that produces world champion shearers, Huntaway working dogs and regrettable jokes about sheep and gumboots.

He is telling his gambler's tale early in the new year of 2018, unspooling a long line of events that happened over nearly five decades. It is an unseasonably hot summer day in New Zealand, one of the hottest of a historically hot spell, but it's cool in the bar of the fishing club sitting on the dock of the bay at New Plymouth, low on the west coast of the North Island.

A breeze drifts in off the Tasman as the yarn spinner, a reformed professional horseman turned dedicated amateur marlin hunter, fetches another frosty longneck of Tui beer and pours a fresh round. He is telling the unlikely story of how horses, luck and nerve bought him his own stud farm and it's thirsty work.

Big marlin and good horses are hard to find, which might be why men like this are so devoted to pitting their wits against nature in the search for them. His name is John Corcoran and he has postponed the fishing tale of the day to describe how he came to get a journeyman stallion called Al Akbar and play his part in breeding Vegas Showgirl, mother of Winx. For him, they're the ones that got away.

Corcoran is a seasoned storyteller and likes to set up the punch line at his own pace from a long run-up. He's happy to talk about Winx's maternal grandsire Al Akbar but these things can't be rushed. First there's the back story of how he came by Grangewilliam Stud, the property he bought decades ago south of New Plymouth, way out in the cow paddocks beyond Waverley.

The Waikato toffs like to think the west coast is not prime horse-stud country like their fertile flats around Cambridge, he says, but they don't know everything. He's a stock and station agent's son from the south and knows about land and livestock, and has a message for the doubters: Grangewilliam Stud and its neighbours in 'the 'Naki' have produced Melbourne Cup winners and plenty of other good gallopers because it is clean, healthy country with hills to exercise the bone and muscle of young horses.

Didn't he himself breed Doriemus, the wiry chestnut 'polo pony' that won the Melbourne Cup in 1995 (then ran sixth the following year before missing by a nostril in 1997), having nailed the Caulfield Cup as well? And isn't it Kiwi, bred and raised just down the road, whose picture has had pride of place in the local pub since he exploded from last at the turn to win the 1983 Cup like a latter day Phar Lap?

No, Honest John Corcoran won't be wearing any criticism of his part of the horse-breeding world, south of Mt Taranaki. He even suggests, mischievously, there are 'no weeds' in the pasture around Waverley but plenty of them up in their wonderful Waikato.

Corcoran, as his fellow Kiwi the late John Clarke would cheerfully confess of himself, favours 'the scenic route' in conversation. But he knows exactly where he's headed, which is the unlikely story of how he came to win the money that paid for the farm to which he eventually managed to lure Al Akbar—and so fluke producing Winx's mother after another stallion dropped dead in the breeding yard at the vital moment.

The odds against those three things happening are longer than hitting a hole in one in the British Open with a broken broomstick, but that's the way it happened.

He starts by describing how his late father, Jack Corcoran, a stock agent and a Gore Racing Club committeeman back home on the South Island, 'would drag me to the races' when he was a schoolboy. It wasn't Corcoran senior's intention to make his son obsessed with racehorses but that's what happened. The sharp-eyed kid would drag a sack around and pick up empty bottles to sell, then bet the pocket money on horses that took his eye.

Young John was soon mad about horses, 'but Dad wouldn't get me one so I borrowed ponies and taught myself to ride'.

When he left St Kevin's boarding school in Oamaru as soon as he legally could, he joined 'the old man's stock agents' as a junior. After serving time as an office boy, he graduated to rocketing a company car around Southland farm districts, picking prime lambs and steers for the export meat market.

He worked with animals every day and could soon distinguish happy, healthy stock from those that weren't thriving. Young people learn fast if they're interested and knowledge soaks deep into uncluttered brains. What he learned of other animals fitted in with his growing interest in racehorses, not just punting on them but also an ambition to ride and train them.

One day ('this would be 1969 or 1970') Corcoran went to Cromwell races. He borrowed $20 from his mother to finance his betting for the day because he was armed with every punter's dream: inside information. A few days earlier he had gone out to check on some store lambs he'd bought for Gore's leading trainer, Ray Cochrane, who fattened sheep to help him through lean times on the racetrack.

When he got to Cochrane's property, he recalls, the boys were just coming back from the track after exercising the horses. One of them was the wise local jockey Steve Allen.

'I rolled down the window and called out, "Steve, what wins at Cromwell on Saturday?" and Steve says, "This one wins—its name is Golden Feathers."'

When Corcoran got to the races he saw that Golden Feathers was the 'roughie' in its field. He took it 'one out' with five favourites in the Pick Six novelty bet, which invited punters to take a shot at the rare feat of picking six winners on the card.

The five favourites all won and so did Golden Feathers at odds so long no one else had put it in the Pick Six. Corcoran had the only live ticket. It paid $33,000 for a total outlay of $8. At the time, he was earning $26 a week. The win was the price of a small farm or a big house and maybe a good car to go with it.

A farm was exactly what he planned to buy—but, wisely, not just yet. Less wisely, he indulged in a series of celebratory parties, one of which ended in him losing his driver's licence for three years. Not being allowed to drive was a hurdle a back-country stock agent could not jump, so he took leave from the agency to pursue what he really wanted, which was to work with horses. He started as a groom at Te Parae Stud at Masterton in the Wairarapa district not far from Wellington.

'I wanted to be a horse trainer—or a jockey,' says the biggest would-be jockey in captivity. 'I borrowed an old mare and taught her to jump and went to the hunts following the hounds. I loved it. I could ride under eleven stone then and wanted to get an amateur jockey's licence.'

He got his chance at Gore races in an amateur riders' steeple-chase. He wasn't booked to ride but took his boots and riding breeches in case he was offered an emergency ride. He didn't have a light racing saddle to help him make the weight.

As he'd hoped, a licensed rider didn't turn up and the course announcer broadcast an appeal for a stand-in. He told the stewards his amateur jockey licence was 'coming through', which was on the grey side of a white lie. They waved him through to the jockeys' room, where he borrowed a saddle from an old hand, Stan Hawthorn.

'At this stage I am shitting myself, wondering what I'd got myself into,' Corcoran says of his much younger self.

The horse was called Hy. Its trainer was one Hector Anderton, who legged him on and said, 'Son, try to keep him handy and if you are up with them with a round to go, get to the front and keep kicking. He's a lazy old bugger.'

He won in a tight finish but confesses there's a story attached to that, too. The hunt steeplechase was run around a course marked by flags and the old horse ducked inside a flag, out of sight of the crowd. It should have disqualified him but the flag steward was an old friend of Corcoran's father and looked the other way.

'He never said anything,' says Corcoran. 'He died a year later and my brother rang to tell me and said, "Billy Green died and even on his death bed he never said a word."'

Winning the race, albeit with a little help from his friends, was a feeling he never forgot. He decided then he would do everything he could to stay around racehorses. Besides, he still didn't have a driver's licence, which meant his options in New Zealand were limited. So he lined up a job in Kentucky and went there to work for the Nuckols brothers at Hurstland Farm, then moved to Tartan Farm in Florida.

'I was trying to soak up knowledge because I wanted to come back to New Zealand and be *the man*,' he says. Meanwhile, horses took him to Europe, or at least to Ireland, where he went as the travelling groom with a 'mongrel bastard' stallion being delivered to a 'toffy' stud owner, Captain Tim Rogers.

Corcoran ended up coming home to New Zealand earlier than planned because his father died. He then spent another year back at his starting point, Te Parae Stud. He still had his Pick Six war chest stashed away—and a consuming interest in international thoroughbred pedigrees and sales.

While he was working overseas, he had made friends with a French groom, Patrice Nicol, who had gone back to Europe to become a bloodstock agent. Corcoran asked Nicol to secure an impeccably bred young stallion named War Hawk II, which had been withdrawn from auction in England after being injured.

Corcoran was still only twenty-six. If War Hawk had been a dud at stud, the failure might have soured him against throwing money at anything as chancy as horses. But War Hawk would become a top sire in New Zealand with a string of winners—and Corcoran was firmly hooked. As War Hawk climbed from the good money of a $600 service fee per mare to a stratospheric $6000, then the second highest fee in New Zealand, the Corcoran bankroll swelled.

He leased a farm on the Wanganui River in the North Island and began building a broodmare band. All the time he had his eye on the property that his old boss in Ireland, Captain Rogers, had bought near Waverley as a southern hemisphere base. It was named Grangewilliam, and its previous owner Ian Parsons had bred good horses as well as stud cattle on paddocks as bright green as Ireland's own, but without the tough winters or terrorist 'troubles'.

Rogers had died, and Corcoran guessed the widow would eventually sell and move back to the old country. He held his nerve and his cash reserve and ended up buying Grangewilliam for half what the estate lawyers had originally wanted.

By then War Hawk had died. Corcoran stood Yachtie, another good stallion that threw winners and brought in full books, so much so that someone made an offer for him that he couldn't refuse. Nearly every horse has a price—though not much in the case of a 'midget' American stallion, Norman Pentaquad, he imported in the 1980s.

Norman's pedigree had saved him from a bullet when he was born not just tiny, but also with a deformity—a tiny extra foot attached to one leg that earned him his name. Instead of the bullet, Norman got the surgeon's scalpel—but only to his deformed foot rather then higher up—and lived to prove that he was no racehorse. But he carried the genes of a great galloping family and paid for his lifeline to New Zealand by siring the Melbourne Cup hero Doriemus before fluking a third life: he became Kerry Packer's favourite polo sire in Australia, Argentina and England. You couldn't make it up.

Corcoran is getting to the part about breeding Winx's mother. But first he admits he considered letting little, unfashionable Norman go with the wild bush horses in the Taranaki ranges before Packer's talent spotter came along and took him back to a long and productive life in the eye-popping luxury of Ellerston in the Hunter Valley, where he impregnated some of the best polo mares on Earth.

So it was that Corcoran had to look for another stallion. He found two. One was Batavian, who came straight off the track from the Graeme Rogerson stable on a share deal.

The other was the Aussie battler Al Akbar, in which he had quietly gathered a majority shareholding.

•

Denise Howell hardly remembers what brought an undistinguished Australian-bred mare named Vegas Magic across the Tasman. She can be excused for this. She is busy—has been for more than forty years and is likely to be for several more yet.

This is what happens when you work for, with and around someone like Graeme Rogerson, which Howell has done ever since the day the master showman of horse training assured her that if she helped run the office at his stables in Hamilton for six months, he would get her a free trip to England on a horse transport plane. 'Roggie' was generous like that, and good at selling the upside to any proposition, especially if it involved horses.

Howell never got to England but she did get to work for Rogerson's intertwined enterprises for the rest of her life. The nearest she got to the free trip in a horse transport was to fly to Australia with What A Nuisance, one of fourteen potential stayers bought as a job lot by Melbourne property tycoon Lloyd Williams in 1984.

What A Nuisance would make the bulk buy worthwhile by winning the 1985 Melbourne Cup, around the time the filly foal was born that would become Vegas Magic, mentioned above. Her mother was Vegas Street, which had never won a race.

THE WRONG STALLION

Vegas Magic's sire was Voodoo Rhythm, a not-so-distinguished member of a distinguished tribe—the Northern Dancer line that has dominated world breeding since the 1970s. Voodoo Rhythm was one of some 200 stallion sons of Northern Dancer. Though he had a name like a Rolling Stones song, as a stallion Voodoo Rhythm was more a suburban pub rocker. But he did leave some good-looking stock, and those looks were passed on to Vegas Magic.

Vegas Magic was a slightly better racehorse than her mother—she at least won two weak races—but was destined to distinguish herself more as a producer than a galloper. For a thorough-bred (notoriously finicky breeders) the failed race mare would become an unusually fertile mother. She left ten 'named produce' in thirteen seasons, meaning that ten of her foals had not only survived but were sound and promising enough to be given official Stud Book names.

Eighth of the ten was the handsome filly that would be called Vegas Showgirl, foaled when Vegas Magic was seventeen years old.

The rule-of-thumb that old mares and old stallions tend to lose the power to transmit quality as they age is supported by statistics showing that horses older than fifteen produce fewer winners than younger parents do. But there are honourable exceptions to this, and Vegas Magic was one of them: her eighth foal, born to her in advanced middle age, was certainly the best of the lot, defying the statistical likelihood that the first two foals are best, more especially the second.

Denise Howell is recalling these things in late January, 2018. It is day two of the Karaka sales but she isn't driving up to the plush sales venue at Auckland's southern outskirts until later in the week. She has plenty to do in the meantime but makes time to talk horses. She arrives at Rogerson's stables out of breath after a swift trip across the outskirts of Hamilton from her home. She wheels her big black Mercedes into the yard next to a dusty Range Rover outside the unpretentious stables where the irrepressible Rogerson trains most of the scores of horses he has in work.

Howell has had to rejig a few things to honour an appointment to talk about her part in breeding Winx's mother. Although she happens to have a yearling up for auction later in the week, she isn't keen on that side of the horse business. She's says she's not a punter or a serious breeder, and dislikes selling young horses she's bred because she gets too fond of them. She would much rather race them but sometimes has to sell a well-bred one to cover the cost of others she races.

As she speaks, she keeps one eye on the television screen in the corner, broadcasting a live feed of the Karaka sales ring. She admits she got the bug early, going to the races with her grandmother Alice and grandpa 'Chum' Howell in the 1960s. That was further south at Paraparaumu—near the Waller family farm at Foxton, as it happens. 'Chum' was a road contractor by profession and a horse fancier by preference.

The racing bug that infected the schoolgirl Denise never left her, to her mother's dismay. She knocked back university entrance to take a job at the Racing Conference, then New Zealand racing's governing body, which meant she looked after the Stud Book entries, among other responsibilities.

Mother superior: Winx's dam Vegas Showgirl does not have a stellar international pedigree but everything else prized in a broodmare: she is beautiful, athletic and maternal, and raised on rich New Zealand soil. Breeder John Camilleri's bloodstock expert had never seen a better head or a broader hip. BRONWEN HEALY PHOTOGRAPHY

Great stallions produce racehorses better than themselves. Street Cry sired not just champions but elite gallopers: from explosive sprinters to a Melbourne Cup winner, all of them tough and easy to train. By the time he died prematurely in 2014 he was the most valued 'shuttle' stallion in two hemispheres. DARLEY

It's 5 February 2013 and Winx is heading back to the paddock after a stay at Tim Boland's boot camp for young horses. Nothing about her shouts 'future champion' but her handlers recall a fast learner who never put a foot wrong. TIM BOLAND/LIMITLESS LODGE

The right choice: by the time Winx hits the line, hard held and alone, Hugh Bowman knows she has what he calls 'the X factor', vindicating his decision to ride her. Nothing she does afterwards astonishes him after her complete dominance of this, her first Cox Plate, in 2015. VINCE CALIGIURI/GETTY IMAGES

Three men in emote: Peter Tighe hugs Chris Waller while Hugh Bowman pats him on the back. They've just won their first Cox Plate and the feeling is pure elation. By the time they reach their third Cox Plate and twenty-two straight wins, the feeling is more like relief. VINCE CALIGIURI/GETTY IMAGES

The winner's circle at Moonee Valley, 2015: Debbie Kepitis and her lucky suit are about to become as famous as the Magic Bloodstock jockey colours. Note Winx's broad hindquarters, which prompted veterinary surgeon Tim Roberts to compare her body shape to an arrowhead. VINCE CALIGIURI/GETTY IMAGES

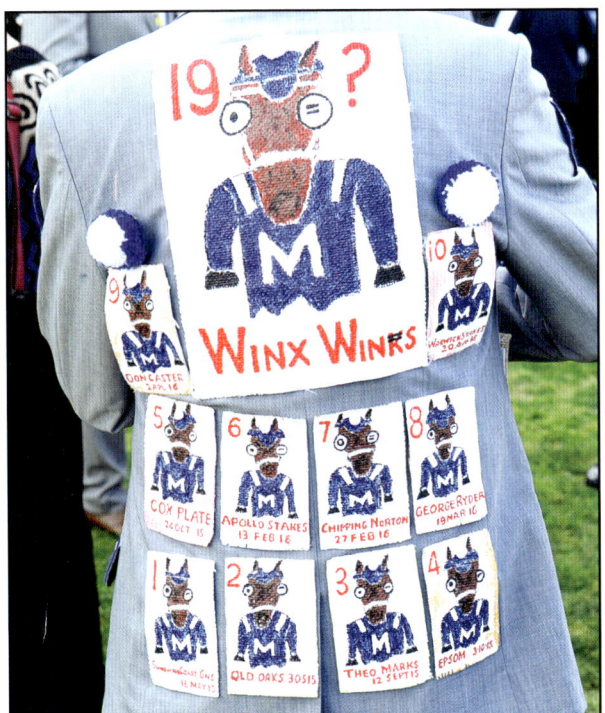

Menz business: Lloyd Menz shows off his homemade victory patches. LISA GRIMM

The second coming: Peter Tighe escorts Debbie Kepitis in her lucky suit after the 2016 Cox Plate. In truth, luck had nothing to do with it. The runaway win crushed any suggestion Winx had been fortunate the first time. MIKE KEATING/RACING PHOTOS VIA GETTY IMAGES

OPPOSITE: Good hands: Hugh Bowman holds his first Cox Plate trophy and makes plans for more. VINCE CALIGIURI/GETTY IMAGES

Team Winx on the podium for the 2016 Longines awards (left to right): Chris and Stephanie Waller, Christine Bowman, Patricia and Peter Tighe, Debbie Kepitis, Lara Kepitis, Hugh Bowman and Paul Kepitis. EAMONN M. McCORMACK/GETTY IMAGES FOR LONGINES

Two Cox Plate campaigns done, a third underway and hopes of a fourth . . . Winx's connections gather in Melbourne for her induction into the Australian Racing Hall of Fame in May 2017. At this point she has won twenty-one races, including twelve Group Ones. FIONA HAMILTON/RACING PHOTOS VIA GETTY IMAGES

Winx in the winner's circle after winning the 2017 Longines Queen Elizabeth Stakes, Randwick. LISA GRIMM

The chosen ones: Umut Odemislioglu came from Turkey via Ireland to learn more about horsemanship. He asked to look after the Street Cry filly before she was named. By the spring of 2017 Umut and Winx have become the latter day Tommy Woodcock and Phar Lap. SHARON LEE CHAPMAN

Another season, another award ceremony: this time the Victorian Racehorse of the Year in September 2017 in Melbourne. Debbie Kepitis's genuine delight is obvious as Winx is announced the winner. FIONA HAMILTON/RACING PHOTOS VIA GETTY IMAGES

After Winx courts disaster with a poor start in the 2017 Warwick Stakes, Chris Waller decides she will race in earmuffs. She is pictured just before the George Main Stakes at Randwick. She looked like a super hero and ran like one, breaking the race record. SHARON LEE CHAPMAN

OPPOSITE: Bowman is the dry, silent type but can't resist stealing a kiss after the 2017 George Main. SHARON LEE CHAPMAN

The day a Queen matched the King: Winx is cheered onto the track before defeating Humidor on 28 October 2017 to equal Kingston Town's trilogy of Cox Plates. VINCE CALIGIURI/GETTY IMAGES

The beat goes on: the crowd gasps as Humidor and Blake Shinn loom on the outside but Bowman knows Winx's third Cox Plate is in the bag. VINCE CALIGIURI/GETTY IMAGES

OPPOSITE: If one image captures the relationship between horse and rider and public this is it: Bowman throws his helmet into an ecstatic crowd after the third Cox Plate victory. It cost him a $1000 fine. MICHAEL DODGE/GETTY IMAGES

The morning after: Winx at Melbourne's Altona Beach with senior track rider Ben Cadden fifteen hours after her third Cox Plate. She looks good enough to run the race all over again. An ominous sign for rivals. SHARON LEE CHAPMAN

As surely as autumn follows spring, Winx wins her first start back after the Cox Plate. It is the 2018 Chipping Norton Stakes at Randwick and she goes around the field in trademark style, like a kelpie heading sheep. SHARON LEE CHAPMAN

Chris Waller says Winx is so docile she can be led with one finger. Debbie Kepitis proves the point as she joins Umut to lead the mare to the winner's circle at Randwick after win twenty-three of the streak, the Chipping Norton. Peter Tighe brings up the rear. SHARON LEE CHAPMAN

Hugh Bowman makes his signature 'she's apples' signal to the crowd after winning the 2018 George Ryder Stakes at Rosehill. Winx pricks her ears and trots back to scale like a show hack. At her home track, she knows she will soon be back in the comfort of her own stable. SHARON LEE CHAPMAN

Winx has just drawn the outside barrier for the 2018 Queen Elizabeth Stakes and 'eases' in the betting from $1.15 to $1.18. Peter Tighe agrees that it could be her toughest test since her first Cox Plate. It doesn't worry the punter who puts $124,500 on her. COLE BENNETTS/ GETTY IMAGES FOR THE ATC

Winx walks back after winning the 2018 Queen Elizabeth Stakes to equal Black Caviar's record of twenty-five straight wins, and Umut clasps hands with Hugh Bowman. The photograph catches the tremendous rein, deep girth and powerful hindquarter of the world's best racehorse at her peak. SHARON LEE CHAPMAN

After the 2018 Queen Elizabeth, Christine Bowman doesn't know whether to laugh or cry or kiss her Hughie so she tries all three. MARK EVANS/GETTY IMAGES

Portrait of an ideal racehorse: combining the speed and grace of her dam, the stamina and grit of her sire, and something else all her own. SHARON LEE CHAPMAN

One of the regular callers was Graeme Rogerson, then going through the bloodstock agent phase of his various identities as a racing entrepreneur, trainer and exporter. Denise was so helpful and efficient he couldn't help stealing her away from the staid office life to the more raffish surroundings of a stable run by the P.T. Barnum of horse racing.

People say plenty about Rogerson but they could never say it was dull working for the best known of New Zealand's many horse wheeler-dealers. He juggled a bewildering number of ventures with the speed and dexterity of a thimble and pea expert: expanding the Hamilton operation by buying extra property and building a new house; opening a Melbourne stable at the old Epsom track; running an international horse sale in the Middle East sponsored by a pearl retailing company; opening a racing stable in Dubai.

Name it, Rogerson did it. And Denise Howell was never far away, a reliable lieutenant in the frantic hustle and bustle at the sharp end of the horse business.

Over four decades Howell's job became her life story. She played a part in the buying and racing of hundreds of horses. Like Rogerson, she was fond of the good ones. One of their joint favourites was a locally bred horse named Batavian, the one they called 'Batman' around the stables.

'He tried hard and he was a sweetie, a lovely-looking horse that raced against the best,' is the way she summarises it. When Batavian was ready to retire from racing, she and Rogerson did a deal with the owners for him to stand as a stallion.

Batavian wasn't high-faluting enough to be fashionable but he had what it took to be a provincial stallion, the sort of journeyman to which Kiwi farmers send mares to get 'home-breds' that could win a trial or a race and so catch the eye of Australian or South-East Asian buyers.

Howell asked the Corcorans at Grangewilliam Stud—far across the ranges from the Waikato horse-breeding heartland—to take Batavian on a share deal. They did. And for one season, it was an excellent arrangement.

Rogerson said he would 'support' the horse and did—sending two mares to him in his first season and another two for his second season in 2001. No one quite remembers the other mare, but Vegas Magic was one of the pair.

Batavian had been lucky just to be there, intact and more or less in demand. Only a handful of racehorse colts get to be stud stallions. But his luck was not all good. Locked inside his genetic make-up, along with the ability to gallop that little bit harder than most of his contemporaries, Batavian carried a time bomb. He was descended on one side from a line of thorough-breds prone to heart attacks, a defect that could be traced back generations to its first known source and which line-breeding had cemented in some families.

If there is such a thing as a horse dying happy, Batavian did. The heart attack hit, as John Corcoran recalls it, while the stallion was serving his first mare of the new season.

Corcoran called Rogerson with the bad news . . . and a cunning plan to salvage at least one full service fee from the disaster. He didn't want to lose both Rogerson's mares so he told him Vegas Magic was in season and ready to be covered, so should imme-diately be served by Corcoran's own stallion (for a modest fee, of course) rather than miss the chance for several weeks while her owners looked around for another sire.

Corcoran's other stallion was Al Akbar.

•

Al Akbar wasn't regarded as top drawer in a world that values aristocratic pedigrees. He was 'colonial bred', as breeders still quaintly refer to stallions bred in Australia or New Zealand, and had earned his right to pass on his genes on the track and on 'type', meaning his looks.

He had been a tough and honest galloper, winning eight races and $255,478, often against horses that had cost far more than he did. And he was regarded as a nice horse in conformation and temperament.

His trainer Chris Wood, from Cambridge, recalls him as 'a lovely horse—a sprinter that won a Group One over a mile as well', suggesting he had guts as well as brilliance. Several jockeys rode the horse and one of them, of course, was a young Larry Cassidy, who would ride Al Akbar's granddaughter Winx twenty years later, starting her winning streak.

Not imported and not fashionably bred, Al Akbar had been good enough on the track to start his stud career at the famous Trelawney Stud in the heart of the Waikato. This being the horse nursery district renowned for Sir Patrick Hogan's Cambridge Stud. Even the Queen came to visit the home of Hogan's world-class stallions Sir Tristram and Zabeel. There is a picture of Her Majesty leaning a little out the window of the big white official car, taking a photograph of the place with her own little old-fashioned camera, the sincerest form of flattery for the stud that Pat built.

Times change and so do horse studs. Trelawney had bred a slew of top horses since its founding in the 1920s but by the end of the century a horse like Al Akbar came to be regarded as nuisance value to the people then running the stud. Standing him was a labour-intensive sideline to Trelawney's core business of sending select broodmares to fashionable outside stallions to breed commercial yearlings for the sales.

It seemed to John Corcoran, the horseman who had learned how to spot 'value' as a stock agent, that the Trelawney people were preoccupied with preparing 'supermodel' yearlings for the auction ring and losing interest in the grind of standing a middle-order stallion.

Corcoran knew Al Akbar would suit Grangewilliam perfectly because he was a relaxed animal who could laze around the paddock next door to a handful of mares, then be led into the stockyards to cover a mare when the time was ripe. Corcoran backed his hunch and approached Trelawney to see if he could buy up a majority of shares in the horse.

The old-time convention with stallions was that they were syndicated to forty owners with each entitled to an annual service, with the stud breeding extra yearlings for sale and selling services above those allocated to the owners.

In his first three years at stud, every 'freshman' stallion is a 'pig in a poke' before his first foals hit the track and prove themselves one way or the other: flying machines or flops.

Some are lucky enough, or prepotent enough, or cleverly managed enough, to get quality mares in their first two seasons and so produce winning offspring. And so some become, 'overnight' (albeit three years later), a new stud sensation.

This transformation is as lucrative as turning lead into gold, as an emerging stallion's first bunch of winners immediately guarantees inflated sales-ring dollars and service fees, often beyond the bounds of logic or prudence as a goldrush mentality takes hold.

A new 'boom' sire sweeps clean for a few seasons but there are always newer ones coming along, most often in the form of any winner of one of the big two-year-old sprints, precocious performances preferably followed by some three-year-old form as well.

Meanwhile, a long backlog of tried stallions ends up languishing between the bottom and mid-market. Owners and stud masters can tire of them, so horses are moved on and percolate down the chain from the mainstream to the margins, victims of ruthless fashions, short attention spans and the promise of the new.

Corcoran reckoned Al Akbar was ideal for his 'bread and butter' operation. So he'd made the horse a takeover target, quietly buying shares in him, then trucking him from Trelawney south to his farm in the undulating dairy and fattening country on the west coast, the district where Kiwi trained to win the 1983 Melbourne Cup. Kiwi hadn't cost much to breed in the late 1970s. Neither did Al Akbar's foals twenty years later.

•

Denise Howell recalls the Rogerson stable was resigned to the last-minute change in breeding plans for Vegas Magic. They were disappointed to lose Batavian but it was a tiny setback for an operation juggling so many balls. Al Akbar hadn't been their horse but he was johnny-on-the-spot, their mare was already there, and it was a long way back on the long and winding road across the mountains to the rich choice of stallions in the Waikato. As the song says, if you can't be with the one you love, love the one you're with.

So it was that Al Akbar got to serve Vegas Magic, a process that took much longer than with most stallions, which tend to follow the wham-bam method of speed dating in the breeding barn. Not that Al Akbar needed a breeding barn. Corcoran ran him across the fence from his mares in a roomy paddock with a rugged old set of cattle yards in the corner next to the main road, hundreds of metres from the homestead and stables.

It was there, in the yards, that the gentlemanly Al Akbar tested Corcoran's patience, as he did with every mare, 'kissing and cuddling and nibbling them for the best part of an hour'.

The later in the day this courtly foreplay took place, the more it annoyed the thirsty Corcoran, keen for a cold one at the local pub.

But, given time, Al Akbar always delivered and his fertility count was high. And so Vegas Magic conceived that day under the sky in the rolling green paddocks of a converted cattle farm tucked against the foothills of the Taranaki ranges.

Eleven months later, in October 2002, she produced the filly foal that would be called Vegas Showgirl. The beautiful foal grew into a crackerjack yearling that looked as if she would 'jump and run', like Al Akbar. She ran second at her first start over 800 metres and won her next over 880, the first two of her nine starts as a two-year-old in New Zealand.

Graeme Rogerson was not shy about racing her. In fact, he was not shy about anything. She would start thirty-four times in four seasons in two countries, winning from 880 to 1400 metres. Her last win was at the Sunshine Coast, on a heavy track in the winter of 2007.

The same track where eight years later her second foal would also win, and begin the greatest winning streak in elite horse racing in 135 years.

8

THE RIGHT STALLION

To buy young, untried racehorses is to confess publicly to being a hopeless optimist, a day dreamer and a gambler—the sort of person who throws money at an 'industry' that runs on compulsive loss making. As one penitent admits, breeding and racing thoroughbreds is mostly like 'climbing beanstalks'.

Many racehorse breeders share some of the fantasies of the buyers they cater for. Nearly everyone in racing does, except maybe feed merchants and farriers, who have their own worries collecting what they're owed by the rest.

Breeders are as different from each other as the Aga Khan is from a Kiwi cow cocky, but they are united by a shared ambition. They all dream of mixing bloodlines, or of refining and reinforcing the same bloodline by line-breeding, to create a creature that does not exist.

The perfect racehorse.

Some people have chased this quixotic quest most of their lives. John Camilleri didn't join them until he was infected in his early forties. He has made up for it since, breeding and racing horses instead of following more conventional hobbies. You might say fishing and golf lost, and racing won, but that would presume Camilleri ever wasted time on such idle pastimes. Like the horses he breeds, he has a lot of nervous energy.

Breeding horses is a chance to play God. It is not only about winning and losing but about plotting excellence and influencing the future. The effect of decisions made in the present trickle down for generations, recorded in stud books the world over. To breed and race thoroughbred horses, especially good ones, is to scribble your name alongside theirs in the margin of history. And it's a chance to profit by winning races or by selling young horses to people who plan to do that. Not a big chance . . . but it can be a big profit.

Even the smallest breeder or owner has a chance of cracking the big time—it happens every season—whereas the weekend hacker has to be resigned to never playing in Grand Slams.

Cecile Smith, who (with a partner) bred Australasia's best middle-distance horse before Winx, keeps a couple of old mares as 'pets' on her eight-acre New Zealand farmlet. The big, plain one she calls 'Large Marge' is Triassic, mother of So You Think, who won two Cox Plates among ten Group One races in two hemispheres and many millions of dollars, euros and pounds.

So You Think was sold to Coolmore in a $50 million deal that spoiled his chance of winning a third Cox Plate. He stands for $44,000 and looks like extending his own handsome branch of the thoroughbred family. Not bad, considering Triassic cost only $16,000 as a cast-for-age mare—discarded as too old and too coarse by the experts, but not by Cecile, who has a soft heart. But not, as it turns out, a soft brain.

John Camilleri is infinitely better resourced than Cecile Smith but, by choice, remains a hobby breeder with a professional attitude: the businessman in him likes his broodmare band to 'wash its own face' by selling enough commercial yearlings to cover the cost of racing some himself.

To call Camilleri's adventures in breeding a 'hobby' undersells his emotional and financial commitment to it. He is more like a weekend golfer who could get Greg Norman to build him a private course and give him putting lessons. He has collected a band of around twenty-five mares worth, between them, more than most houses. Though probably not more than his own house.

Camilleri can afford to do things well but that does not make the task of choosing which stallion for which mare any easier. This conundrum is universal for breeders—the same as for Cecile Smith with 'Large Marge' or a show rider trying to breed a hack as it is for Camilleri or the biggest breeders in the world.

The first year, Camilleri wanted to give Vegas Showgirl the best chance to justify her price tag by sending her to a proven stallion. He sent her to Encosta De Lago, one of the most consistently successful sires in the land, with a solid pedigree. His reasoning, sharpened in discussion with Peter O'Brien, was that his mare was high, wide and handsome, so would be better matched with a horse that was a little 'neater' to balance the result. It is a rule of thumb in breeding not to breed big horses together because 'they get elephants', just as it is thought unwise to breed stayers together because 'they get slow horses'.

In everything he does, says O'Brien, Camilleri wants to excel. 'He's used to sourcing the best bloodlines for chickens, so he has an innate understanding of breeding animals.'

Vegas Showgirl was big as well as beautiful so they didn't want her to 'throw a big, gawky foal'. O'Brien explains, 'Encosta was the best choice for her because he's physically very powerful, with a short back and big shoulders and big hip. Very robust.'

The plan was to breed a rockstar foal by a proven and popular establishment stallion. With horses, words like 'plan' should be replaced with 'hope', but the match with Encosta De Lago worked nearly as well as hoped: Vegas Showgirl's first foal was a bright bay filly that seemed in most ways the ideal blend of her parents.

Camilleri and O'Brien sent the filly to New Zealand to be prepared for the 2012 Karaka yearling sales, playing a hunch that Vegas Showgirl would appeal as a mother more in the country where she raced so well and so often, and that Encosta De Lago progeny were more of a novelty there than in Australia, where scores of his yearlings crowded auctions.

The filly was muscular and strong, proof that the prejudice against first foals is not always warranted. But she wasn't quite 'correct' in conformation, and the middling price of $NZ150,000 was only a fair return on the investment to breed her.

Tim Martin, a Sydney trainer, liked the filly enough to forgive her being a little 'back at the knee' (his words) and brought her home, completing the trans-Tasman merry-go-round that started with Vegas Showgirl leaving New Zealand in 2008 to improve her sales appeal by racing in Australia. Not to mention her mother Vegas Magic heading the opposite way years earlier.

Martin the knockabout, instinctive horseman—part breaker, part farrier, part track rider—kept half ownership of the filly. This pleased him more every day. Once he'd broken her in, he knew she wasn't run-of-the-mill. She was so explosively fast the co-owners named her Miss Atom Bomb.

Martin spoke to Peter O'Brien about her before that Christmas, telling him she 'had an engine' and 'blinding speed'.

The connections started dreaming about the Golden Slipper, as the connections of fast early two-year-olds often do.

As it turned out, Miss Atom Bomb's not-quite-perfect knees didn't bother her at all, but her apparently perfect 'wind' suddenly did. She had to have an operation for a breathing problem but it didn't work. So the flying filly would become a broodmare—much the same as with Black Caviar's dam Helsinge, yet another case of an injury diverting a promising filly to the breeding shed untried in a race.

Martin, whose fortunes fluctuated as many trainers' do, would sell out his share in the filly. But he stayed keen on her family. Apart from Miss Atom Bomb's raw ability, he respected her breeder. He knew John Camilleri would keep on breeding to the best stallions he could from the filly's mother, and so anything he sold should be well 'protected' in the market in future.

He was right about that. By the time Martin bought Miss Atom Bomb, Vegas Showgirl had a weanling filly. This time not by an Australian sprinting sire but by an international middle-distance star: Irish by way of Dubai and America, shut-tling to Australia to scoop up extra revenue. His name was Street Cry and, as horses go, he was a world heavyweight contender.

•

The Darley Arabian is the Genghis Khan of horses. Science tells us that the Mongolian warlord has more than sixteen million direct male descendants, mostly spread from Asia across to central Europe and the Middle East, a legacy of his appetite for wives, concubines and slaves as his Tartar hordes invaded most of the known world in the twelfth century.

Likewise, the Darley Arabian has become the daddy of them all: nineteen of every twenty thoroughbreds in the world are directly descended from him by male lineage, the rest related on the female side. The thoroughbred has contributed to several breeds—quarter horses, standardbreds, Australian stock horses—and countless 'non-stud book' and 'half-bred' horses used for hunting, polo, showjumping, stock work and so on, so the Darley Arabian (and his contemporaries the Byerley Turk and the Godolphin Barb) have millions of inter-related descendants the world over.

The Darley horse was named after the shrewd but ill-fated English merchant Thomas Darley, who bought the colt from a Bedouin chief near Aleppo in 1702. The Bedouin tribesmen were poor but led the world in horse breeding and training, keeping pedigrees tracing back to the time of the Prophet.

Times change but the allure of horses doesn't. The day would come when another Bedouin family, the Maktoums of Dubai, came into billions of dollars worth of oil and used some of it to claim the Darley name—and Godolphin as well—after they started racing horses in Britain in the 1970s.

The thoroughbreds the oil sheikhs started to buy and breed owed their stamina and beauty to their Arabian male forebears, and their speed to line-breeding of the fastest in each generation. Since the Maktoums and other ultra-wealthy Arab sheikhs started to sift through the world's best thoroughbred nurseries, they have bought and bred thousands of horses around the world. Wherever thoroughbreds are bred and raced at an elite level, the royal Maktoums of Dubai (they are affectionately known as 'the Doobie Brothers' at the Kentucky yearling sales) have set up stables and studs under their Darley and Godolphin banners.

In 1997 Sheikh Mohammed bin Rashid al Maktoum had an English mare named Helen Street covered by the American-bred Machiavellian at stud in Newmarket, England. The mare foaled a colt in Ireland and he was later taken to the United States to begin his racing life. They named him Street Cry.

Street Cry was a heavyweight international horse the way Joe Frazier was a heavyweight international boxer. He was heavy-set and dark and intimidating and although he didn't win every outing, he won when it counted and was never disgraced against the best. Street Cry was powerful and precocious enough to win his first start at two years old, durable enough to win at three and four, honest enough never to run further back than third. Stud masters love horses that do that, even if they are not pretty.

At three, Street Cry won the United Arab Emirates Derby in Dubai. And at four, he crushed the opposition in the fabulously wealthy Dubai World Cup when he unleashed an unmatchable run far from home. He did the same to win the Stephen Foster Handicap at Churchill Downs. He won five of his twelve starts, ran second six times and third once, and went to stud at Godolphin's Jonabell Stud in Kentucky at a fee of $US150,000.

In his first season, he sired Zenyatta, although that meant nothing until she started to race some five years after she was conceived. If the stamp of a stallion is that he can get at least one horse better than himself and several as good, then Street Cry was a rare sire. The giant Zenyatta, bought by a wealthy Californian record producer, Jerry Moss, would become not only the dominant mare of the first decade of the new century but the dominant middle-distance racehorse, retiring just as Frankel started his unbeaten streak in England.

Named after The Police's album *Zenyatta Mondatta* (Jerry Moss is Sting's long-time producer), Zenyatta would win her first nineteen starts. At her twentieth she failed by a nostril width in her second Breeders' Cup after giving the leaders a fifteen-length start on an unfamiliar track and surface. Americans might suggest she beat better horses more often than her contemporary Black Caviar did in Australia. Australians would disagree. But she was freakishly brilliant.

Street Cry had raced on dirt—superbly—but later produced stock that won on any surface over any distance, from Group One sprinters like Street Boss to classic winners like Street Sense to fast stayers like Shocking, the 2009 Melbourne Cup winner.

When Street Cry first came to Australia, though, his dirt form—dominating the 2002 Dubai World Cup, notably—didn't impress Australian breeders. It might even have prejudiced them against him. Some experts believe the most successful dirt horses have a slightly different galloping action from turf horses: a 'grabbing' with the front legs rather than the 'daisy-cutting' movement that is the ideal on turf.

When Street Cry was unloaded from his flight in 2003, he was still unproven and Darley struggled to find any love for him at a fee of $38,500, a third of his American price. Darley manager Alastair Pulford recalls: 'He covered just seventy-two mares. In 2004 we slashed his fee and he covered 123 mares. From this crop he got Whobegotyou and Shocking. He had one season in Victoria when we purchased the stud there in 2006. He had two years off before resuming his shuttle duties in 2009 at a fee of $110,000.' This would rise to $125,000.

Call it the Zenyatta effect. Street Cry's rising popularity and the quadrupling of his fee when he returned to Australia came after his unbeaten daughter won her first races in 2007. By 2009 she was at her stratospheric best. By this time Shocking and Whobegotyou and others were winning races in Australia and local breeders had swallowed their initial distaste. Dirt-track form wasn't dirty anymore.

If Street Cry had been a dud at stud, he would have been called plain, maybe even coarse. When he succeeded from limited opportunities, people looked harder and found more to like.

Standing still, Street Cry seemed 'just another horse', recalls Melbourne bloodstock adviser and writer Danny Power. It wasn't until he walked, head down and with purpose, business-like and bold, that you could see that the big, lazy bouncer was an athlete in disguise. He was a deep bay colour, so dark he looked almost black when he was sweaty or wet, the way So You Think does and many of Lonhro's offspring do. That colour was unrelieved except for a tiny crescent moon between his eyes and two white hind feet, adding to the impression of 'blackness'. Dapples showed through his summer coat when he was in peak condition, a trait he would pass on to both Zenyatta and Winx.

Alastair Pulford agrees Street Cry was no 'oil painting to look at'. He describes him as: 'A professional no-nonsense horse who was never nasty . . . a heavy-topped, strong horse who threw a lot of substance into his progeny. He was a great mover who walked with purpose, something a few smart breeders latched onto early on in his career. It is very rare to find a Street Cry without strength. His pedigree suggested he should have been a turf horse; his lineage is all turf.'

Street Cry's American trainer Eoin Harty told Pulford he'd seen the colt as a youngster and admired his strength and physique, and that's why Sheikh Mohammed gave him the horse to train for his starts in the United States. (He returned to the sheikh's main man Saeed bin Suroor for his Dubai campaign.)

At stud, Street Cry ended up heading the General Sires List in both hemispheres, a reign cut short by his premature death in 2014 at age sixteen. But his reputation lives on, especially because of the feats of his two extraordinary daughters.

Alastair Pulford wrote an epitaph for him at the author's request: 'Born in Ireland, raced in America and Dubai, stood in America and Australia and sired major winners in America,

Australia, England, South America and South Africa. Truly a horse of the world.'

Pulford means it. Replays of Street Cry's wins and footage of him being paraded at stud stirs memories of the Australian champion of the late 1970s, Kingston Town. Anyone who looked at Kingston Town up close was left with an impression of unusual power and leverage, muscle and bone: the deep girth, mighty shoulder, and length and strength of that great galloper comes to mind when you see Street Cry. There's an air of brute strength about both horses. For all their incestuous origins, thoroughbreds vary as much as the cousins in any big family. Street Cry and Kingston Town make you think of warhorses, not show ponies.

Not that they were similar in temperament. Street Cry was a gentleman. 'The King' was a fiery character swiftly gelded as a youngster by Tommy Smith to stop him kicking the stable down to fight the other colts over the fillies. Until the appointment with the knife, he was more interested in being a stallion than a racehorse. What would have happened if he hadn't been 'cut' is one of those questions that must still keep members of his owner's family awake sometimes.

The similarity between the two extends to the way they raced: Street Cry was a middle-distance horse but with the acceleration to be dangerous at almost any distance. He could come from well back and pick up Group One fields and crush them, dominating the last furlong in the lung-bursting rush to the line. That's what Kingston Town did. It's what Zenyatta invariably did, and from suicidally distant back marks. And it's what Winx so often does.

Combining the high cruising speed of the elite stayer with the closing rush of the top-class sprinter, an attribute most prized in racing: turn of foot. It's why canny breeders breed for speed as well as stamina.

It might have been Banjo Paterson who first wrote the line 'speed from the sire, stamina from the dam', but it was a horse-breeding axiom long before that. John Camilleri went with the formula but in reverse. Because his mare had speed to burn, he chose Street Cry for his stamina.

On 27 September 2010, Coolmore's stockman and head driver, Craig Atkinson, backed a truck to the loading ramp and led up Vegas Showgirl and her filly foal by Encosta De Lago. Vegas Showgirl was in season and Peter O'Brien had set up a 'drive on' appointment with Street Cry along the valley at Darley.

Half an hour later, the truck turned into Darley's elegant driveway. Atkinson waited while Street Cry performed what has been called (at least with elite stallions) 'the most expensive minute in sport', then took the mare home to Coolmore's river paddocks to wait her time.

That was a Monday. The following Saturday, at Hollywood Park in California, Street Cry's astonishing daughter Zenyatta won her nineteenth consecutive race. It would be her last victory before her only loss—by inches—and immediate retirement the following month. By then the tiny embryo inside Vegas Showgirl was taking shape.

As one astounding career was ending, on the other side of the world another was conceived.

9

THE STANDING START

Not *every* foal is born in the midnight hour but for every one born in daylight, dozens arrive in the middle of the night. No midwife would be surprised that most foals are born between 11 pm and 2 am and almost all the rest before dawn. We mammals tend to give birth under cover of darkness, a prehistoric survival tactic. This is why the bigger horse studs are as busy as maternity hospitals overnight: they have paddock lights and closed-circuit cameras monitored around the clock and nightshift staff on patrol, with veterinarians on call.

Several thousand years of selective breeding and feeding have domesticated the horse, and three centuries have refined the thoroughbred into an animal as dependent on humans as a caged budgerigar. But inside the hand-reared aristocrat's satin skin the wild still lurks. Each horse is born knowing only it is a prey animal, a target for predators that in the modern pastoral world no longer exist except in the horse's small but well-programmed brain. You can't wipe out a million years of instinct with a few centuries of polishing.

At the end of August 2011, a month before Vegas Showgirl's time neared, the handlers brought her group of mares, those with similar foaling dates, up from distant river paddocks where they'd been running free.

From then on they were treated as if foaling could happen at any time because, as with humans, gestation periods can vary by days or weeks. They were put in floodlit yards at night and released into the paddocks each day at daybreak.

Vegas Showgirl showed no sign of foaling on her notional date of 1 September but the Coolmore staff watched and waited. They could tell with a glance at her udder that she was only days away from foaling. It was starting to fill but the teats hadn't developed the waxy discharge that happens when a mare is set to foal. That all happened two weeks late, which wasn't all that unusual. What was unusual was that the foal arrived in broad daylight, at 9.20 am.

On the morning of 14 September, the handlers noticed Vegas Showgirl was 'sweating up' and brought her into the foaling yards near the homestead, then into what's called 'Hospital 2' foaling area.

As stud manager, Peter O'Brien was ultimately responsible for every horse on the place. But he'd had an eye peeled for Vegas Showgirl since he'd fallen for her at the Magic Millions broodmare sale three years earlier.

Because she was no longer a 'maiden mare', and had given birth easily the first time, she was not seen as a high risk. But no one takes chances with half-a-million dollars worth of mare and foal. Unlike cattle, horses are delicate creatures: without swift expert intervention a difficult birth can be fatal for both mare and foal.

O'Brien and a vet, John Freestone, were checking mares nearby when Vegas Showgirl delivered. The foaling manager Paddy Sheehan and his assistant Julie Danet handled the birth, which O'Brien could tell was going smoothly.

A foal should be upside down in the womb and be born feet and head first, like a diver. Vegas Showgirl's filly must have read the textbook.

O'Brien and the vet went over to admire the foal and check the paperwork while the others gave the new arrival an enema to clear her gut, ready for her first drink of colostrum.

At the top of the foaling report, which is filled out for every foal born on the stud, are three diagrams of a horse, both right and left profile and a front-on outline of the head. These diagrams are filled in to identify each foal with the markings they are born with and will carry for the rest of their lives.

Paddy Sheehan studied the newborn foal and swiftly marked the diagrams on her report, starting with an X in the centre of the face in line with the bottom of the eyes, indicating a 'whorl' in the hair. Then he inked in two more whorls the same way: one high on the neck on the near side (the left side) and the other on the off side (the right), closer to the wither. Then he marked both near-side feet to indicate some white in the hoof and two barely perceptible white markings—on the coronet (the band just above the hoof) of the front foot, and on the heel (just behind the hoof) of the back foot. Apart from this, the filly's dark bay coat didn't have a white hair on it. Even less than Street Cry, with his tiny crescent moon between the eyes and a couple of white socks.

In the space on the report for Foal Weight, Sheehan wrote '60½ kgs'. This was heavier than the average of fifty-three kilograms for a mare that had foaled before, but O'Brien credits the extra weight mainly to her tallness rather than bulk.

In the remarks section, O'Brien took over the pen, and wrote: 'Tall leggy filly with good strength + bone. Quality foal. Deviates in slightly RK (will be fine with time).' This cryptic notation meant her right knee turned in a little but was nothing to worry about.

Thoroughbred foals are born with spindly legs nearly as long as they will ever be, nature's way of making sure they can keep up with their mothers in the race to stay ahead of predators. But long legs mean they usually take longer to stand after being born than other hoofed animals. Many of them take hours to master the wobbly 'stilts' before they can keep up with Mum. They look like drunks at closing time, doing pratfalls.

But this foal was different. O'Brien noticed how quickly she jumped to her feet, which she did in the first ten minutes while the mare was still cleaning off the afterbirth. Twenty minutes after that, the filly was walking around as if she had been doing it all night. Most new foals are unsteady on rickety legs for hours.

Even the great Secretariat, the template against which modern champions are measured, took forty-five minutes to stand, which was quicker than most. But Vegas Showgirl's filly was something else—more like Northern Dancer, the breed-shaping progenitor that the freakish athlete Secretariat never managed to be at stud.

Tough little 'Dancer', competitive to the core, climbed to his feet within ten minutes of his birth. Not as well known as either Northern Dancer or Secretariat is the colt that came within a fraction of equalling Secretariat's all-time speed record in the Kentucky Derby. His name was Monarchos. He, too, stood and walked around ten minutes after his birth.

Such instant physical poise is rare among thoroughbreds, bred for so long for speed alone that Nature's law of survival of the fittest has been lost in all but a few hardy individuals. To look at, the Street Cry–Vegas Showgirl filly was just another gawky foal but she was strong, active and agile from the minute she hit the ground. No sabre-tooth tiger was going to catch her.

There wasn't much wrong with her and much that was right. And, as O'Brien had predicted of the creature he'd helped create, she would be 'fine with time'.

But no one could have imagined she was another Zenyatta— or better. That would be lunacy.

•

In the paddock, foals canter in circles around their mothers; in tight circles, at first, because they don't want to stray too far in case of emergency. A lion attack, say, or the sudden urge for a drink of milk.

As the babies get bigger and bolder, which they do daily, the circles get bigger and they go a little further until they move in different circles with other foals and frolic with them, testing the boundaries of maternal influence.

At Coolmore, as on any similar professional stud, staff are relatively plentiful and extremely knowledgeable or they wouldn't be there. Being Irish-based, Coolmore relies on some permanent and several visiting horsemen and -women from the old country, where blood horses have been bred in numbers for centuries, and where horse-related occupations can run in families for generations.

And then there are the locals. In the Hunter Valley, many of them have grown up around horses and livestock. Between them all, there are plenty of people who make sure that valuable foals are handled well. They are haltered and taught to lead a little before they are strong enough to pit their strength against a human.

By the time the busiest horse brander in New South Wales, Tim Cone, turns up in January 2012 to brand the previous spring's foal crop, Vegas Showgirl's filly is not the heaviest foal in the paddock but she's one of the tallest. She behaves herself well: no rearing over backwards or kicking or striking or any of the other things that make horse branding a tiring trade for a strong man.

Each foal is branded, by convention and the rules of racing, according to who its owner or breeder is and the year it was born. The breeder's brand goes low on the left shoulder. A number denoting the year of birth goes on the right shoulder, and above that is another number usually denoting the foal's birth order for that breeder that season. There is no obligation to number them in birth order, though this is the most common practice, only to ensure each foal is branded differently from its contemporaries.

Since fire-branding was phased out, branding irons have been super-chilled with liquid nitrogen to make them so cold it permanently whitens the hair and discolours the skin without any injury and with minimal discomfort.

When John Camilleri named his breeding enterprise Fairway Thoroughbreds after his Derby winner, he registered as a brand what is formally known as a 'script capital F'. The brand is an elegant piece of copperplate script forged by a skilled smith like so: $\mathscr{F}$.

Cone is a different sort of brand manager from the ones found in advertising agencies. He swiftly shaves off a patch of hair with electric clippers on each shoulder and swabs it with alcohol to stop the brand sticking. Then he puts the ultra-cold iron on the bare patch of the foal's left shoulder and counts roughly six seconds, by which time the $\mathscr{F}$ has appeared. Then he swaps sides and repeats the process, this time putting a number 6 above a number 1 on the right shoulder, denoting that the foal is Fairway's sixth of the 2011 season.

Compared with a human tattoo the whole process is swift, painless and inexpensive but leaves a permanent identity marker—unique to the filly for the rest of her life. Then it's back to the mare paddocks to do more eating and drinking and cantering in ever-bigger circles.

•

Evaluating horses is as uncertain as evaluating art. Value is one thing, price quite another. Horses are worth whatever someone will pay for them, which can vary wildly, especially at auction.

If (hypothetically speaking) Vegas Showgirl had been returned to the sales ring a few months after making $455,000, it is quite conceivable she'd fetch half that price. In other words, the mid-$200,000 sum Camilleri and O'Brien thought she was worth until they got into a bidding duel with Gerry Harvey for her.

Competition, not logic, fuels extremely high auction prices— and lack of it leads to extremely low ones.

Naturally enough, serious breeders are like big-time art dealers but more so: they take steps behind the scenes to guard their investment in a commodity, the 'value' of which is volatile, vulnerable and often short-lived. Deals are done and understandings reached to protect the commercial standing of stallions, especially, but also broodmares.

A breeder of John Camilleri's calibre, keen to run his multimillion-dollar hobby on a business footing, has to decide which yearlings to sell and which to race. His gamble is not in the betting ring but the sales ring. But someone in his position is not going to risk devaluing his breeding stock by letting the vagaries of the market dictate a 'low-ball' price. He would far rather keep Vegas Showgirl's leggy daughter than accept less than he thinks she is worth.

Street Cry's Australian fee was around $100,000 or a little more, depending who was asking. But that was for owners coming in 'off the street' with mares that did not strike Darley as a prize opportunity to throw a commercial foal, which would sell for plenty and bolster the stallion's perceived value.

In just a decade Camilleri had emerged as a long-term player with high-quality mares and the resources to do things properly—and he had the experienced horseman O'Brien in his corner. They negotiated a foal-share deal with Darley: no money would change hands but Darley would eventually take half of whatever price the foal made as a yearling.

This arrangement cut the capital outlay and the risk for Camilleri. And Darley, in return for nothing but its stallion's valuable biological input for a hectic minute in the breeding shed, got the chance to share the 'upside' when the gavel came down.

It hardly needs saying that an owner with the resources to protect future profits would put a floor in the market for the 'share' yearling, cutting Darley's risk almost to nothing. Given Street Cry's stud fee was $100,000, the breeder could afford to 'buy back' his own filly for twice that much at auction and still be no worse off than if he had actually paid up the service fee in cash eighteen months earlier.

So that's what happened. Camilleri was keen to retain the filly but willing to let the market decide if he raced her or someone else did. If she made $200,000 in the ring, he would take her home at a net cost of $100,000 and race her. But if she made more, he would just be an interested spectator, wishing the successful bidders luck and pocketing half the proceeds.

It was like tossing a coin.

•

It's true that the late Kerry Packer once dropped $7 million betting against his own horse Major Drive in the 1987 Sydney Cup, but the bookmakers got only one Packer in a lifetime.

Since the big man's death, and possibly to the relief of twitchy bookies and trainers, it's fair to say the biggest gamblers in racing are not punters but the people who buy yearlings for big prices, followed by those who sell them for not big-enough prices. And this lottery starts in the breeding shed.

When Vegas Showgirl's filly was foaled in the spring of 2011, she was one of 15,540 live thoroughbreds born in Australia, most of them within weeks of each other. Add more than 4000 foals in New Zealand and she is one in nearly 20,000 foaled in the combined Australasian pool for that season.

The success–loss ratio is tough from the jump, so to speak. It takes about 28,000 broodmares, each individually covered by one of hundreds of stallions in an international and eye-wateringly expensive speed-dating exercise, to produce those 20,000 foals.

According to Victorian bookmaker, owner and former track jockey 'Honest John' Dow, those figures mean breeders take 'board odds' of 11 to 8 against getting a live foal. And the birth (or not) of a foal is the beginning of the great annual raffle of horse breeding and buying. The attrition rate from foaling day onwards is enough to give bank managers a nervous twitch and keep divorce lawyers and veterinarians in a style guaranteed to make them rich—unless they, too, fall for the voluntary wealth-redistribution scheme known as the 'racing industry'.

Despite the number of planned foals not born at all and the number of foals that are born but don't make the cut, there are still thousands of well-bred, highly fed, hand-polished yearlings 'pimped' for sale eighteen months later.

But some animals are more equal than others: in any group of mammals, from field mice to field marshals, there is a hierarchy. At the top of the pyramid are the few that combine the conventional markers of physical correctness with famous and fashionable pedigrees.

In the shorthand of the sales ring and mounting yard, a horse that has a desirable pedigree is said to have 'a great page'. This refers to the carefully structured page of notes under each lot number in the sale catalogue, outlining the achievements of its parents—sire and dam—whether on the track or in breeding winners.

The names of maternal forebears and their progeny that have won stakes races are highlighted in bold type in the catalogue, which inspires another shorthand term: 'black type'. And so a 'great type' (a yearling of excellent conformation) with plenty of 'black type' (close relatives that won stakes races) is the Holy Grail of the sales ring: an animal of beauty, strength and balance born to a family of high achievers.

Thoroughbred horses are an aristocracy cultivated from a ruthlessly enforced meritocracy. With occasional exceptions, those males that don't perform on the track do not get to breed. The females that do not perform have to produce offspring that do. Geldings, of course, are the eunuchs in the harem.

In effect, top-end yearling sales, such as the Inglis Premier sales in Sydney and Melbourne, the Magic Millions Gold Coast sale in January and the premium Karaka sales in New Zealand each summer, are like beauty competitions for the primped and preened but wholly untested teenage offspring of an A-list of famous athletes and their glamorous partners.

The auction ring is a fascinatingly random way to select— or search for—future champions but no one has thought of a better one, a situation that suits those watchful sellers who cater to the passing parade of occasionally excitable buyers competing for yearlings.

Whoever pays $2 million for one of those golden babies in Australia and New Zealand is effectively taking odds of around 10,000 to 1 that it will win a Golden Slipper, a Blue Diamond or a Guineas—meaning one of the 'stallion-making' races. That's if it's a colt.

Winning one of these stratospheric races would put the buyer ahead of the game in one hit but the odds against are eye-popping. This is well understood by the people in the game yet tacitly ignored by big spenders excited by bidding duels, which is why there are million dollar-plus sale toppers every season.

Some studs generate the fashionably bred animals as well as the competition and the publicity to grab headlines. Some trainers spending other people's money, or hoping to attract it into syndicates, see big bidding battles for blue-blood babies as self-promotion.

Chris Waller is not that trainer.

A cynic once said racing has plenty of shrewd people but not many prudent ones. Waller might be the exception, being both shrewd and prudent. That's if 'prudent' is a word that can ever be used about paying the price of a Rolls Royce for fragile flight animals with an inbuilt tendency to cripple themselves and each other.

Waller mostly buys in the middle of the market—expensive enough, but not recklessly so. He might have gone beyond looking for 'cheapies' but he can't help wanting value, and buys to budgets, often strict ones. With certain exceptions, he tends to buy horses with 'scope', the potential to grow into middle-distance gallopers or stayers that need time to mature.

One yearling sale regular says approvingly of Waller that he mostly buys horses bred to run 2000 metres so that 'the fast ones are Guineas horses and the slower ones are Derby horses'. (Needless to add, the slowest of all are country race hacks on the way to being hobby hacks.) These stamina-bred horses can take time—years, for some—to show what's in them, and not everyone has the patience for that. But Waller does and so his owners do, too. That's a sweeping simplification but there's truth in it.

Which is why, at the Magic Millions sale on the Gold Coast in the new year of 2013, Waller and his bloodstock adviser and long-time friend Guy Mulcaster looked carefully and often at the sort of horses in which many keen buyers at that sale weren't much interested.

Most Magic Millions buyers (and therefore their trainers, taking a cue from those who pay the bills) are looking for pre-cocious speed horses, the ball-of-muscle 'early comers' that have influenced Australian breeding ever since the Golden Slipper began as the world's richest two-year-old race in 1957.

Australia can now export world-class sprinters but tends to import stayers, if not from New Zealand then from Europe.

In the middle are the versatile middle-distance horses Waller seems to like, horses with potential that might not be tapped inside the first year, and not tested properly for months after that. If it takes two years to get a horse going properly, he will take that time.

Lot 329 was one of that sort. There was nothing overly eye-catching about her, either on the page or in the flesh, but she had quiet admirers. The catalogue showed that her dam, Vegas Showgirl, was moderately bred but a tough and well-performed New Zealand race mare, a minor Group winner that had changed hands for big money when Graeme Rogerson sold her after bringing her to Australia to win a swansong race.

Her first foal, the Encosta De Lago filly Miss Atom Bomb, went wrong in a barrier trial and never raced. But the filly must have showed plenty of promise because her trainer Tim Martin liked her so much that he looked at Lot 329 closely, wishing he had the backers to buy this yearling even though she was rather different from the type Miss Atom Bomb had been.

Guy Mulcaster had seen Vegas Showgirl race in New Zealand. And he would recall her as the smashing broodmare for which John Camilleri had outbid Gerry Harvey.

There are, as the story goes about every future champion, 'twenty people' who claim to have been underbidders on the Street Cry–Vegas Showgirl filly. One who doesn't make that claim but can be believed when he says he wanted her is the trainer Gerald Ryan.

His problem, Ryan explains nearly five years later in the Rosehill trainers' hut, was that he couldn't interest owners at the sale who were looking for Golden Slipper types.

Ryan is known as one of Australia's most astute judges of young horses for the reason that he has found and trained so many of them. For instance, at the same Magic Millions sale where he saw the Street Cry filly, he bid close to half a million dollars ('And we were prepared to go to 600 grand') to buy the colt that raced as Rubick—brilliantly bred, beautiful-looking and fast—and would soon become a sire at Coolmore. Ryan also bought a $300,000 colt that, racing as Washington Heights, has earned $676,000 in Australia and Hong Kong.

Rubick and Washington Heights looked like sprinters and so sold to enthusiastic bidding. By contrast, to the majority of Magic Millions buyers, the Street Cry filly looked 'correct' but not covetable. To the casual observer, she seemed leggy and narrow and immature and nothing like the Golden Slipper hopefuls.

But Gerald Ryan and Guy Mulcaster are what you might call horse watchers: they don't so much whisper to horses as mutter about them, possibly in their sleep. Among yearling drafts from elite studs, Lot 329 was just another immature filly, but something about her appealed to each of them, as well as to the luckless Tim Martin, whose best owner was heading to New Zealand to buy at the Karaka sales instead. Martin reckons he was willing to risk $150,000 on his own account but to go any higher without a backer would have been foolhardy. Risks like that send trainers broke, as even the great Bart Cummings found.

Ryan's pool of owners was eager to buy speed but Mulcaster's friend and client Chris Waller was looking for stamina as well. It is possible the canny Kiwis thought they could pick up some bargains by playing against type and trends and the market bias for precocious 'early goers'.

'I had her led out [for inspection] maybe four times,' Ryan told me years later, expertly thumbing the Magic Millions catalogue he keeps with dozens of others beside his binoculars on a bench in the Rosehill training tower. 'A real athletic horse. Moved good.'

But Lot 329 didn't have the rockstar looks and aristocratic maternal pedigree and 'presence' of the future Rubick, so no one wanted to pony up big bucks for her.

To people other than Ryan and Mulcaster and Melbourne bloodstock agent Damon Gabbedy, who would be the eventual underbidder, the Street Cry filly might have had something of the wallflower about her. She looked a little like a teenage netballer in a beauty pageant. But the horse mutterers value things others might overlook.

Ryan is a remnant of the old school, from that part of Victoria's Western District that could be the most 'Irish' area in the southern hemisphere. He was apprenticed to Owen Lynch, an old-time trainer, and he took notice of that generation. He doesn't pull out tape measures or bother too much about the theory and science of sizing up horses. He just looks at them and trusts his instinct and his eye—which, of course, subconsciously computes bone and muscle and angles. Describing the filly as she was in 2013, he drops into horseman's shorthand practised over thirty years of chasing the sales and many years of race riding before that.

'Athletic, strong behind, strong hind leg, moved well,' he intones, dragging hard on another cigarette cupped in his workers' hands. It wasn't just him who fancied her, he says. 'My foreman Sterling Alexiou, he loved her, too.'

But love doesn't pay bills—and, Ryan adds, 'Street Cry wasn't as popular here then.' Owners with the cash to buy speedy-looking colts like the future Rubick and Washington Heights have their own ideas about what type of horse they want and what type of races they want to contest, even if they don't quibble too much with the experts about the merits of an individual animal.

For Mulcaster, things were a little different because Chris Waller is a little different, brought up in New Zealand, imbued with a love for stayers and jumpers. Lot 329 was one of a list of horses Mulcaster had marked for Waller to show his owners.

That's how they do it: narrow down the field to a long list then encourage prospective owners to pick and choose to help cut the list. Because, in the end, choosing one horse over another is always a toss-up when it comes to racing ability. So if owners with buying power don't like chestnuts or white feet or lop ears or 'baldy' blazes, then they get to choose something else on the list of preferred candidates. That way, the people who pay the bills get to claim some responsibility for sales-ring choices, for better or worse. This helps a trainer, who needs the diplomacy of a courtier to keep everyone happy . . . and who knows deep down that even after you've cut out the supposed 'riff-raff' on pedigree, conformation and type, it's still a raffle.

The good thing for Waller and Mulcaster was that they had a tight group of three owners looking at Lot 329, not a football team of clashing opinions and egos. Even better, the three got along well and were experienced enough to know what they didn't know and to trust the professionals.

If he'd been asked, the oldest of them, Richard Treweeke, might have summed it up with a saying from his boyhood on the family sheep stations: 'Don't keep a dog and bark yourself.'

The other two, Peter Tighe and Debbie Kepitis, had been around racing and in business long enough to know it is good advice.

10

THE WINNING SMILE

When Debbie Kepitis's mobile phone rings it quacks like a duck, and this tells you something: the woman in the winners' circle with the dash of purple in her dark hair is irreverent and likes colour, movement and fun.

Meet her once and you jot down 'extroverted, cheerful, glass half-full, gregarious, confident'. Meet her again and you see no need to change any of that, just add a little.

She is both hearty and kind-hearted but also an Ingham, which means she is alert. Anyone who deals with her on the business side of horse ownership would probably learn that the lady with the ready laugh is no mug. And she has done quite a bit of horse business in the last decade, and there's more where that came from.

The way things are going, Debra Norma Kepitis could be the best-known female face in Australian racing alongside the ever-green Gai Waterhouse, the ubiquitous Michelle Payne and the steely businesswoman Katie Page of Magic Millions and Harvey Norman. In a couple of years, Debbie Kepitis has become more recognisable to the wider public and more widely quoted in the mainstream media than either her father Bob or her late uncle Jack, the Ingham brothers who were giants in both racing and business.

The odd thing is that her earliest memories of racehorses are mostly of the other sort. When little Debbie Ingham was a kid living on market-garden acres near Casula in Sydney's outer west, her dad had trotters as well as gallopers. It was a natural thing to do in that time and place.

The Ingham brothers and their father Walter had concentrated on pigs before a wonderful stroke of bad luck, an outbreak of a swine disease, meant the porkers had to be destroyed or removed from the family property.

Denied the income from their pigs, the industrious Inghams concentrated on breeding poultry, first layers and then 'broilers', that would ultimately make their business one of the world's great poultry meat producers. The story goes that the original flock started with a cockerel and six hens that Walter Ingham obtained in 1918. This might be true.

In the Inghams' early days they used delivery horses to collect restaurant and pub 'slops' and stale bread as pig feed and to get produce to market—much like their contemporary and sometime competitor Charlie Baiada, John Camilleri's grandfather, across the paddocks at Pendle Hill.

It's not a big jump from delivery horses to trotters, especially in the days when standardbred harness horses were more like workhorses than pampered and pedigreed playthings. By the mid-1970s the Ingham brothers were the biggest harness-racing owners in Australia but they fell out of love with 'the trots'. Jack turned entirely to gallopers before Bob did, too.

Bob Ingham wanted to help reform the harness code but was rebuffed, so he turned his back on the sport, selling all his harness horses. And so the Inghams switched from Harold Park to the Hunter Valley, altering the trajectory of both racing codes. Losing 'the chicken kings' might have been the single most short-sighted move by any sporting body in the country's history, another nail in harness racing's coffin.

It is now history that Bob and Jack Ingham built a formidable dynasty of gallopers at their racing stables, Crown Lodge, and later at their own huge breeding operation. Starting with Valiant Rose, a mare they inherited in the 1950s, they would eventually breed and buy thousands of thoroughbreds over decades and race horses on a scale only a handful of oligarchs, landed aristocrats and 'oil sheikhs' could match overseas.

By the time Jack died at seventy-five in 2003, the brothers had 400 broodmares, ten world-class stallions, and 800 young horses on three properties, Woodlands Stud in the Hunter Valley, another farm at Cootamundra and Belmont Park on the Hawkesbury for pre-training and spelling. That season, more than 200 winners had passed the post in their vivid all-cerise colours.

As poultry producers who understood livestock breeding and management on an industrial scale, the brothers imposed business discipline on the racing enterprises. Because they mastered systems of bulk feed production and of purchasing and animal husbandry, they could make a giant stud operation run as smoothly as a small one, but far more cost-efficiently.

The result, as the most casual racegoer might recall, was that the cerise colours became the best known in Australia, mainly through the feats of their champions Octagonal and his son Lonhro but also through dozens of other notable gallopers, many bred at Woodlands and trained at Crown Lodge. There was a time when you could hardly go to a racetrack anywhere in Australia without seeing their crown-shaped brand on horses.

A few years after Jack died, Bob grasped the chance to get out of the family's massive investment in racing at a profit, or close to it. In 2008 he pulled off the sale of the century, selling the entire breeding and training complex across four states to one of the few people on Earth who could afford the $500 million price tag, Sheikh Mohammed bin Rashid al Maktoum of Dubai. The sheikh headed the global sports and racing leviathan Godolphin, mothership to the Darley stallion and breeding arm.

Bob Ingham sold everything, walk-in walk-out, right down to the stable cats. The 'hobby' had grown into a complex breeding business he no longer wanted to worry about. But he still loved the animal and wanted to keep racing.

The young Debbie had watched her father and uncle's addiction to racing with interest and pleasure but some detachment. She had ridden ponies as a child until a fall put her off riding at an age when many girls move from pony club to the show ring. So she wasn't infected with the horse bug by constant close-up exposure to them, or peer pressure from pony-mad friends, but she was brought up aware of the vagaries of racing as the news of wins and losses trickled down from her elders.

Meanwhile, she had her own life to lead.

Debbie started work at Avco finance company in Fairfield in 1977, fresh from school. A young Paul Kepitis was assistant manager there. Paul, son of Latvian parents, had grown up at West Pennant Hills and was amused to find out later that he'd had something in common with the new girl: Paul's father, a market gardener, had also raised chickens—and, in fact, had once grown them on contract for Inghams.

When they first started dating, Paul copped a bit from his workmates who would nudge him and joke about who he was going out with and Paul, puzzled, would shrug it off. He didn't know that the girl with the winning smile and the chirpy banter was one of THE Inghams. By the time he did realise, they were an item.

Their first real date was going to see the champion Kingston Town run in 1978. Some horse. Some date. They married in May 1980 at the Ingham home in Liverpool. Nearly forty years and three daughters later, they're still going to the races together to see a champion.

'We have two granddaughters now,' Debbie says. 'We're very strong on the female line!'

Until 1987, 'I was much more a mother than a racegoer,' Debbie recalls. Paul became a member of both Sydney race clubs before they were joined at the hip to become the ATC, but Bob leased a private box at Rosehill in 1987. After the birth of their second daughter Lara in 1987 (the oldest, Alinta, was born in 1984), there was a luxurious gap before baby Talia turned up, and Debbie had time to go to the races more often. Until then, she says, the track had been more something for the men in the family.

'My dad was a man's man,' she says. When she was young—she's one of four—her brothers Robby and John would go to the races with their father. It didn't interest her or her sister Lyn much then but as she grew up that changed.

In the beginning, she and Paul followed racing 'more from the periphery'. The races were a Saturday afternoon social outing. But a casual interest turned into something more passionate after Bob and Jack Ingham made the huge commitment of buying Woodlands Stud in the Hunter Valley in 1985.

Debbie, Paul and the two girls stayed there on holidays the following year, when Lara was a toddler. The stud, with its mares and foals and stallions, added a new and more personal dimension to racing. Debbie liked the property, it was hard not to, but fell in love with the horses, something the young Peter O'Brien noticed when he met her while working for Inghams at Woodlands.

She had given up any idea of going to gymkhanas and the like after the scare when her pony, Valentine, threw her off as a child. But now, a mother herself, she felt drawn to the breeding side of racing. To see horses born, grow up and be educated and eventually make their way onto the track fascinated her, as it did Paul and their girls.

While Woodlands was producing so many horses and while in-house trainers were training them at Crown Lodge, now developed into a huge state-of-the-art private training complex next to Warwick Farm racecourse, there was no call for the Kepitis family to be more 'hands on'. But when her father sold the lot to Darley, things changed.

Like the suddenly enforced end of the pigs on the family farm back in Grandpa Walter's day, the sale of Woodlands and Crown Lodge might have seemed a loss at the time but it worked out brilliantly.

In fact, Debbie's late mother Norma sensed even before the big sell-up that while 'it was great following Dad's horses it would be nice for us in the family to buy a horse together'.

So that's what they did. They went to the 2004 Inglis Easter sales and bought a colt Gerry Harvey had bred, by their old family favourite Octagonal out of Light Up The World.

'Mum gave all of us a job. I designed the colours. Mum's a Scorpio so they were black and red. Brother Robby had to come up with a list of names. John would handle the marketing if it got famous. And Lyn had to make sure all the reports were accurate.'

Robby decided to call the colt By Boon, a jokey acronym standing for 'by Bob out of Norma', which was the Ingham siblings' pedigree.

Despite his breeding, his name and his brilliant new racing colours, as a racehorse By Boon made a good family-bonding project. By Ingham standards, he didn't do much: ran maybe nine times for two wins and $32,000. 'He didn't light up the world,' Debbie jokes.

'After that Mum decided to get one a year. Next we got one by Danzero out of Professionale.' They called it Hoystar, a nod to Norma's maiden name of Hoy. 'A black, beautiful horse. John Hawkes trained him.'

When Norma died, Robby took over the striking red and black colours, which were easy to see at a distance. They raced a few more horses between the siblings, then Paul and Debbie decided to branch out on their own account.

They went into a few syndications with the usual strike rate of success: not much. Then there was a fundraiser for a Warwick Farm trainer, Tony Wildman, who had terminal cancer. Lee Freedman of Makybe Diva fame donated a year of training to be auctioned and Debbie and Paul bought it.

It meant they then had to buy a horse for Freedman to train. So they bought a filly by Danzero from Campbell Fever at the 2007 Inglis sales. Their old friend and long-time Woodlands employee Suzanne Philcox came up with the name Woppitt because the once-famous speed record enthusiast Sir Donald Campbell had kept a mascot teddy bear with that name.

Woppitt wasn't big but she was fast and tough and took the Kepitis family 'on a great ride', Debbie says. She won her first trial by five lengths and turned into a Moonee Valley specialist, hitting the front and staying there to win on the short course around the tight track. Debbie thinks that if the recent innovation of 955-metre sprints at the Valley had been around then, Woppitt would have won them.

She was a city winner who won enough stakes money to cover her price of around $230,000 and the $35,000 they'd paid at the charity auction for Freedman's training. This put little Woppitt well ahead of thousands of slow racehorses.

'She hooked us hook, line and sinker. She even won a listed race in Adelaide—a bit of black type.'

The fact that Debbie had selected Woppitt (from a list of six that Freedman had drawn up with a bloodstock agent) made her keen for another go at the lucky dip. Maybe she could pluck another winner?

Woppitt retired to the paddock at four to become a foundation member of a broodmare band owned by the newly formed Woppitt Bloodstock. So far she has produced horses as compact as herself but none quite as fast. Her third foal, the tiny Broodwar, went to an equestrian as a hack after she won $56,000 on the track.

The sale of the family's racing empire in 2008 left a gap that disappointed the Ingham siblings. They missed the heady days of 'Occy' and Lonhro and going to Rosehill to cheer on the stream of Golden Slipper runners the Ingham brothers bred: one year they started half a dozen runners in the Slipper.

Bob Ingham was firm in his resolve to sell the lot. His business instincts told him that everything is for sale at a price and that, at his age, he might not find another multibillionaire sheikh. A decade later, that decision has been vindicated. But, back then, he was conscious of the family sentiment. So he suggested filling the gap by buying a small team of horses and including the four kids in it.

The string of horses might have been small by Ingham standards but was quite big enough, and select enough, to be noticed. Ingham Racing bought twenty-four yearlings at the Easter sales for around $19 million.

But who was to train them?

The Ingham brothers had maintained a long relationship with the private trainers at Crown Lodge: John Hawkes, who was at the helm of their success for thirty-plus years, and then with the rock-solid Peter Snowden, who had been with them almost as long. But Hawkes had left before the sale to start a training partnership with his sons, and Snowden now worked exclusively for Darley under the new ownership arrangement and couldn't take outside clients. Bob wanted a completely fresh start with the family 'team'. It was as if he enjoyed the task of finding and auditioning a rising star.

He had noticed a young Kiwi named Waller over the previous couple of years, mostly on post-race interviews on television. At first he was a subject of mild curiosity—previously unknown in Sydney, bobbing up and winning a mid-week race here and there and a lot of placings.

In one sense Waller was just another hopeful, scratching a toehold. But the old businessman saw something in him. He liked the way Waller presented, as poised and polished as a Hayes or a Freedman but humble with it.

Although he was still strictly small time, he didn't act that way. He projected upwards: he was always impeccably but conservatively dressed, in a suit with just the right tie, and he spoke well but thoughtfully, without bluster or boastfulness or resorting to the slanguage of the track and stable yard. As a horse trainer he sounded less like a reformed jockey and more like the sort of middle-ground political candidate people might vote for.

And he always used the best jockeys, classes better than his horses. It was a combination that intrigued Ingham.

'This young New Zealand trainer kept shining on TV, the way he handled himself,' Debbie explains it. And away from the television cameras, he was friendly and polite. 'Chris always said "Hello".'

There were good reports from people the Inghams trusted. Peter Snowden was especially impressed with Waller's attitude, his reputation for paying his bills and his way of doing everything properly.

Bob Ingham had heard enough.

•

Stephanie Waller remembers the phone call clearly. She and Chris were in their hotel on the Gold Coast for the 2008 Magic Million yearling sales, which were in March that year, three months late because of the equine influenza outbreak.

When Chris's phone rang, she saw his eyes 'go big'—but with amazement, not alarm. The conversation didn't last too long. When it was finished, Chris said to Stephanie: 'That was Mr Ingham.'

Ingham had explained that because Peter Snowden would be contracted to train exclusively for Darley, he and the family would need a new trainer for a string of horses they were planning to buy.

Would Waller step up?

It was the moment that turbo-charged Waller's career. The twenty-four horses the Inghams bought for $19 million would push him up the trainer ranks. More importantly, as it turned out, the powerful new connection meant Debbie and Paul Kepitis would be in the Waller camp.

The alliance with the Ingham family was a version of Waller's policy of engaging the best jockeys: not only do they ride well but they are not riding against you. Having the Ingham and Kepitis horses in the stable would send the right signal to other heavyweight owners—and every well-bred youngster they sent him would not be boosting a rival. It meant that instead of gaining steadily on the trainers ahead of him, as he already was, he leapfrogged them.

Bob Ingham had found a man half his age whose experience was limited to dairy farming and training horses but whose ideas of running a business chimed with his own.

Waller believed in setting up systems that worked efficiently and predictably regardless of whether he had ten horses or hundreds. Inghams had built their empire on systems: if one thing fails when you handle millions of live chickens, the results can be catastrophic in a matter of hours, so they learned business discipline the hardest way.

Waller's years of hard work and scraping by were turning into 'luck' at last. Two weeks after the Inghams decided to send horses to Waller, he won his first Group One when Glen Boss 'threaded the needle' between horses to win the 2008 Doncaster on Triple Honour. The signs were good.

With a Doncaster winner in the stable and twenty-four Ingham horses heading to the breakers, Waller had worked his way up and onto the launching pad.

•

A difference of opinion is what makes horse racing and missionaries, someone once said. Well before Chris Waller's stable got the influx of Ingham blue bloods, Debbie Kepitis knew enough to know what she didn't know about racehorses. But she also knew her own mind and was keen to back her judgement of horses, trainers and jockeys. She had been exposed to the wisdom and prejudices of her father, her uncle and successful horsemen like John Hawkes and Peter Snowden and the stud experts at Woodlands. She knew the ones to trust and what questions to ask.

The Inghams were a robust lot and Debbie, with two brothers and male cousins, was used to sticking up for herself in what her father probably considered a man's world. What's more, she had a subtle incentive to prove a point raised in a dinner party conversation at Muswellbrook in 2003.

It was there, over a wine or two, that a *bona fide* bloodstock expert, who'd been exposed possibly too long to his boss John Singleton's gift for a pithy turn-of-phrase, forgot the need for diplomacy at the dinner table.

They'd all had enough to drink to discuss their mutual passion passionately, and along the way the expert pooh-poohed Debbie's grasp of racing and breeding.

She recalls he said something like, 'It's not natural to you.' Which, she admits, was fair enough in the sense that she was not (and still isn't) an expert whereas he is a professional, and known as a good one. But the exchange got her competitive instincts flowing.

It was those instincts that kept her going back for more after the pleasant experience of selecting and racing Woppitt. And it kept her keen to have some side ventures apart from the shared commitment to the Ingham family horses. Woppitt Bloodstock is Paul and Debbie and their daughters. But Debbie also looked at going into horses with Waller on her own account.

As her father grew older and more frail, he looked to her to keep an eye on the horses in training and so she had got used to fielding monthly bills and weekly updates from Waller about how each horse was going. This made her comfortable with the idea of joining the trainer and other potential owners to look over horses before the sales.

That's how Debbie and Paul came to meet a Brisbane couple with the same idea. Their names were Peter and Patty Tighe. The Tighes had already raced horses with a handful of others.

One of them was a retired grazier, Richard Treweeke. The Tighes didn't know him well yet but they noticed that the horses raced on the shares with him had won races. Maybe he was lucky?

He was. Born to it, some might say.

11

THE TIGHE CONNECTION

Chicago isn't the only city with a South Side. Brisbane has one, too. It's where the fruit and vegetable markets are. It's where Peter and Patty Tighe first met as teenagers, then drifted apart, then met up again and married twenty years later. And it's where they live now, when they're not travelling together.

That's one sort of love story. The other is with racing.

The Tighes have an enviable life but it hasn't happened overnight and might not have happened at all. Peter is old school. He started in his father's market business after three years as a teenage bank teller.

He was eighteen when he made his first venture into racing as an owner with Barley Sugar, a greyhound he raced with her trainer Alf Shorter. She ran at all the biggest Queensland tracks and sometimes in New South Wales. She had cost $4200, a lot of money in the 1970s, but won back half her cost in one hit.

Everything is relative: that stake might have meant as much or more than the millions he would win a lifetime later. It was a lot harder to find, and took more nerve, than the $75,000 for his share of the yearling that would become Winx.

After her racing days, Barley Sugar had several litters of pups, which meant young Tighe owned close to twenty greyhounds by the time he was twenty. But he gave 'the dogs' away as his responsibilities at the market grew.

Meanwhile, his father was treasurer at Rocklea Trotting Club, not far from the markets. The club ran meetings every Saturday, and everyone at 'the trots' could bet on gallops races all over Australia at a time when other methods of betting were limited or illegal.

'I loved a bet and still do,' says Tighe, who caught the habit of studying form from his father. 'I have my own system,' he says drily. 'Fifty per cent form study and fifty per cent luck.'

It's a great system while the luck holds.

•

It's three sleeps since the 2017 Cox Plate and Peter Tighe is sipping water after a late breakfast and, possibly, another late night. At fifty-nine he's tall, lean and fit-looking, dressed in black jumper, skinny-leg blue pants and slip-on shoes. He's blond and suntanned with a ready smile and could pass as John Singleton's younger, taller, more athletic and less noisy brother. That description flatters Singleton more than it does Tighe, who's more laconic than lairy, and quite happy not to be the centre of attention.

The Cox Plate celebrations are over but the Cup carnival isn't and he's pacing himself so he can stay the distance. The Tighes are staying at Crown Towers, as they have for every carnival for nearly twenty years.

Other people play golf in exotic places or buy boats, Tighe says. When they're not home in Brisbane he and Patty are happy to spend their spare time following the yearling sales and racing carnivals.

It's a long way from where he started in racing. It's been a rapid rise the last few years but it all began, for Tighe at least, at home in Queensland with his late father.

Kevin Tighe, described by his son as 'a very proud Queens-lander', spent his working life in the Brisbane wholesale fruit and vegetable markets, moving with them from the old city site to the present one on a floodplain at Rocklea in 1964. Kevin had worked at several businesses in the markets before eventually buying J.H. Leavy the firm, when Mr Leavy the man died just months short of getting the Queen's telegram for his 100th birthday.

'My father had an older partner in the business with him who retired in September 1978,' Peter says. 'I resigned from the bank that day and was out there within two weeks. I'd always loved the markets. I'd spent almost my entire childhood school holidays there.'

Peter had done two and a half years in the Commonwealth Bank after leaving school but always hankered for the market life. Not that he got to do much wheeling and dealing when he quit bank telling and joined his father at nineteen.

'I swept a lot of floors and nailed a lot of boxes,' he says of the days when fruit and vegetables were packed in timber cases instead of cardboard. They dealt in almost everything except, oddly enough, the Queensland staple of bananas.

'I was a bit of a clone of Dad. He taught me well about racing, about odds and reading the form.' And about the wholesale fruit and vegetable game, from farm gate to shop door.

When his father died in October 1986, Peter was only twenty-six years old. If he had a choice then—to sell out and work for someone else or go back to the bank—he didn't take it.

He stepped up, survived, and ended up running J.H. Leavy for thirty years. He still does, but now he gets a salary.

In 2016, he sold the business to an international produce company based in New Zealand, but stayed on as head of the Australian division, which ships produce all over Australia and across the Tasman. Even without his share of a river of stakes money, he wouldn't be lying awake worrying about how to pay the bills.

The broom boy who became the boss knows how the business works from the ground up, and has introduced and overseen each improvement in efficiency and scale over four decades. He knows that well-tested systems—as well as unique knowledge— make other businesses run well.

As an expert in his own field, Tighe respects experts in others, which might be why he's not one of those owners who tries to tell trainers how to train their horses. He knows a lot more about racehorses than when he bought into his first one, but has never thought he should harass the specialists.

His father had worked his whole life in the markets, juggling figures to stay ahead of the game: weights, volumes and prices. Kevin Tighe was good with the numbers, so it was natural he did some starting price bookmaking on the side, being trusted enough to take bets from friends and workers around the markets in the era before governments set up the off-course tote.

'It was the culture of the markets,' says Tighe of his dad's era. They bet on cards, dogs, trots and gallopers. The way the market was run meant those who worked there could get to the races on Wednesday and Saturday afternoons. 'That was their outlet.' A lot of people in the market owned horses—and still do. Nearly all of them have a bet. It comes naturally to those whose livelihood relies on calculating probabilities and percentages and punting on the weather and other variables.

Kevin dabbled in trotters but was more interested in punting or taking bets than owning horses. Peter was a punter, too, but took a more direct interest in owning the animals, which is why he ended up buying into greyhounds like Barley Sugar and her progeny. But he had no time for that once his father died.

His life turned serious almost overnight. Looking back on that decade and the young man he was, he muses: 'I probably put 100 per cent into the business.'

He had no time to spend with greyhounds the way he used to. He couldn't really afford to pay for racehorses. And without his father around to chew over the form, even punting lost its flavour for a while. Mere betting on horses and dogs didn't compare with the big gamble he was taking by backing himself to keep the business afloat.

'For ten years I lived and breathed the business and built it up.'

After that, he came up for air. A couple of things happened. The first was the return of the girl who used to live over the road from the Tighes. Her name was Patricia, but everyone called her Patty. She was tall and elegant and—this time he noticed—beautiful.

Patty and her mother and brother had arrived in Brisbane from Wangaratta in Victoria when she was fourteen and Peter was sixteen. They'd moved in opposite the Tighes in Osric Street, Yeronga. Patty was soon friends with Peter's younger sister Ann Maree, who studied with her at the local tertiary college.

He and Patty were never more than friends as teenagers and they drifted apart as life took them in different directions. Patty married and had a couple of children. Peter didn't. He was working too hard.

But when he was in his mid-thirties the business started to pay him back. His luck held. When he ran into Patty again, she was newly single. It wasn't quite school sweethearts finding each other but it was a second chance with the girl-next-door. They married and later had their son James, who completed the family with Patty's two older children, Nicole and Andrew.

Life was pretty good. But there was another itch to scratch.

•

Some bookmakers and punters rely on their judgement of 'heads' (the human kind) rather than of horses—a version of 'follow the money'. This works because some people seem better informed than others and so they are well worth watching. Some might even be more intuitive, a quicksilver quality between luck and judgement. Peter Tighe knew someone like that. His name was Ivio Vedelago.

The Vedelagos were well-known fruit growers from Stanthorpe on the downs south-west of Brisbane. Ivio had branched out from the orchard business 'and was a very successful man at whatever he touched', says Tighe.

One weekend around 1995 Vedelago invited him to a Brisbane Broncos Rugby League match. The Broncos must have been playing well because when Vedelago offered Tighe a half-share in a young racehorse, he accepted. They had often done business together and Vedelago seemed sure-footed. The half-share was $8000 and the horse was a homebred filly. She raced as Franciscan Magic.

Time warps memories slightly, although Tighe has an impeccable excuse when it comes to Franciscan Magic's early starts. He recalls that her first win was 'at Eagle Farm at 25 to 1', the day before their son James was born. He was right about all of it except that it was in fact the filly's second win: she'd won a maiden at Toowoomba a few weeks earlier.

'I couldn't be at the races because I wanted to be with Patty,' he says, about as genuine a declaration of love and devotion as a punter can make. But he didn't miss out on the generous odds, backing the filly each way and in trifectas.

Franciscan Magic was no world-beater but she won four races and more than $60,000 in stakes, a far better return on Tighe's

$8000 than most horses sold for fifty times the price. And good enough that her name would live on in Magic Bloodstock, the family syndicate Tighe registered in 2003.

'We were chuffed,' he says of the filly's success. Meanwhile, Patty 'had been bitten by the bug of the social side' of racing.

Tighe and another part-owner of Franciscan Magic, a local painting contractor named Eddie Edwards, went to the Brisbane Bloodstock sales with their trainer Mark Dale to look for their next horse.

'I just wanted to buy a grey horse,' says Tighe, who was working on the impeccable logic that greys are easy to pick in a field. No one else was terribly interested in the grey filly by Canadian Silver, an unfashionable stallion headed for obscurity. They got her for $8000, meaning she was valued at half the price of the mare they had just retired. Tighe kept a three-quarter share of the new horse. At that price, why not?

They named her Where's The Magic and she won her first four starts and $75,000—and might have won more if she hadn't been injured. The Tighes were well ahead on so-far modest investments in their hobby. They weren't pedigree bores, still aren't, but anyone who notices how horses are related—as all thoroughbreds are—might have noticed that Where's The Magic's great-grandmother was the super matriarch Micheline, mother of Surround, one of the greatest fillies ever to race anywhere, any time.

Surround was a grey like Where's The Magic and, like her distant relative, had just twenty-eight starts before retiring injured—but that's where the comparison ends between the two grey descendants of Micheline.

Surround is still the only three-year-old filly to win the Cox Plate—not to mention a clean sweep of Oaks in three states— and no one knows what she might have done if she hadn't been injured soon afterwards. Surround was a freak in her era, and would have dominated any other. No female racehorse before her could have matched Surround over her pet middle distances in Australia, albeit in her three-year-old season. And there has been only one since—and she races in the blue colours that Tighe had made back when he raced the 'Magic' line of horses.

Sandra Pegler, who bred Where's The Magic, knew she had a ready-made buyer for another grey by Canadian Silver. How could they refuse? The Tighes and Eddie Edwards the painter paid $12,000 for the colt, gelded him and named him Make Mine Magic.

In eight seasons he won his first six starts on the way to fourteen wins and 'just shy of a million dollars prize money'. He ran in Stradbroke Handicaps against the best horses in the land, which is special for Queenslanders. They even tried to run him in a Cox Plate but he didn't like Moonee Valley's tight track and the Melbourne way of going.

The handsome grey, who turned out to be Canadian Silver's most successful offspring, was given an honourable retirement: the clerk of the course used him at Eagle Farm race meetings. When he died, they buried his ashes there.

'He was probably the catalyst,' Peter Tighe says. 'The bug bit us.'

People can race horses all their lives and not get one as good as Make Mine Magic. But the Tighes did.

●

Just beneath the surface of Peter Tighe the amiable Queenslander is the cool decision-maker who likes everything he handles to be done well. This restless quest for excellence is instinctive.

By the time the Tighes raced their second horse, Where's The Magic, Peter was looking for ways of doing it better, as he did in business. He sent the filly to Alan Bailey, the Gold Coast trainer then regarded as one of Queensland's shrewdest.

It was Bailey who would sustain the long and successful career of Make Mine Magic, keeping him fresh and sound season after season. And it was Bailey to whom the Tighes turned in order to feed their new interest.

But the racing gods, having lured them on with beginner's luck, went missing for a few years. The Tighes went to yearling sales—only the Queensland ones at this stage—and bought a series of youngsters on Bailey's recommendation. They started to pay more, shares in horses costing up to $200,000, usually with other syndicate members. None of the new horses made the returns that Make Mine Magic had. Despite that, it was the gallant grey horse's 'shout': they were playing with his winnings.

Along the way, Bailey introduced them to one of his other clients, a retired Sydney man holidaying on the Gold Coast. Richard Treweeke was a generation older than the Tighes, had grazing interests in the Hunter Valley and New Zealand, and was one of those old-time 'sports' who nearly always had a racehorse in his name. Which was why, when the Tighes bought a filly by Noverre for $80,000 at the 2007 Magic Millions sale, their new acquaintance took a half-share.

High Roll'n Woman, as they named her, won her first three starts and ran third in the 2008 Magic Millions 2YO Classic, which put them $250,000 'in the black' immediately and ensured her resale value as a broodmare—another $220,000, as it turned out.

Apart from giving them a thrilling two-year-old season of racegoing, the fast filly brought in roughly $400,000 more than she cost. It was a good start to the relationship between the Tighes and Treweeke. It's not that all racehorse owners are superstitious, exactly, but most are. And it's a rare owner who doesn't want to stick with winning riders, trainers and partners. If they didn't believe in luck ahead of logic, they wouldn't be racing horses.

'I never owned a horse with Richard that never won a race,' says Tighe about his southern partner. Although it was a close-run thing with a filly called Ruth's Secret—'the name's something to do with an old girlfriend of Richard's, I think'. This filly, bred by Tony Santic of Makybe Diva fame, won only one race and $7400 before being injured. Treweeke, a romantic at heart, gallantly kept her as a broodmare.

Treweeke wasn't the only Sydney connection that Alan Bailey made for the Tighes. Having a good horse helped. When Make Mine Magic raced in Sydney, Bailey stabled him with Kevin Moses at Randwick. The former jockey and his wife Jenny were sociable people and got along well with the Tighes. When Jenny and Kevin Moses bought a colt to be raced by a women-only syndicate, they asked Patty Tighe to take a share.

It was a disparate group. Besides Patty Tighe, Jenny Moses and Kim Beadman, wife of the fine jockey Darren, there were seven others. One of them was Debbie Kepitis.

The colt the women raced cost $85,000. They named him Perchance. He turned into a serial bridesmaid, running second an unlikely number of times before breaking through in a $100,000 feature maiden race in Brisbane—the Brisbane Plate—put on to commemorate the amalgamation of the two main race clubs there. He won one other race in fifteen outings.

Debbie couldn't be in Brisbane for Perchance's good win— the one that paid for him—but the Tighes saw her at the races in Melbourne that spring and struck up a friendship that waxed over the seasons. They all stayed at Crown Towers. It would become an annual get-together.

'Debbie was looking to get into horses—but not at any cost,' recalls Tighe. 'I think the first one was Loophole, which we bought in New Zealand. Waller wanted to put together a group of owners and put up a million dollars to buy several horses in New Zealand.'

They went to the Karaka sales in 2011 to execute Waller's scheme to buy staying stock specifically aimed at the classics— Oaks and Derbies.

The horse that would race as Loophole was by Lonhro from Better Alternative. 'Deb was very keen to buy him,' says Tighe, because of the Ingham family attachment to Lonhro and

Lonhro's sire Octagonal. It turned out as good a reason as any to buy a particular horse.

Loophole cost $260,000. Debbie Kepitis signed up for him at the auction and he would go back to Sydney to be broken in and raced in partnership by her family's Woppitt Bloodstock and Tighe's Magic Bloodstock.

Loophole would eventually start sixty-three times over seven seasons and win $471,500. By 2013 he was promising enough that when they returned to New Zealand with Waller and the same plan, a syndicate that included Kepitis and Tighe bought his half-brother (a foal of the same mother, Better Alternative) by the then-ancient Zabeel.

The valid prejudice that says old stallions lose their ability to throw as many winners as they used to might have kept the price reasonable. Zabeel wasn't just any old stallion but the slashing colt was a bargain at $190,000. They called him Preferment.

In any other year in any other decade, to buy such a well-bred colt, one that went on to win Group One races and $3.6 million in prize money, would have been the coup of a lifetime, beginner's luck never to be topped. When Preferment won a Derby then shaped as a class-staying four-year-old, it was ludicrous to think he'd soon be overshadowed by a filly they'd bought the same month.

12

THE RIGHT STATION
IN LIFE

If you had to choose one story about Richard Treweeke that shows where he's from, it is the one about his first trip abroad. It was on a ship, for a start. The tiny percentage of Australians who went overseas in the decade after World War II went by sea, a voyage more in keeping with world travel a century earlier than that of a few years later.

These were the days when Prime Minister Menzies would spend five weeks on an ocean liner, dining at the captain's table, then spend weeks in England watching cricket and attending to affairs of state, then take another five weeks steaming home. There were, of course, telegrams for national emergencies more urgent than Test Cricket and Buckingham Palace garden parties.

It was a different world, hard for anyone born since the 1960s to imagine, and young Treweeke had a first-class view of it.

Richard was born on 29 November 1930 in the family's Sydney house at Tamarama. His mother insisted on summoning a doctor to the house for each birth because she was afraid of her babies being 'swapped' if she ventured to a hospital. After delivering each baby she would return to whichever station her husband was running.

In January 1949, a few weeks out of Australia's oldest boarding school, The King's School, Richard boarded the spanking new British liner SS *Orcades* in Sydney for the return leg of its maiden voyage. He was travelling with his grandfather George Treweeke and his grandmother, the former Hattie Swift.

Hattie, he mentions in passing, was descended from the family of Jonathan Swift. Her forebear was a Theophilus Swift, who survived an attack by the notorious bushranger Martin Cash—the Irish convict who had worked for a pioneer farmer named George Bowman in New South Wales before being sent to Van Diemen's Land. George Bowman being the direct forebear of the jockey Hugh Bowman and occupier of the Hunter Valley property where Winx would be bred generations later. Owner, rider and horse are connected by their origins in the pastoral age, which makes theirs a very Australian story.

The *Orcades* was 28,000 tons and the last word in floating luxury, the pride of the Orient Line with a crew of 600 and what contemporary newspapers reported admiringly as a power plant big enough 'to light a city'.

The Treweeke party disembarked in Melbourne to take in the races at Flemington. That day the great Scobie Breasley rode five winners and young Richard backed all of them, according to his much older self.

'I won about 2600 pounds!' he says, reliving the pleasure of a magical afternoon in a vanished world. It was a fantastic sum for a teenager, even one as well off as he was. His grandfather, who owned a string of sheep and cattle stations in New South Wales, had been giving him £10 a week allowance—'but I opened my big gob and he stopped paying me until it [the winnings] was all gone!'

That might seem like a lot of spending, and it was. But, he explains, there were girls on the *Orcades*, and more in London and Europe, to help him spread his good fortune. Even as a youngster, Treweeke was fond of female company, and spent generously.

His daughter Elizabeth cuts in mischievously at this point of his life story to underline the point that age did not cure him of this tendency.

'At Dad's eightieth there was a line of women all desperate to tell me they had known him biblically. He was a lover—and maintained friendships with all of them. He loves to have a good time and is incredibly generous and kind.'

All of which is unquestionably true of the retired grazier who is trawling his memory for anecdotes from a fortunate life.

'We travelled all over England,' Richard continues with his tale. 'Went to Cornwall and spent a bit of time [there].' The Cornwall side trip was because the original Treweekes, who'd founded the family's grazing dynasty after the 1850s gold rushes, had come from the district of Breage.

Old George and young Richard also went to the races at Ascot, as one might. It was a break from inspecting stud cattle and arranging to ship the now rare Devon breed home to one of the family properties near Orange.

Importing Devons, cattle that are dark red all over with no white markings, was Grandfather Treweeke's cunning plan. In those days everyone 'out west' had the same common beef breeds, predominantly Herefords and shorthorns, so anonymous it was easy for stock thieves to get away with stealing them.

'Grandfather brought in Devon bulls so when these shifty buggers started to pinch your cattle, you'd know by looking at them,' Richard explains. 'We had three properties at Bourke, one at Scone and four at Orange, one being Uralla, where I grew up.'

Travelling around a worn-out Britain and war-torn Europe wasn't always easy but they did their best to dodge the worst bits. 'Grandfather bought a Humber Super Snipe and hired a chauffeur who drove us all over France, Italy and Spain.'

When they got home, Richard went jackarooing, mostly on sheep stations. The first was Egelabra near Warren, one of the finest merino studs in Australia. Then he went to Condobolin and worked for Banjo Paterson's son Hugh, who was 'married to a White from Scone'.

He doesn't bother mentioning this is the same White family that produced Patrick White the novelist and Nobel laureate. In his time the Whites were better known as polo players and stock breeders than writers. They possibly still are.

Richard spent a lot of time with horses and dogs and inherited the family's fondness for breeding and racing thoroughbreds. Grandfather George had always liked having well-bred horses. In the 1940s, he part-owned a mare named Hesione, half-sister to the world-famous Ajax, probably the best horse bred at Widden

Stud before Kingston Town and eventually sold to Bing Crosby and his Hollywood friends in California.

Treweekes have been around gallopers for more than a century and the family has many racing connections.

Richard's distant cousin Jean Treweeke married Germaine 'Winks' McMicking, one of the four owners of Gunsynd, the 1970s hero horse that won the Cox Plate and the Doncaster and plenty more. The public loved the handsome grey, which was tough as well as talented and caught the eye.

Another cousin, Bill Treweeke, owned Maidenhead, a top horse in the 1960s. And Richard reckons one of the old-time Treweekes won a Grand National in the 1920s.

The Treweeke family, in other words, have been in many ways blessed by fortune. But the stations and the wool cheques, the Randwick Members Stand and Tattersalls Club couldn't save them from the consequences of war.

The old man jumps up to show off a framed black and white photograph of a handsome man in an Australian officer's uniform, in pride of place on one wall of his airy apartment on Sydney's North Shore.

It is his father Lieutenant George Swift Treweeke, known as 'Swift', of the 6th Light Horse and 13/33 Infantry. He survived two years in Bougainville and New Guinea in World War II but was killed in a car crash on his way home to Bourke in 1950, aged forty-three, only days after he buried his own father, George senior. His beloved brother, Richard's uncle, Lieutenant Fred Treweeke, had been killed at Tobruk on 28 October 1942.

Richard doesn't dwell on the war's lingering effects on the family, preferring to remember a happy childhood riding his pony five miles to and from school in Orange before going to board at King's in Sydney in 1943. He played rugby, did athletics and target shooting in the school cadets, but he never forgot his pony mare—only her name, which is excusable after eight decades and the names of so many female friends of the human variety.

'She was a little chestnut mare with a white blaze,' he says, eyes lighting up. 'I've always liked mares and fillies. It's difficult to get rid of a stallion or a gelding.'

As a livestock man, he thinks, he was better at breeding merinos than cattle or horses. But back at Orange in the 1950s, after his jackaroo phase, he 'had a bit more money' and became a life member of the Orange Jockey Club.

'All my mates had horses,' he says. From then on, he usually had a share of a racehorse, too.

He jumps up again and shows off a trophy wall of race-finish photographs. Nearly every one is a mare and their names are as racy as they are . . . Ruth's Secret, Midnight Minx, Champagne Cath, Night Rogues, Jitterbug, Midnight Dancer.

He has so many photographs they've spilled out of the study and are marching up other walls. Two are leaning against the skirting board, waiting to be hung.

The best of the lot has the sauciest name of all, he explains, shoulders shaking with mirth. He should know because he named her Winx.

'Each of us had to put names in. One of mine was Winx . . .

when you see the showgirls in Vegas, they wink at you.' That's his story and he's sticking to it.

His memory is getting a little patchy but he is firm about some things. Such as his opinion that, from Phar Lap to Black Caviar, there's never been a better horse in the land than Winx.

The first time he clapped eyes on her was in the horse wash at the Magic Millions sales complex straight after the auction. It's hot in Queensland in January and the handler was hosing the yearling to cool her after her first public outing.

Richard remembers how calmly she stood, a professional already. It made him want to stick around long enough to see her race. So he did.

13

THE SOUND ADVICE

Bloodstock agents are part anatomists, part salesmen, part sooth-sayers and, in the case of the Irish subspecies, possibly part horse. Many of them are passably honest.

When the late Robert Sangster led the boldest and shrewdest buying team across the Atlantic late last century to mount raids on the Kentucky yearling sales, the crew would take with them a wizened Irish horse whisperer who had trouble deciphering the written word but could read young horses fluently.

The story goes that this leprechaun could not work out how to turn off an ice-cream machine in the Keeneland sales dining room and so let it run on the floor, to the bemusement of all. He was delighted with the novelty of hot and cold running water in the hotel. And yet the sharpest multimillionaires and racing men who have ever traded in thoroughbreds, renowned people with names like Magnier and O'Brien, trusted this Paddy O'Rainman to help divine which expensive babies they should buy for the price of houses and yachts and Rollers. This is racing.

It is clear that the relationship between trainers, owners and their bloodstock advisers is close, right up until it's not. Things can change when the money runs faster than the horses. Until that point, they have to trust one another almost implicitly in a business that can shake people's faith in human nature and horses' legs.

Chris Waller does not merely trust his long-time bloodstock adviser Guy Mulcaster. He believes in him. He privately describes him as 'the best judge of a horse in the world' and means it. One reason for Mulcaster's acumen is that he's had plenty of practice since he left the family farm near Hawke's Bay a long time ago to work with horses, a journey that brought him into contact with another Kiwi farm boy, the younger Waller. Now they've joined forces again, climbing rather higher up the totem pole.

The relationship is close but not cosy. It runs on action and results. So, back in December 2012, Mulcaster is not lazing on a beach somewhere contemplating Christmas. It turns out that the week he spends on the road, inspecting yearlings at Hunter Valley studs, is the start of a purple patch that seals his reputation and Waller's high opinion of him. At the time, of course, it's just a daily grind, with the results nearly two years off.

For a bloodstock agent that means time in dull motel rooms, a dusty car, an uncomfortably warm mobile phone and an overworked tablet device crammed with downloads of every conceivable bloodstock catalogue, stud book and racing database. Some people still carry the hard copy 'books' but, like Waller, this agent is an early adopter of electronic aids.

Mulcaster is a watcher. See him at yearling sales or races and he is watching horses and sometimes people, eyes narrowed in thought and flicking from the horses to phone to tablet screen.

Now and again he slips away for a smoke but that doesn't distract him. He's taking pictures in his head, filing some and discarding most in an endless chain, a routine Waller tires of after a couple of days of inspecting yearlings. The agent backs up his memory by tapping cryptic notes onto each catalogue page.

By the time he reaches the Magic Millions venue on the Gold Coast, ready for the yearling sale that January, he's already spent days going over hundreds of yearlings in the Hunter Valley. One of them was Lot 329, Vegas Showgirl's filly at Coolmore Stud. She didn't stand out enough for him to recall much about her later but obviously she passed the first audition.

This whistlestop tour isn't so Mulcaster can be the first to identify a few hot prospects but to eliminate the many that aren't. This cuts down the workload at the sale, which is a quietly frantic climax of the quest for the best at the right price.

More than 900 yearlings are to be auctioned over a week, so he has had to prune the numbers to a long list then help turn it into a short one. A bloodstock agent's task is like a detective's: eliminate 'suspects' to find the few likely candidates to concentrate on. Then call in forensics.

Enter Waller with his trusted Sydney vet Tim Roberts, who arrive on the Sunday before the sale starts on Wednesday. It's good cop, bad cop time. Roberts gets to be bad cop. As he wisecracks later, if they manage to find a Group One winner, agents are 'at the races high-fiving everyone'—but if one breaks down it's the vet's fault and agents are nowhere to be seen. As with most jokes, it works because there's a grain of truth in it.

Like all trainers, Waller has likes and dislikes about young horses but doesn't shout them for reasons of diplomacy. Some entrenched ideas come from personal experience, others are inherited from trusted mentors all the way back to his grandfather, Colin Waller. Some biases are temporary because racetrack success and failures overturn them: stallions shunned one season can be cock of the walk in the next, a process that happens even faster in reverse as roosters become feather dusters.

Waller is wary of unproven first-season sires, unlike buyers who gamble on 'freshmen' stallions in the hope that one is the next genetic superstar. He likes a proven stallion, one that produces horses with good temperaments and natural athleticism. He looks for runners, not body builders with false muscles.

'I love a good temperament because I am working with them,' he says. 'I like horses that move well, but I leave the conformation to Guy and Tim. And I like value: the best horse you can get for the money because I respect people's money—it's after-tax money that they could be spending elsewhere. We need people to come back and re-invest.'

This is code for 'Don't burn the people who pay for the party' and it ties in with his other dislike: 'I'm not a big fan of people forcing a horse on me, saying they will keep a share.'

He'd rather buy outright at the true market price and pass on the saving to owners instead of propping up an artificially big price by leaving sellers with big chunks of ownership. 'If Guy likes a horse and Tim says it's sound, we will try to buy it.'

Changing fashions bemuse him but they are a fact of life in the annual sales lottery. At the time of writing, the unfashionably bred but aptly named Queensland sprinter Spirit Of Boom has been elevated into a boom stallion. And on the other end of the seesaw, the once expensive and briefly popular Newmarket Handicap winner Wanted has become unwanted, exiled to rural Queensland where he is a bargain for breeders who could never have afforded him in his first four 'pop star' seasons in Victoria.

Whether either horse entirely deserves his fate doesn't matter because the market is fickle and usually unforgiving: it won't take much for Spirit Of Boom to lose his shine but it would take a slew of late-blooming, spring-heeled offspring to make Wanted wanted again. It can happen.

Thoroughbred stallions rise and fall faster than football coaches. Statistics aside, Waller suggests, trainers can't help liking tractable, 'trainable' horses—always providing these sensible animals are not also slow.

The same trainers like to dodge stock with a reputation for being nasty and skittish, erratic trackworkers and 'bad doers' that go off their feed at the least sign of stress—unless, of course, the alley cat becomes a lion in a race. Winners are forgiven much and losers are soon on the truck.

Because they can't actually see what's in a young horse's head or its heart, trainers and their advisers look very hard at their legs. Particularly front legs from the knee down. Some are more forgiving of faults than others but the longtime veterinary surgeon Tim Roberts is not the forgiving type.

Except, of course, the year he advised Nick Moraitis to take a punt on a rough yearling by a first-season sire. The yearling came cheap at $40,000, turned into the champion Might And Power, and his sire Zabeel became one of the greatest stamina stallions in the world.

But Might And Power's Caulfield–Melbourne Cup double and Cox Plate make him the exception to the Roberts rule.

'I'm the conformation Nazi,' he says from the vantage point of forty years in the business, including twenty in South Africa. 'My job is to make sure we buy horses that don't break down.' He studies the entrants in an equine beauty pageant as dispassionately as a butcher buying bullocks, looking for the ones the judges have the *least chance* of breaking down.

To hear Roberts tell it (part of a routine of friendly rivalry), a bloodstock agent is a connoisseur who follows the pseudo-science of pedigrees and abstract notions like type and quality and whether or not a yearling shares desirable traits with its most successful near-relatives, preferably ones grown in a particular district. Much like a wine buff.

By contrast, Roberts suggests tongue-in-cheek, the veterinary surgeon is a scientist, an impartial professional above mere theories, anecdotal evidence and subjective judgements. He looks at just the facts, ma'am: the biomechanical structure of the animal, using X-rays and surgical scoping gear that can detect and measure any deviation from ideal textbook anatomy.

The 'conformation Nazi' is like the laboratory boffin who can tell you exactly how much alcohol and acidity and sulphites are in the connoisseur's latest wine vintage, ignoring the price tag and fancy label. He doesn't care much about pedigrees but checks nutritional history, hearts and airways and, most of all, their legs to make sure 'the wheels don't fall off'.

Judging how the bone and muscle of a young horse will flow together later in its life—another year, maybe two—is where science meets theory and practice. Does the sum of the parts look like an athlete or just another handsome also-ran?

Disagreements over that question make the yearling market—and racing itself.

•

Mulcaster has cut the original 900-plus babies to 100. The next cut is from 100 to sixty-one. Of those, Tim Roberts approves about forty as sound enough to buy. The vet's job is not to select horses, which Roberts is very capable of doing, but to veto any selections that don't meet strict physical standards.

From this lot of prospects they hope to win 'four or five' at auction, the final move in the relentless sieving process that reduces thousands of available yearlings to the few to buy and try.

Inevitably, compromises must be made. The agent can covet some horses and the vet can knock them out as risks, but Waller still has to find horses to fit inside certain price brackets. Buying the 'best in show' for the biggest money has never been his thing. He buys like a farmer, not a promoter. He wants good value and sound animals and doesn't judge a horse by its price tag.

There is a rule-of-thumb that around '200 grand' is a natural limit for careful buyers because up to that price, it is feasible a useful galloper might pay its way with a few provincial wins and a couple of races 'in town'. Pay much more than $200,000 and the horse has to be much classier to 'wash its own face', let alone turn a profit.

Richard Treweeke has met Debbie Kepitis through Peter Tighe and is happy to throw in his lot with them. They agree that $70,000 each makes a round figure that should land them a nice horse. But which one?

In the thoroughbred business, it helps to be born with a silver spoon in your mouth, even if it doesn't help for long. Horses (and people) born with a wooden spoon can kick on through natural ability. But that's once they get to the racetrack and looks and pedigree and price stop mattering so much. Before racetrack reality bites, yearlings have to fit market conventions to appeal to buyers.

Buyers generally want big, shiny, well-muscled, loose-walking yearling colts that look like their sires, preferably in bays or browns with not too much 'white paint'. Some of these biases might strike an outsider as something between superstition and fashion, like thinking green cars are bad luck or blue is better than beige.

If pressed, buyers have to concede that winners come in all shapes and sizes and colours. But that doesn't alter the fact that at the Magic Millions sale, where most people are after 'early 'speed', a lanky filly like Lot 329 looks a little like a fifteen-year-old netballer standing next to seventeen-year-old wrestlers. She is never going to get near the sale toppers.

When Waller's group work through the list and get to her, Waller and Roberts see nothing to alarm them and plenty to tick: nice-enough head, kind eye and generous nostril, long rein (neck), deep girth, powerful hindquarter, good demeanour, good walk. And, most importantly: flawless legs.

The slight turn in the right knee that Peter O'Brien noticed in the hour-old foal has long gone, as he said it would. Had potential buyers asked O'Brien, he could have told them something else for nothing.

'She'd eat stones,' he says, which is Irish for 'her appetite and digestion are excellent', a great asset in racehorses because it means they can take the work to reach the fitness they need.

Significantly, Mulcaster is more impressed by her dam Vegas Showgirl than the pedigree purists are because he remembers seeing her race in New Zealand. Aussies and others might look down on Kiwi form but Mulcaster knows exactly what he saw galloping on the green, green grass of home, and he liked it.

'You wouldn't have called her top class but she was good,' he is to recall. 'She was tough and resilient—and history shows these good New Zealand race mares can leave good horses.'

But it isn't as if Lot 329 is his favourite Street Cry at the sale. That would be Lot 340, due in the ring thirty minutes later. This one is not a lean, light filly. It's an imposing black colt that looks like Street Cry himself but more elegant, the right pitch of power and poise.

The colt reminds the then boom Melbourne trainer Mark Kavanagh of Shocking, his electrifying 2009 Melbourne Cup winner by Street Cry, which is why he pays $550,000 on behalf of a coterie of Melbourne business people wanting a Cup contender. Kavanagh also pays big bucks for another Street Cry colt later in the sale.

Both prices are outside the Waller group's budgets, although Debbie Kepitis puts up $100,000 for a fifth share of the expensive Fastnet Rock filly that is to race successfully as Amicus.

Tim Roberts the vet is looking only at the anatomy that's put in front of him. Lot 329 passes. But he is to say later that if he were buying, he might have gone to $160,000 but no more than $180,000 for her. He doesn't rate New Zealand form or Al Akbar ('basically a failed stallion'), which he reckons restricts the 'residual value' of the filly to what she does on the track.

Potential buyers circling the filly probably privately agree with this valuation but hope she goes for less.

Tim Martin, the knockabout horseman who befriended Waller when he came to Rosehill, is counting on the Al Akbar factor to discourage pedigree devotees who prefer 'the page' to the animal. He wants her because he rates her two-year-old half-sister, but can't risk more than $150,000 because his key owners would rather buy in New Zealand this season.

Martin's fellow Rosehill trainer Gerald Ryan is in the same boat: he fancies the filly but without backers sharing his enthusiasm for a non-sprinting, slow developer, his only chance of getting her is if she's friendless in the ring.

Both bargain hunters are shot ducks well before the filly is led in front of the auctioneer. At least three keen buyers with deeper pockets are eyeing Lot 329.

Damon Gabbedy of Belmont Bloodstock is looking at her for a New South Wales breeder whose identity he doesn't reveal then or later, but whom ringside regulars later suggest is Peter Orton of Vinery Stud.

Gabbedy is known as a straight shooter and a shrewd judge of fillies, although top of his CV is the fact he bought the colt turned star racehorse turned great stallion, Encosta De Lago.

What none of them know is that the filly's breeder John Camilleri is prepared to buy her back for $200,000 at auction to fulfil his obligation under the foal-share deal with Street Cry's owners, Darley. He likes the filly but if he wants to keep her he has to meet the market.

Then there's Debbie Kepitis and Peter Tighe—and Tighe's 'lucky' horse partner Richard Treweeke, who is dropping into the sales late because he is on holiday on the Gold Coast. At the time Treweeke and Tighe part-own a star juvenile, Champagne Cath, tipped as Waller's Golden Slipper chance that season. This very promising filly is by Street Sense, the best son of Street Cry, and another reason for this crew to like Lot 329's breeding.

Debbie Kepitis's blunt summary of the big yearling sales is that you go to Karaka for 'the long distance horse', to the Inglis Easter sales for 'the great page' (meaning fashionable and expensive pedigrees) and to the Gold Coast to get something 'up and running for a reasonable price'.

Richard Treweeke has suggested getting something 'up and running' because, he tells them disarmingly, he's not young and won't be around forever.

Debbie likes the charming old-timer. She's met him once through the Champagne Cath owners and concludes: 'He would have been a very suave young man once, a very smooth operator.' Even better, she says, 'He's a good payer and we don't argue. We don't want to train the horses. Richard had the same attitude to horses and training as we did.'

Lot 329 passes Debbie's criteria but doesn't look better than others she has earmarked. Looking back, she is not tempted to rewrite history. Neither are the rest of them. The Street Cry filly was high on the list but never a 'must buy'.

'I did my thing,' Debbie recalls. 'I get a list of horses from Guy—about thirty—and look at them. Paul did, too. We cut off the ones we don't like. It might be the colour, the socks, the eye.

'She [Lot 329] was beautiful but she didn't stand out. She's the right colour and stood tall and held herself well. Had a good eye. But nothing outstanding.'

By 'right colour', she means not a flashy chestnut but a dark bay with hardly a white hair on her. Debbie doesn't like odd numbers of white socks and prefers none at all.

'On the first day of the sale we thought $180,000 would be the mark. But the ones I wanted the first day were going higher than expected. So we decided we would have to go higher than that.'

Mulcaster could not recall much about Lot 329. He'd seen her at Coolmore on his sweep of the Hunter Valley studs and obviously approved her to be vetted. Talking about it later, he scrolls back to the catalogue page, which tells the tale in shorthand.

Next to 'Vet' he has typed *low-medium*. Next to 'Type' is *medium size, good head*. Then he's put his own code: *NB++*.

'It's not top secret,' he grins. 'Stands for "Not Bad".'

It's a pretty laconic description for a lot of horse. It's the same notation he put on Lot 597, the crackerjack Fastnet Rock filly which the Waller team bought two days later for $500,000 on behalf of several lucky co-owners . . . including the Kepitis family's Woppitt Bloodstock and a Brisbane friend of Peter Tighe's, Noel Greenhalgh.

That's the one that will race as Amicus, win the Thousand Guineas and be sold to Europe for top money to go to the world's leading sire Galileo. In other words, she proves an extraordinarily good result. Yet Amicus is a distant third behind two other horses Debbie Kepitis signed for (as part-owner) in just over two weeks.

Peter Tighe has been looking at the horses on the vetted list but he's the first to admit that by this stage, they all 'look like beautiful creatures' to him, and that the subtleties of tiny faults evade him, as they do most people. He's pretty happy to leave it to the experts. Debbie Kepitis, on the other hand, loves looking at horses and is keen to know as much as she can.

'The years Inghams didn't buy horses, Paul and I would buy, so we slowly went into it that way,' she later explains. They did the sales circuit with Waller's team 'with us learning by seeing a lot'.

'I don't buy a horse over the phone generally—I like to get the excitement of it all.'

She refers to 'doing the book' (catalogue) with Waller, Mulcaster and Roberts. By the start of 2013, she has been going to sales with them for at least three years, which means looking at hundreds of horses—a crash course in bloodstock that lets her play a part in selecting a handful of horses at the Gold Coast and at Karaka two weeks later.

Debra Norma Kepitis, grandmother, has just turned into a grand horse buyer. Within a couple of weeks she will have taken big shares in the winners of more than $20 million, one of them a stallion with a future. A fact that must be of great interest and slight embarrassment to the expert who'd suggested she wasn't up for it.

•

Lot 329 walks into the tiny ring in front of the auctioneer's podium at 3.47 pm on Thursday, 10 January 2013, as if she has done it every day for months. A blonde French girl in Coolmore livery leads her clockwise around the ring. For once, it's the easiest job in the room.

Yearling sales can be hard on young horses and their handlers. The horses are taken from familiar surroundings and put into strange ones, dragged in and out of their looseboxes many times each day to be paraded in front of strangers. No wonder some soon become as jaded and irritated as riding-school hacks.

Damon Gabbedy detected a little 'attitude' in the filly earlier in the week. There is no sign of it now, when it counts more. She walks perfectly and effortlessly, as easily led as a crowd-wise old police horse, head down and businesslike but never 'walking over' her handler or reefing at the lead, no plunging or rearing or spooking. Peter O'Brien noticed the same thing in the horse-walking area outside the ring.

Her back feet 'step through' in the approved way, easily overstepping the spot her front feet have just left. She moves her tail and ears gently, at ease with the crowd, the auctioneer's amplified voice and other potentially alarming sights and sounds—a good sign in a budding racehorse. You want them to walk like a panther but behave like a pussy cat, and she does.

The auctioneer, Grant Burns, has plenty to work with for the three minutes she's in the ring.

'One of the great fillies of the world, of course, Zenyatta—by the same sire! Gets a great filly . . . second foal of a good stakes-winning mare as well . . . bit of scope about her . . .'

Then he pops the question: 'What for her? Up to you to judge. Six figures? A hundred? A hundred? Eighty? Fifty?'

Someone down the back of the auditorium calls 'Forty' and it starts, slowly at first.

'Then fifty? All done? Then eighty, all done? On the market at ninety . . . for sale all the way . . . Right at the very back, a hundred.'

Then the serious bids kick in, spurred by John Camilleri's decision to go to $200,000 in the hope of retaining the filly. Gabbedy and Tighe follow it up, ready to go on with it. The pace slackens once the $200,000 mark passes and Camilleri's bids stop. Gabbedy has also set the '200 grand' limit but allows 'plus a bid', another ten per cent.

'I'll take tens!' yells the auctioneer. And he does.

Peter Tighe and Debbie Kepitis confer for a second. They are sitting with the Waller camp at a table well over on the auctioneer's left.

Debbie recalls, 'Peter and I looked at Guy and Chris and one of us said, "Do you think we should?"'

Tighe hardly hesitates, telling the others he's prepared to carry the extra margin himself if need be. They bid $210,000 and hope it ends there.

Gebbedy counters: $220,000. Tighe goes one more: $230,000. They are $30,000 over their estimate of value, and $20,000 over the $70,000 each agreed to toss in the pot.

'Another dollar and we wouldn't have bought her,' Tighe is to recall. But there is no more. Vegas Showgirl's daughter is theirs.

•

At Karaka two weeks later, Debbie Kepitis and Peter Tighe are again with Waller and Mulcaster. They are looking to buy stayers. One is by the grand old man of New Zealand breeding, Zabeel, out of the mother of a tough horse named Loophole they bought two years earlier and race together.

Loophole will end up running for six seasons and winning $470,000 but his half-brother by Zabeel puts that in the shade in half the time. He becomes Preferment, a Derby winner that goes on to win the Australian Cup, Turnbull Stakes and the BMW, before retiring to stud.

Either Debbie Kepitis and Peter Tighe are very lucky or Waller is right in thinking Guy Mulcaster, Tim Roberts and his

New Zealand vet Tim Pearce are the best in the business. Or maybe both propositions are true, and excellence attracts luck.

Meanwhile, the bloodstock man who made fun of Debbie Kepitis has made his peace with her and now makes fun of himself. In his circles, it's the perfect dinner party story, a bit like the one about the manager who said the Beatles wouldn't last. You could dine out on it for years.

Still, every time the bloodstock man's wife sees Debbie, she can't help apologising. And Debbie laughs and says: 'Don't worry—look what he did for me!'

But that all comes later. By the end of the Magic Millions sales, Lot 329 has left the Gold Coast and gone back south to be educated.

As the truck rolls down the Pacific Highway, it bypasses the Hunter Valley where she was conceived and foaled and raised. Behind her is the land and a lineage stretching back through generations of thoroughbred horses, all the way to England, Ireland and America. All those distant fields and stables, all those gavels dropping at auction, all the way back to when a few aristocrats and industrialists bred fine horses for their own amusement.

From those rich men's playthings of the past have descended a host of beautiful creatures, an endless supply of moving parts for a modern gaming industry. Occasionally one soars higher than even the best of the rest.

14

THE BREAKER

It's a warm morning in early summer but the paddocks beside Yarramalong Road near Wyong are a brilliant green, lush under a slightly overcast sky. Perfect snake weather, you might think, not something to mention to connections of the million-dollar babes up here to further their education.

Black painted timber fences saddle-stitch the landscape into squares, chessboard neat, the straight lines running across perfectly curated pastures, a golf course without bunkers. A tractor is mowing one to keep the grass at ideal height, not long and rank. Hard to believe all this was bare cow paddocks ringed with barbed wire and derelict sheds as recently as 2006. Such a total makeover could have its own reality television show.

Cream summer-weight horse rugs hang in rows on an oversized clothesline behind a stable block. Others, spotless as hotel linen, are rolled neatly and stacked with military precision beside other gear in a vast tack room. The barns are big and new and there are plenty of them on this model pre-training property. It is one arm of Limitless Lodge; the 'babies' come here from the sister property up the road where they start being educated after the sales.

The enterprise is named for Limitless, the owner's great eventer that is buried here. Not a bad memorial for a good horse.

The stable blocks have cream walls with dark green roofs and wide central passages. They are high, dry and airy, pleasant for man or beast. The building is modern but its purpose isn't: you hear the high-pitched, hollow tapping of a farrier's fine-nosed hammer, the timeless tune heard around stables as long as horses have been shod.

There's another sort of song, not quite so timeless: a radio is playing music quietly. Horse trainers and dairy farmers know the soothing quality of music for animals, apart from breaking the monotony of a repetitious job. Speaking of which, there's the rhythmic scraping of shovel on concrete as a stablehand heaps manure into a barrow—a task that hasn't changed much since Hercules had to clean out the Augean stables, although he didn't have a Bunnings barrow with a rubber tyre.

Between the barns is a circular water-walker that cost the price of a farmhouse and costs plenty extra to keep in perfect working order. A technician drives from Wyong every day to make sure everything is just so: the water clean and chilled, the right amount of salt mixed in to discourage any bacteria and promote healthy healing of any scratches.

Nothing is left to chance at the boot camp for beautiful horses. And, unlike a human boot camp, there is no one here yelling at the rookies.

The boss sees to that. He hires new staff as casuals for a month or two to see if they conform to the establishment's calm, quiet way of handling sensitive animals. That way, if he catches them losing their temper, they are soon looking for another job. Only the trusted get to work in horse heaven.

The boss is Tim Boland, one of Australia's better-known equestrian figures. His reputation has spread from the Olympic sport of three-day events to the racing industry. Excellence is its own advertisement. That, and the fact Boland is an extreme worker in all ways: he works himself, he works horses, he works his staff and, not least, he works the room.

He strides from one impeccable barn to another at even time, talking at the gallop. He is wearing an Australian Equestrian Team polo shirt, which is fair enough, as he has been a highly competitive horseman—an eventer—all his adult life. This choice of vocation came as a surprise to his parents, who once expected a more conventional profession.

Boland, a lawyer's son, grew up in Sydney's northern suburbs. He went to Knox Grammar, and was a 'sport-crazy' teen, playing cricket and rugby. But his grandfather had a farm at Tumut, where his interest in horses was hatched. For several years, he says, 'that was our holidays'.

He and his sister Sarah had a couple of 'mongrel ponies', Gus and Paddy. They graduated to pony club in Sydney. Sarah was 'the gun': an excellent rider and a serious student, now an equine vet in England. Her brother has taken the more precarious scenic route to the top of his profession.

'I got into vet science but then got accepted into the Australian Young Riders team to go to New Zealand.' So he quit study, much to his father's dismay. Worse, his horse was injured, ruling him out of the competition. But it was the start of a new career.

'My dad thought I was an idiot—wanted to disinherit me. My parents had a five-acre place at Duffys Forest. We had stables for eight horses. After we grew out of Gus and Paddy, we got ourselves eventing horses.'

Eventing is for neither the faint-hearted nor the leisure rider. At the top level, each competition is held over three days. Horse and rider compete in a different discipline on each day: dressage then cross-country and finally showjumping. The winner is the best overall. It's a talented and tough horse that can excel in all three phases.

Boland's first competition horse was Parkview Lad, which he found advertised in the Horses, Vehicles & Livestock columns of the *Sydney Morning Herald* on 22 March 1985. He was 'the stockhorse type, about 15-2 hands and seven or eight years old' and cost $3500. Tim was fifteen and delighted.

'He was fantastic. He got me going and helped get me selected.'

Then came Waratah, the horse that made young Boland's name. He first saw him at a performance horse auction but could not outbid an experienced rider who bought him. But that woman was then selected for the Seoul Olympics and needed the money more than she needed that particular horse so she contacted the underbidder—Tim Boland.

By now, his father was resigned to his career choice—if that's what it was—and wrote a cheque for $17,000 for Waratah. In 1988 that was the price of a superior new motorcar. But Waratah was better than a car: he became an international star in eventing.

'It was amazingly good of my parents,' Boland says. 'They had soon come around when they saw I was making a red hot go at it. I loved finding horses and producing them and making them better and selling them. The thrill was a bit of both—of teaching and dealing.'

He started the Australian Event Horse Centre, selling horses all over the world on his own account. 'I probably became Australia's biggest eventer-dealer, getting horses going and then selling them. It's an expensive sport. You need nice horses.'

After a spell overseas teaching and buying horses for the Dubai royal family (the Maktoums of Darley and Godolphin fame), he became a manager for one of them, Sheikh Mohammed bin Khalifa al Maktoum, which meant travelling the world buying and selling horses.

Boland had an eye for spotting talent—and the ability to polish it. When international riders came to Australia looking for horses, 'their first port of call was me'. He went to a lot of places, made a lot of friends. 'One thing leads to another.' What it led to was combining his sportsman's quest for Olympic selection with the business of retraining thoroughbreds off the racetrack.

He saw horses that might have been half-million dollar yearlings being moved on for a song after going wrong. He was happy to re-educate some suitable ex-gallopers as eventers and show horses. But he reckoned he could do more at the front end of the business: having first crack at educating the horses as youngsters. It struck him that people who paid huge money for elite horses would like the idea of an elite education so they could protect their investment as much as possible. Call it the accredited Ferrari workshop principle: if you're paying for a Ferrari, you don't take it to the grease monkey down the street. You want specialists.

Boland was confident he could hand young gallopers to racing trainers with a guarantee that each horse was educated systematically and thoroughly to a high standard, like a well-tuned motor. And that consistent excellence would guarantee a consistently excellent return.

'Plenty of Olympic gold medallists live in a tent,' he says. 'They make those sacrifices. But that's not for me. I've been in no rush [to compete internationally]. I could sensibly sit back and wait.'

There are only four horse-and-rider combinations in each Olympic eventing team, but fifteen in the Australian squad. Boland was disappointed not to get a guernsey for the London Games in 2012 because his horse GV Billy Elliott, although in hot form, was overlooked for reasons he can't fathom and doesn't dwell on.

'I soon realised it [not competing at the Games] wasn't so bad if that's the worst thing that happened!'

He doesn't say that the best revenge is to succeed but that's his attitude. He works hard to live well. Most of the bigger Sydney trainers send yearlings to him to break in and to pre-train.

Walk around the barns and there are familiar trainer names beside each horse's name: Joseph Pride, John Size, Gerald Ryan, the Hawkes . . . and C.J. Waller.

The breaking in starts as soon as the sale season opens in January, and runs for six months. The yearlings come in waves from the various sales, and the process begins, day by structured day.

It's disciplined, organised and predictable: the results can usually be replicated month after month, season after season. Horses stay until they hit the mark.

Which is exactly what Chris Waller wants.

•

By the time the filly steps off the truck the day after being bought and sold, she is no longer Lot 329. She will be known for the coming months as 'the Vegas Showgirl', after her mother. After nine hours on the Pacific Highway, travelling overnight to beat the heat, she arrives two hours before dawn on 11 January, a Friday, with some others.

The yearlings are unloaded at one of Boland's four virtually side-by-side properties run under the Limitless Lodge banner. It's the one he calls the spelling farm, managed by his mother-in-law Sonia Adams.

Standing still for the standard first-day mug shot, the bay filly is what Boland and other horsepeople call a 'bum-high yearling' that still has to grow into her head. An immature yearling like this one has not yet developed a prominent wither, the point where the mane ends in front of the saddle, so the rump stands higher than the wither. She weighs 448 kilograms that day. She's a fraction taller than average but lighter than some 'pumped up' yearlings.

She is calm and kind enough but keeps 'herself to herself', not as affectionate and playful as some youngsters, a character trait that stays with her. The yearlings are as different as children.

Boland recalls the grey Catkins, raced by the Ingham family, as 'a lovely thing'. Whereas another grey filly, Foxplay, 'could be a bitch', a description said with a grin that takes the sting out of it.

The short version is that Foxplay needed re-education before she injured herself or someone else. Her worst antisocial habit was lying down on the track with trackwork riders, but she had others. This had nothing to do with how she had been handled, which was exactly the same as her contemporaries.

'Nurture and love is the best way with horses, but it doesn't always work for every horse,' Boland says.

Foxplay had to learn to cooperate with those who fed and shod and exercised her so she could shine at what she was bred to do. If that meant picking up her feet without kicking, not biting, not lying down when saddled, and not 'jacking up' then that was what had to be done.

When she arrived at Limitless Lodge, she had the makings of a rogue. By the time she left, she was a racehorse—and a good one. In any other era, Foxplay would have been a cracker. As it happened, she was one of the elite fillies of her year overshadowed by the aloof older bay mare that would become her mate.

Day one at the breaker's is like a child's first day at school, except that the child is nearly as tall as its parents, at least five times the size of its teacher and ten times as strong, and its schooling will be compressed into a few crowded months.

The teachers don't lose a minute. On the first day, they handle each of the new arrivals.

On the same truck as Vegas Showgirl's filly are three others that will later race as Treasurable, Flying Brit and Max It Out.

One of Boland's leading hands that year is Amirali Attaollahi, known as Amir, who comes from a family of horsemen in Bangalore, India. Amir's great-grandfather trained horses for the Aga Khan in Mumbai, his brother Sulaman is a leading trainer in Bangalore, and Amir himself worked for Frankel's trainer, the late Sir Henry Cecil, at Newmarket in England for two years. He handles batches of fourteen expensive yearlings a fortnight the way a Formula One mechanic tunes race cars: it's not easy but he has the necessary skills.

Amir likes the chestnut filly by More Than Ready that will race as Treasurable. 'She was more sparky,' he recalls, and is pleased to hear she briefly lives up to her early promise before going wrong.

The Street Cry–Vegas Showgirl filly, by comparison, is 'very casual, very calm, no dramas', probably as easy to handle as any of the hundreds he educates in his six years with Boland.

'She was the best one of the group,' Amir says. 'Never gave any trouble.'

The first thing fitted on the filly (and her fellow pupils) is a roller around the body just behind her front legs where a saddle girth will soon go. The roller is no novelty to yearlings that have been professionally prepared for the sales: the stud grooms fed and exercised them as expertly as if they were beauty show entrants—which, in a sense, they were. But now they're heading from the beauty pageant towards being professional athletes, and handsome is as handsome does.

The roller acts as a dummy saddle but has other uses, too: it has metal rings attached so that long, light reins can pass through and extend well behind the horse's rump, enabling a handler to steer her on foot, walking out of range of flying hoofs.

Amir picks up her feet and handles her all over—again, no novelty to a yearling professionally 'prepped' for sale. Some might be a little spooked because of the new surroundings and new people, but not this wise bay filly.

The lessons start, not in a rush but as inexorable as the sun rising. Amir bridles her, toying gently with her ears and lips to ease any fears, coaxing a plain snaffle bit into her mouth, clipping the long reins to the bit rings ready to guide her. He leads her to a safe, closed-in work area with a solid fence and a sandy base and starts work. This is steering, starting and stopping time. The youngster learns to respond to the gentle pressure of the reins— to turn each way, to walk and to halt on command.

The words that handlers use don't matter in themselves but the tone does, and consistency does. Each word—'steady' or 'whoa' or 'come on'—could be in Mongolian as long as it was repeated in the same way for the same reasons at the same time. Their tone and rhythm, reinforced with physical cues, reassure the young horse.

Late in the first week Amir replaces the roller with a big stock saddle and takes her into a round yard: the absence of corners makes circle work easy and natural and keeps a horse moving forward without any chance of being jammed in a tight space.

Tim Boland handles and rides a lot of the youngsters at Limitless Lodge. But there are far too many for any one rider, so he employs several other skilled horsepeople besides Amir, many of them eventers like himself, adept at everything from formal 'strictly ballroom' dressage to riding horses over huge jumps at speed. As all-round riders, they are extraordinarily capable.

They are also disciplined and conscientious or they don't last.

'Our staff start on time, not wandering in with a mug of coffee a few minutes late,' says Boland. 'No rough and tough or hurly burly. All just gentle and quiet. The secret, as top trainers say, is just happy horses.'

Boland explains that before they first ride the young horse, 'you put yourself all over them so they get used to it'. Amir is an accomplished 'first-on' rider because he did a lot of it at Henry Cecil's stables. He leans across the horse's back and leans backwards and forwards, then straddles them carefully. Some breakers might start off leading a skittish youngster with a bag stuffed full of straw, or even cans, in the saddle to get the animal used to something bulky on its back that makes a noise. This filly doesn't need any extra effort. She's a natural.

Next, another handler leads the filly around the yard with Amir in the saddle. Some nervy yearlings might spook at this so having the extra handler helps dampen their potentially explosive reactions—the rear, the buck or the plunge.

The Vegas Showgirl just gets on with it. And when she is put back in her stable she eats like a workhorse, not a fashion model.

By day five or six, most yearlings are ready to be ridden around. The tempo goes up a little at a time. They walk then trot and, finally, canter slowly in circles then, in the dressage arena, do figure-eights.

Working a young horse clockwise and counter-clockwise teaches it to 'change legs'. When going clockwise the horse leads with its right foreleg, the way a swimmer doing sidestroke leads with one arm. It switches to the left foreleg when it goes the opposite way. When the rider steers the horse in a figure-eight, it changes the lead leg as it changes direction.

Changing legs is a basic lesson but it matters because a horse tires leading on one leg, just as a person would tire carrying a heavy bag in one hand. In a race, a horse can win a small respite from fatigue by changing legs. Because most racetracks are roughly circular, seasoned racehorses lead on the inside leg (nearest the rail) then change legs in the straight to settle into the run home. Jockeys cue them to do this.

By the end of the first week, the youngsters are ridden all over the farm, always in company with other horses. It is too confronting for a young horse to be taken alone from the 'herd' until it is more seasoned and trusts a rider's guidance as much as its own instincts. The rogues are the ones that trust their own instincts the longest.

By the end of week two, they are trucked down the road to the pre-training property for the next phase. At the height of the season, batches of ten 'babies' are trucked across from one Limitless Lodge property to the other every Monday. Loading and unloading from the truck is all part of their education.

Colts and fillies are kept separate, and each trainer's lots are kept together so they 'mate up' for when they graduate to the racing stables. No matter how finely bred and crazily expensive, elite thoroughbred horses are no different from bush brumbies or their pre-historic ancestors: they are herd animals and creatures of habit.

So from the start, the Street Cry–Vegas Showgirl filly is kept with Waller's other youngsters. This is common sense, or horse sense, sharpened by constant practice.

By the start of the third week, by now at the pre-training property, the big stock saddle comes off and the light exercise saddle goes on for daily riding sessions, to simulate the months or years of early-morning workouts ahead.

After a working session, the filly is led into the water-walker. This is partly to exercise and tone young muscles without stressing young bones and tendons, and partly because she needs to be familiar with everything ahead of her in a racing stable.

'All the constant handling is ideal,' says Boland. He's an enthusiast and bubbles with energy and ideas. You see why he was good at finding and training performance horses and selling them on.

Every other day, the filly and her mates learn and repeat new lessons: from walking under saddle, to trotting, to cantering slowly. Vegas Showgirl's filly doesn't buck or rear or shy or do anything faintly menacing. She behaves with aplomb.

'There is no speed in that first preparation,' explains Boland, referring to the pace at which the youngsters work. 'We make sure they travel kindly on the bridle, that they are comfortable about going into the pool and are quiet in the barriers.'

By 'travel kindly on the bridle', he means the youngster will walk, trot or canter at an even pace without 'pulling': not straining against the bit to go faster, instead accepting the pace the rider sets. This ability to conserve energy by maintaining a precise pace is vital in the battle to make a racehorse gallop a fraction faster for a fraction longer. Not every yearling accepts these behaviour modifications readily but 'the Vegas Showgirl' gives a textbook example of each lesson learned. She shows the poise she had in the sale ring.

Experience shows how much a young thoroughbred can handle, not just physically but mentally. On day twenty-six, the filly and her batch of classmates are worked on their fourth and final Friday then trucked to the spelling farm for a break. All part of the system.

The youngsters have a spell—a holiday—for between four and six weeks to give them time to rest and mature before they return for pre-training. 'We start with dressage,' Boland says. This is a point of difference between Boland the equestrian and more basic forms of horsemanship seen in racing's other echelons. Dressage is considered the classical method of horse training, a thorough and time-consuming form of education that teaches the horse to use its body powerfully, as an athlete, responding precisely to cues from the rider.

'It's very easy to get a horse to bowl around the track but you need them to go around in a considered way,' is how Boland puts it.

Vegas Showgirl's daughter does that as calmly as she does everything else.

When Waller asks Boland to rate each of the new kids, he reports that she is straightforward and switched on—but no more.

'There were no bells saying, "She's a star",' he recalls. 'We never said, "Stop Press!"

'On type, there was nothing to get carried away about: just another well-bred horse bought by the Waller team. She looked athletic, all right. But we get a bunch of horses looking like that.'

Occasionally, a young horse is so forward, so unusually precocious, that the breakers wait for its progress on the racetrack and rush to have a bet at its debut. There wasn't one of those in the bay filly's class of 2013.

Of the three she arrives with, the cheapest (at $60,000) wins three moderate races in Queensland as Max It Out; the 'sparky' chestnut that becomes Treasurable (cost $165,000) never wins a race and is sold to New Zealand in 2015; and the Flying Spur filly that becomes Flying Brit, which cost $75,000, never races and later changes hands for $8000 as a backblocks broodmare.

As for 'the Vegas Showgirl', all that Boland and Amir could recall later is that she was tractable but aloof. 'She'd always stand down the back of her loosebox,' says Boland.

It takes another year before anyone knows if she is better than the other three.

15

THE WRONG FOOT

When she'd arrived at Limitless Lodge to learn to be a racehorse, it was mid-summer and she was barely sixteen months old. By the time she gets on the truck to leave, it is almost spring. She is officially a two-year-old, although still a month short by the calendar.

Seven months of education, spelling and pre-training have transformed the baby into something else—not yet a mature animal but a version of what she will become.

On 12 August 2013, Chris Waller dictates one of the briefest of the routine weekly updates he has relayed to the owners through the long lull since the gavel fell. It is just six words: 'She will travel to Rosehill today.'

For the owners, all that has happened since summer is that they have paid monthly bills. Soon they need to think about naming her.

Richard Treweeke, man of leisure and good with words, has written a list of suggested names. Peter Tighe, practical man, has checked them against the racing database to cull ineligible ones: none that has been used in the previous seventeen years is available, for a start, which knocks out probably quarter of a million possibilities. There are other restrictions, too. Names are limited to eighteen character spacings and cannot be commercial brand names or, theoretically, the name of a living person. And the registrar can approve or reject any name at his or her discretion. A good name is much easier to think of than it is to register, which is why there are so many bad ones.

By the time the Tighes and Kepitises meet over dinner after the races in Melbourne, Peter has a short list of names to show Debbie. They boil it down to three names they all like. Even after they submit them, the process takes some time. The filly will be identified by either or both of her parents' names for a while yet.

Debbie always admired the way Suzanne Philcox, who ran the office of Woodlands Stud for years, named hundreds of horses during the Ingham brothers' heyday. Suzanne stayed in the job when Inghams sold to Darley and kept up the tradition, still naming horses for Debbie and her siblings when asked to: one-word names that are easy to pronounce, usually with a nod to the breeding or some quirky historical link.

It was Suzanne who named the great Octagonal, from Eight Carat by Zabeel. But even she couldn't have topped the four-letter word Richard Treweeke had high on his list, at least for brevity and irreverence.

Being in your ninth decade has its little compensations: the old 'man of the world' could get away with a name that had a subtle double entendre, at least the way he explained it later. But it wasn't obvious and it was short and sharp and sounded fine to the registrar. So after two years of being known by her parents' names, the Street Cry–Vegas Showgirl filly eventually becomes Winx.

To Sydney's busiest trainer it's just another youngster on the roster, a unit occupying a numbered space until it does enough to make its name stand out. C.J. Waller might not be running a factory but it is an extremely big hotel, his Rosehill racehorse Hilton.

Waller sees the filly after she arrives for the first time since the Magic Millions sale. It's hardly a revealing moment—revelations good or bad don't come until later, after a preparation, pacework and trials against horses of known ability. But it is a chance to look over the equivalent of a young adult last seen heading off to school as a raw 'tweenager'.

Any precocious ones who went through the sales with her are already being set for early two-year-old races that are auditions—eliminations, really—for all the juvenile speedsters aimed at the world's richest two-year-old race, the Golden Slipper, in autumn.

Despite Waller's ambitions with Champagne Cath the previous summer, the Slipper is not his usual territory and this leggy, immature filly by the middle-distance horse Street Cry is hardly likely to be mentioned in the same sentence as the big race. But when he sees her work on the track, he doesn't rule her out of two-year-old races altogether. In fact, over two weeks his reports flag his growing interest in trying her sooner rather than later. The way she moved must have caught his eye just enough to intrigue him.

The first report, on 13 August, is diplomatically upbeat but non-committal:

She only came in yesterday so I haven't had much of a chance to spend time with her but my first impressions are that she's a beautiful filly and has certainly grown and strengthened since I last saw her so I was very impressed. This morning she went to the barriers and behaved herself well. At the end of the week she'll have a 3/4 pace gallop; I won't get too serious with her but will try to learn as much as I can about her and give her a good insight into stable life.

A week later, on 21 August, he dictates:

She is doing everything right although she's still quite a soft filly therefore I only want to do some basic education with her. It's likely to be completed early next week and then she can go out for a break. With her I would like her to have a start as a 2yo but being by Street Cry, we don't want her put under too much pressure. She will have nice gradual preparations and that will allow her to tell us when she would like to be racing rather than us pushing her.

But by next day there's another development:

We did some X Rays on our 2YO's yesterday to look at their joints and to give us an indication on how they are growing.

To give you a very brief explanation they have a big gap in their knees when they are growing and once they stop growing the gaps close up. When they do close up you can put them under more pressure but until they do so I am very cautious about sending them along quickly. The vet was very happy with the X Rays and said we can put her under more pressure now.

Five days later, he says:

She is going very well and is a lovely filly who has coped very well over the past seven days. She's not going to be an early 2 year old but that's not to say she won't race as a 2 year old. My thoughts are to take her a little bit further and possibly turn her out at the end of the week for a six week spell to then give her a chance to get to the races pre-Christmas which I think would be a real possibility. Pushing her any further now would only be wasting time and money. Once again she's been a pleasant horse to deal with and certainly does have ability hence the reason for getting her out early and then back in with a pre-Christmas preparation in mind if she allows us.

In two weeks Sydney's best and probably 'kindest' trainer has gone from 'won't get too serious with her' to planning a pre-Christmas race. This isn't a whim but a sign that she's thrived in the stable and done everything right on the track. As the breakers have noticed, every time she's asked to take the next step, she does it.

The idea is that she will go to Boynton Park, a spelling property at Berry, south of Sydney, owned by Waller's senior vet Tim Roberts and his wife Cheryl. After five weeks in the paddock, she will start pre-training at the same property then return to Waller HQ.

For two months everything is on track. Then comes the first sign of a setback that seems minor but gets steadily worse, a scenario most racehorse owners get to experience at some stage.

On 4 November, Waller's office emails the owners:

> She is working well however she has a hoof abscess which is currently being treated. We don't expect it to be a big problem however and will hardly hold up her progress at Boynton Park.

In another week, on 11 November, it's harder to sound positive:

> Her hoof abscess is still lingering unfortunately but the team at Boynton Park are working hard to get on top of it so that it doesn't hold up her preparation.

By next day, the news is even less cheerful:

> She came in with a very sore foot but it is just an abscess. It is not anybody's fault but it is certainly going to hold her up. She is still quite tender on it and because it has burst out the top of the foot, it can often take a while

to grow down. I don't know how far we will get this preparation and if it is going to hold us up I would quickly turn her back out and send her back to the paddock to ensure that she is not just treading water so to speak. She will be fine as it is not a long term problem but it is an issue that if it did happen to make her sore while under a bit of pressure, I would try to avoid that and turn her out.

18 November:

Our staff have done a good job with this filly's foot and she is now back working on the training tracks and moving fairly well. We will give her a few more days to be 100% and if she's not, we will obviously have to back off her work load and could be worth spelling her to ensure that she gets over the problem 100%. At this stage she is 95% and heading in the right direction. It will take some careful care and management of the area where the abscess burst out the foot to ensure that the hoof growth over the next 3 months is not affected. If anything changes we will get back to you. In terms of getting to a trial, if she did stay in work we would be about 5 to 6 weeks away from that.

26 November:

Her foot is almost 100% now and she's working along normally. She had a three quarter pace gallop on

Saturday and is a very nice mover. That's about all I got out of the work as it's hard to find out more at that pace. She went to the barriers for the first time this morning and as you would expect, she was pretty slow out but she will learn quickly. We will take one week at a time and gradually step up her workload without putting her under too much pressure. She will do a bit more barrier work each week and we will intensify her work with each week. She's a nice filly and that foot problem has set her back a bit so we won't rush her to make up time, we will let her get there gradually.

3 December:

We are still having some problems with that hind foot and it might require complete rest. She is going to lose part of that hoof and it will be a month or so before new hoof grows down to replace the missing part. It is nothing serious although it does sound quite nasty but it will grow back to a normal shape and certainly a stronger wall. It hasn't affected her workload to this stage. She has been working at three quarter pace and also went to the barriers again this morning but as we step her up to full pace galloping it may have some [effect]. At this stage we will push on but if we do need to spell her, obviously I will and I will report this to you if she does go out for a break. With all that aside she is certainly a very nice filly.

9 December:

I am going to turn her out for 3 to 4 weeks and let this foot grow back properly as on and off she is still having good and bad days and a little bit reluctant to stretch out when we get her up to full speed. As a result she is not using that hind leg as much as she should be and the muscle development there is not as good as the other legs. I think we should pull up now, allow the foot to grow back properly, get some weight on her and next preparation we can push on with her. She is a very nice filly, very well bred and has a bright future ahead so let's give her every chance.

Waller sends her back to Limitless Lodge. Tim Boland's regular farrier Chris debrides the hoof wall of the bad foot and shapes a special shoe for her. Four years later, he still clearly recalls the crack in the hoof left by the burst abscess.

'I had to cut it out and fit a zee-bar shoe to get her weight off the heel,' Chris says, rasping and trimming feet in the colts' barn. He walks over to the travelling blacksmiths' workshop on the back of his ute and grabs an example of the zee-bar horseshoe from his collection. It has a boomerang-shaped bar across the middle, designed to relieve stress on the affected part.

Time and decisive treatment were the only way to deal with the abscess. But it would take many more weeks for the hoof to grow out. At the time it was mildly frustrating for the owners, already facing extra expense.

Looking back, it's hard to know whether the hoof problem cost an early win—or was a delayed blessing for the filly. Maybe the answer is 'Both'. But the enforced absence from the hurly-burly of the track meant extra months of gentle exercise, rather than testing pacework, and time to grow.

Hindsight is a tease. Later, Waller's mind strays to the road not travelled. By then he knows what he half-suspected well before Christmas—that Winx could have run in the Golden Slipper. But he also knows that such a run would have been at a cost, and the fact it didn't happen is soothing. Almost.

'Her class would have got her into the Slipper,' he is to say much later. 'But her form until she turned four suggests she wouldn't have won it. She probably would have been just another runner—and it would have been a different story for her after that.'

Meaning, running in Golden Slippers is not good for longevity.

Waller adds that 'she's a better horse now than she would have been' if she'd run in the Golden Slipper. He says, 'It's a good selling point about why two-year-old races are not the be-all and end-all.'

As Christmas 2013 becomes New Year 2014, Winx's foot recovers slowly. If the Slipper had ever been a real chance, it's well gone now.

On 20 January 2014 Waller relays a message to the owners from Limitless Lodge to say Winx will start pre-training there on 3 February. He also reports: 'Her feet are improving.'

It's a year almost to the day since she started under saddle. And no one knows for sure yet if she can outrun the ambulance.

16

THE NATURAL

By the time she finally returns to Rosehill on 25 March 2014, her arrival is just another necessary chore in the pressure cooker of the autumn carnival. Somehow Waller finds time to look at her and dictate a message that is typed into an email to the owners.

Every Monday and Tuesday, except maybe Christmas Day, no matter where he is, Waller takes out a digital recorder and composes a report on each horse. What it has eaten, the work it has done, its daily temperature and weekly weight are recorded on a spreadsheet as diligently as a private hospital patient's might be.

'Her foot appears to be back to normal and the pre-trainers have given her a good report card,' Waller dictates. 'I would expect her to be ready for a jump-out around the 22nd of April and a trial on the 28th of April.'

On 8 April, his report says Winx is 'a lovely filly' but she had 'lost all of her muscle tone over her hindquarters when she had the foot problem. Now that her foot is 100% and she has had the time to recover, the muscle mass has built up beautifully over her hindquarters. I am very happy with the way she is heading.'

A week later, he reiterates she has 'rounded up nicely and her foot is perfect now' then adds:

> She had a gallop on Saturday and again this morning and both pieces of work were good. She will progress to a jump out on April 22 followed by a trial on April 28. I am looking forward to getting her through to the jump out and I would expect her to do well . . . If she does need extra time we will certainly give it to her but I could not see why she would need the extra time at this stage. I think she will be more than competitive.

Behind the scenes, the stable's regular farrier, Jason Brettle, has filled the hollow left by the hoof abscess with a synthetic filler, then rasped it down to make it perfect, something between panel beating and plastic surgery. He's good at it. Brettle grew up in a family of trotting trainers, a code that above all requires an intimate knowledge of horses' feet and how to correct them. No hoof, no horse.

After the jump-out, Waller reports, 'She loaded into the barriers well but jumped quite slow.' Jumping slowly is a sign of the only flaw in her armour, something the breakers hadn't noticed when giving her gentle barrier practice at Limitless Lodge.

Waller decides against giving her a full trial immediately, instead opting for another jump-out:

We will only take a backward step if we trial her now
which is not what we want.

He suggests that some unofficial trials at Rosehill on 29 April might suit.

If not I will just give her a jump out on the 6th of
May before trialling her on the 12th of May. The most
important thing is that she is showing us quite a bit of
ability and is coping well with her weight. She is also
mentally coping well which is great to see.

The filly is still almost anonymous in the hierarchy of a big city stable, where she is one of about 100 horses Waller has at Rosehill, with more elsewhere. She is like the teenage footballer down from the bush to train in the reserves: she has a name but not many know it yet. Still, a couple of people around the stable take a little notice.

One is the man everyone calls simply 'Umut' because his Turkish surname is long and hard for English-speakers to wrap their tongues around.

The path that led Umut Odemislioglu to Rosehill begins in a distant province of Turkey. He is not the first Turkish national to work in Australian racing. Punters know the well-liked provincial jockey Ibrahim Gundogdu, who rode mostly in Victoria until a fall later interrupted his career. But Umut is almost certainly the only stablehand in the land to have trained as a dramaturge on the stage in Turkey, where he also acted in a television series.

Acting didn't thrill him the way racehorses had since he was a boy helping his grandfather, an olive farmer and hobbyist horse breeder in the province of Izmir on the Aegean coast. Umut went from school to study theatre but helped his grandfather with his horses at weekends. He eventually quit drama and went to Istanbul to do a two-year degree in horse management and worked in stables. But he wanted to learn more about the different training techniques used elsewhere.

One of his teachers arranged a job on an Irish farm, J. K. Thoroughbreds at Corbally Stud in County Kildare. There, Umut realised how much he had to learn. One day he saw a Coolmore Stud promotional video about the Australian stallion Choisir and decided to go to Australia.

He arrived on 1 April 2006 and found work through a company that set up stud and stable placements for overseas workers. After nine months at Attunga Stud near Scone, Umut joined Tim Martin's stable at Rosehill.

Exposure to the hyperactive Martin was a fast learning curve that lasted five years. In that time, working with around ninety horses, Umut went from stablehand to assistant foreman to foreman to assistant trainer—and learned Australian racetrack English, which differed from the version of English he'd learned at school.

He realised that Martin, the gifted bush horseman who'd graduated from horse breaking and rodeos and the like, 'is not a business person like Chris'. When he first met Waller at Rosehill, he saw him 'as a young person who has a good system—a routine'.

Umut's way of comparing trainers is to say: 'In horse racing they are like tennis players—they don't all speak English but they can all play. Every year Chris got more horses—from twenty to forty to ninety. His connection with workers and owners is different because he is a different character.

'I start [at Waller's] as a stablehand again because I like to spend time with horses instead of people. Six months later a foreman left so I got his barn—seventeen horses, like quarantine and babies.'

By 'quarantine' he means the barn used for horses new to the stable, kept separate for a time in case they have brought coughs or colds or more serious ailments from elsewhere. This includes overseas purchases and the 'babies', early two-year-olds fresh from the breakers.

He first sees the Street Cry–Vegas Showgirl filly just after she officially turns two. Her breeding interests him.

'Many of the babies are unnamed,' he says. 'You spend a couple of weeks with them. Some you notice—the naughty ones. But she was one of the quiet ones. She was small, narrow but tall enough. I noticed her because she was by Street Cry, like [American champion] Zenyatta. I was most interested in the breeding part. So I ask for this unnamed filly, the Vegas Showgirl. I wrote on a piece of paper "Vegas Showgirl" and "Waltzing Willie", both by Street Cry.'

Waltzing Willie is later gelded, and eventually wins a couple of races and runs several placings before being moved on to a Newcastle stable, where he pays his way. Umut's other interest, the narrow filly, doesn't look like a 'jump and run' type, either. She's as light as a feather but she does show signs of class.

Umut observes that experienced trackwork riders are neutral or even negative about most young horses in case they seem over-enthusiastic and are then proven wrong, as optimists often are about young horses. Pessimism is a far safer default. But one relative novice, a young Frenchwoman, is sufficiently naïve or frank to be impressed and to say so.

Her name is Lucie Pontoir. She is not familiar with the Australian reliance on pacework because she comes from a place where horses are exercised relatively slowly, often up slopes, and rarely tested against a stopwatch in training.

Lucie gets to ride some of the 'babies' because for the first few weeks they are being exercised quietly rather than worked hard. The senior track riders are mostly concentrating on proven horses being set for spring races.

How Lucie the 'tourist' stablehand rates an unnamed young-ster is hardly going to set the trainers' hut alight in the lead-up to the spring carnivals. The harder heads present assume novice track riders think everything they get on is better than it is. Despite that, Umut is struck by something the French girl says about the Street Cry filly he's chosen to look after.

One morning Lucie walks the filly into his barn after track-work and says, 'This horse is a superstar.'

'It's then,' Umut says later, 'I think I choose the right one.'

The taciturn Turk has reason to think about the chatty French girl's intuition soon after. That season, while the Street Cry filly is back in the paddock, an aristocratically bred English horse—black sheep of a distinguished line—arrives after one of Waller's European buying trips.

The horse is out of a famous blue-blood mare, Ouija Board, and will race in Australia as Our Voodoo Prince. He has been found wanting as a classics candidate in Britain but has some staying talent to go with his lineage. But Waller and Mulcaster's justified faith in his ability doesn't mean the Rosehill track riders have to be impressed with what they see as a 'spoilt' English horse.

'No one liked the tried horse from Ouija Board—but Lucie did,' recalls Umut.

After running last in a trial at Rosehill, Our Voodoo Prince wins three city races in Melbourne in one busy month, presumably recouping his purchase price and more besides: proof of the buying team's skill at finding tried horses and Waller's skill in turning them around.

Our Voodoo Prince starts his hat-trick on 22 March and ends it on 19 April. For Umut, this performance franks Lucie Pontoir's judgement.

Three weeks later, by now officially named, Winx has her first official barrier trial, Jimmy Cassidy up, and runs nicely mid-field after being slow away. Winning trials is not high on Waller's priorities.

Umut guesses that if Lucie's instincts are right, the skinny filly is worth watching in her first race. The more experienced riders like her but don't 'declare' her a winner.

Cassidy 'kicked up' for the debut race but the ride goes to another Kiwi, a quiet lad less than half Jimmy's age who has ridden 200 winners in New Zealand but is still entitled to claim an allowance in Sydney. Another shrewd Waller import.

•

'The promising two-year-olds on a racetrack are the gold men covet', wrote the sports writer William Nack in his study of the great Secretariat, the horse that was the love of his professional life in the way that Muhammad Ali was for some of his Press Room contemporaries.

A good two-year-old might be a good three-year-old and four-year-old, so to have a two-year-old 'is to have a future'.

Winx ran as if she had a future, even if she didn't look the part yet. But experienced trainers, Nack observes, have 'emotional brakes that draw them up short before allowing them to make the mistake of liking a two-year-old too much too early'. Trainers insulate themselves from disappointment by staying sceptical because they know their young winner beats, by definition, other green young non-winners: horses that will mostly not make it.

Plenty of horses break their maidens and never hit the front again. The flash-in-the-pan of false promise is as old as racing. Another truth is that not all great racehorses, let alone the merely good ones, win their first races. This is especially so in Australia, where trainers often race horses into fitness instead of getting them race fit 'at home', as they tend to in England and Ireland.

Phar Lap didn't win his first four starts. On breeding and type he was a rangy stayer that looked like a 'chaser in search of a steeple, so he could hardly be expected to win two-year-old races. Accordingly, he ran last at his first outing and finished a long way back in the next three. It is proof of Phar Lap's class and his connections' lack of it that the raw-boned youngster was prodded and punished into winning his final two-year-old race, in April 1929.

Kingston Town? He ran last at his first start, famously prompting Tommy Smith to geld him. Bernborough wasn't first past the post in his first race, a Toowoomba maiden, only getting the race on protest from a horse that didn't much trouble the scorekeeper afterwards. The great Tulloch started favourite at his first start, the AJC Breeders Plate, and was beaten.

So when a freshly named Winx steps into barrier four at the 1100-metre mark at Warwick Farm on 4 June 2014, she doesn't carry the weight of history as well as her allotted 55 kilograms.

The six youngsters drawn on her outside include the top fancy, Felines, which has won two juvenile races already and is destined to be a sharp sprinter. There are a few other smart ones in the field, as happens in a state where thousands of youngsters are bred for the Golden Slipper and hundreds aimed at it from the day they're first saddled.

Waller's competent and calm Kiwi recruit Jason Collett is aboard, not long out of an apprenticeship with horses that began around the time he could talk. Winx has tightened in the betting from $7 to $5 but it's no plunge, more a case of keeping a first starter from a strong stable 'safe', despite her well-known tardiness about jumping out.

Collett later can't recall who legs him on but it isn't Waller. He knows 'nothing about her' apart from the fact she's 'a first starter for Chris'. He hasn't ridden her in work or in trials. He's heard the stable staff reckon 'she was pretty good' but he's not excited.

'She didn't grab me. She was just a horse like others in the race. She wasn't quick from the barrier.'

In the first half of the race, she is lengths behind the leading group, dominated by the speedy Aperture and the classy Felines, which shape as first and second a long way from home.

Collett settles just ahead of the tail-enders but has to 'squeeze her most of the way' to improve his position. Then it changes. Before the leaders hit the turn 'they started stopping in front of me—and she went up a gear. I knew I was going to win at the top of the straight.'

At that stage the caller notices Winx has joined the race and is streaming down the middle of the track. At the fifty-metre mark, Felines is still in front and galloping better than everything in sight—except the one forging past on her outside.

The caller sees what's going to happen just before it happens and in the rush momentarily skips the winner's name.

It's finishing very fast! Gets up! Good win!

He retells the tale in machine-gun bursts.

Showed no early speed, as it has done at the barrier trials, but she was very strong at the finish, coming home all over Felines, who didn't look like it stopped; it sat outside the leaders and sprinted away—but Winx has put up a big performance on debut.

A bigger performance on debut, as it happens, than Phar Lap or Bernborough or Kingston Town or Tulloch, the undisputed Australasian champions of the previous century. But no one is thinking along those lines on a winter Wednesday at Warwick Farm, including the winning jockey, though he concedes it was good to beat a smart filly like Felines so easily.

'I thought she was pretty handy,' Collett says years later, too honest to gild his recollection. 'She had a bit of bottom to her, the way she could be squeezed for so long and then "find" again.'

Which, in his laconic way, sums up the difference between this first-start winner and so many others. Under pressure she kept 'finding'. And she did it over a short sprint course that didn't really suit her, against peers who not only looked more mature but looked *better*.

The whiff of prejudice in favour of handsome, precocious youngsters over plain, immature ones still lingers over her as she stands calmly in the winner's stall. It's the wallflower's revenge and it's just beginning.

At ground level, Umut is more impressed than the rider. Like a proud parent, he thinks 'his' girl is a natural: 'She comes from nearly last, stuck in traffic but still gets through to win. That was very impressive. If a horse wins its first race, it's a good horse.'

Waller's eyes and ears that day are Liam Prior, the former cadet steward from Port Macquarie who started with the trainer in 2009 and has ended up like his younger brother. Prior, racing manager and future stable business manager, tells a favourite client, Brian Agnew, his filly Lucy's Luck is hard to split from Winx on their work. Lucy's Luck runs well back and is headed nowhere. Agnew pokes fun at Prior: 'Some judge you are.' Just more proof that horses make fools of people.

Collett rides Winx's next start, over 1400 metres at Rosehill. This time the market says there's no doubt—she starts $1.60 favourite—and the money gets it right.

But then the young jockey makes a choice. 'I got off her, for her third race, to ride a filly called Alpha Miss that I rode in the Slipper. She was taking the same path as Winx and I elected to ride her. I think it ran third,' he adds.

'I remember seeing Winx winning it and thought "Fuck!" but it was a wet track and I thought the wet helped her. Next, I think Hugh Bowman was suspended and I took the ride. She ran second to First Seal. She had every chance but First Seal was superior that day.'

Which First Seal was, that day and several others. Study a photograph of First Seal taken that season and you see a ball of muscle, heavier and stronger than the skinny filly she so regularly beats. Winx is running on class and stamina and First Seal on maturity and natural speediness, and at this stage that's enough.

During their three-year-old season, First Seal wins three of their clashes and finishes ahead of her twice more, the way a teenage boy who shaves at fifteen beats the other youngsters until their hormones kick in, too.

Luck is never far away in racing. Both sorts. 'I get suspended and Bowman jumps back on her,' recalls Collett. 'Runs second to First Seal, over a mile.'

Then comes her sixth start, Collett's fourth ride on her. 'This is her first start back in her autumn preparation. It was a good field. She was slow to begin. She just wasn't sharp, as if the penny hadn't dropped.

'I thought she was a chance but at that stage I still didn't think she was going to be that good. She didn't jump, didn't travel comfortably, went out wide and I think got home good [to run seventh of eleven]. Next start she ran fifth of twelve. I can't even remember it, to be honest.'

He smiles and pulls out his phone and calls up the replays. It is as he described in each case, though the two down-the-order placings don't reflect how close she finished to the winner.

Both times she started slowly and came home strongly. The second time, he recalls thoughtfully as he studies the video clip, he switched her back to the inside—and the inside turned out to be 'off' that day. Bad luck or pilot error or both, just another of racing's many variables. None of it a big deal at the time, when the two losses reinforce his impression that Winx is just another good young horse, no champion.

Speaking of which, Alpha Miss doesn't win another race in Sydney after Collett elects to stick with her. To be fair to him, he'd ridden her since her first trial the previous spring, winning four races on her before riding her into twelfth place in the Golden Slipper.

As it turns out, Alpha Miss doesn't win again for more than a year and then only after switching to the stable of the enigmatic Robert Smerdon at Caulfield. Smerdon finds a tonic to galvanise Alpha Miss's elusive will to win—but only once. She wins the Schillaci Stakes with Craig Williams aboard then melts away, just another flying filly that looked like a contender for a few months.

Collett, meanwhile, has lost any claim he had on Winx. After her two losses with Collett steering early in 2015, Tommy Berry takes the ride and wins on her—her fourth victory in eight runs—then loses at the next start. But Collett doesn't get reinstated when Berry gets off.

Those who back her to favouritism in the Australian Oaks that autumn might wish he had, on the grounds he knows where the rails are at Randwick.

Instead, the Brazilian they call the world's best jockey, Hong Kong's 'Magic Man' Joao Moreira gets the plum ride on the favourite. Coming up to her tenth start, Winx is a promising middle-distance filly, although well-beaten over shorter distances by First Seal and still barely known outside Sydney.

Waller sticks to his policy of using big-name jockeys and that autumn the visiting Moreira has star billing. The other international rider, Ryan Moore, is booked for Waller's other fancied runner, third favourite Ballet Suite.

Hugh Bowman rides $7 shot Candelara for Bjorn Baker and runs third with a ride as neat as the Brazilian's seems extravagant. There are only ten starters and Collett isn't on any of them.

The on-again, off-again partnership with Winx has already ended for Collett. As he puts it with perfect economy, 'Her career was going a bit quicker than I was in mine.'

The quiet Kiwi has no hard feelings towards Hugh Bowman, who's set to get back on Winx—though not at her next start, it turns out. As Collett muses, Bowman won on her at the right time, 'and you don't change what's not broken. He's proven.'

Winx running second in the Oaks grates on Umut but doesn't shake his faith in his favourite filly. He pauses when asked about the loss.

'Maybe too much confidence by the rider,' he says. 'The Oaks was a disappointment.'

It was disappointing for the connections, too, though not all blamed the jockey's judgement as much as punters did. Waller would say later that Moreira got the filly to settle well, in striking range of the leaders, but had elected to come off the fence to make his run on a day when there was a track bias towards rail runners.

So while Winx seemed to bog down after going wide, the 'bolter' Gust Of Wind compounded her advantage by railing like a greyhound. A year later, Winx would have overcome such a disadvantage, but as a three-year-old she could not quite pull off the superhero feats that would become her trademark at four and five.

The Australian Oaks was supposed to be her grand final. After it, Waller had planned on sending her to the paddock before setting her for the Caulfield Cup in the spring, six months later. If she'd won the Oaks—or been well beaten—that's what would have happened.

But to miss out on a Group One win so narrowly because of track bias was neither one thing nor the other. ('Once they turn four,' Waller muses, 'it only gets harder to win a Group One.')

At the time, in his usual email report to the owners, Waller goes to some trouble to explain the Moreira ride: 'She was very unlucky in the fact that we came off the fence at the 1600m mark.' He says he 'had a good chat to Joao Moreira after the race' in which the Brazilian explained his reason for coming off the fence:

> He nearly got put through the running rail going past the winning post for the first time. He said from that point on her action wasn't the same, she was very tense and felt claustrophobic, so when the opportunity arose at the half mile he came off the fence and gave her a bit of galloping room. I accept that, but on the day you had to be on the fence and we got caught in behind slow horses, which was out of Joao's control. It is a little disappointing for me and you as the owners knowing that our filly was

the better filly on the day and we only ran second. We have been in the opposite position when we have won races and I am sure there have been unlucky horses behind us. I am still not convinced that she is fully mature and developed yet so that is going to make going to the paddock for a spell the main option.

But Waller is already weighing alternatives.

The other option is to proceed to Brisbane for the Queensland Oaks which is going to be run over 2200m this year, from what I understand, at Doomben. It is a big ask to take a filly up there but they are only a three-year-old once and she is fairly lightly raced really. We will keep her in the stable for a few days and make a decision later in the week.

It's tempting to say the most careful trainer in the game changed his mind overnight. In fact, it took two nights.

On the Monday after the Oaks, Waller recalls, 'We looked at her and said, "There's not much left of you." But probably the only chance to win a Group One was to grit our teeth and go to Queensland.'

As a kid, he'd always been a fiercely competitive cricketer. Now he was going to throw the ball at the stumps. This would not surprise those who knew him as a child on the farm at Foxton.

17

THE GOOD KEEN MAN

When Chris Waller is twelve, his grandfather Colin Waller legs him onto a racehorse named Abyssinia.

They are in a cow paddock next to Chris's parents' farmhouse, down the road from where his grandparents live. They've hatched a plan to pre-train the mare for a month before she goes back to a professional, Noel Eales.

Chris the budding businessman charges $3 a day to feed her, sending out weekly bills to his aunts, who race the mare with their father. Now Chris the novice track rider has his feet in the stirrups and his heart in his mouth.

The boy can ride a little. He started out on the arm of the couch using his mother's knitting needle as a whip then graduated to a pot-bellied Shetland pony. Lately he has practised on a retired galloper named Vandalize, a bigger rogue than Snow Lupton, the Melbourne Cup-winning trainer who sold it to them 'cheap'.

Vandalize, big and black, is 'a bugger of an animal' and has taught Chris plenty about being careful when handling horses.

Abyssinia is better in all respects but a 'fresh' galloper fired up on hard feed is a tricky proposition for the boy to ride on a light exercise saddle. Like stepping up from a tractor to a sports car with bad brakes.

The paddock is L-shaped with a pond in the corner and fenced with barbed wire to keep cows in. He starts cautiously, keeping the mare to a canter. But the work is not hard enough to get her fit.

'My grandfather was giving me advice on what to do,' Chris recalls. 'He says, "Go a bit quicker."'

The boy niggles her with his heels and clicks at her. She takes off and he can't hold her. As she gallops into the corner of the L-shaped paddock, he wonders if he will end up in the barbed wire or the pond.

'It took my breath away. My grandfather closed his eyes, thinking: "What have I done to my grandson?" But someone up there must have been helping me. I made the turn. It was the fright of my life. When my grandfather told the story later he said I was as white as a ghost.'

Somehow Abyssinia keeps her feet and somehow the boy clings on. The fright doesn't last long. What does last is the after-glow of achievement. Fear of falling does not scare him as much as fear of failure.

'Anyway, she won first-up a few weeks later, so we must have done something right.'

Chris Waller's first win. With a little help from Grandpa and Noel Eales.

If Colin Waller had lived long enough to see his grandson succeed so well, you'd guess he would be pleased but not altogether surprised.

•

Everyone in the family has a story about their Chris. His aunt Christine Cunningham, a teacher, tells one about when the boy used to help his grandmother Elizabeth.

He liked to help her cook but he liked to save time in everything he did. One day, they were making an apple pie. He was peeling and cutting up apples on the bench—and set up a bowl on the floor below so he could push the apple wedges over the edge to fall into it. Look, Gran, no double handling.

Elizabeth Waller reckoned the apple-pie making was an insight into the way her grandson thought. He was endlessly curious about doing something a better way—and a sponge for information. 'He was always a genius!' she would tell an interviewer decades later, heart on sleeve.

Elizabeth is biased in favour of her grandson, not least because he flew back to New Zealand for her 100th birthday in May 2018. And possibly because she sees in him a touch of her renowned grandfather Professor John Shand, a Scottish-born mathematics and physics lecturer who helped set up New Zealand's first university in 1871. Shand was a towering figure in New Zealand education, renowned for the financial acumen that made the University of Otago a success.

In racing, obsessed as it is with mixing and matching blood-lines, having a professor in the pedigree catches the eye. The

Wallers sometimes wonder if their boy wonder, self-taught professor of horse training, is a throwback to that flinty old Scot with a Presbyterian work ethic to match his intellect.

When Chris was not yet four years old, his father was late getting home from the races one afternoon to start milking—a rare occurrence for a farmer as conscientious as John Waller. His mother Marilyn, a teacher by profession and a gardener for pleasure, mostly left the livestock to her husband but this night she decided to get the milking started before dark.

As the cows filed in from the paddock to wait in the yard, udders swollen with milk, Marilyn walked across from the brown brick veneer house to the cowshed with her little boy holding her hand. He led her into the engine room in the shed and showed her the switches to turn on to get the machine running.

As it hummed to life, he said encouragingly: 'You've done it, Mum! You've done it!'

But she hadn't, she says, telling the story. *He* had. Without him, she couldn't have started the machine. She describes a boy who was always busy, always striving—except in the classroom, which didn't interest him the way the real world did.

Chris went to Oroua Downs primary school down the road, where Marilyn taught, and later on the bus to Manawatu College in nearby Foxton. It was a neat high school in a drowsy rural backwater (population 2040) on the coastal plains half an hour from Palmerston North and 112 kilometres north of Wellington.

Palmerston North, 'Palmy' to its friends, is a city just big enough to have a university and a few suburbs sprawled over the flat dairy country.

Waller's future boss, the horse trainer Paddy Busuttin, calls Foxton 'a working-class town', a leftover from a time when it had a carpet factory that processed wool, when agriculture provided profits and jobs now long gone.

Manawatu College rates two on the government's socio-economic scale, with one being the poorest socio-economic group and ten the wealthiest. There aren't many rich kids at school in Foxton but there are a few battling ones, perhaps just enough of a contrast to encourage ambition rather than complacency.

The school is around the corner from Waller's other local influence—Foxton racecourse. Helen Weller, wife of the clerk of the course there, ran Waller's stable when he went to Sydney in 2000. It has a sign on the gate: 'Warning! No hunting in this reserve'. 'Hunting' refers to rabbit shooting, not horses and hounds.

In the quiet main street, wide enough to turn a bullock team around in early times, is the Castletown Motel, which has a huge sign depicting a horse's head. This is the hometown's tribute to the champion that Paddy Busuttin trained (and a young Chris Waller briefly strapped) in the early 1990s.

Castletown is a bona fide Kiwi hero, along with Busuttin and his regular strapper Rata Prince. He had 100 starts between the age of two and eight, won three Wellington Cups and an Auckland Cup, and ran third in the Melbourne Cup behind Subzero in 1992. The old horse was Foxton's most famous son until his sometime strapper C.J. Waller joined him in the New Zealand Racing Hall of Fame in 2018.

As a high school student, Waller made a good sportsman. He was wiry and fit, a handy runner, keen rugby player and a good all-rounder at cricket. When he took up squash he trained himself to be good enough to represent the club at distant tournaments.

Sport aside, his passion was for animals. His parents and grandparents spoke about trainers and jockeys and great horses, but their interest in racing was not to do with punting so much as with the animal. They were what he calls 'stock people', who bred and raised cattle and horses, pigs and dogs. Chris grew up knowing about animals—and believing they were *worth* knowing about. He didn't ignore his father's farmer values, he embraced them.

He would feed calves and help milk cows and do his other chores, his mind attracting bits of knowledge the way a magnet grabs iron filings. Decades later, he recalls things that might seem obscure—but not to him—such as the fact that some New Zealand soils lack trace elements like selenium and copper.

'It was a sin to lose an animal—you had to be ahead of the game,' he recalls of the lessons of farm life. 'A horse is the same as a farm animal. Prevention is better than cure. We take their temperature regularly and treat them with antibiotic drugs. We treat a sore leg aggressively—don't turn a blind eye.' He learned early that if you ignore a small problem, it will turn into a big one.

'My dad was always big on hygiene in the dairy shed— keeping it clean.' It would have been a form of disgrace as well as a financial setback if their bulk milk 'rating' had been marked down because of a high bacteria count. It became second nature to keep the calf-feeding equipment perfectly clean, one of the methodical habits of animal husbandry he soaked up from boyhood, along with the seasonal rhythms of farm life.

'We'd make hay in the summer, cut grass hay. My dad was a real worker. He'd never take a day off or employ staff. He did it all himself. It was just part of life and a good way to learn to work when you are around people like that.'

Looking back, Waller doesn't overplay the rugged childhood angle—nor go the other way and paint things as grander than they were. He is still too busy building the present to be bothered with embroidering his past, which is still too recent to interest him more than the future does.

The Wallers' farm had about 160 cows on 230 acres, run single-handedly by Chris's father John. They milked the usual Holstein-Friesian cows and ran a few beef cattle, mostly Angus. Chris reared calves 'on the bucket' after their mothers went back into the milking herd.

Feeding calves before and after school was 'a pretty quick and easy job', he says. He would get some milk from the vat after each milking and add 'some herbs and spices to make their coats shiny'. It's a jocular reference to filching the feed additives the dairy cows got in their grain and some horse molasses from the feed shed then thinning it with hot water to mix into a 'caramel milk shake' for the calves.

He studied cattle pedigrees 'of all the bulls available for AI', the elite stud bulls whose semen was for sale for artificial insemination of farm herds. This was despite the fact his dad was 'old-fashioned and stuck to the traditional way' and would buy bulls to breed his own replacements. In other words, studying the AI pedigrees was information for its own sake, a way of feeding a mind hungry for knowledge.

Meanwhile, his only sister Megan—older, arty and articulate—would be 'reading five books at a time', says their mother. Megan would go on to be a hotel manager in Auckland, to study at university and later to set up her own international business making and selling 'stack' bracelets in Sydney.

Megan is proud of her little brother but hardly surprised at his progress. She saw how competitive and determined he was, from the moment his feet hit the floor each morning.

'We never walked across to the cowshed from the house,' she recalls. 'We always ran because everything was a race for Chris. I was more athletic but he was more competitive.

'He was always hands on. He couldn't watch the All Blacks playing on television without going outside and playing. He had a goal post set up in the paddock. And a long jump pit! And a running track, all mowed and rolled. And a cricket pitch—with boundaries, all mowed and rolled. Every Christmas Day we had to have an international match, with all the relatives forced to play. And every night after school in summer I had to play cricket with him. Running was more my thing and I got plenty of practice with Chris.'

She describes a boy who would fidget in class, bursting with energy and ambition to do something for himself, not listen to others drone on about subjects that didn't interest him.

But his energy was constructive, not always the way with hyperactive boys. 'Right from the start he attracted a lot of people around him,' Megan says, and he was involved in the student council at school. However, she adds: 'He always marched to his own tune. He was never swayed by peers or anything.

And he had a work ethic that made him take pride in his work as a stablehand. He's on his own trajectory. He puts in two hundred per cent.'

When they were little, she recalls, they would put their grandfather's racing saddles on the wood box and perch on them, listening to the local race caller Alan Bright on the radio. These childhood memories of her brother, which Megan later writes about, reveal the man he would become:

He liked to construct steeplechase courses around my Grand-parents' lawn . . . overturned boxes, benches, shrubs . . . and would spend hours jumping them. Never content to watch a rugby or cricket game, he had to run outside and emulate his many sporting heroes. Richard Hadlee and Lance Cairns meant backyard cricket games most summer nights until dark. Dad and I had to face medium-fast and spin bowls and search for wild sixes in the hedge and horse paddock. Cows suffered in between our limited overs at the cowshed. My touch rugby mate Thomas used to tell me I had good hands and was impressed that I never let anyone past or was never bluffed by dummy passes. A result of facing Chris and his rugby ball for as long as I could stand. Even though perfectly capable of pumping up his rugby ball, Chris would take it into All Black, Mark Donaldson's sports shop and chat to him and get his ball autographed. His obsessions extended beyond rugby or cricket too.

He had a tennis phase when I received a tennis rebounder for Christmas. I didn't even play tennis but he convinced

Mum that I really wanted one for Christmas. Tennis was later extended to squash which intensified when he discovered some of the local jockeys played at the Foxton Squash Club.

Anything he saw on TV became an obsession. Yachting when Peter Blake et al were achieving remarkable feats. His calves for Calf Club Day suffered these obsessions with names like Swasibubble [a yacht] before he moved onto racehorse names (Librici and Tredici). His greatest heroes were involved in racing. Jockeys were our rock stars. Lance Robinson who used to come to our farm en route to riding Grandfather and Uncle Bob's horses at the beach and Jimmy Cassidy and Noel Harris were the top of our list. Later, Noel Harris rode Chris's first winner Go Morgan and Noel told me at the Hall of Fame dinner that he still had a hand-written letter that Chris had sent thanking him very much for riding his horse.

Trainers were pretty important too and Noel Eales our Grandfather's trainer, Snow Lupton and Paddy Busuttin had god-like status. Their achievements on the exciting Australian stage made big impressions. Kiwi winning the Melbourne Cup and Lomondy winning the Caulfield Cup no doubt planted seeds for what was possible if you dared to dream.

One of the pair's aunts, Robyn Waller, recalls that when Chris was at high school, she was touched by his concern when she cut her hand at a family gathering at the farm, one of the get-togethers at which Chris would spend time teaching his younger cousins to play cricket.

The injury meant she would have trouble driving a manual car, opening doors, cooking and so on when she went home to Auckland. So teenage Chris booked himself onto her flight back to Auckland to help her for the week. He changed gear for her in the car, did the washing and cooked roast dinners.

Chris's maternal grandfather Don Johnston died when the boy was very young, and his mother always nursed a dream that her son would be like him. 'Grandpop' Johnston had studied agricultural science and become a specialist consultant to dairy farmers, all while he ran his own property.

Marilyn fancied Chris might go to Lincoln University in Christchurch and study agricultural science like her father, and learn the latest techniques of pasture improvement, animal genetics and milk production. But classrooms still made him restless; his practical mind blocked out academic abstractions, and he felt at ease among older and (in his eyes) wiser people, farmers and horse trainers, who had learned by *doing* and taught by showing.

The boy who'd raised calves and pigs liked all livestock but he was drawn to horses, perhaps because they seemed to promise something to an ambitious lad whose ambition made him restless. He was itching to get on with improving himself— and, perhaps, proving himself. Someone who knew him then might have sensed in him a hunger to be 'somebody' without yet knowing who or what.

Marilyn mentions in an interview many years later how her schoolboy son once said he'd 'have a Mercedes one day'. Perhaps 'that tells you something', she adds, smiling at her boy's fierce ambition.

He might have inherited his 'Grandpop' Johnston's thoughtful approach to problem solving but, in the end, he chose horses over cows.

That might have had something to do with his other grandfather, Colin Waller.

•

By the time Chris knew his grandfather Waller, the old man was a retired farmer, a careful and conservative family elder. But as a young man, Colin had been a dashing horseman in a family full of them.

Every family has its stories, some of them true. The family legend about Colin was that he'd taken his bride Elizabeth to the races on their honeymoon—and ridden a winner there. This interesting start to married life in the bleak 1940s was mildly profitable, close to home and rather romantic, especially given the bridegroom had not lost the race or fallen off and injured himself.

The Wallers still speak of Colin's father, Chris's great-grandfather Fred Waller, as a remarkable horse and dog handler in a time and place when thousands of people handled horses, dogs and other livestock every day.

These days, Erewhon Station is known as the wild, otherworldly location where filmmaker Peter Jackson shot *Lord of the Rings*. Before World War I, Erewhon—an anagram of 'Nowhere'—comprised 35,000 acres of jagged peaks, ridges and gullies in one of the remotest corners of the British Empire's most remote dominion.

It was at Erewhon that young Fred was recognised as an out-standing horseman, as his brother Jim already was.

Dozens of stationhands camped in huts for months at a time on the lonely mountain sheep runs. The only alternative to hard work was sheer boredom, which gave rise to some unusual bets to break the tedium.

The station workers used stock horses to ride the ridges and draught horses to pull supply wagons and cart bales of wool, but Fred Waller stood out in his handling of green horses and rogues.

His mates made a bet he couldn't catch a distinctive palomino that had escaped the home paddocks and joined the wild horses in the ranges. It was much the same scenario as Banjo Paterson's 'The Man From Snowy River' in Australia the previous decade: crack riders gathered to pursue an escaped thoroughbred colt running with a brumby mob in the Snowy Mountains. But in this real-life Kiwi case, Fred Waller went out alone with a rope and, presumably, his best working dog.

Three days later, the story goes, he rode the runaway out of the ranges back to the station. Job done, bet won.

It wasn't the last time Chris Waller's great-grandfather won a wager involving animals.

•

The pioneer Wallers had arrived in New Zealand in the mid-nineteenth century from Ipswich in Suffolk. They settled first in the Rangiora district outside Christchurch on the northern edge of the Canterbury Plains on the South Island's east coast.

Robert Waller was born in 1863 and married Jane Bush in the Presbyterian Church at Ashley near Christchurch in 1889. Their son Fred was born in 1891, one of four sons and three daughters. There is still a Wallers Road at a tiny place named Loburn near Rangiora, although the family long ago spread around New Zealand, mainly to the Palmerston North region of the North Island.

Like many farmers' sons, Fred did time 'shepherding' on the huge sheep stations sprawled across the Southern Alps, which is what took him to Erewhon, biggest of them all.

The shepherds were more dependent on dogs than on horses to bring in mobs of half-wild sheep from ridges so steep it was impossible to ride over many of them. They had bred a strain of collie-cross dogs, forerunners of the Huntaway breed, that were tough and intelligent enough to work out of sight in the mountains, guided by nothing but whistles from their handlers.

Fred had a dog named Doon that understood him so acutely he took a bet he could stand outside a double-storey pub in a country town and whistle the dog through the building, room by room to the stairwell, then upstairs to a hallway, through another room and onto the front balcony overlooking the street. He won the bet.

Fred would move to the North Island and establish the family farm at Himatangi near Foxton and go on to own and train racehorses in the 1920s and 1930s, as did his brothers J.J. (Jim) and Hilton 'Fats' Waller.

Jim was an amateur jockey, a handy athlete, clerk of the course, showjumping rider and a successful public trainer. Apart from his other accomplishments, he owned an extraordinary 'high jumping' pony named Riot, which regularly leapt over obstacles taller than he was but was known for clearing huge jumps running free without a rider.

Both Jim and Fred would become well-known as trainers, especially of jumpers and stayers. Jim was the first to train three winners of the Wellington Steeplechase. By the time he won the third leg of the hat trick with Gaiety in 1949, brother Fred was dead but the stories about him were not. It was Fred the farmer who owned and trained Aurora Borealis, arguably the finest jumping mare New Zealand has ever produced. She was so small they called her 'the pony' but she won the 1930 Great Northern Steeplechase and the New Zealand Grand National the same year.

'She could hardly see over the brush fences,' says John Waller, grandson of Fred and father of Chris. The story of how Aurora Borealis won thirteen races at the height of the Depression, carrying huge weights, is an epic chapter of Waller family history. Life was tough and the brave little mare helped feed them.

John and Marilyn Waller don't have many racing photographs around their new home, the second they've had since selling the old Waller farm. One picture, prominently displayed, is of Chris's first Group One winner, Triple Honour. The other is a faded black and white picture of little Aurora Borealis, set up in the impeccable living room of the impeccable architect-designed house overlooking Awapuni Racecourse on Palmerston North's outskirts.

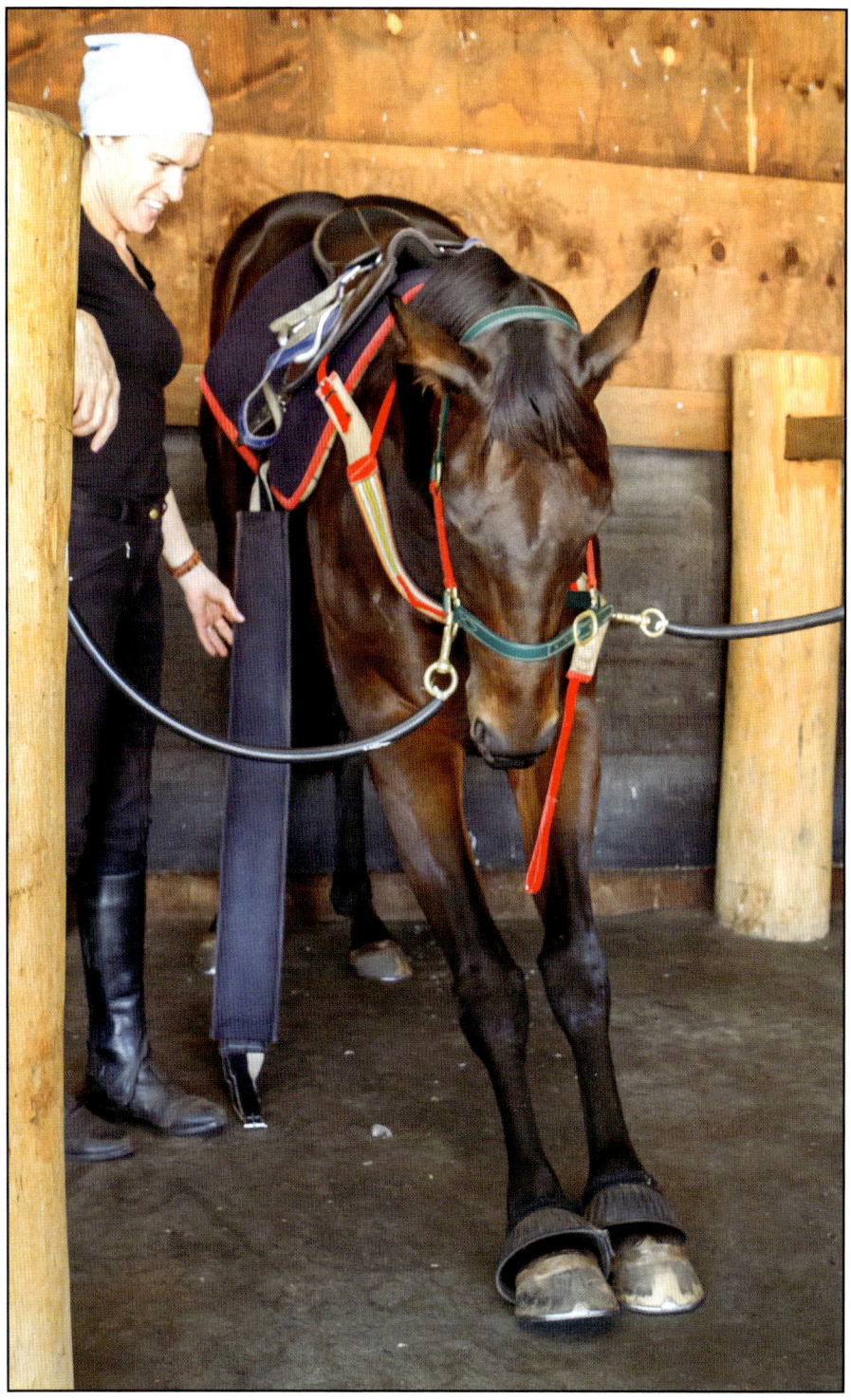

Stretch those legs . . . exercises are part of Winx's daily routine before pre-training work begins at the Hermitage, the property west of Sydney where she and other elite racehorses spell. Track rider Karen Koolman looks on. IMAGES IN THIS SECTION BY DEB PARSONAGE UNLESS OTHERWISE CREDITED

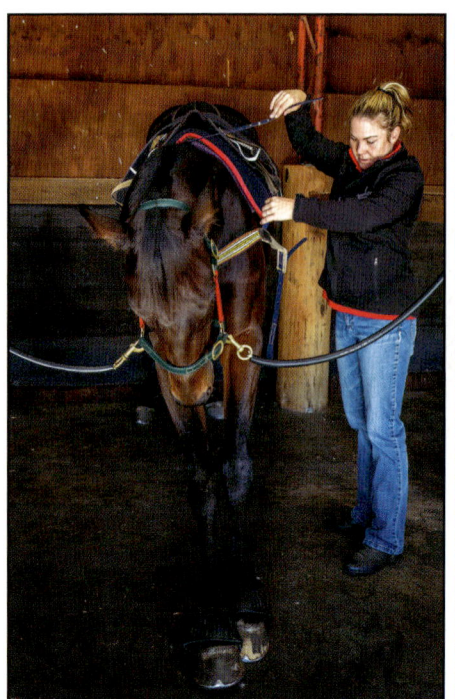

ABOVE: Horses are creatures of habit and a quiet routine is essential: in the tie-up shed, Winx is saddled then bridled (above right) the same way in the same place at the same time every day. Pre-training track riders Karen Koolman and Shannon Beasley swap horses on alternate days so they can compare notes.

RIGHT: Olly Koolman leads Winx off the uphill 1600-metre training track he had built from scratch in paddocks beside the forest. The track is graded into a gentle crown, planted with a thick pad of kikuyu turf and perfectly drained.

OPPOSITE: No hurry—Shannon walks the star guest a long way to warm her up before she starts her work.

Winx mooches along on a loose rein looking to snatch a mouthful of grass as her latest workmate Unforgotten goes on ahead. Each mate she has spelled with since her winning streak began has gone on to be a Group winner.

Trotting on the flat section of the track. Trotting is a good low-impact exercise for gallopers. Winx is often trotted downhill, a dressage technique to extend her stride.

Head on: Karen Koolman works Winx uphill to build aerobic fitness and muscle strength with little risk of injury. Some Australian trainers are starting to agree with their English and Irish counterparts about the value of straight tracks and hill work, especially for pretraining.

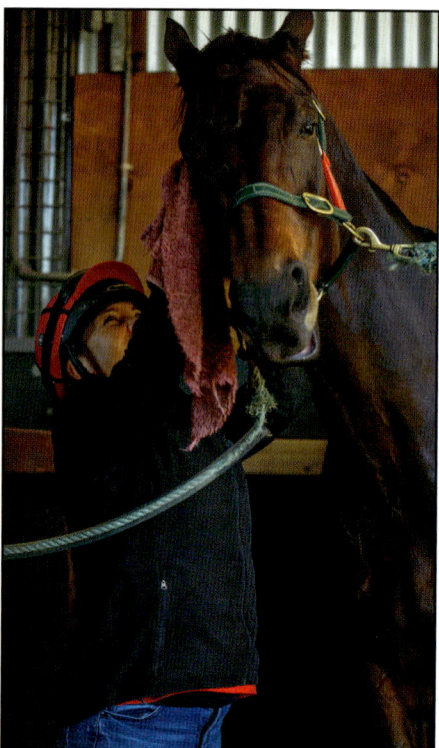

A drink of water in the wash bay (above left), and getting dried off by Shannon Beasley (above right).

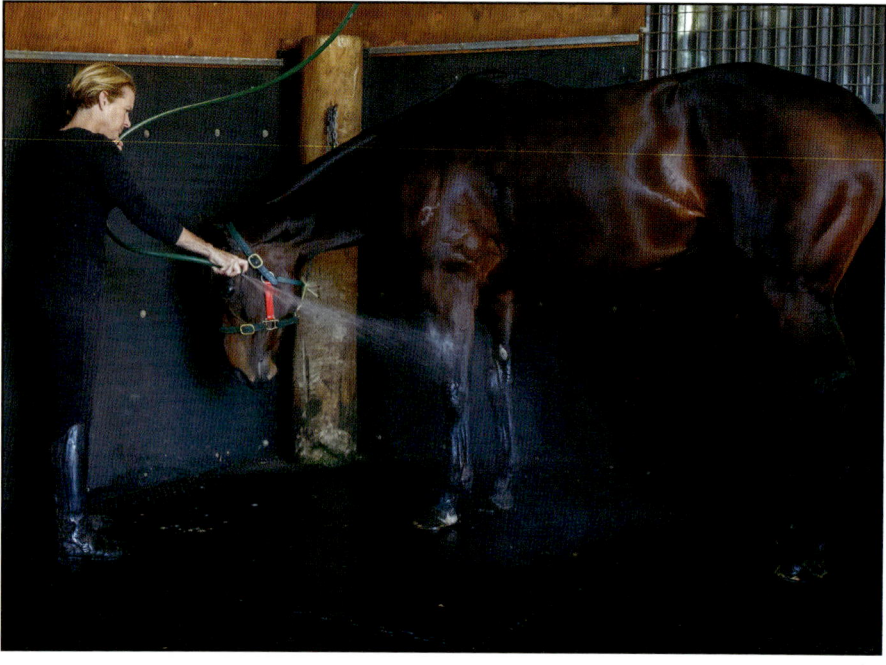

The usual hose-down to wash off sweat and dust after a morning workout, to be followed by a rubdown.

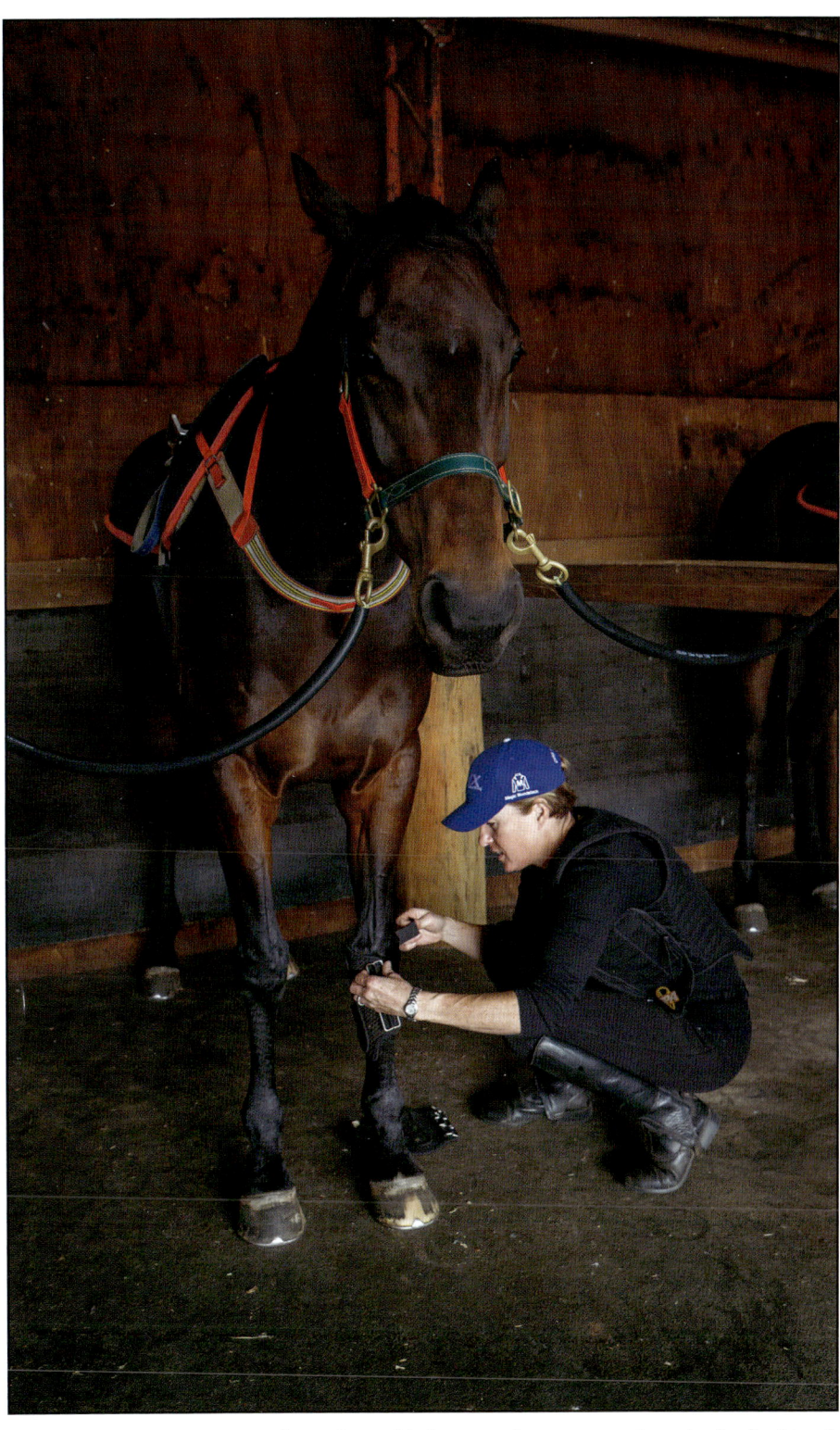

No foot, no horse. Karen Koolman fits padded exercise boots to cut the risk of a shod hind foot injuring the lower front leg, a racehorse's most vulnerable spot.

Back in the paddock after work, rug left off until later to get the midday sun on her back.

Winx exercises in the mechanical walker, another way to stop her putting on too much weight. Although she looks lean, she has always had a healthy appetite and needs work to stay close to racing trim.

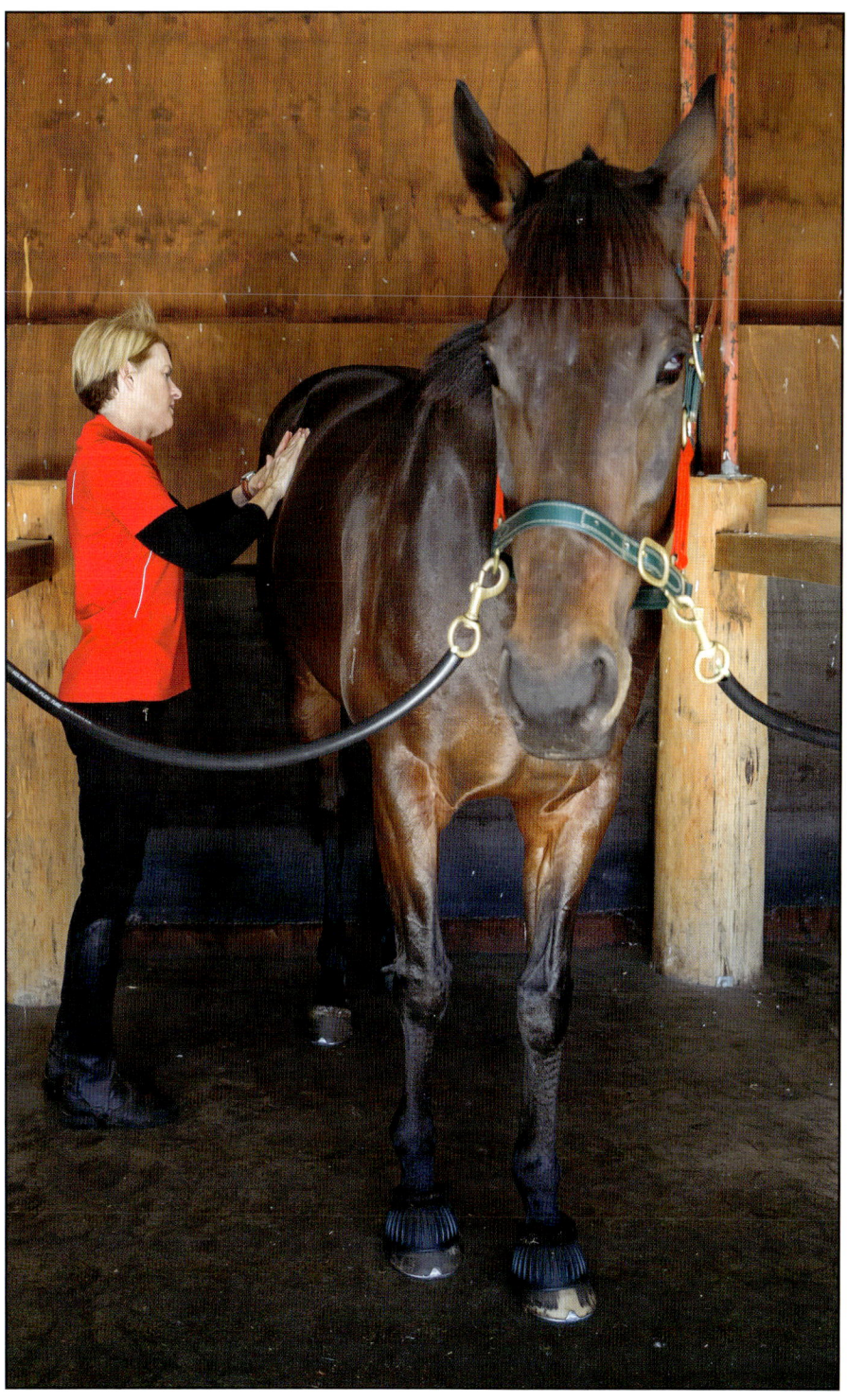

Hands on: Karen rubs Winx's hindquarters using Bowen massage techniques, something her husband Olly describes as 'one of the many one-per-centers' that go into keeping the mare fit and keen for racing.

Winx walks out of the pool at Flemington after swimming one or two laps, which she often does before she works. DARRYL SHERER

Shannon Beasley and Olly Koolman watch Winx in the Icelandic aqua-treadmill that was so helpful in getting her fit to a deadline after her bone-chip surgery in 2016.

A sight to lift a trainer's heart: the champion races around her paddock, a picture of physical freshness and mental fitness, ready to tackle the task ahead.

Pulling a power turn, proof of the natural athlete Hugh Bowman admires. He says he has never ridden a more balanced horse in any discipline.

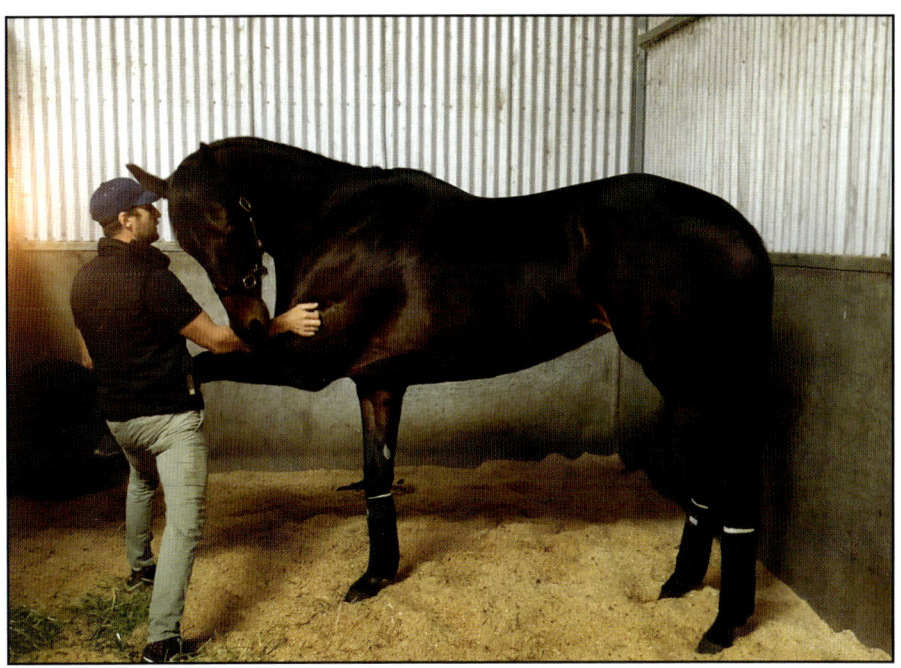

Winx in her Rosehill home, box 51, with her physio Tom Simpson. CHRIS WALLER RACING

Rider Ben Cadden works Winx on the track at Flemington in her lead-up to the 2017 Cox Plate. DARRYL SHERER

ABOVE: Carrot and apple 'cake' for Winx on 1 August 2018, birthday for all horses in the southern hemisphere. CHRIS WALLER RACING

OPPOSITE: Olly's son Kian has grown up seeing Winx several months a year. Winx has been on the property for every birthday Kian can remember.

A steady walk back to the tie-up shed after another workout.

The photographs of Aurora Borealis are a reminder of Fred, who died tragically in 1940, but not before passing on the love of good horseflesh to his sons Colin and Bob, who rode as amateur jockeys then bred horses on the farm—and trained the occasional one at home if it wasn't good enough to send to a professional trainer.

'My father and Uncle Bob both rode winners,' says John. 'Dad once paid someone to milk the cows and went all the way to Ellerslie by train to ride some rich bugger's horse and won—and the owner only gave him a fiver, which was pretty miserable. He worked out he would have been better to stay home.'

Despite his own lifelong attachment to racehorses, Colin didn't promote racing to his children. But John and his sisters Christine, Alison and Robyn dabbled in it anyway. As a young man, John would 'test pilot' horses his father and Uncle Bob broke in.

Chris grew up often seeing his dad hacking a young galloper around the cow paddocks to educate it. John was what Chris calls a 'good stockman'. He ran the farm singlehanded, treating his own livestock for any injuries or illnesses.

Because Colin lived next door, Chris grew up learning about horses from him. He soaked up information as children do, and as intelligent and impressionable children do even more. He went to the yearling sales with his grandparents and saw young horses through his grandfather's wise eyes, then later how they went on the racetrack.

One of New Zealand's finest trainers, Noel Eales, was a family friend who trusted Colin to 'babysit' his stables at Awapuni near Palmerston North when he had to campaign a horse elsewhere, back in the days when he raided Australian carnivals. Chris would help his grandparents with the Eales' horses and it left an impression.

Kiwi's 1983 Melbourne Cup and Mr Lomondy's 1986 Caulfield Cup were feats of mythic proportions to a boy soaked in sports history. Local heroes did not come any bigger unless they were All Blacks. For his grandfather to know Mr Lomondy's trainer Noel Eales well enough to be asked to help out at his stables was a source of wonder and delight. 'I got the bug then,' Chris says.

He still describes Eales with sincere respect: 'As good a trainer as they come, a very professional fifty-horse stable, a good strike rate. He was old school. I tagged along and watched the strappers do their job, and would see good jockeys ride work—Noel Harris and David Walsh and Maurice Campbell.'

Some describe Noel Eales as New Zealand's Bart Cummings—except that Eales never bought expensive yearlings to syndicate. Owners tended to bring him homebreds, and he trained for longevity rather than a quick turnaround, rarely racing two-year-olds.

The old Wallers were 'staying' men—jumpers, for preference—and so that classic view of the thoroughbred wormed its way into young Chris's fertile mind, the way it did with the great Irish trainers who came from jumping backgrounds, Vincent O'Brien and the unrelated Aidan O'Brien. The sort of people who can prepare horses to go over fences and stay long distances might have an edge on others.

The horse sense and accumulated experience of great-grandfather Fred the amateur steeplechase jockey filtered through the generations. It could explain why the C.J. Waller name, though prolific in form guides, has until recently appeared only rarely beside entries in two-year-old races and big sprints—but regularly figures in middle-distance and staying races.

The link between the brilliant modern trainer and his forebears' traditional horse lore might not be obvious but it is there.

Chris's aunt Alison Horrocks recalls her father Colin had an old recipe for a rubbing mixture that treated horses for bad tendons or ligaments. It was a concoction of Epsom salts, vinegar, saltpetre and a patent liniment sold as 'Penetrene'. He kept the mixture in a flagon. In his last years on the farm, in the late 1990s, the old man had a horse named Rand, a homebred out of a good Waller mare, recovering from lameness. Every day he would go to the paddock gate and call the horse, which would trot over to him. Colin would produce a neatly folded handkerchief, soak it in the mixture from the flagon and swab the bad leg.

Rand recovered completely and, as Chris was moving to Sydney to train by then, was sent to jumps specialist Mark Oulaghan down the road at Awapuni.

The horse went on to win a total of ten races and almost $700,000—most of that in Japan and America in international jumps races as a six-year-old in 2000–01. Colin Waller lived just long enough to see his homespun methods and his homebred horse vindicated. The horse's recovery was probably a tribute to his patience and skill.

When Colin was dying, in 2001, he spoke of his father Fred, who had died suddenly in 1940, well before any of his grandchildren were born.

'When Dad was in hospital, he told us these stories with tears in his eyes,' says Alison.

By that time, Chris was a struggling rookie trainer in Australia, juggling feed bills and credit cards. But he flew home to see his grandfather one more time. The old horseman was so frail they thought he might not last 'but he hung on to see Chris', says Alison, her voice catching.

Colin had been like a second father to Chris. The one, perhaps, who with his race saddles and silks and jockey boots and tales of past glories had unwittingly steered him towards racehorses and the outside world and away from cows and the family farm.

But others, too, played a part in training the man who would train Winx perhaps as well as any champion ever has been trained.

•

Most people who breed horses in New Zealand are farmers by origin or inclination. When New Zealand's greatest thorough-bred breeder—the world-renowned Sir Patrick Hogan—was a child, before horses bewitched him, he used to memorise the pedigrees of Jersey cattle.

Hogan's innovative ways of preparing and presenting young horses for market revolutionised the way yearlings were sold in New Zealand and Australia. Before Hogan's era, half-handled yearlings would have the paddock mud brushed off them before being chivvied into the ring by farmhands in gumboots.

His innovations went back to his childhood, when he made a point of grooming and feeding and handling dairy calves better to compete with other farm children in the 'Calf Club' competitions of rural schools. He also fattened pigs to sell, always chasing an edge to produce animals better than the rest.

Even at the height of his fame—and considerable fortune— as an elite thoroughbred breeder, Sir Patrick still devoted some of his properties in the Waikato stud heartland to dairy farming. He never lost sight of the fact it was the land that raised the cattle and horses and supported the empire of chance he built. A generation later, Chris Waller sensed the same thing.

In New Zealand, perhaps the most truly agrarian western nation left, even more so than Ireland, the link between horse and land was still clear. Not many Kiwi farmers are far from a horse.

When Chris Waller waited for the school bus on weekday mornings at quarter to eight, he would see an old horse truck go past.

'I'd wave to the driver, as you do in New Zealand,' he recalls. One day he got to talk to the driver. 'I said I'd like to come with him when he was taking horses to the beach. Then he advertised in a local shop window for part-time help, and I answered.

'His name was Alister Good. He was a farmer and a semi-professional trainer, ten minutes from home. I used to go there at weekends and holidays. He taught me to ride with a bit more confidence. He was a very good horseman, who loved his animals.

'The day I turned fifteen I got a driver's licence and drove his truck. I'd milk cows and work horses. I started riding trackwork, and learned everything I needed to know in a basic way.

'I was starting to struggle a bit at school so I applied for my first full-time job. It was at Waverley with Bill Thurlow, whose parents had horses with Alister Good. He also had cows and horses on his farm.'

Waller had bought an old Honda Civic with money he had made from rearing some Murray Grey calves to sell as steers. He packed a few clothes and drove north to South Taranaki on the south-west coast of the North Island.

·

Bill Thurlow is a fit, active, middle-aged man, king of all he surveys on his smart property near the Corcorans' Grangewilliam Stud where Vegas Showgirl was bred, on the highway that passes through the Waverley district down the coast.

Thurlow has done well over the thirty years since he was briefly Chris Waller's boss. As he leans on his garden fence to chat, a farmhand buzzes back and forth on a ride-on mower, making the grounds neat. It wasn't always this way.

In 1989 Thurlow was a lively young bachelor, a share farmer who needed a hand to help milk a herd of someone else's cows and to work with his 'stable'. He had hired the teenager straight from school on the recommendation of Alister Good.

Thurlow knew of the boy by his family name, as people do in rural New Zealand. Chris Waller's aunt Christine Cunningham had taught Thurlow at primary school and Wallers had been farmers and horsemen as long as anyone could remember.

The trouble was, Thurlow admits with a grin, 'I had one horse and a whole lotta cows.'

There were 140 Friesians to milk but only one old steeple-chaser to exercise. It was hardly the key to the glamorous world of racing.

The cows had to be laboriously milked in a little, old-fashioned cowshed with only fourteen stands. To illustrate his story Thurlow jumps in his ute and heads down back roads to the old cowshed, no longer used. He points out the corner of a tired shed next to it where he'd rigged up a makeshift loosebox for his steeplechaser, Lord Kamaran.

Working for him in 1989 was no picnic, he admits. The best bit, if you could call it that, would be exercising Lord Kamaran around the cow paddocks after milking.

The accommodation was a ramshackle old farmhouse—since burned down, fortunately. Thurlow, then in his late twenties, had been better at pouring beer than cooking or cleaning for a relatively innocent and naturally fastidious employee.

'I was single, so it was a bit of a party house,' he says. All in all, he concludes cheerfully, it was no wonder the teenage Waller lasted only a couple of weeks before politely quitting. It was Waller's first time living away from home and he was homesick. Thurlow could hardly blame him and has watched the progress of his former farmhand ever since with interest and some affection.

These days, Thurlow buys and educates young gallopers to re-sell—a star of 2017, Gingernuts, was one of his, and he has done well enough to race a couple of horses himself. One of them in 2018 is Midnight Delight, which Waller trains at Rosehill.

Of Waller, he concludes: 'He was obviously a nice, polite boy—pretty articulate and not rough around the edges. Everyone's proud of him here.'

•

Working at Bill Thurlow's was only a detour for the homesick teenager. He went home and worked with Alister Good's horses in the morning and milked cows with his father in the afternoons.

'I thought that was pretty good. It lasted three months. Dad knew Paddy Busuttin and asked him if he had any work, so I went and worked for Paddy in Foxton. I now realise how much my home life and working for Alister Good influenced my life.

'Paddy Busuttin was all professionalism and a brilliant trainer. He was the new kid on the block—training Group One winners and very good on the public relations side. He had a big team of horses and a lot of staff.'

Busuttin couldn't believe what he saw on Waller's first morning at his stables. The new boy pulled out a notebook and pen and started taking notes.

Busuttin had trained hundreds of horses and known scores of stablehands, a broad church ranging from burglars to beauty queens, but he had never seen one take notes before. John Waller's boy was different. He had a sort of missionary zeal.

The harder he worked, the more responsibility he was given. First, it was travelling horses to races around the North Island. Then over to the South Island. Then Australia.

He had become a thoroughly competent horseman on the ground and a useful work rider, but there were plenty of those. His reliability and practical intelligence counted more. If he'd been out late with the other stablehands, which wasn't often, he wouldn't short-change the horses next day: the feed and the work were on time and everything was done as meticulously as if the boss and the owners were supervising it.

Waller was young but he was a farm boy and smart with it: he'd been treated like an adult since he was big enough to reach the clutch on the Fergie tractor. Long before he could vote he'd treated sick cows, delivered breech-birth calves, handled bulls, driven trucks and used guns. He didn't smoke, rarely drank too much.

By his twenty-first birthday he was the ideal foreman and assistant trainer. Which is why, two years later, he was asked to take over the stable when Paddy Busuttin was offered a position training in Singapore.

It was a chance to run a ready-made stable so Waller of course agreed.

Looking back, he suspects he was probably too young, at least in the eyes of some horse owners. But what he endured taught him more than if it had come easily. He knew exactly how to look after the horses Busuttin left but he was not yet old enough and confident enough to command the respect of their owners.

It wasn't until he was in charge that he realised how unsentimental racing can be.

'It was a big learning curve,' he says, about owner loyalty and lack of it. A lot of people who said they would stay with him didn't. If they didn't have a win or didn't like being told their horse wasn't good enough, they would ditch the young trainer. Waller realised something that constantly combative people never learn: don't nurse grudges.

Some owners stayed, many went. But Waller remained polite to all. He didn't argue or complain about those who took their horses, and always greeted them later as if nothing had changed.

'They respect you for not getting upset—and it always keeps the door open,' he muses.

Some owners came back when they realised they'd sold him short and had done no better elsewhere—and because he'd made it easy for them to return without embarrassment. The experience taught him more about handling people than it did about horses. It taught him that relationships and communication with owners (and media and race clubs and breeders) matter as much to a trainer as conditioning horses, because without good owners you don't get good horses. And good horses—or lack of them—are the biggest difference between one trainer and another. His battle to stay afloat also taught him how lonely it is, but how vital, to make constant hard decisions: to buy, sell and sack.

He had to borrow $40,000 to stay in business, but it was gone within a month. Then he took out an overdraft and knuckled down to surviving hand to mouth.

The struggle might have cowed a less resilient character. The prospect of failure hardened his resolve. Only those who knew him then would realise that his overnight success took fifteen years of brutally hard work and self-imposed poverty. The workload hasn't improved since then—but the scale of success has.

By the time he was thirty he was a man of flexible intellect but rigid determination. If that is not *the* recipe for success, it runs a close second.

There is no better witness to that success than the partner who shared the load. Her name is Stephanie.

•

They went to the same school but weren't 'schoolyard sweet-hearts'. He was two years older and wrapped up in work but found time to form the opinion she was the most beautiful girl between Palmerston North and New York, where she went to work as a model just after he steeled the nerve to ask her out.

The story they tell is that Chris's father, a man with a sense of humour and a twinkle in his eye, told Stephanie his son was keen to meet her. She was singing in a band called Hokio at a local race meeting at the time.

Stephanie Titcombe, daughter of the Foxton carpet mill accountant, was not yet twenty then but she had already been spotted by a talent scout. She soon took advice that she could go further as a model than as a singer.

One job led to another and she ended up working in New York with assignments in Japan and Europe. But all the while she stayed in touch with her long-distance admirer. Stephanie enjoyed working overseas but loved going home to Foxton. So much so that when Chris first suggested leaving for Sydney in the late 1990s, she didn't want to move.

As the Waller stable wobbled on foal legs for the first few seasons, Stephanie's modelling jobs paid the bills. Another important female in Waller's life also played a part at that crucial time.

Her name was Party Belle, though in truth she was no belle. Waller is kind about her: 'a nice, big New Zealand mare—plain but with a good constitution'. He broke her in himself after he and his father leased her from the breeders. She could not quite win a race in New Zealand—Waller's first official winner, in fact, was Go Morgan at Trentham in 1997, ridden by Noel Harris. But she made up for that across the Tasman.

When Waller's strongest supporters, Tony Muollo and his father Tony senior, agreed to send their promising three-year-old Ocean Run to Australia in 1998 to aim him at the Gloaming Stakes, they also agreed to pay for the four-year-old Party Belle to go along, as much travelling companion as second stringer. And the trainer got a $40,000 overdraft from a bank manager who took a chance on him.

Ocean Run ran 'a blinder' in his first race at Rosehill but pulled a muscle, which scuppered his tilt at Group race glory. But the homely Party Belle blossomed. She ran placings at Kembla Grange and then Goulburn. As Waller went back and forth to New Zealand to run the stable there, he left Party Belle with Analese Trollope at Paul O'Sullivan's Rosehill stables. The mare won three provincial races straight, then returned to New Zealand after failing twice in town.

Again, Party Belle didn't win in New Zealand. But she returned to Sydney the following season and excelled herself. In five weeks she won three straight and ran third in a Listed race. Larry Cassidy rode her in the wins.

Party Belle never did much after that but her job was done. The wins kept Waller afloat when he needed it most. If any one thing prompted his move to Australia, it was probably Party Belle's two strings of wins. A young trainer producing a horse to win three straight, including two races at Randwick, demanded attention: in this case from the people running Rosehill. The Sydney Turf Club was planning a new barn of twenty looseboxes and asked Waller if he would apply for them.

'Of course,' he said, 'I'll take those boxes.' But he explained that he couldn't fill twenty boxes so they asked if he would take ten and another ten in six months, and he agreed.

And so the man who says he has never been a gambling trainer ('Couldn't afford it') took the biggest punt of his life. He fetched his five best horses from Foxton. One was the faithful Party Belle. She couldn't get warm again but she'd paid her way.

As for Analese Trollope, she would become Waller's longest-standing employee, head foreperson at his Rosehill headquarters. Joining his stable was an act of faith for her. Waller had no money but she knew he paid his bills.

The ten boxes at Rosehill were meant to be ready on 1 January 2000, the day the 'Y2K bug' was supposedly going to cripple civilisation. The Y2K bug didn't arrive but neither did the stables, which weren't ready until 1 April, the first April Fool's Day of the new millennium. At the time Waller wondered if that was an omen, but things worked out.

'Our first runner was Our Cracker—he won at Rosehill. A good old horse. I had five average horses I had to get the best out of. I think it formed the way I trained. Don't break them down—you need longevity. I couldn't get finances [in Australia]. No bank manager. Still had a stable in New Zealand. All in all, I trained about eighty winners in New Zealand.'

The story of Waller's 'maxed-out' credit cards and sleeping on friends' couches has become a standard, like Tommy Smith and his first good winner, the rogue Bragger. It's not long enough ago to have become a legend but already the Wallers' two children might find it hard to believe how different their parents' lives were as new arrivals in Sydney.

Chris and Stephanie rented a two-bedroom flat at Rosehill within walking distance of the racetrack and the railway station. This was handy because they did not own a car for two years, Waller says. He worked out a quick way to jog to work—straight over the back fence and down a lane and across the highway.

The flat was cheap but had no air-conditioning—a rookie error for Kiwis—so they moved to another one with air-con that cost an extra $10 a week. Stephanie had enough singing and modelling work to cover the rent, and Chris earned almost enough in training fees to pay the feed, farrier and veterinary bills. Any stakes money was the difference between barely existing and having a little left over at the end of the month.

Stephanie would rather have been home in Foxton.

'It took me a couple of years to accept living in Sydney,' she says. One reason was that they could hardly have been more broke. They slept on a mattress on the floor. On weekends they would borrow an old car from fellow Kiwi trainer Shaune Ritchie to do the grocery shopping.

They couldn't afford to buy a flat but eventually scraped up the deposit for one in North Parramatta—they could never have imagined that, in 2011, they would be able to buy a house in Baulkham Hills. Along the way, they finally found a weekend to get married, back home in the little Anglican church in Foxton on 12 February 2005. They are proud but unpretentious people.

'We were happy when we had no money,' Stephanie says. 'We have the same friends now we had then. Chris was always generous: he would shout everyone and spend the rent. Lucky we had a good landlord.'

Buying yearlings was almost out of the question. Waller had to improvise with what he had, training carefully to reduce the chance of breaking them down. He thinks it taught him to train for longevity—an insight into keeping Winx sound season after season.

'I learned how to run the business in Australia pretty quick. Learnt I had to use good jockeys: they could tell an owner a horse had every chance but wasn't good enough.' It was the lesson learned from his dealings with skittish owners over the previous couple of years: better a respected jockey with a reputation to tell owners bad news than a young trainer trying to maintain diplomatic relations.

'Back then, I'd ring Larry [Cassidy] first. Then I would ring the next best and so on, so I usually had a top-flight jock riding for me. Darren Beadman was a massive influence. He was my idol. He was just as good in winter at Warwick Farm as in a Group One. Good jockeys are a big part of my success. A young, unknown trainer using good jockeys attracts attention.'

Because he was an outsider, he wasn't a hostage to his own history. As an outsider he started with a clean slate, not owing anyone and with some novelty value. By hiring reliable track riders to work his horses, he could cherry-pick the best freelancers at the races.

'A five per cent better jockey is a lot [of upside] over a year. Their feedback is better; owners get value for their money.'

It wasn't just a case of projecting a professional aura on race days. Back in the stable, although starting out with only ten horses, he applied his system of feeding, grooming and exercise that would work just as efficiently with double that number— and with double that again. He set up his corner shop as if it were already a big store, which meant he was primed for expansion, not overwhelmed by it.

He was steeped in dairy farm discipline: routines had to be established to keep animals content and standards of hygiene and treatment high.

'Looking after dairy cattle you get to know about condition, if they're happy or if they're hungry and calling out. You get to understand if they've got a sore foot and doing it tough. Whether they're too hot or too cold. You can see how they are.'

Unlike a lot of trainers, Waller had never really been a horse hobbyist who'd infiltrated racing, learning by trial and error, nor a broken-down jockey with no other trade. By applying high standards of animal husbandry and client management from the start, he stood apart.

Looking after thoroughbreds requires the same discipline and care that looking after any group of animals does, from an aviary to a piggery to a zoo. An analytical attitude comes with that. He was taking a big chance by setting up at Rosehill but it was a calculated risk by an entrepreneur, not a gambler.

Waller has sentiment—anyone who sees him choke up after big wins knows that—but he's not sentimental.

At the 2004 New Zealand yearling sales, Melbourne bloodstock agent and writer Danny Power saw a strong filly out of Waller's brave mare, Party Belle. He bid. So did Waller. But Waller pulled out at $20,000 and Power got the yearling for $22,000. Power was intrigued because Waller obviously liked the horse and was attached to its mother—but wasn't tempted to bid more than a rigid budget of $20,000.

As Partysinga, Party Belle's daughter would win four country races and be placed ten times in Victoria. She was no champion but she paid her way. A decade later, Waller would be paying half a million for some yearlings, but still sticking to a budget. His business principles haven't changed but his clients have. Their pockets are much deeper.

18

THE STREAK BEGINS

No one knows when a streak begins, only when it ends. When an apprentice from Perth rides a first starter for Peter Moody at Flemington in the autumn of 2009, everyone knows the hulking filly has won trials but that's no guarantee of success. The same filly's $300,000 mother never made it through a preparation, let alone won a race.

Moody's debutante looks like Serena Williams serving against schoolgirls and that's how it plays out. The kid, Jarrad Noske, holds her under double wraps then humiliates the field at a canter. But no one is expecting her to go on to win ten straight, let alone twenty-five, because that's crazy talk. And what sort of a name is Black Caviar, anyway?

Every last-start winner could be on its way to a streak, the way every pensioner leaving a TattsLotto agency clutching a ticket could be winning the lottery. Truth is, winning streaks that run to double figures at the track are far scarcer than lottery wins, which happen every week.

A streak grows bit by bit before it's noticed. It goes from beginner's luck to novelty to talking point to marketing angle before it becomes something else, something bigger than another racehorse in another horse race. It takes on a life of its own—a promoter's dream but not a promoter's invention. It has an authentic star power that can't be contrived.

That's why on the night Black Caviar wins her eleventh race, the William Reid Stakes, Moonee Valley is jammed. There are many new faces among the regulars to see this living legend with the now unforgettable name and those striking colours—black dots on salmon background, isn't it?

Something happens that night that you don't often see: the jockeys' room empties out as the riders without a ride in the big race come outside and find vantage points. Some climb the ladder of the stewards' tower opposite the post.

The great mare's ten straight wins have turned even these hard-bitten professionals into fans. They know they're witnesses to history in the making and, for once, a television screen isn't enough. Tonight they want to be ringside with the punters, the waiters, the tote staff and the strappers, all elbow to elbow with the public, like Collingwood supporters in a premiership year or Springsteen fans queuing for tickets.

Promise of a pure spectacle beats what brings people to a normal race meeting at other times, when those who turn up at all are either paid to be there or hoping to profit from being there. Run-of-the-mill racehorses, even good ones, have backers. But the freak with the streak attracts fans—more with every win.

When a streak gets to double figures, public fascination is amplified and so is the pressure. It becomes a highwire act: hard not to look at, impossible to ignore.

•

Caloundra, 16 May 2015. Sunshine Coast Guineas. #1

On the day of the 2015 Sunshine Coast Guineas, all that is still ahead for the new highwire act, the horse no one yet knows is set to follow Black Caviar so soon. First, she has to make it safely without falling.

The longest journey begins with a step, the saying goes, and for Winx this is it. But Hugh Bowman misses it because he hasn't got a crystal ball. There's no way then of knowing the filly's journey isn't going to end soon enough, the way most do.

Bowman is happy to hand the reins to his old friend Larry Cassidy for the Sunshine Coast sideshow because he has a big book of good rides on the big stage in Sydney, mostly for Chris Waller. The young Winx just has to take her place down the queue of Waller–Bowman priorities.

Bowman will be back in the saddle for a slightly off-Broadway version of a Group One classic, the Queensland Oaks, two weeks later. After that, he is entitled to imagine, the filly will probably go to the paddock while the connections do some head-scratching over how to snaffle a decent race with her in spring and get enough kudos to breed from her.

Punters and bookmakers might see it differently but, for the stable, the 1600 metres of the Sunshine Coast Guineas is more a pipe opener to get ready for another tilt at black type, consolation for losing the Australian Oaks in Sydney.

'It was always the plan to spell her,' Peter Tighe says later. 'It's funny. On the Saturday we thought the campaign was all over, but a few days later Chris rang us and said we should give her a quick break and set her for Queensland.'

Her new target is a sawn-off edition of the Queensland Oaks, with 200 metres shaved from the 'mile and a half' classic because its usual home, Eagle Farm, is under repair.

Given that Winx is coming off a stiff 2400-metre loss at Randwick and is due to run 2200 metres in Brisbane, no one in Wallerland is counting on a big result over the shorter distance at Caloundra, even if the market fancies her chances.

Proof of this is that, of the owners and trainer, only the Tighes go to see her race. They live in Brisbane, so it's close and they know people who'll be at the races. Win or lose, for them it's a social day out with local friends.

Still, Larry Cassidy drives to Caloundra, agreeing with punters that the drop in class means his 'pick-up ride' will be hard to beat. He holds the thought right up until she hacks out of the barrier as reluctantly as some old steeplechaser contemplating three miles of hedges.

As the race unfolds a long way in front of him, Cassidy reckons she has blown her chance by blowing the start. At the 600-metre mark he is resigned to a distant placing. He eases to the outside rather than risk being bagged if she tries to go inside horses and gets blocked for a run. Better a smooth fifth place than to crash and burn trying to run an heroic third.

Then the X factor kicks in.

Two minutes later, the *Courier Mail*'s Nathan Exelby is interviewing a grinning Peter Tighe. Guess what? He's looking forward to the Queensland Oaks in his hometown more than ever.

'She got a bit far behind them,' he says. 'I thought it would be a nice Oaks trial if she could finish in the first four.'

Standard happy owner stuff. Racing writers interview dozens of winning connections as happy as Tighe. But not as happy as he's going to be.

Looking back on it three years on, he says: 'Patty and I were the only ones from the camp there. We went there with no expectations and she came out and bloused them. There was a wow factor that day.'

•

Doomben, 30 May 2015. Queensland Oaks. #2

With 600 metres to go in the Oaks, the caller suddenly sounds almost relieved. He's just spotted Bowman making his move on Winx and his voice rises to mark his appreciation of a new plot development.

'Winx is on her way forward now,' he chants, letting an army of punters know how their favourite is travelling. As he switches back to running through the field, the ones watching on screens can see the white bridle and the blue colours cruising past horse after horse, silhouetted against the high cream fence blocking Doomben from the surrounding suburban sprawl.

Winx has pulled to the outside, 300 metres to go.

Seconds later, she passes the 200 metres.

Here's Winx. She's winding up and look at her go! Inside the 200-metre mark and Winx has raced to the lead from Imperial Lass and Ungrateful Ellen.

She overhauls the leaders at the 100 metres and wins by three lengths, Bowman already easing her before the line ahead of Ungrateful Ellen, an interestingly named filly (her sire is Grey Swallow, her dam Degeneres) owned by John 'Dr Turf' Rothfield, comedian Russell Gilbert and David Price, Hong Kong-based bloodstock trader from Melbourne.

Craig Williams, on Ungrateful Ellen, says she ran home well but the winner was in a different class.

Bowman agrees. He says he could have settled Winx closer to the leaders but she was comfortable racing back in the field. He didn't need to add that he was confident she could come from a long way back, provided she could get out.

'She has a real turn of foot. I think there is a genuine upside to her as well,' he tells reporters. 'She's done it with authority.'

It is Winx's first Group One, Waller's thirteenth for the season. The Tighes have won their first hometown big one. Peter Tighe says Waller is 'a genius' for setting her to win an Oaks with one lead-up run. Waller ducks the compliment and says it's more down to Winx's resilience and brilliance than to his training.

'A quality filly like her just needs to be kept fit without being flattened,' he says in a post-race interview.

Fit without being flattened. The craft of horse training distilled into just four words. It's that simple and that hard. But first find your quality filly.

Waller knew Winx had ability. But each start revises his estimate of her quality. Before the Australian Oaks he thought she was shaping as a handicap stayer but now he has ditched the idea of campaigning her as a lightweight Caulfield Cup chance because the Queensland double makes her look like a brilliant weight-for-age 'miler'. He discounts the idea of running her in the Queensland Derby against the colts the following week because, he says, winning it wouldn't prove anything—or improve her value. He is careful not to back her up too quickly.

Instead, he says, he will spell her ready for spring. His target is the Myer Classic, a Group One mares race at Flemington on Derby Day. It's the biggest and best day in Australian racing and Waller is thinking Winx is up there with the biggest and best mares in the land.

He is getting no argument from the media yet. Paul Joice, writing for Racenet, files a piece on the Queensland Oaks that begins 'Explosive, exciting, dominant—the superlatives abound when describing the win of odds-on favourite Winx . . .'

She goes to Warrina Lodge in the Guanaba Valley in the Gold Coast hinterland for a month, then back to Tim Boland's Limitless Lodge at Wyong for pre-training. Whatever they do there seems to suit her. She had been whittled down to 480 kilograms after her Oaks campaign in April but thrives after the Queensland campaign. Warmth can help young horses grow.

Boland's records show she leaves Limitless Lodge for the last time on 23 July weighing 507 kilograms. And she 'hasn't been beaten since', he notes. As with each spell and preparation afterwards, she has put on weight—and barely loses any of it in work.

•

Rosehill, 12 September 2015. Theo Marks Stakes. #3

When James McDonald gets the call to ride Winx in the first start of her four-year-old season, he might be as talented a young jockey as anyone. The two facts are connected.

Hugh Bowman is suspended and Waller is quick to ask McDonald to step in. Waller being Waller, he leaves nothing to chance and asks McDonald to ride some fast work on the mare when she arrives at his stables after spelling and pre-training.

McDonald finds her quirky and 'not the normal racehorse'. She is quiet enough but when he rides her out of the barn to the track 'she would hump up and down on the spot'. It's not a full-blown buck. 'She wouldn't throw you off but she'd unsettle you,' he is to recall.

Which is what she does going out of the mounting yard onto the track for the Theo Marks Stakes. Officially, she turned four many weeks earlier on the 'horse's birthday' but by the calendar she is a couple of days short of the milestone.

Despite the training and racing she has done in the previous two years, she is still a frisky young horse fresh out of the paddock, 'feeling her oats', as they say of the high-energy diet that makes horses toey. None of it is going to worry the seasoned horseman Ben Cadden, her regular trackwork rider, let alone a world-class race jockey like McDonald, but it is 'quirky' enough that he remembers it.

'J Mac' feels no great pressure riding her in the Theo Marks because in the normal scheme of things, on a normal horse, it would be only a preparatory run. Besides, he wouldn't be able to ride her regularly (even if Bowman could not for some reason) because of his commitment to the giant Godolphin stable—and to horses that would often be racing against her, notably the English horse, Hartnell.

She's an Oaks filly resuming in her four-year-old year. Racing convention says this is just a 1300-metre warm-up race for a stayer whose last win was over 2200 metres. It's a standard first-up run to build fitness for later, all the more reason why Bowman wouldn't be worried about missing it.

Winx hasn't read that script.

'No one knew what she was capable of,' McDonald muses later. 'She jumped out of the gates slowly and settled back. Not a lot of pressure to do much . . . she copped a lot of interference on the turn.'

By 'interference' he means she almost slams into the rump of another horse and has to take evasive action. She goes from second last to last as he hooks her around the trouble to come down the outside.

'To tell the truth, I gave up any hope of winning the race but I gave her a whack and she just took off. Then I thought "At least I will finish in the money" and she balanced up and ended up picking them up.'

It's a fairly bald description of a nerve-tingling, logic-defying run. Play back the tape, as McDonald and his mates have many times, and it is astonishing every time.

McDonald admits he didn't ride her vigorously before and after the interference, which was why the chief steward Ray Murrihy hauls him in to explain his tactics. He tells the truth: he thought the interference had cost him any chance and didn't want to knock her about with a gut-buster from way back.

At the 250-metre mark she is last. At the 200-metre mark she is in front of only four horses with nine in front of her, strung out over many lengths. She is five lengths from the leader at the 100-metre mark. That 100 metres represents less than six seconds' galloping time in a fast finish and she has to make up a second to win. Racetrack arithmetic says flesh and blood can't go that much faster than these good gallopers already are. But this mare explodes.

The caller is going through the leaders—*Sons Of John is driving through*—when he sees the blue flash down the outside.

There are still three horses ahead of her at the fifty-metre mark. She can't win. In his last breath before the post, the caller yells *Winx flying!* and by the time the *-ing* syllable is out of his mouth she hits the line in what looks like a dead heat. He can't pick it.

Oh, did she get there? Oh, Winx has flown at Sons Of John. What a powerhouse finish! It's a photo.

And it was.

The camera freezes one of racing's minor miracles. Winx has come from the clouds to win by the barest of margins, giving

McDonald a hat-trick of consecutive wins that day. His mates still tease him about being the guy who could have killed the Winx streak right there. It's only later—as she keeps winning, and winning—that the significance of this small miracle becomes clear

On the day there's no thought of a streak. She is just a very good middle-distance filly who has turned in a surprise first-up performance in a sprint after being left at the start and running into interference.

It reminds younger people like Umut of Street Cry's greatest offspring Zenyatta in America. But there is something about overcoming every obstacle and still winning that throws up memories of another horse: Kingston Town, the champion someone once defined as a horse that could win any race from any position.

McDonald remembers Vegas Showgirl in New Zealand as 'a tough thing, a fantastic bodied mare . . . can't believe what Roggie put her through'. Meaning that Graeme Rogerson gave her nine starts as a two-year-old. McDonald says she was like the best Al Akbars: honest, tough and amazing wet trackers. On a wet track Al Akbar's progeny were a chance even if they were 80 to 1, he says. Which is why McDonald has never doubted Winx could handle any going. (His only regret, later, is that he has to ride against her so often. He calls it a 'love–hate relationship'.)

But it is early days and the Theo Marks is just the latest of a series of surprise endings. There is not yet a great weight of expectation on the Oaks filly with the lightning finish.

Peter Tighe, in fact, hasn't got there that day. It's the one Winx win that he wasn't on the course to see.

As for Waller, after the race, he is almost cracking jokes.

'We might have to change her name to Wings,' he says.

•

The significance of the Theo Marks win takes a little while to sink in. Paul and Debbie Kepitis don't start a scrapbook until her next start, in the Epsom. Even then, it's not all about Winx. She's not yet the centre of their world.

In a piece headed 'Scream Queen' in the *Sportsman* of 2 October, Ray Hickson predicts Debbie's voice will be heard if either Winx or Sadler's Lake wins the Epsom next day. Debbie informs Hickson she 'grew up on acreage' and has a 'five-acre voice'.

Hickson sketches a story that becomes increasingly familiar over the following two seasons, about the daughter who's keeping up the Ingham racing tradition since her father's big sale to Sheikh Mohammed in 2008.

The story is more about Sadler's Lake than Winx, despite her being favourite in the 150th Epsom. The Kepitis family had bred Sadler's Lake from a young mare named Mingshan, retired early because she was a 'bleeder'.

Debbie is quoted: 'I think he has a great chance and I think he is going to be a very good horse for us.' But she doesn't dispute the punters' high opinion of Winx, given the win in the Theo Marks despite interference.

Of the Theo Marks finish, she says: 'I was astounded. From where she was getting knocked down, I thought she'd run a great third or possibly second.'

In the Epsom, she predicts: 'She'll be the one storming down the outside and hopefully the jockey can make sure she has free running, and keep out of trouble.'

Then she turns to the Turnbull Stakes at Flemington where their Derby winner Preferment is set to win on his way to a Melbourne Cup start. In other words, the first big story featuring Winx is not so much about her as about the others in the Ingham revival.

There is reason to be cautious about Winx's Epsom chances despite her being $2.80 favourite. The Theo Marks win has pushed her handicap weight up to 57 kilograms, which would make a weight-carrying record for a mare to win the Epsom.

History says she can't win with the weight. But Hugh Bowman says she can and that she is 'a genuine Group One horse'. The punters believe Bowman and back her to start at $3 after she's drifted to $3.10. Waller wouldn't be running her if he didn't think she could win. The Epsom has been boosted to a million-dollar race, worth five times more to the winner than the Theo Marks, but it's not five times harder. The boy from Foxton can do the arithmetic.

•

Randwick, 3 October 2015. Epsom Handicap. #4

By the time he leads his favourite female around before the Epsom, three weeks after her third straight win, Umut the taciturn Turk has a new mobile telephone ringtone: the climax of the Theo Marks race call.

By now people are starting to agree with Umut's firm conviction he chose the right youngster to look after two years earlier.

Punters and the bookmakers have an opinion of her, too, keeping her safe around the $3 mark. It's a $1 million Group One mile race, theoretically of higher quality than the Group Two Theo Marks but, again, Sons Of John proves her strongest opponent and he's no champion.

Bowman is back on Winx (and never gets off, apart from one exhibition gallop) but she tests his resolve. On the way to the barrier she bucks and nearly 'drops' the man who knows a bit about riding buckjumpers but preferably not in a saddle the size and weight of a straw hat. It's a warning to him to be ready next time she 'humps up'.

Bowman gets her away safely from the wide barrier but soon finds trouble. Whereas she struck interference in the Theo Marks, this time she finds a scrimmage that would flatten an All Black.

She's won three straight in eye-catching style so the caller knows to keep an eye open for the swooper in blue while calling the leaders.

Entirely Platinum at the 700 metres leads by three-quarters to Ecuador . . . Bowman starts to get a little bit closer now as they come to the home turn.

She is closing fast on the leading bunch, then you see her head go up and Bowman rise in the irons in the sort of split-second collision that can so easily end in a fall. But she is agile and her rider's balance and nerve is ingrained by a boyhood of camp-drafting cattle, playing polocrosse and cross-country jumping. He instantly weaves her around slower horses and through the mob in a display that marks him out from the typical jockey.

During this drama his elbow connects with Blake Shinn on Kirramosa.

Hooked and Sons Of John but Winx is starting to unleash with her powerful sprint! And Winx races up to hit the lead! She's shot away in the Epsom. It's all over.

Bowman stands high in the stirrups as she cruises over the line and gives a salute that's going to earn a fine, but it's worth it. He's about to trouser $30,000 in jockey's percentage and everything he knows about horses tells him that this one is going to step up to a new level every time she races.

Waller admits closing his eyes when Winx almost fell on the turn. The first thing he says to Bowman after he dismounts is: 'I was scared for you at the 400 metres.'

Then he tells reporters, 'It was an awful scrimmage turning for home. For her to pick herself up after that and put herself back in the race before bursting through like she did, it was pretty special.' He pauses, then repeats: 'It is pretty special.'

Bowman, among the most measured of jockeys, describes how she 'got stood on her head at the 450 metres', then adds: 'Look, I don't like to get carried away but she is a superstar in the making.'

The ease of the win, given the interference she suffered, probably helps Bowman survive the inquiry into how his elbow came into contact with Shinn as Kirramosa whipped past at the turn. Shinn tells the stewards he didn't feel the elbow but film of the race suggests the contact must have given him amnesia.

Bowman's explanation to the stewards summarised the race and Winx's part in it:

You could see how much horse I had under me by the way she won. I was awkwardly placed.

She was still on [the] bit and I hadn't gone for her and that saved me. Everything had gone well until then. I hadn't used anything to get there . . .

She got unbalanced and stood on her head but I was able to get her to re-gather herself and once she got to the outside she was ready to go. It was just like the other day and she got herself out of it.

Bowman survived Elbowgate to retain his forty-fourth Group One but was fined $500 for the celebratory salute before the post. It didn't worry him. He was pictured kissing his wife Christine afterwards. Not just a peck on the cheek, either. Apparently the bloke from Dunedoo is a romantic as well as a bit of a rodeo rider. Who knew?

The Kepitis–Ingham homebred, Sadler's Lake, with the veteran Jim Cassidy in the famous Ingham cerise, has run ninth of the fourteen runners. Winx is the new heroine, at least in Sydney.

The artful tipster Ron Dufficy summarises it: 'She is a very serious mare who may have put her cards on the table for the Cox Plate.'

Privately, Waller is almost jubilant. His email message to the owners goes like this:

What can we say, she was the deserved winner and it
is about the only thing that needs to be said. Well done

to you all, to own a very special horse. Barrier draws, distances, track conditions, luck in running, she seems to overcome it all. I think what fools us is that she is just a horse getting better and better and raising the bar every time that it is in front of her. Her last four wins have been nothing short of devastating, she has the makings of a very special horse and where will she stop improving? It is scary to think! Let's enjoy today, we will get back to you as per normal on Monday with an update and we look forward to the next run wherever it may be.

Next day, they go public. If she pulls up well and stays bright during the week, says Waller with characteristic caution, she might run in the Cox Plate and not the Myer Classic on Victoria Derby Day. But if she doesn't bounce back from the hard run, she will run in neither.

She pulls up a treat, as they say in racing. Her price tightens to single-figure odds in Cox Plate betting. The punters say she's a contender. This leaves Bowman with a problem. Waller also has the well-fancied Kermadec and Preferment in the race and Bowman has ridden them both.

He has to weigh up whether Winx's demolition of second-tier gallopers like Sons Of John makes her a better chance than Preferment's known ability to match the best on his day—such as winning the Turnbull Stakes the day after the Epsom, Bowman aboard.

He watches how Winx settles so well at Flemington. Her regular morning rider Ben Cadden has gone back to his young family in Sydney and Justine Hales is riding work on her and Preferment. Justine says she is working perfectly. And, as Peter O'Brien once put it so well, she'd still 'eat stones', which makes her easy to train.

Bowman doesn't rush his decision. His patience is rewarded. Winx works so well at the 'breakfast with the best' session at Moonee Valley the Tuesday before the Cox Plate that she makes the decision for him.

Justine Hales had galloped her around the Valley the week before and confirms what is obvious to any keen watchers: the tight turns don't worry her in the least. That reassures Bowman but doesn't surprise him. The scrimmage in the Epsom told him how agile she is, a trait she often shows him afterwards.

So he puts her ahead of Preferment, telling the *Herald Sun*'s Lauren Wood he is gambling on Winx's potential to run the last section of her middle-distance races at sprinting speed: the weapon he calls 'the X factor'.

Jockeys can be wrong. But Hugh Bowman is right this time.

•

Moonee Valley, 24 October 2015. Cox Plate. #5
Winx's powerful finishes have already made her a favourite with punters in her hometown but that's not yet enough to make her favourite in a Cox Plate. Melbourne racegoers don't get a real look at the young mystery mare from the north until the promotional trackwork breakfast at the Valley on the Tuesday.

She looks good even to bleary-eyed reporters who aren't yet sure how to spell her name. To anyone with knowledge and a dog in the same fight, she looks lethal.

After Winx's quiet gallop at the Valley the previous week, with Justine Hales steering, Criterion's trainer David Hayes looks thoughtful. He tells Hales at Flemington later that week he'd never seen a horse go around Moonee Valley's tight turns so well at its first time on the track.

Until that moment Hayes had every reason to think he had the best horse in the race. Now he's just seen one that might upset his calculations.

At the televised barrier draw held during the breakfast, Winx gets the number-one alley, next to The Cleaner. The top fancy Highland Reel draws perfectly in four.

The evergreen racing writer Max Presnell thinks enough of Winx's claims to write a thoughtful piece pointing out that she's one of a tiny handful of mares (and one filly, Surround) with the credentials to win the Cox Plate. But he wonders whether she has the stamina of a Makybe Diva.

'Can she sustain a long run under the pressure? Bowman figures she can as he chose Winx rather than Preferment, a Victorian Derby winner with no distance doubts.'

His punchline: that Bowman has more in common with the great 'Demon' Darby Munro than the fact they share the second name Hugh. Presnell admits his own doubts but allows that Bowman might know better. It's the perfectly hedged bet by a seasoned campaigner.

The *Telegraph* sticks with the Sydney mare, possibly because it can't resist the irresistible rhyme of the headline: WINX TO

BREAK JINX. Ray Thomas is on a roll. He boldly discounts the inside barrier as an obstacle: 'I doubt any horse in Australia has her finishing speed in races of 1600 metres and further.'

But tipster Ron Dufficy plays devil's advocate. Someone has to. 'Winx has been winning fillies' races and handicaps but now she is at the elite level at weight-for-age.' Dufficy also discounts Highland Reel and Criterion, preferring Kermadec, Preferment and Hartnell. These are not crazy ideas or bad horses but he brings to mind two sayings: that all horse racing is a difference of opinion and that all punters die broke.

With any luck, 'The Duff' doesn't back his own tips. Hartnell runs fifth, Preferment is ninth and Kermadec beats one home.

Bowman turns the number-one alley from a supposed negative into a positive. What the form 'experts' said about the inside gate doesn't matter because Winx can't read and Bowman pretends he can't. Without the interference that has plagued her up north, she has the field at her mercy. She runs her last 400 metres in 23.94, much faster than any other horse in the race.

It's hard for merely good horses to compete with the new superstar. She is the first mare to win the Epsom–Cox Plate double in the same season. The only previous horse to do it in half a century was the great Noholme in 1959.

For Waller, it is career-defining. Not that he strays too far from the script. 'This is pretty special, a dream come true, really.'

•

It's not only that she runs the Cox Plate distance faster than it has been in the seventeen years since the track was re-configured.

The stopwatch doesn't reveal that she runs such a slick time without being pushed, so comfortably within herself that even those who know her best are surprised.

Something about her complete assurance suggests she might compare with any of the great Cox Plate winners before Might And Power. This might be seen as heresy in the beginning but will become a confident assertion over the following two years.

The difference between this bravura performer and the scrawny three-year-old who couldn't catch First Seal is one of racing's many mysteries. She simply matured later and improved much more than her contemporaries did.

Before the Cox Plate, she had many racehorse virtues. Now she's a virtuoso.

Waller hasn't got to where he is by over-estimating horses. He goes the other way: sticking to the old racing maxim that recommends keeping yourself in the best company and your horses in the worst, which is why he'd sent her to the Sunshine Coast Guineas at Caloundra while he stayed in Sydney.

But he is only human. Privately, he can't help showing some enthusiasm. On the Tuesday after the race, he emails the owners:

I have spent a bit of time with her over the past 24 hours and she looks well. She has been eating well since her run and the vet trotted her up yesterday and couldn't find any faults with her. She is going to the paddock as a sound horse ready for a nice break. I am no closer to working out a preparation for her apart from the fact that it will be geared towards the Queen Elizabeth most

likely at her fourth run back. We will find three lead up
races that we will endeavour to win with her to keep her
winning run intact.

He then goes into the necessary housekeeping, mentioning
the 'invitation overnight' to the Japan Cup but underlining that
it's time for the mare to have a break, and asking the owners to
make a diplomatic withdrawal ('It's a privilege to be asked . . .
but I don't think it's wise') in the hope they can take up the invitation the following year. The good news is that precautionary
X-rays of her main joints show no sign of damage.

It is good to be going to the paddock with a horse like
her knowing that there is nothing that needs tidying up
and she can enjoy her break.

It's the first time in his reports he mentions not only 'the
winning run' but keeping it 'intact'.

In Waller's mind, the seed has been planted, the streak taken
shape and the ordeal has begun. He has sensed not only the
truth but its consequences: Winx probably has the ability to win
anything she is set for—but only with flawless fitness, perfect
planning and the absence of bad luck. You can train horses all
your life and not face that exquisite pressure.

On the evening of Wednesday, 28 October, the stable's new
star is led onto the truck and chauffeured up the Hume to the
Hermitage. Olly Koolman is waiting for her. For nearly two
months, the pressure is his. Mostly.

19

THE SHOW REEL

Make a film about Winx the wonder horse and the director has a dilemma: how to extract drama out of something as predictable as Bradman making centuries every season. As a film star she makes a good racehorse: she doesn't talk, let alone do drugs or sex. Doesn't even like being patted.

The freak with the streak is a force of nature, like a river, but that's not great box office. Her prowess and progress grow more remarkable with every win—but is another Group race necessarily much different or better than the last or the next? Answer: only sometimes and then mostly for connoisseurs. A film about a racehorse that sticks strictly to facts and action is like the telephone book: plenty of characters but a lousy plot.

For the audience, the context of the contest is everything. Without context, watching *Australia II* inching past a distant marker in a distant ocean in 1983 is like watching paint dry.

Public interest in Winx is in her tightrope act: the degree of difficulty of keeping up the winning sequence. To show this, a filmmaker has to compress into a few minutes a string of triumphs that in real time take months or years. It's about bottling the excitement of victory after victory without the boring bits in between—the biographical version of cutting to the car chase.

The classic way to do this is to screen the image of newspapers rolling off the press: front page after front page, each flashed on screen with our hero featuring above the fold. The other way is the film-clip montage of climactic moments spliced together: knockouts, boundary shots, winning goals—and, in this case, race finishes.

From 'Rocky' icing his opponents and a rock band acing stadiums to a racehorse winning races, the montage makes fast work of Zero To Hero.

The Winx show reel begins after her first Cox Plate.

●

Exterior. Day. Winx is led onto Waller Racing truck at country location. Truck moves off towards Sydney skyline.

Cut to Rosehill stables. Winx reunites with regular attendants, cast as smouldering and exotic 'Umut', blonde and perky 'Candice', and 'Ben' the wiry Aussie track rider.

Cut to 'Waller' character in his office above the stables doing busy trainer stuff, gazing at screen with glasses on. Guy Pearce could play him. Close-up of computer screen shows a report from the spelling farm that makes the trainer character happy for a moment. He calls over other staff to read it.

They crowd around and someone reads the report aloud. It says Winx is now 544 kilograms. 'Waller' points out this is nearly 100 kilograms more than when she was broken in. Proof she is still growing, still getting stronger.

A bit character gets his or her line: 'A hundred kilos—that's the size of Buddy Franklin!' And it is, all that extra bone and muscle to hone into a galloping machine for the autumn carnival, then the spring carnival . . .

So much for the imaginary Winx film, although that scene is based pretty well on the facts. Apart from Buddy Franklin, who weighs a little more than 100 kilograms these days.

In the real world, Olly Koolman's glowing December report not only mentions Winx's bulking up but her winning attitude:

After a 25 day holiday she has handled the last 22 days of trot and canters up the hill and she is absolutely bursting with energy. When she goes back to her paddock each day after work she actually puts on quite a show of excess energy kicking her heels up for a couple of laps before getting back to her breakfast. She is looking particularly well right now and seems to have strengthened to my eye. I'm as excited as anyone for the Autumn.

Two more months pass in Wallerland. Cut to the horse race.

•

Randwick, 13 February 2016. Apollo Stakes. #6

Two weeks before Winx's racetrack return, commentators are already debating whether a four-year-old mare that has won nine of fifteen starts is a 'champion'. Some say the word is cheapened by overuse by lazy hacks.

An earnest Sydney scribe puts the question: 'So when does an elite racehorse deserve acknowledgement as a champion and what is the criteria for that ranking?'

Longevity matters, for a start. Winx has proved her excellence but not that it will last. Then there's consistency, as in consistently beating the best. Apart from a few below-par runs as an immature youngster, she's done that. Trainer and jockeys concede in retrospect that some human error might have helped get her beaten as a three-year-old. Do things a bit differently back then and her early record would look a lot smarter.

Then there is versatility, acceleration and brilliance.

Ron Dufficy, whose tips she smashed on Cox Plate day, is undeterred: he plays the game by voicing reservations about her champion credentials.

'You can't do it in one spring campaign,' he tut-tuts to Ray Thomas in the *Telegraph*. 'To be a champion, a horse has to back it up next campaign and keep doing it.'

Dufficy is presumably tent-boxing for the entertainment of readers, although he stops winking for a second and makes a shrewd point about the reliability of race mares: 'I remember John Hawkes told me that with mares, one day you have them and the next day they are gone.'

Still playing contrarian, the Duff splashes a little lukewarm liquid on the Cox Plate win—saying it might have *looked* like a Kingston Town performance but, in fact, Winx and Bowman conspired to take advantage of a 'terribly biased track'. What's more, he says, Criterion's jockey Michael Walker was hard done by: he'd come in complaining Bowman had almost put him over the rail.

Walker's main problem, given the winning margin, was more likely windburn. Still, Dufficy allows that if Winx wins the $4 million Queen Elizabeth Stakes at Randwick in April then she's a champ.

Form 'guru' Gary Crispe, compiler of Australian Timeform ratings, does his sums and says Winx adds up better than Sunline at the same stage of her career. Crispe says if she scores another big win against all comers, she gets the numbers to be a champion.

None of the hypotheticals matter to Bowman, whose opinion was formed in the straight in the Cox Plate. He won't be getting off Winx again. He'd ride her in the Tour de France if she entered.

Waller has good reason to start the campaign with the Apollo Stakes. Like the cat that ate the canary, he knows exactly the sequence of actions that scored last time and so he replicates them as precisely as possible.

The aim is a second Cox Plate. Waller uses her previous preparation as a template: start with a shorter race (but not a pure sprint) and a class notionally below her best, followed at two- or three-week intervals with races that step up in distance and class. It's conventional except for one thing: a conventional Cox Plate horse first-up after a spell can be excused for not winning against speedsters. But Winx is no longer a conventional horse.

The Apollo Stakes is 1400 metres and Group Two. It's a version of the Theo Marks over 1300 metres the previous spring, with the extra 100 metres slightly in Winx's favour. Some super-fit sprinters might just hang on to the lead at 1300 metres but the extra ground means Winx can swamp them with that freakish finish.

On the day, Bowman rides her more like a good horse than a champion. The field is not big enough to throw up a traffic jam, and he keeps her within reach of the fence, not yet warily circling the bunch as he will in future.

As she straightens for home, she is only one horse width off the rail, inside other contenders, including the leader Solicit. About 200 metres out, the white bridle ranges up alongside Solicit and the caller takes the cue:

Now Winx is being called upon by Bowman—and here comes Winx going after Solicit—Solicit a head in front but Winx is going through her gears and look at her go! Oh, Winx! She's certainly the best. A great return to racing.

Job done. She's back safely from another preparation, the fourth of her career. She's run a tick over 35 seconds for the last 600 metres on a good track, bothering to do just enough to beat Solicit and Hauraki. She can finish much faster if she needs to. Like ten lengths better.

Ray Thomas's first paragraph nails it: 'Winx does what all elite athletes do—she makes winning look easy.' He urges racing administrators to hang every marketing campaign for the autumn carnival on Winx 'because the super mare is genuine box-office gold'.

Waller opts for humility, gently suggesting that more Group wins will be for the greater good: '. . . it is important for racing that she keeps winning.' He avoids the 'champion' bandwagon.

'She's not there yet,' he says soberly. 'She's got to win two Cox Plates; she has got to come up for another prep or two.'

But signs of the strain of training not-quite-a-champion are starting to show. He admits he has begun 'second guessing and looking at her and thinking "Is she too big; is she ready?"'

The Apollo Stakes shows she's not too big and plenty ready. Solicit has given her something to chase, the way a greyhound chases a tin hare. When Bowman gives her an inch of rein, she smokes the hare.

Bowman has never before experienced the sort of scenes that happened in racing's golden age, before he was born. Spectators actually run across to the fence to watch the mare go onto the track. It's folk hero stuff, the way it was with Gunsynd and Tulloch, Bernborough and Ajax, all the way back to Phar Lap and Carbine. Bowman has hardly seen Black Caviar race so it's his first real exposure to fans rather then punters and spectators. Not that fans don't bet: after the Apollo, they cluster in the betting ring and along the tote windows to collect their sixty cents above every dollar staked.

Waller warns later, 'She will improve a lot.' He can no longer treat her like any other good horse and set her for races three or four weeks ahead. She is now a long-range project, the almost champion.

'With a horse like her, she is expected to win every start so we have to ensure we try to keep her winning,' Waller tells reporters. 'I don't know how Black Caviar did it.'

The pressure hasn't distracted the perfectionist from his vocation. The Randwick double with Winx and Springbok Flyer takes Waller Racing to ninety-nine wins for the season, with the Cox Plate and other Group races in the tally.

The boy from Foxton is training as well as anyone in the world.

•

Randwick, 27 February 2016. Chipping Norton Stakes. #7 Boxing promoters and their cousins, carnival barkers, know the importance of 'making a gate'. In the absence of bearded ladies or two-headed kittens, you need competition: if not the real thing, something close. Old-time boxing tent operators like Roy Bell and Jimmy Sharman used to plant 'gee-up' men in the crowd to stir the pot among the paying public. Similarly, in the interests of spinning newspaper yarns and turnstiles, racing writers and racing clubs tend to conjure a challenger for every champ.

On the eve of the Chipping Norton Stakes, that role falls to 'New Zealand's best galloper' Mongolian Khan. The horse's connections are alleged to be 'confident they can give superstar Winx a run for her money'. Of course, the Mongolian Khan camp has plenty of reasons to be proud of the 2015 Caulfield Cup and dual Derby winner, robbed of a Melbourne Cup start by a colic attack.

The wily Kiwi Murray Baker trains Mongolian Khan but has sent him across to finish his preparation with his son Bjorn, a natural-born showman whose Warwick Farm stable was the launching pad for a splendid animal, It's A Dundeel, to win the three-year-olds' triple crown in 2013: that comprising the Rand-wick Guineas (1600 metres), the Rosehill Guineas (2000 metres) and the Australian Derby (2400 metres). Dundeel, as he was known in New Zealand, would end up winning six Group Ones, including the first $4 million Queen Elizabeth in 2014, and retire guns blazing to stud at Arrowfield.

Now the same crew has Mongolian Khan, and Bjorn Baker isn't missing the chance to score a publicity point for the supposed heavyweight clash with Winx, not to mention his own training enterprise.

'I could make a case that Murray's horses tend to improve when they come to me,' the fabulous Baker boy says mischievously. 'But if I did that I'd probably never see another one again,' he jokes. 'In all seriousness, he's sent this horse over in magnificent condi-tion and there's not really much I need to do other than keep him ticking over. We worked him over 1400 metres on Tuesday and, my word, it was as good a work as I've seen in quite a while.'

Kerrin McEvoy, the boy from Streaky Bay in rural South Australia who's become an international jockey, goes to Warwick Farm to ride Mongolian Khan that morning.

'He was nice and bright, which is what you want to see from a horse on the comeback,' he says noncommittally. In other words: roll up, ladies and gentlemen, and see what they're touting as the heavyweight clash of the autumn.

The crowd, good by Sydney standards, is confronted by con-tradictory facts and figures for the 'clash'.

On one hand is the compelling record that no odds-on favourite has been beaten in the Chipping Norton in thirty years.

On the other is the hoodoo that no reigning Cox Plate winner has won the Chipping Norton since Carbon Copy in 1949.

But the supposed hoodoo isn't as statistically sound as it first seems because in seven decades hardly any Cox Plate winners have actually run in the Sydney race the following autumn. Among the few Cox Plate heroes who swung and missed in the Chipping Norton are stars like Gunsynd and Flight.

Not everyone buys that the scene is set for a showdown. Racing writer Chris Roots suggests the fact Mongolian Khan was fighting for life at the Werribee Veterinary Clinic with colic around the time Winx staged her Cox Plate demolition is a good predictor of their respective fortunes in the race.

And when Roots has a quiet chat with Murray Baker instead of his ebullient son Bjorn, he finds the canny Kiwi isn't tilting for glory, only to ease Mongolian Khan back into the game.

Baker senior is frank: 'Winx, she's a superstar; I don't think she will be beaten on the weekend.'

The public agrees. Winx's odds are so short (starting price $1.35) the TAB opens a novelty market offering $5, odds of 4 to 1 against Winx going unbeaten to the end of April. It is the first of several bets offered against the mare reaching certain future milestones unbeaten.

Chris Waller's sister Megan plays the Winx 'futures market' twice, later on, and wins the price of a snazzy new car. Her brother doesn't bet but she knows how much he hates losing. So he is not taking chances on the $600,000 stakes getting away: besides Winx, he enters Preferment, Grand Marshal, Who Shot Thebarman and Storm The Stars. It is an astonishing display of firepower. Seven months into the season, the Waller team has already won ten Group One races, putting it in reach of Bart Cummings' record of twenty Group Ones in 1974–75.

To get a record tally of Group races demands more than big numbers of horses in training—something Waller has built at an unprecedented pace. A trainer also needs a champion to win a string of stakes races the way Kingston Town did for Tommy Smith and the way Leilani did for Bart Cummings. Now Waller seems to have that angle covered. Winx can gallop at least like Kingston Town and better than Leilani, though not everyone knows it yet.

On 26 February, Gary Crispe is quoted saying Winx's Timeform rating has 'soared to a lofty 126' and still climbing, putting her in elite company. He says only Black Caviar (136), Sunline and Makybe Diva (129), Atlantic Jewel and More Joyous (128), and Miss Andretti (127) sit above her: rare air for a young mare that has raced four times since her three-year-old year.

She draws eight of twelve and at least jumps better than Hauraki, which misses the start. But she settles well back, one off the fence, while Magic Hurricane and Dibayani lead from Mongolian Khan and Hartnell.

In drama, the hero has to overcome an obstacle. The nearest Winx has to an obstacle is that when the field claps on pace early, she settles seventh of the dozen runners, further behind the speed than her supporters might wish.

Bowman gets going on Winx. He starts his run at the 600, inching closer.

Winx is four wide in a tight field, horses packed like sardines in a can.

Magic Hurricane swings in front from Dibayani but Winx is starting to stride up on the outside . . . Bowman sits quietly on Winx as it starts to put its head in front from Dibayani—it's under immense pressure—but now Winx is starting to extend from Dibayani and Hauraki. Oh! She's a wrecking ball, Winx! And there's the seventh picket in the fence.

After Bowman steers her back to the winner's stall and the cheering dies, he has something to say.

'She's the best I have had anything to do with,' says the man who rode So You Think twice as a youngster, though not in either of the Cox Plates that the Adonis of a horse won before being sold overseas to boost his stallion CV. Bowman explains his preference for Winx over the colt: 'I have had more to do with her and she is definitely closer to my heart.'

The result is expected and welcomed—and not only by those who have had big bets to win not much.

'That was a real race,' Bowman says. 'They went along and I don't think anyone expected that.' By this he means the other horses clapped on more early speed than expected, so it wasn't a dawdle followed by a sprint.

'I didn't expect to be back that far but I didn't see the need to disrupt her gait just to be where everyone thinks she should be. But, knowing she is the horse she is, I was able to pull her out and she put herself there. I would be more inclined to wait on any other horse but she has that X factor about her.'

He says a few other things but sums it up this way: 'She got herself into gear; I didn't ask her to go. She just put herself into the race. She is a dream to ride; she is the perfect woman.'

It is easier to ride horses than train them. 'It's not enjoyable,' Waller says that afternoon, describing the strain of wondering if and when Winx will produce the unnerving burst of speed that euthanises top-class opponents in the last 200 metres.

By now, sheer superiority puts her beyond normal criticism or jealousy. Bowman's keenest opponent, Blake Shinn, is beaten into second place on Dibayani. He says his mount was 'brave in defeat, just ran into a champion', the gun jockey readily dishing the accolade the armchair experts are still bickering about.

And that morning's *Sydney Morning Herald* carries a piece on Guy Mulcaster, the bloodstock diviner who liked her as a yearling. The intro says: 'He dreamt of finding a champion. Now after the success of Winx, he can say he has.' Seven straight wins nails it.

The hoodoo was hoohaa. As for Mongolian Khan, he beat one horse home.

•

Rosehill, 19 March 2016. George Ryder Stakes. #8
After the faux showdown with Mongolian Khan, this might be billed the real thing. For the first time since the precocious three-year-old First Seal beat Winx in five starts, the two mares meet again. *Best Bets* tipster Kevin Casey tickles up the story, saying 'in its own way' the clash is 'as big a challenge for the great mare as was the Cox Plate. First Seal has a 5–0 record against her though—and they meet for the first time in twelve months.'

A year is a long time to nurse a rivalry in racing. Much can happen to anything as fragile as a racehorse, let alone form. Some fillies hit their physical peak by the time they turn four and First Seal is one of them. Winx was nowhere near it as a three-year-old, her immaturity masked by innate ability: her baby steps were just so much better than most.

By the time First Seal jumps out to take up second spot behind Turn Me Loose in the opening stages of the Ryder, she's been relegated from gun filly to just a good mare—the sort that can hold her own in a crack field of weight-for-age horses until the whips start cracking.

Behind her, Bowman buys his way out of potential trouble by spending some horsepower: from barrier seven he lets Winx stride three wide in the eight-horse field to avoid the kickback from the track and any chance of interference. He uses her acceleration to move up to be one off the fence, then asks her to go again from the 600-metre mark. Once Winx finds her rhythm, it is like watching a cat ready to pounce on a pigeon: she is totally alert but not making the move until the moment is right.

It comes as they round the turn. Winx slides past Fast Seal, who slips to fourth place, then she spears out four wide and runs down Kermadec and Press Statement at the 200-metre mark. She hits the front at the 100 metres to make a perfect Waller trifecta a certainty. The relatively small winning margin of a length and a half makes it look closer than it is, so well calibrated is her superiority in the closing seconds of the race.

The Golden Slipper is hard to upstage on its big day but watching Winx this time comes close.

'I've never ridden a horse that has the crowd behind her like Winx does,' Bowman says afterwards. 'It is very special. At the 400 metres, I was confident she was going to win and she left them in her wake the last 100 metres.

'I could enjoy the moment, I could hear the crowd; it was just me and her and it was ever so sweet.'

But for Bowman, as with Waller, exultation is starting to be tinged with relief. It creeps into his summary of the race. 'I was a little bit more apprehensive today than [in] recent starts just because of the draw and the set-up of the race.' This meant, he says, he called on Winx's turn of foot twice in running—something you can't do with horses more closely matched in ability.

'We've come to expect it [but] I certainly feel as though it is up to me to put her in the right spot. I know she is going to deliver but I still need to put her in a position where she can. So far, I've been able to do that.'

Waller admits it looked awkward early but 'Hugh made it look easy when he got her into a beautiful position and found a nice rhythm. She ambled up to them turning for home which is always a good sign but it's hard when you are trying to put away a field like today, a field of superstars, but she was just dominant again . . . She is beating horses like Kermadec and Press Statement and they are dead-set superstars in their own right and she has beaten them pretty easily.'

First Seal isn't mentioned, underlining the point that a year is a long time in racing. And thirty-two years is a lot longer: a mare hasn't won the Ryder since the wonderfully named Emancipation in 1984.

They don't come along often, the tomboys who beat all comers, all ages and both sexes. When one does, it can outshine even the million-dollar babies in the Slipper.

The precocious colt Capitalist goes for a spell after winning the Slipper. Winx goes back to work to prepare for her next bout two weeks later.

•

Randwick, 2 April 2016. Doncaster Mile. #9

The only time Winx raced on a heavy track before this, she won the Furious Stakes at her third start in 2014. But her last defeat, in the Australian Oaks at Randwick, was on a soft track, even if that loss was not directly caused by the going so much as the winner finding the firm part of the track that Winx's jockey didn't. Still, the prospect of a heavy track worries the Winx camp before the Doncaster, the main event on the opening day of Sydney racing's new brainchild, The Championships.

'If the track happened to come up extremely wet then it would hold some concern,' Bowman says two days out, answering a question rather then volunteering a statement. His concern is more a case of wanting everything ideal for Winx, rather than genuine worries about the going.

'I know the turn of foot she can show on a dry track; it's amazing. It's like holding a trump card. In an ideal world we would get a reasonably dry track again this weekend.'

With the likelihood of at least soft going, Bowman is happy with barrier eleven. 'You wouldn't want her hemmed away on the Randwick fence looking for a run, especially when it's wet.'

Then there is the weight. Under the Doncaster's handicap conditions, Winx has to be close to top weight and give away up to 6.5 kilograms to some male rivals, a big concession for a mare with a slight edge under the weight-for-age scale applying in most of her races.

But track conditions and weight do not shake the betting. The punters have almost unnerving belief in her. She eases only a fraction from $1.80 to $1.85 after the barrier draw. The betting says she will overcome the big field, the wide barrier, the weight and the track surface then star in the marquee race of The Championships series, the Queen Elizabeth Stakes, a week later.

For Racing NSW supremo Peter V'landys, Winx's dominance since the previous autumn carnival could hardly be better if he'd dreamed it up to push The Championships to a public increasingly indifferent to racing. In eleven months, her winning streak stands at eight and marks her as one of the rare ones that transcend the sport. Like Black Caviar and Bart Cummings, her appeal is seeping outside the pool of die-hard followers.

V'landys doesn't miss the chance to jump on the Winx platform to push The Championships, launched in 2014 to turn Royal Randwick's autumn meetings back into a carnival to draw uncommitted people outside 'the industry'.

'Derby–Doncaster Day on Saturday is one of the great race meetings but the story of week one of The Championships is Winx going for nine in a row,' V'landys purrs in a preview. There is plenty more in this promotional vein as he name-checks highlights such as the T.J. Smith Stakes ('the richest and highest-rating sprint in the country'), the Doncaster, the Derby and the excellent idea of a Country Championships Final for what reporters dub 'the best from the bush'.

V'landys is calling it Australian racing's 'Grand Final' because, he says, it brings together the outstanding horses of each age group to compete over various distances to determine the best of the best.

Which is all very well but it is the Winx factor the Australian Turf Club is betting on to drag 30,000 people to the track—*if* the weather holds. Sydney sports fans are a tough sell.

The punting bible *Winning Post* carries a Doncaster 'by the numbers' segment in a special supplement. In Winx's favour is that runners from wide barriers have the best strike rate, even if not specifically from barrier eleven.

The bad news is that Cox Plate winners have a poor record in the Doncaster of the same season. Of a dozen to try the double, only Tobin Bronze managed it, in 1967. Sunline ran second, meaning no mare has ever pulled off the double since the Cox Plate began in the 1920s. The other ten horses to attempt it finished unplaced.

No pressure, then.

•

Two days out from the Doncaster, Winx works at Rosehill before dawn. It's dark but, figuratively at least, she is bathed in the glare of public and media attention—an audience of reporters and cameras. And not just the usual suspects but the sort that rarely gather for a racehorse at that hour. Winx is starting to draw moths to the flame of her growing fame.

As Ben Cadden pilots her on the course proper, the watchers and their cameras can make out the effortless, economical action, head tucked neatly. She sails where others toil. Look closer and they see Cadden—a strong horseman at least ten kilograms heavier than race-day jockeys—concentrating on holding her to the steady pace Waller wants. His forearms and biceps swell like Popeye's from the strain. She doesn't reef and throw her head but, like most great natural athletes, she is strong for her size. Every jockey who rides her mentions her power and balance.

The presence of the media pack reminds Waller of what his contemporary Peter Moody has endured with Black Caviar. Waller is wise enough to see that racing needs all the help it can get but the day-to-day reality of training a star is another layer of difficulty in the exhausting business of training 200 horses saddled with the expectations of potentially thousands of part-owners, given the number of syndicates.

The difference in scale is frightening: if training one horse is putting up a tent, training 200 is building a skyscraper. Then along comes Winx, which is like having to guard the Crown Jewels on the building site.

Waller is grappling with the growing public interest—and sense of public 'ownership'. He handles it gracefully by the standards of a business where trainers tend to be divided between P.T. Barnum boosterism and the ingrained suspicion and secrecy of the old-time betting stables.

The boosters played the press and the public as mugs and the plunge trainers were suspicious of everyone. But Waller is emerging as a 'third way' trainer, a modern man running a modern business, not a public circus or a private casino, and he treats the media almost as well as he treats clients and horses.

So here he is at dawn on the last day of March, with as many microphones in front of him as the prime minister doing a doorstop. Reporters, the ones from outside racing's closed society, find the polite trainer does more than dress neatly: he has the diplomat's knack of sounding thoughtful, friendly and frank without giving too much away. If it's true that he's had a public-speaking coach, it has worked.

'She's starting to capture at least the Australian imagination,' he says of the popularity of the mare by then being led back to the stables for the next phase of her morning ritual.

'At the moment it's certainly a new level of pressure for me, but fortunately the horse does the talking and makes my job a bit easier.'

Two days out, she is $1.80 favourite. If she wins, she'll be the shortest-priced favourite Doncaster winner in exactly ninety years, since Valicare at 4 to 5 odds in 1926.

'Her trackwork over the last two weeks has been faultless,' Waller continues, rolling out words needed to mortar the gaps between the images the hungry media beast needs. The trackwork has been 'possibly even the best of her work she's ever shown according to her track riders this week'.

It is the 'grab' the cameras need—and also true.

But, underneath, Waller is wrestling with the laws of probability, which say that if a top-class mare is ever going to be beaten, it will be against all ages and both sexes in a handicap in which she has to lump a champion's 'impost'. It would have been easier, even tempting, to duck the Doncaster and stick to weight-for-age races.

Weight will stop a train but, this time, it doesn't stop the trainer. Waller sticks with his decision not to 'cherry-pick' weight-for-age races because, he says, the public expect to see her on the track. Privately, he's confident she can stamp herself extraordinary by pulling off a win that no other Cox Plate-winning mare ever has. But it is a risk.

Coming from this cautious and pragmatic man, it is a gesture of sportsmanship that also extends to the owners, who have the right to veto but have left the decision to Waller.

'It wasn't a money thing,' says Peter Tighe of the decision to run. 'There was no pressure from the owners.'

Waller explains, 'You can't just keep them in cotton wool and let them run every six months, such as a heavyweight world champion boxer. She's got to race every two or three weeks.'

Which is a nice way of saying what all trainers know: away from the hoopla, a Doncaster favourite or a Birdsville bush maiden is a horse, bred and fed to run against its kind the way Friesian cows are bred and fed to milk.

Starting Winx twice in eight days is, at a logical level, no different from doing the same with a picnic galloper. Apart, that is, from the difference of several million dollars in stakes—and the growing obligation of trying to extend an unbroken streak, a load becoming heavier with every success.

It's a good problem to have, certainly. But that doesn't make it any easier to carry in the countdown to the next contest, each now more like a duel than a horse race—Winx v. the Best of the Rest, promoted like a title fight.

In a preview the day before the race, Richard Treweeke tells the *Telegraph*: 'She has won us a lot of money but we don't worry about that so much. For us, it is more the joy that people get from watching her race. The fans love her. It is amazing how many people I haven't heard from in years who have called and said they feel a part of it because they know me.'

The old man says he's raced horses since 1957 and never actually seen any of them win before Winx. 'It got to the point where I thought, "If I stay away from the races they might win."'

Winx broke the jinx when he went to see her second start in a two-year-old race at Rosehill. She bolted in.

Treweeke wasn't well enough to go to Melbourne for the Cox Plate or to see her in the Ryder Stakes. But he reckons he'll get to Randwick this time.

'Whoever beats her will need to be something special,' the old woolgrower declares. 'There's no way I am going to miss the Doncaster.'

That Waller has trained five Doncaster winners in eight years helps persuade the owners he can do it again. But she has to defy history and 6.5 kilograms more than the bottom weight for him to acknowledge publicly that the lady is a champ.

•

Race day. Royal Randwick has the theatre of the horse but there is nothing staged about the dangers of riding there. Despite the glitz and the glamour off the track, once the horses are on it the risk is as real as anywhere else. It is no respecter of reputations.

Early in the day Bowman limps into the stewards' room wearing only his left boot. The right boot, a featherweight thing, was destroyed when Bowman's foot was jammed in the barrier as his mount Pera Pera jumped askew in the Country Championships Final.

Chief steward Ray Murrihy asks if he wants to see a doctor about the battered foot.

'No, I'm right,' Bowman says quickly. An amputation would make him break his appointment with Winx in three hours' time, but this won't. And the bruised foot isn't his only worry that afternoon.

Winx is fractious in the barriers—her one occasional fault as a racehorse—and jumps away slowly, beating only Azkadellia, left badly at the start. Winx is bumped by Volkstok'n'barrell, which has been bumped by Turn Me Loose. She settles in front of only Azkadellia until the first turn. Bowman eases her past two horses, staying away from the rail to avoid being pocketed. But as the field banks up after rounding the first turn, she faces a wall of rumps. The caller's voice goes up an octave.

Bowman's riding for luck on Winx, looking to slice his way through the centre of the field . . . Winx is bottled up, Bowman goes back to the inside!

The crowd noise rises and bleeds into the broadcast microphone in a way that only happens on big occasions. The spectators sense Bowman's desperation. He veers one way then another, looking for the way out.

Three seconds is a long time at speed: by the time the caller has framed the sentence, Winx isn't bottled up anymore. After fanning wide, he switches her back inside and forces a hole in the wall.

Later, people talk about 'threading the needle' to describe how the mare splits two tiring horses who part like a pair of drunks shouldered by a bouncer. The race isn't over but Winx owns it now she has clear air.

The brave Happy Clapper charges down the outside and even braver Azkadellia flies from last along the rail. Winx hunts down Vergara, which has stolen a six-length lead but melts like an ice-cream in the oven when the two good horses and one champion range up.

Happy Clapper tries, so does Azkadellia but Winx has drawn clear in the Doncaster. Here's nine in a row! She breaks all the records today. She's a champion, Winx!

Her old nemesis First Seal finishes twelfth of fifteen. About the time First Seal hacks past the post, the caller is adding a postscript:

Today is the day she's declared the champion of the turf, Winx.

Bowman says later it is the first time he has ridden her where he felt the track conditions were so unsuitable he feared she could not win. But 'the fact that she wasn't comfortable and still produced that finish is something only a horse of champion qualities can do. I'm elated. She's a once in a lifetime horse. I can't believe I'm actually sitting on her.'

Waller, more relieved than elated, is surrounded by racing writers and well-wishers as the mare returns to the yard. 'I thought she was beaten at the half mile, let alone the 600-metre mark,' he says. 'She was going nowhere and I have never seen Hughie have to niggle her. Even after a few hundred metres, she never gets right back there unless we are taking her back from wide draws but that was not the plan.

'She just looked like she was skipping a few strides on the track, maybe she wasn't. But gee she showed some guts that last 200 metres.'

Then, finally, the acknowledgement he's ducked so long: 'We took on the handicapper. She's a champion. Does it get any better?'

Chris Roots writes that the degree of difficulty was higher than in her Cox Plate. He dares compare it with Kingston Town's miraculous win in the 1983 Cox Plate after caller Bill Collins said the black horse couldn't win. His point being that champions find a way.

Next morning Winx goes to the beach to paddle in the shallows with the Sydney Cup favourite Libran. She seems not to have taken any harm from the hard run but wise and kind trainers know not to go to the well too often. On Monday morning Waller announces Winx won't be backing up in the Queen Elizabeth Stakes the next Saturday.

Lost in the hype for Winx as The Championships headline act is the fact she has never run seven days after a race, let alone one as gruelling as the Doncaster was, followed by one as competitive as the Queen Elizabeth Stakes would be.

The Queen Elizabeth Stakes' new $4 million status as The Championships centrepiece makes it Sydney's richest race and, at some level, money talks. But when the Winx connections say they never put money ahead of the horse's welfare, they mean it.

On Tuesday morning Waller announces the decision that has been percolating in his mind since the 800-metre mark of the Doncaster—and maybe even before that. Winx isn't quite her normal self, he says. The implication is that she's off to the paddock but the reality is slightly more complicated.

As for the Queen Elizabeth, the stable's hopes now rest on Preferment, the impeccable Zabeel entire part-owned by the Kepitis and Tighe families.

As it turns out, the crowd gets to see a dominant mare streak past the field and swoop on the leaders, superbly piloted by a seasoned world-class jockey. But it isn't Hugh Bowman on Winx. It is Damien Oliver on Lucia Valentina.

Preferment and Bowman run twelfth. Bowman's bruised foot has recovered. It is not him that's going under the scalpel. It's Winx.

20

THE SECOND COMING

The day after Waller steels himself for criticism for the painfully public decision to scratch the Queen of racing from the Queen Elizabeth Stakes, he has to make another hard call about Winx. But this time it has to be done secretly to ensure no one connects it with the first decision.

Of the Queen Elizabeth scratching he will later reflect: 'I copped criticism for it but I knew it wasn't right to back her up. I'm proud of pulling up stumps.'

It takes him months to be as confident of the second decision. It's a gamble and, until Winx resumes fast work for the spring, he can't be entirely sure it has come off.

The hidden drama starts in the days after the Doncaster, when he orders a set of leg X-rays. This is routine. The mare is sound, with no sign of lameness or any other ill effects from her torrid race. It is merely a check-up before she goes for a spell.

Winx's day-to-day veterinary surgeon Ross Alexander, who works with Tim Roberts at their Centennial Park practice, comes to the stables and does the X-rays and 'scopes' her spectacularly healthy airways and scans her flawless tendons. This complete check-up is known in the business as a 'Hong Kong' vetting, as horses sold for high prices to Hong Kong buyers must pass stringent checks.

Everything is fine with Winx . . . except for a tiny floating bone chip in her near fore fetlock, the fist-sized joint above the hoof where sloping pastern meets vertical cannon bone. In a human, it's the left ankle.

The chip is barely the size of a child's fingernail and about as harmless—unless it moves from where it has flaked off the bone and becomes a risk, like a tack working its way into a Ferrari tyre.

It is what Ross Alexander calls an 'incidental find'. But he and his boss, Tim Roberts, urge Waller to act on the stitch-in-time principle. Remove it now and it *might* not interrupt her second Cox Plate campaign. But don't remove it, and the chip moves, it could inflame her joint and derail her spring preparation. Or whole career.

Waller is torn. He weighs the possibility of the chip turning bad against the probability that surgery will work well. It is belief in science versus fear of bad luck. Both instincts are in him but science wins. So does his secretive streak.

Only those who need to know are told because the connections are worried the coincidence will make it look as if Winx has been pulled from the Queen Elizabeth because of a hidden injury when, in truth, it is only a precaution following a random find. No one in the Winx camp wants to muddy her mystique with the sort of headlines the story would make. Waller, already spread thin over fifteen-hour days, doesn't want to be sidetracked by the inevitable hullabaloo.

Randwick equine specialist surgeon Jonathan Lumsden operates on her leg on Monday morning, 11 April. Alexander and Roberts are in the theatre to watch their most famous patient. The keyhole surgery takes maybe seven minutes, although Winx is under a general anaesthetic much longer.

As soon as she recovers she is trucked to the Hermitage as planned—but not under her own name. Like a rock star headed for rehab, she travels incognito.

She is transported to the Hermitage under the name 'Skinner'. Olly Koolman unloads her. Later, a stablehand asks him about moving the bay mare with the bandaged leg. She adds, deadpan, 'I thought you'd do it yourself—she looks a lot like Winx.'

You can fool some of the people some of the time but not stablehands who have handled Winx before. Koolman calls the staff together and explains that for the duration of her stay, the bay mare is 'Skinner', especially if there are any visitors or contractors around.

For Koolman and his wife Karen and the staff, it's a delicate assignment. Even the Koolman children Riaan and Kian know Winx by sight from earlier visits but they understand not to mention her at school. For ten weeks, the kids keep it as quiet as if Mum and Dad are hiding John Dillinger. It's possible their Uncle Chris Waller will lobby Santa to reward such good children at Christmas time.

Meanwhile, the patient is to recuperate and 'do rehab', much like a footballer who's had a niggling injury cleaned up at the end of the season. Not that there's a footballer in the land with Winx's earning capacity.

She can't ride an exercise bike or follow the simplest instructions but, on the other hand, nightclubs and pizzas are not a problem. She has only one 'girlfriend' and that is the unnamed, half-broken-in, half-lame yearling in the stall next to her—which, like all Winx's spelling paddock mates, will end up a Group One winner.

Waller won't commit anything important to email in case it leaks. Having taken expert advice to do the bone chip operation, he now faces the ticklish task of getting Winx back into work sooner than the textbook suggests. For someone who doesn't punt, it's a gamble that takes nerves of steel—and owners who trust his judgement.

It's a race against the calendar. Waller knows that to run in the 2016 Cox Plate she needs to be fit to win certain lead-up races spaced well apart. He cannot rush that end of her preparation but, to make the deadline, he will have to shave her rehabilitation time by accelerating the program.

He modifies the formal veterinary advice according to his own experience and instincts, the way his dad would have with dairy cows and his grandfather Colin did with his homebred gallopers. He scrawls his plan in point form on a piece of paper then gets Ross Alexander to take a photograph of the note with his phone and send it to Olly Koolman.

The plan rests heavily on using an exotic machine Koolman has installed at the property. It is an 'Aqua Icelander' water-walker—a

WK 1
CUT BACK HARD FEED
PLENTY OF CUT GRASS.
IF POSSIBLE WEIGH MON & FRIDAYS EACH WEEK

WK 2
START H WALKING 10 MIN X 2 DAILY

WK 3
ONCE STITCHES OUT CAN GO ON WALKER.
20 MINS X 2 DAILY.   AS WELL AS
HAND WALKING. (JUST TO KEEP HER HAPPY)

AT 3½ WKS
INTO A SMALL YARD & KEEP WALKING ON
WALKER.

AT 5½ WKS (THUR 19 MAY) START ON
AQUA WALKER BUT NOT TO DEEP
SPEAK TO ROSS REGARDING TIME FRAME
ON AQUA WALKER.

ON 3 JUNE (FRIDAY)
START RIDDEN WORK (WITH CAUTION)
ON GRASS & STRAIGH TRACK IF POSSIBLE

✱   FEED COSEQUIN DAILY.

✱   ONCE STITCHES OUT START WEEKLY PENTOSAN

22 OCT FREE TRIP TO COX PLATE!

treadmill built into a sleek stainless steel and Perspex tank that
fills to any level with cold water as a horse walks at pre-set speeds
and gradients. The machine, then rare in Australia, costs more
than a Range Rover to import from Iceland. Waller sees it as a

way to safely replicate going to the beach daily, which would be difficult anywhere and impossible from the farm.

The treadmill, created by an Icelandic marine engineering firm, stimulates muscle groups so they do not lose their 'memory' of certain exercise patterns. Olly Koolman reckons it proved its value in two weeks.

Every half-day counts in Waller's pruned schedule. Halfway through the sixth week Koolman has Winx walking every day in the cold water on the treadmill, strengthening her leg and back muscles and managing her body weight without the strain of carrying a rider. The now almost invisible surgical wound needs to be healed perfectly, without enforced idleness robbing her of residual fitness.

Seventeen days before she is scheduled to return to Rosehill, Winx is saddled for the first time since Bowman's tiny race saddle came off her after the Doncaster nearly two months before. Olly legs up a light trackwork rider and watches 'Skinner' hack up the property's long, straight uphill track on a cushion of springy kikuyu.

He thinks to himself she's never looked better. But it's too soon to go the early crow.

In the ten weeks Winx is at the farm, Waller emails the owners with only a few cryptic lines on her progress couched in the most general terms. He doesn't want anything finding its way into the public domain until he is sure Operation Bone Chip is a success. One of the messages has a photograph of her working on the uphill track, which is a wordless code for 'everything normal in Winx world'.

It is nearly two years since the enforced lay-off with a foot abscess left her in the paddock to grow instead of being raced as an early two-year-old. It might again be a case of a black cloud with a silver lining. The absolute peace and quiet of the farm stable mixed with paddock grazing in idyllic surroundings seems to suit her. The treadmill exercise is like gym work without the stress of carrying a rider's weight.

Winx is 'rising five', an age when many mares have finished growing and stop improving and sometimes become cantankerous. But when she returns to Rosehill in late June, it strikes everyone who knows her that she is bigger and stronger than she was in her autumn preparation. Getting back to work in the relative warmth of the stable in the coldest months will help her do well.

Waller sends an expansive message to the owners the day after she returns to Rosehill on 20 June. There is a sense of relief in it—and anticipation.

She has arrived safely back in to the stable yesterday and she looks well and went out for a quiet canter this morning. Her regular rider Ben Cadden was very happy with the way that she felt and also commented on how she has come back stronger, so pleasing comments to hear. It is great to have her back. Everything seems to be fine with her and we have allowed plenty of time just for a gradual build up towards trialling which I expect to be around the 29th July, second trial on the 9th August and hopefully a first up run on the 20th August which will be the [Warwick Stakes], but obviously a lot of water to go under the bridge prior to then. We will do our best to keep you updated and have plenty of fun and hopefully win lots more races.

After that, he let the stewards know about the bone chip operation. There was no obligation to do that—and with an ordinary horse no more would have been said. But the Winx factor meant the story got oxygen and the stewards reacted nervously to publicity by calling an 'inquiry' into why they had not been told about the operation earlier.

With Winx, Waller says, people are always 'looking for a talking point'. From then on, he says, 'I realised Winx wasn't just our horse anymore.' She was public property.

•

Waller leaves nothing to chance. He gives Winx five weeks of steady work, calibrated to build fitness little by little, like a master craftsman applying a coat of varnish to a teak hull then rubbing it back before laying down another coat.

The not-quite-final polish is in the form of two trials, the first over 850 metres at Randwick on 29 July. Bowman holds her to fourth of ten, which isn't as easy as it looks. As Ben Cadden says about riding her trackwork, 'When she sees a bum in front of her she just wants to beat it.' All part of her dominant female personality.

Eleven days later, another trial, same place, same distance, same placing, different bums to chase. Bowman puts her exactly where the boss wants, which is never winning trials. It is just enough work to give her a little blow out before her first-up in the Warwick Stakes on 20 August—two months since resuming training at Rosehill.

As Umut says of his boss, Waller turns over every stone. The Saturday before the Warwick Stakes the Sydney races are at Rosehill. Winx has a quiet gallop on the course proper in the morning but her day isn't over. Waller asks Umut to lead her over from her barn to the tie-up stalls to reacquaint her with the sights and sounds of race day so nothing strange will stir her up the following Saturday when she is back on stage. Waller reports:

> This afternoon she has been at the races and just had a quiet walk around in the stall area, just keeping her under the radar and getting a few of the butterflies out of her system. She was nice and calm, she went back to the stables after being here for 40min and then got tucked in for bed.

The following Tuesday she is due for a solid gallop with Bowman up, followed on Thursday with a media breakfast put on by the Australian Turf Club. This is purely a public relations exercise. The other sort of exercise has all been done, starting when she stepped confidently into the water-treadmill at the farm exactly three months earlier.

•

Randwick, 20 August 2016. Warwick Stakes. #10
A year before this, she was a young mare leapfrogging from win to win so nimbly no one was sure how high she could go, how

long she would stay there. Now everyone knows it wasn't beginner's luck. Now the races Waller chooses for her are not so much targets as stepping stones, paid appearances on the way to Cox Plate II, her grand final.

Not that this means he can take the stepping stones for granted or change the way he trains her, which is the way he trains all his horses: bringing them along steadily without gut-busting track gallops.

Waller's methods come from having to keep a handful of ordinary horses sound enough to eke a living from provincial and mid-week meetings. He couldn't afford to break them down so he didn't. Now it's part of his character, like a Depression-era grandmother who never wastes string or electricity. His rise is gratifying but his work ethic is a hair shirt. The reward for success is to shoulder an even bigger load: training more and more horses as well as managing the Winx phenomenon. Two juggernauts he has to harness together.

The Warwick Stakes might be a stepping stone or a bonanza or a bonus for the connections but for the horse it is simply the first run back after a spell. And there's always the tiny doubt with a maturing mare going into spring: maybe tomorrow her hormones will tell her she wants to quit work and start chasing boys instead of beating them.

Even a sober, single-minded workaholic like Chris Waller couldn't resist romance. He fitted marriage and fatherhood into his secret master plan to dominate world horse training. But it's different for a thoroughbred mare: sex and motherhood is a one-way ticket off the track.

The 1400 metres of the Warwick Stakes is the ideal starting point for a Winx campaign. She bounces out of the barrier like a sprinter and takes up second place to the speedy Rebel Dane. It is, the caller notes, 'a soft run in second for Winx'. She's one off the fence in the tiny field, the perfect place to stay out of trouble and be poised to pounce. If she doesn't fall, she wins. Even by her stratospheric standards she is totally dominant from the jump.

As the two leaders cruise past the 400-metre mark, Bowman sits as chilly as a statue as she idles past Rebel Dane and into the footnotes of racing history. The crowd starts cheering. She's a neck ahead at the 200-metre mark and two lengths ahead at the 100-metre mark and wins by nearly double that margin. There's no contest so the caller paints the context:

Here's the season premiere of Winx and what a blockbuster season we're in for . . . she toys with her rivals in the Warwick Stakes . . . the first in a stepping stone to defending the Cox Plate.

The streak has hit double figures. A version of luck might win five straight but ten has nothing to do with luck, apart from absence of the bad sort. Winx is now knocking on a door that has legends' names on it.

Waller the all-sports fan just happens to have a metaphor handy. 'That is the heats of the Olympics over and done with, and we just have the semi-final and final to come,' he says.

Waller the diplomat plugs Sydney racing. 'I am pleased we chose Sydney to resume, that's her home, and there are a few more runs to come in Sydney before she takes on Melbourne.'

Waller the conscientious correspondent dictates a glowing report to glowing owners.

Obviously she resumed today with a very impressive win, I don't need to say much more than that. You guys have travelled the journey with me, sure there has been a little bit of pressure over the past couple of weeks and I copped a bit of criticism but in hindsight I think we have done the right thing and the horse, within the ten days of that scrutiny, has done the talking and certainly received all the accolades she deserves when winning today. Let's get her through the race and on Monday I will get back to you with a more in-depth update but what an impressive win! The way she jumped and put herself up on the speed, it wasn't a great field but Rebel Dane is no slouch and is in form with a run under its belt and Lucia Valentina is a very good horse and Hartnell is also a Group 1 winner. It wouldn't have been much different wherever she went with similar horses to these and she would have beaten them just as easy. Well done to you all, I am sorry I didn't get a chance to stay after the race but I have a big 24 hours ahead of me as I am going up to the stallion parades tomorrow and I need to get a lot of work done tonight.

Hugh Bowman is by now looking for different ways to say the same things. This time he goes with: 'It's just an honour to be on her back.'

Oh, and she ran her last 600 metres faster than the field's 32.89 seconds with Bowman smoking a pipe, as the saying goes. That sort of speed is Black Caviar territory.

•

Randwick, 17 September 2016. George Main Stakes. #11

It might as well have been an exhibition gallop. In fact, it is. After scratching from the Chelmsford Stakes two weeks earlier because of the bog track, she needs the gallop and this is it, with a $300,000 winner's cheque thrown in. She rears coming out of the barrier and settles back further than expected but shrugs it off. By taking the streak to eleven and her Group One tally to seven, she matches Kingston Town's purple patch. In Melbourne, she has another exhibition gallop to be match fit for the Cox Plate. It's called the Caulfield Stakes.

•

Caulfield, 8 October 2016. Caulfield Stakes. #12

'Caulfield is probably not perfect for a Sydney horse first time but she just has got that ability to put herself around and finish off,' is the way Waller previews it. Caller Greg Miles puts it a little more bluntly after the deed is done. 'She scared her rivals away and she blew them away when they got there.'

There are two other starters and only one of them, Darren Weir's Black Heart Bart, has any claim to be in the same sentence as Winx. The Hayes-trained He Or She is going around for the third place money, and why not? There is a good living to be made running behind Winx. Brad Rawiller on Black Heart Bart uses the lead to hold the trio to track gallop pace then puts on a good show of making a race of it in the straight. It is the perfect pipe-opener for the Cox Plate favourite, adding an eighth Group One and another $360,000 for a couple of minutes work. Her $1.20 price seems generous—and almost as safe as bank interest.

•

Moonee Valley, 22 October 2016. Cox Plate. #13
The Saturday before the race, Cox Plate horses and their work-mates get to work on the course proper at Moonee Valley. Anyone who sees Winx work that morning—and hears the riders talking—wouldn't bother speculating about anything beating her.

Winx's regular track rider Ben Cadden has handed over to Bowman and is riding a handy Waller mare, Lady Le Fay, set to run in a race before the Cox Plate. Cadden has Lady Le Fay six lengths in front and travelling well when he hears Winx's distinctive breathing looming behind him, Bowman holding her.

'She goes past me like I'm in the slow lane of the autobahn,' Cadden recalls. 'We've both got grins on our faces.'

Just then Dean Yendall comes along on the tiny three-year-old Yankee Rose. Yendall might be the lightest senior jockey in the land and can make Yankee Rose's bottom weight of 47.5 kilograms in the Cox Plate. As he approaches, Bowman can't help teasing him.

'Ten kilos isn't going to be enough!' he calls.

Bowman has six rides before the main event, including one on Lady Le Fay. He wins on none of the six, but each loss informs him of how the track—and the wind—is playing.

He sticks to the fence on Lady Le Fay and is well beaten, which tells him the cold, cross wind is buffeting rail runners.

He leads from a wide gate on Luiza and she fades badly, he guesses for the same reason: exposure to the wind, first sideways and then head on. Then, from another outside draw, on Sezanne, he stays wide and charges late down the outside to be narrowly pipped by something that got a lucky break inside the field.

Sezanne, as one observer notes drily, is in 'different post-codes' from the rails ride on Lady Le Fay. It's an instructive result reinforcing Bowman's growing confidence in the need to shelter from the wind as long as possible before making a dash down the centre of the track like a bike rider streaking out of the peloton.

By the time the clock counts down to the big one, it's clear that gate three is not the advantage it might be nearly any other year.

Bowman has done his homework and is almost relaxed. So is Winx. This time she doesn't play up going to the start. The only threat to their combined composure is that when the crowd cheers them onto the track, Bowman is unexpectedly moved and has to 'regather' his emotions when he gets to the barriers.

Winx is not the emotional type. She jumps cleanly and parks in fifth place outside little Yankee Rose, who looks like a bantam-weight at a bouncers' convention as Black Heart Bart and the flashy Awesome Rock slide to the front in what caller Greg Miles tags as 'a leisurely pace'.

Awesome Rock was the $575,000 matinee idol of the same yearling sale where Winx was a wallflower but price and looks aren't going to help him today.

The French visitor Vadamos streaks to the front and stretches the lead like the sharp miler he is, but Miles isn't distracted by tourist exhibitionism. The man calling his last Cox Plate is intent on Winx and Hartnell, the English horse that seems able to win anything except when Winx is in it.

The French horse surrenders as Hartnell moves up and Winx and Bowman follow him with deadly intent. That's when Miles knows he has the one-on-one contest that's been playing in his mind's eye for weeks.

The two great champions together at the 800-metre turn . . . Hartnell's hit the front and Winx is going with him and they've turned it on. The great race is on here . . . Hartnell the leader, Winx striding up to join him from Black Heart Bart and Awesome Rock.

The Hartnell tactics fold up as Bowman's strategy unfolds. He fans her out from three wide to the middle of the track as they round the turn and aims her straight down the fast lane with the wind in his face and joy in his heart. In his eyrie in the stand, Greg Miles describes a scene he will savour long into retirement.

This is a blitz! It's a Winx blitz! Two in a row and she joins the all-time greats of the turf. Winx has won it by six lengths.

In fact, it's more like eight. By the time Hartnell and game little Yankee Rose hit the line locked together, Winx is out of sight behind the judge's tower, heading around the bend. It's a Secretariat moment, without the drugs.

It's also Winx's thirteenth straight win. The stable staff reckon Waller won't write '13' on a work sheet but maybe this result could cure him. The only bad luck around the world's greatest mare is for those that run against her.

It leaves the professional watchers groping for new super-latives. Bruce McAvaney keeps his cool and says it best, even before Bowman turns her around to ride back to the winner's stall.

'It's hard to imagine we have seen a better horse win a Cox Plate and that says it all,' he says on Seven's television coverage. 'We weren't around for Phar Lap. We saw Kingston Town and we've seen all of them [since] but never seen anything better than that in a Cox Plate.'

Waiting by the winner's stall, Christine Bowman is crying. As he rides back, her husband is trying not to. And Winx? She looks as if she could go around again.

21

THE THIRD ACT

Win two Cox Plates and you are in rarefied air. After the dazzling So You Think won his second, he was sold to Irish interests in a deal that valued him at $50 million—and which proved that Bart Cummings had a heart. We know this because losing the big beautiful horse nearly broke it.

That price tag shows the race has international standing, otherwise So You Think might have ended up back near where he came from: a farm somewhere in New Zealand.

As Melbourne racing writer Matt Stewart once put it, the Cox Plate is not a salad plate. Occasionally, a merely good horse does a Steven Bradbury and flukes one. But to win two the arrogant way Winx wins hers puts her next to modern greats such as Sunline and Kingston Town. And when watchers with the calibrated sense of sports history of Les Carlyon and Bruce McAvaney make calm comparisons with Phar Lap and Tulloch, it tells us champions are not better just because they're dead.

Winx's pure heroine appeal is hard to resist after her second Cox Plate. Even Waller, a professional realist, wrestles to mask his emotion that day, and loses. Having hidden from public view to watch the win he'd plotted for a year, he is so rapt he does a Bart Cummings and says what he likes.

Asked what is next for the champion, Waller looks around the Valley's amphitheatre and says it straight: 'Win a third one.'

Waller unplugged is on a roll. 'This is Australia's big race. Getting to the other side [of the world] would be good but she'll be back next year. That's what we're in the game for. She was in the zone today and when she's in the zone she would beat any horse in the world.'

The heat of the moment melts his usual polite deflections. He belts the inevitable Royal Ascot query like swatting a mosquito. 'Why would you want to go overseas for one race?' he says. 'Maybe the world could come to us, if they're good enough.'

In the ensuing months, of course, he dials up the diplomacy and is careful not to rule out Ascot completely, but decisive actions outweigh careful words: nothing he does with Winx deviates from the target of a third Cox Plate.

The only thing that *might* have changed that, he is to reflect much later, is if she'd lost a race and broken the golden shackles of the winning streak without losing her ability or appetite for racing. 'Then we might have thrown the ball at the stumps and gone for a Japan Cup or the Arc or a race in America somewhere,' he admits in 2018.

Meanwhile, in late 2016, away from all the speculation and the marketing motivations of others, he has to look after the animal. She's a horse, and horses that gallop at speed with other horses can hurt themselves. The day after the Cox Plate, the world's finest race mare has a swollen leg.

Waller Inc. swings into action. Treating the leg is routine—bathing and bandaging, ice and antibiotics. And there's something Waller didn't have to worry about pre-Winx: the public relations element. He puts out a press release, like a politician or small corporation. Image and perception are starting to matter as well as the usual breakables such as tendon, muscle and bone.

On the Tuesday after the race, Waller's report to the owners reflects the added layer of responsibility:

> The swelling is reducing and the little bit of the heat is also dis-appearing, indicating that already the antibiotics are starting to have an effect. She is no longer sore on the leg when walking, it is a little painful still to touch but certainly on the improve and it was good to take the aggressive approach to eliminate any risk. I am not saying we are completely out of the woods yet but she is certainly a lot happier and therefore I am today as well. I think our press release has been well received, I have had nothing but positive feedback and to get the message across early, rather than prolonging it, I think has been easier for all of us and the general public.

The injury is minor and on the mend but Waller is as painstaking as if the mare is a family member. He keeps her at Flemington for another week of treatment, observation and tests.

On Melbourne Cup Day, 1 November, he reports she has a 'clear blood profile' and can travel back to Sydney next day to start her spell. Later that afternoon, his opinion of Kerrin McEvoy's riding ability rises further when the Streaky Bay wonder wins his second Cup, this time on Lloyd Williams' well-fancied Almandin.

The Winx connections might notice something familiar about the Cup result: the second placegetter, the aptly named Irish entry Heartbreak City, is piloted by Joao 'Magic Man' Moreira, whose acrobatic balance and stylishness throughout the 3200-metre trip are not quite matched by tactical finesse in the final furlong.

The Irish horse's trainer Tony Martin, like Waller, is a good sport and generous soul and doesn't comment in public. But he confides to friends later that the Brazilian spoiled an exemplary display by going 'too early' on Heartbreak City in the long straight, a trap for foreign riders at Flemington. It's a 'what if' moment: a Melbourne Cup would be life-changing for the Irish visitors in the way that it clearly isn't for the multimillionaire winner Lloyd Williams, who collects them like tea cups.

If Moreira *had* won the Australian Oaks on Winx the previous year, what path would the mare have taken? The likely answer is: one that didn't lead to two Cox Plates and confident preparations for a third. This is racing.

Waller is already mapping out the autumn campaign. He talks to the owners about the Chipping Norton, George Ryder and Queen Elizabeth Stakes, which means the mare must be back in work soon enough to kick off with the Apollo Stakes in mid-February. He has to think like an elite coach who mulls over strategy in the summer break while his players are on a beach somewhere. This suits him. The boy who rolled cricket pitches in cow paddocks and played competition squash has never restricted his thinking to racing alone: he sees himself more as a sports executive who trains athletes. Like the best coaches, he thinks outside the conventions and customs of his craft, which span generations, even centuries.

Back in 2007, the equine influenza crisis that grounded racing across Australia prompted Waller to take his first trip to England. The mission: to buy tried European stayers that might appeal to some buyers more than the long-range raffle of buying yearlings. Waller, Guy Mulcaster and Tim Roberts flew on the cheapest economy tickets he could find. There weren't many Melbourne Cup prospects in their modest budget but they did buy horses that could win moderate city races and, for lucky owners, pay for themselves within months. Waller didn't need a Harvard MBA to learn lateral thinking.

It was a tough year, the one before he got the life-changing Bob Ingham phone call offering a barn full of million-dollar babes. Because Rosehill was the last track to be closed down by the equine flu outbreak, it was the last to re-open, which froze training there. Waller didn't have any money but he had ten days he could never have spared otherwise. On the way back from England he stopped at Milan to visit a former Sydney goalkeeper, Zeljko Kalac, who had just joined AC Milan. It was a chance to study elite athletes training and playing, a subject that fascinates Waller.

Back in Sydney, he found that while he was in the air, Stephanie had fallen ill and was in intensive care after a six-hour operation.

'It puts it all in perspective,' he says of the gut-wrenching homecoming. But it also focused his aim. He decided he would train horses as well as he could for as long as he could do it well—but no longer. He doesn't want his children in the same business working the way he does and he doesn't want to keep up the suicidal hours forever.

But those decisions will be made long after Winx retires. As spring heads into summer in 2016, Waller's long-term plans are still exactly that: not invisible but distant. Winx, by contrast, is a little over an hour away and will soon be back.

The first Monday after the Cup carnival, Koolman reports from the Hermitage.

Winx has settled back in super and is eating the place down. I can't believe how bloody good she looks. She is on fresh cut grass rather than relying on Lucerne hay as she tends to hog it and fatten. She has a new built yard this time and away from all contact with other horses other than Kinema. She goes out to the paddock at 7 am with breakfast, after-noon feed at 3 pm and back into the stables after a full day of sunshine and for a safer night at about 7 pm. She enjoys the paddock but loves the stable, she gets agitated in the paddock if she is left out too long and in the past we have observed that she tended to lock herself away in the shelter for most of the day anyway. This routine seems to suit her best . . .

Her feet are in better condition this time, in fact the best I've seen them in two years.

We are loving having her here again, it's a real privilege and gives everyone a boost. We were brought to tears watching her win the Cox Plate.

In her previous preparation Winx was 519 kilograms. She comes back to Rosehill on 9 December at 533 kilograms, bigger and stronger—yet to Waller's sharp eye she looks fitter than he expected, so he shaves back her workload a little. At five years old, she is still filling out: a sign, perhaps, that her physical peak is ahead of her, a scary thought for rivals. Waller tells the owners she 'looks tremendous' and 'picture perfect':

Everything will be geared towards the first up run . . . second up into the mile race which is the Chipping Norton so to be going second up into a mile with her status she needs to be pretty fit, hence the reason why she is back in.

By 'status' Waller means her unbroken streak. A normal trainer with a normal horse can happily use the first run as a tune-up but celebrity changes that. Winx the superhorse can't afford a near-miss any more than Kate Middleton can be caught wearing fluffy slippers at Royal Ascot.

In each preparation Waller has to divine how to get her fit enough at home to win first-up and yet stay fresh enough to peak at the end of the campaign. This does not get easier. The only living trainer in Australia to have experienced this particular stress is Peter Moody, who lost sleep, his hair and occasionally his cool doing a brilliant job of making sure Black Caviar didn't lose anything at all.

In the stable, it's Groundhog Day. Winx runs in the usual two trials a fortnight apart in January. Both times, Bowman quietly steers her to be third of nine runners. Bowman, crowned the world's top jockey before Christmas, flies to London to meet the Winx connections for the Longines Horse of the Year awards. Waller leaves late on Saturday night after watching Winx work that morning and gets back the following Thursday.

It's enjoyable but not a holiday. Waller dictates a detailed report from London that runs through her preparation gallops and reveals the international media are turning up for interviews. He is pleased that this includes *Time* magazine. The glittering international event is a world away from his bargain horse-buying trip a decade earlier, and light years from milking Friesians in Foxton.

Winx is judged third behind the American horses Arrogate and California Chrome, a result not every commentator agrees with but excellent for the stud prospects of both entires. Australians wonder if 'dirt horses' being judged ahead of 'turf horses' in a global competition defies logic because only American horses race on dirt, and the rest of the world races on turf.

Back home, the world's greatest race mare—and best galloper on turf—is eating like a draught horse and working like a dream.

Waller reports he 'couldn't be happier with her' but cautions that her preparation 'does include three Group One races at the highest level and we will take each run as it comes'.

•

THE THIRD ACT

Randwick, 13 February 2017. Apollo Stakes. #14

The platitude about taking 'each run as it comes' suddenly has some meaning, because the first run comes two days late. The authorities postpone the Apollo Stakes from Saturday to Monday because of the extreme hot weather forecast. The delay doesn't bother Waller or Winx. It does bother a man who flies a round trip of 31,000 kilometres to see her win her fourteenth straight.

His name is Martin Wickins. He is a Canadian tax accountant and if he is not Winx's most devoted fan, it's a dead heat with the retired public servant who sews a homemade badge on his 'Winx' suit for each of her wins. But the badge man travels from Canberra, not Canada.

Catching the Apollo Stakes is the first of ten times the amiable Wickins will fly to Australia to see her race between this sweltering weekend and when she wins the 2018 Queen Elizabeth Stakes fourteen months later. (At the time of writing he is planning lightning visits number eleven and upwards to take in her entire 2018 Cox Plate campaign.)

Wickins is happy to fly across the world for a weekend to catch a champion run. He did it for Frankel and for the great French mare Treve. He calculates (in early 2018) he has so far flown 220,000 miles to see Winx—which he points out is almost the distance to the moon. He pleads guilty to obsessing about racing since the day he went to the races in Toronto with a high school buddy.

'I put two dollars to win on a horse called Rock Walk at 99 to 1. It was a terrible horse but I got hooked on the sport and

317

the beauty of the horses,' is the way he explains it. That $2 loss has turned into an eye-wateringly expensive hobby.

As a student he took a part-time job 'hot walking' horses after exercise gallops. Once he established his career, he bought into horses. Now he breeds them in Kentucky, races them in Canada and flies to Australia to watch the best galloper in the world when he's not following his ice-hockey team, the Pittsburgh Dolphins.

Wickins bought the saddle Larry Cassidy used on Winx in the first race of her streak. It cost enough to pay Cassidy's tax bill, though nothing like the amount Wickins has spent on oil paintings, rare books and other racing memorabilia he has gathered in Toronto.

On the weekend of the Apollo Stakes, Wickins manages to stretch his stay to make it to the postponed race meeting. It is worth the lost time, he says later.

'She lived up to the hype as she of course cruised to win in the same manner she always does,' he recalls. 'It was a big field with Hartnell running second. It was a legit race and perfect to set up the rest of the season . . . she thrashes the only horse anyone thought could challenge her. She set the tone quickly and emphatically . . . almost like it would be her against herself the rest of the year, which it was.'

The 'breathtaking experience' sets the seal on a long-distance infatuation. 'I was convinced she was the real deal. You get those goosebumps and teary-eyed and very thankful that you got to witness it.'

After the Apollo, Wickins promises himself he will return for every race Winx contests. In fact, he has to miss one, the

Turnbull Stakes, but spends the equivalent on the Cassidy saddle with the money 'saved' on the airfare.

Racing NSW and the club turn the postponed race into a marketing gimmick, making admission free and moving the Apollo Stakes to 5.40 pm with a promotional push labelled 'Winxafterwork', a campaign to persuade people to knock off work to get to the track—or pub or club or home—to watch her comeback run. She doesn't let them down.

Waller's view of the Apollo Stakes is sober, considering the way Winx takes Hartnell apart, duplicating the Cox Plate result. Hartnell usually beats the best of the rest and Winx always flogs Hartnell.

> She bounced back to winning form today with a good win in the Apollo Stakes. She stepped a touch slow and settled midfield, travelling nicely, and I was just hoping that she was going to stay out of trouble. Turning for home Hugh managed to get her out into the open, she got a nice cart into the race off the stable mate's back and at the 300m mark Hugh was asking for an effort and she quickened nicely. Hartnell finished off strongly behind her.

•

Randwick, 25 February 2017. Chipping Norton Stakes. #15 Waller does not run a 'tipping service' for his owners but his dispassionate dissection of form is instructive. He tells them Winx has drawn perfectly in barrier four, that there are only three or four chances and the rest of the field is made up of stayers using the 1600 metres as a stepping stone for longer events that will not feature Winx or Hartnell.

In an earlier report he has pointed out that smart three-year-olds can be the trickiest known unknowns, a hint not to dismiss Victorian Oaks winner Lasqueti Spirit.

Against that, he says, 'Winx is very well, she has come back in good form and her work since her last start has been good.'

She jumps well enough, slipping back from midfield to sit seventh of ten with the Oaks filly Lasqueti Spirit making light of her featherweight in the lead. As Waller predicts, the challenge won't be from any of the dour stayers resuming their preparations but from the cheeky three-year-old that has to be run down.

Bowman is drifting Winx wide around the field, stalking the leaders before the turn, when the caller turns his attention to her, voice rising in anticipation.

He pulls to the passing lane as they round the corner . . . Lasqueti Spirit in front of Endless Drama but Winx moves straight up on the outside. She went straight past Hartnell . . . They've got 200 metres to run. He hasn't even pushed the button yet on the mighty mare Winx and she's really starting to pull away . . . Oh, isn't she great to watch, back-to-back wins in the Chipping Norton! It's been won by some of the legends and that she is. Winx by two lengths.

•

Rosehill, 11 March 2017. Exhibition gallop between races
Kerrin McEvoy has proven a cool, level-headed jockey against the best in the world. When Waller asks him to gallop Winx between

races at Rosehill because Bowman is riding in Melbourne, McEvoy is as delighted as an apprentice getting his first ride in town. He has a full book of rides, including Winx's stablemate Foxplay and other good chances, but it's hard to concentrate on them.

Normally, he runs through each race while driving to the track, picturing the likely scenario from homework already done. But the thought of riding Winx in front of a big crowd of fans there to see her pushes everything else out of his mind. He tells himself not to let her go too hard: don't spin the wheels of the Ferrari just to show off.

'It was just a routine gallop—but you could feel the X factor,' he is to recall a year later. 'All I could think of was her, and the following she's created.' McEvoy has seen racegoers and punters and owners all over the world but these fans are different.

One person knows how he's feeling: Hugh Bowman, at Flemington to ride Jameka in the Australian Cup. About the time McEvoy pulls into the jockeys' carpark at Rosehill, his mobile pings. It's a message from Bowman, whose thoughts are obviously straying, too.

Good morning. Winx - very straight forward. She will want to roll from 500m, however if you keep a good hold until 350 she will really quicken for you & don't be afraid to give her a squeeze inside last 75.

Buckle up

Good luck

McEvoy wins two races that afternoon, including the Phar Lap Stakes on Foxplay, but his exhibition gallop on Winx is the highlight.

'The first thing that struck me about her was how much "bigger" she rides than she looks. She has balance and length; she's so smooth and well-balanced when she's galloping, she's like a snooker table. In human athletes we say "core strength". That's what she replicates. It's hard to pinpoint.'

McEvoy the consummate professional can't contain his awe: 'Just to sit on her in a gallop—it was a great day for me to have that.'

•

Rosehill, 18 March 2017. George Ryder Stakes. #16
Some Group One races are stronger than others. The George Ryder, on Golden Slipper day, is shaping as a heavyweight match race that threatens to overshadow the world's richest two-year-old contest.

The Ryder is not only worth nearly double the stakes of the Chipping Norton but is 100 metres shorter. At 1500 metres and a million bucks, it attracts dangerous characters of a sprinting nature. Anything less than a mile is their turf and sprint specialists can be difficult for even brilliant generalists to handle.

Enter Chautauqua, top of the food chain over the short course with a finish like a charging lion that suggests he could be dangerous if he gets the distance. If the big grey horse were a full forward, he would be 'Plugger' Lockett. If he were a cricketer, he would bowl bouncers to scare batsmen. He appears never to have quite forgiven the world for the eminently sensible decision to geld him. He has, after all, won $8 million in stakes.

For a sprinter, Chautauqua finishes like a middle-distance 'swooper'—what the Americans call a 'stretch-running sprinter'. He drops out of races like a sulky steeplechaser then, when it seems too late, cuts loose and comes at the leaders like a runaway truck. Sometimes he mows them down before the line and sometimes he just frightens them, the villain in the pantomime. Even at the peak of his considerable powers, which includes winning against world-class horses in Hong Kong, no one is quite sure which Chautauqua will turn up: hero or villain.

By the time of the 2017 Ryder the grey eminence is an enigma, the old heavyweight champ who's possibly past his peak but still lethal. Matching the tough sprinter with the brilliant middle-distance star at the in-between distance of 1500 metres is a promoter's joy.

Then there's Le Romain, a horse that makes a handsome living in high-class sprints. He doesn't win many Group Ones but is a reliable yardstick for those that do: he runs enough placings behind champions to have earned seven figures. He isn't Chautauqua but he *is* consistent. On a good day he can beat Chautauqua if the moody grey gets the blues.

But whoever writes the script for the Ryder cranks up the weather. It has been so wet the Rosehill track is a Heavy 10. Any wetter and ducks will land on the course proper.

Convention says there is an extra degree of difficulty for Winx: she is dropping back in distance (from 1600 metres to 1500) in preparation for a grand final over 2000 metres. This is unorthodox. But her connections now have faith in her to overcome any of the elements that worry lesser horses.

They calculate that 1500 metres is 200 too far for sprinters—and that she is faster than any horse in the land over the last 600. It is also possible one of the Kiwi mafia recalls that her mother Vegas Showgirl loved the wet and everything sired by Al Akbar was the same.

Winx v. Chautauqua discourages also-rans. There are only five other runners. Winx jumps awkwardly and shares the tail end with Chautauqua the habitual backmarker, who's on the fence. Bowman angles out to avoid the 'kickback' of wet sand and turf that can half-blind a jockey and discourage a horse. Winx picks up speed on the outside while Chautauqua cuts the corner, then Tommy Berry spears the grey across to the middle in search of better going to chase her. It doesn't help. Nothing can, as the call makes clear:

Bowman sits motionless yet again . . . Look at her rip clear inside the 200. Le Romain can't go on, nor can Hauraki. Chautauqua is out of the pack but all conditions, all distances, all challenges—here's sweet sixteen for Winx making it back to back wins in the George Ryder. Le Romain six lengths away second, Chautauqua third.

It is a comprehensive humbling of Chautauqua, who finishes more than eight lengths behind Winx and only six lengths ahead of the last horse. Darren Flindell the caller catches his breath and adds an editorial:

Winx is simply the best—a cutaway, storm-home victory yet again, on the heavy ten. Bowman does carry a whip. He never needs it. He just sits up on Winx as she destroys her rivals. Bring on the grand final in the Queen Elizabeth.

The performance is one of her best. She has run a phenomenal time for the last 600 metres. Her last 200 metres was by far the best by any horse on the day at 11.69 seconds, and the sectional between the 400 and 200 metres was 11.25 seconds: times so astonishing on a bog track that if they were hand-timed, people would doubt them. But the Longines timing devices in each saddlecloth are accurate to the tiniest fraction.

'She's a hovercraft,' racing writer Matt Stewart deadpans later.

Apart from all the other superlatives, offers Hall of Fame trainer Lee Freedman, she's just proven herself the best wet tracker in the land, over any distance.

Two weeks later, on April Fool's Day, Chautauqua makes the Ryder form seem even better by winning his third T.J. Smith Stakes with a heroic last to first run. To the naked eye, it looks as electrifying as any of Winx's best efforts. The stopwatch disagrees.

It turns out the grey runs the last 600 metres (of his pet 1200-metre sprint) much slower than Winx's equivalent sectional in the Ryder—a time difference that accounts for about seven lengths of her huge winning margin over him.

Chautauqua's time for the 1200 metres is slower than that of an obscure mare named Diddums winning over the identical distance earlier that afternoon—her third win for total stakes of less than $200,000.

Such crude comparisons are risky because reluctant heroes like Chautauqua only ever do what they must to win. He beats horses, not stopwatches. But he couldn't get near Winx and maybe never could have. There's no shame in that.

•

Randwick, 8 April 2017. Queen Elizabeth Stakes. #17

It wasn't quite the elaborate secret that Winx's bone chip operation had been, but the little stone bruise (which later turns into a hoof abscess) was a quiet drama before the Queen Elizabeth—a problem that had to be solved fast under pressure, like plugging a leak in a submarine before the crew panics.

It started simply enough. The mare was tender in one foot around a horseshoe nail. When they pulled out the nail, it relieved the pain but not the cause. Such a bruise can eventually push up through the hoof wall and become an abscess. It would later burst through the coronet, the bony ridge where hoof meets hairline.

None of it would matter much to a horse in the paddock but this one had to stay fit to race the best horses in Australasia within days. Missing work will derail a preparation 'timed to the minute'.

As this miniature drama unfolds Waller doesn't want to underplay the problem. Neither does he want to start an avalanche of alarmist publicity. It's a fine line. Ten days before the race he reports it to the owners matter-of-factly and in the past tense, blunting the sense of emergency:

> She had a minor foot issue and obviously mid preparation it is something that needs to be carefully managed with a horse like her. From time to time all horses get foot problems and they are

exaggerated when you have got wet weather and they can pick up infections with their feet. Again, it is nothing serious—we identified that, around a nail hole, where the farrier obviously puts the shoes on the feet, there was a little bit of sensitivity. We removed the nail and it gave her instant relief. It was a touch tender for a few days but it hasn't meant that she has missed any work at all.

All true. Two days earlier, on the Sunday, he has sent Winx to the beach, followed by a normal working gallop on Monday. Bowman declares her 'perfect' but Waller worries it might return as the sort of problem he'll have to make public. While she works normally she is sound and the bruise stays 'in house'.

We just want to keep a low key approach as best we can and as you are all well aware, low key isn't easy to achieve with a horse like this. Saturday at Randwick will give me a good chance to give her a nice hit out.

She draws barrier three of nine runners, Hartnell and Exospheric on her inside. In theory, those two will jump smartly and hold their positions and Winx will settle behind them midfield, one off the fence. In practice, she jumps on level terms then drifts back with Exospheric to sit exactly midfield one off the fence, well ahead of three tail-enders. Hartnell is facing his seventh clash with Winx, but his English jockey James Doyle is out to stretch her by stealing a big lead.

The small field lets Bowman do everything to plan. There is no helter-skelter of horses jostling for position. He has reduced this to such a predictable pattern each call is sounding the same. As the field reaches the turn:

Winx is three wide. She's starting to inch a little bit closer . . . Doyle's first to make his move on Hartnell. But here she comes around the field, Winx. Bowman hasn't moved a muscle. Doyle has on Hartnell. Here she comes. Winx moves up on the outside of Hartnell then the United States and Happy Clapper but away she goes now, Winx in the Queen Elizabeth Stakes. She puts two lengths on Hartnell. She's racing royalty this mare. That's seventeen in a row. The grandstand is shaking. She wins it by four and a half to Hartnell.

Afterwards, Waller underlines how seriously the stable had taken the hoof trouble. The preparation 'wasn't without its ups and downs', he reports, but taking a 'very professional' line had stopped 'small issues' blowing up into big ones. 'It would have appeared from the outside that it was a seamless operation but it wasn't quite that simple.'

But, he adds, 'We have a very healthy horse ready to continue on with her dominance in the spring.' He proposes lunch with the owners so they can watch the replay again and reflect on 'what a great horse she is'.

Three days later Winx goes to the farm to recover properly, the final act in a remarkable piece of horse training and husbandry. The abscess drains through the opening in the coronet and her foot recovers completely.

Grandfather Waller with his bottle of liniment and folded handkerchief could hardly have done it better.

•

THE THIRD ACT

Randwick, 19 August 2017. Bob Ingham Warwick Stakes. #18

Four days out from the race, Waller is sweating on whether she still looks a fraction burly. She has come back into work at 533 kilograms again, but Waller's eye tells him something the scales don't: he describes her to the owners as 'a slightly bigger and stronger version of what we had in her last preparation'.

He judges the field of eight as moderate with only two real dangers—the 1400-metre specialist Ecuador and Winx's stable-mate and 'pal' Foxplay, a Group One winner. Apart from the speedy Red Excitement, the rest are stayers running to get fit and pose no risk. It's a perfect starting point for Winx, especially from barrier two. But Waller is uneasy about her barrier manners. He senses they are not getting better—and might be worse.

He has reason to worry. She has played up in the barriers at trials. He reveals afterwards it's the subtle pressure to keep her 'sharp': he has kept her fresh enough to sprint well in this 1400-metre race as a guide for whether to take her to Ascot to run over 1200 metres.

She goes into the barriers for the Warwick Stakes toey from short, sharp work and not a lot of it. When the gates open, seven horses jump and for a split-second it doesn't compute that Winx is not one of them. Finally, she lunges out. It turns out she reared when the field jumped.

The mare's missed the start by four lengths in a sensation. Winx is last and Ecuador is going to lead comfortably.

Meanwhile, reformed rogue Foxplay is tucked on the fence in third spot, perfectly positioned by McEvoy to capitalise on her stablemate's nightmare start. Winx settles six lengths off the leader but pegs back the margin so that at the 500-metre mark Bowman has her starting the trademark arc around the field, the one like a dog heading sheep.

Little Foxplay, McEvoy low in the saddle, corners like a whippet on the rails, flying with her ears pinned back, busting a gut to pull off the upset of the year. As Ecuador drifts off the fence on the corner, Foxplay darts inside him and takes the lead. Red Excitement is making ground on Ecuador, too. But that would only matter if Winx wasn't on her way.

She's cutting loose now! . . . Winx is down the outside. It's going to get desperate. Winx is going to Foxplay. Winx dives! Yes! She got up! Winx got up to beat Foxplay. There's eighteen in a row but what about the drama today . . . It went so close to going pear-shaped today but Winx got up where it counts. Happy eighteenth, Winx!

Below the caller's box an excited reporter is pushing a microphone at Debbie Kepitis, who can't quite believe they've dodged a bullet.

Waller credits Bowman's horsemanship in the barrier when Winx plunged: 'Hugh Bowman never panicked and fortunately stayed on her as she could have easily dislodged him and that would have been a tragedy.'

It is a day for fast times. The race time for the last 600 metres is 32.93 seconds, which means Winx—running well behind the point where the leader trips the timer—must have run 31.9 seconds.

'I have never seen those times before by any horse,' says Waller, shaking his head. In one mad minute the rodeo horse in the barrier turned into the world's fastest galloper.

Foxplay took weeks to get over the hard run. Winx pulled up as if she'd been for a jog.

Looking back much later, Waller is relieved to have got away with it. 'Too fresh,' he says. 'Simple as that.'

•

Randwick, 2 September 2017. Chelmsford Stakes. #19
It's the day she matches Zenyatta's record of nineteen straight. She jumps almost perfectly, by her standards, and in the end wins with a length to spare. But, 400 metres out, Bowman is more worried than he ever was playing catch-up in the Warwick Stakes. Today, it's catch-me-if-you-can, a game put in play by Josh Parr on Red Excitement.

Parr takes Red Excitement straight to the front and starts building a lead, stringing out the field to cover maybe sixteen lengths. He's four lengths in front, then eight. When horses go that hard in a mile race, they are supposed to fold up as if they are shot. This horse doesn't. Going around the turn with 400 metres to run, he is eight lengths in front and suddenly this is serious. It could be the Zenyatta day when the champ doesn't reel back the leader until just after the post, losing the photo finish by the width of a nostril.

When Winx plays a home game, she gets a good turnout. The full contingent of owners and families and Waller and his family are there, along with a bigger crowd than usual. With twenty seconds to go, they aren't feeling good. More importantly, neither is Bowman.

At this point Winx is three off the fence and overtaking the third and second horses. Everything looks fine except for the huge gap between them and the leader. Arithmetic says it's going to be hard unless Red Excitement finally surrenders to the lactic acid in his legs and the burning in his lungs. At the 200 metres he is showing no signs of it. The caller's leisurely early style is replaced with an Ozzy Osbourne scream:

Red Excitement is clear. Winx is now going after Red Excitement and she is now starting to get into her gears. Can Red Excitement pinch it? Winx is flying home! Winx is getting to Red Excitement! . . . She gave us a scare again but she has won easily.

Seconds later, Waller is speaking as calmly and drily as if it is a Gosford maiden. It's big wins that make him emotional. A near-loss he is steeled for.

'Yeah, very exciting,' he says, looking as excited as an undertaker. 'They turned the race on, I guess, tried to break us up.'

He says he was more worried than in the Warwick Stakes. Given that the mare jumped on level terms this time, it's a tribute to the plan almost perfectly executed by Josh Parr and Red Excitement's trainer Gerald Ryan.

Waller compliments his fellow Rosehill trainer: 'Well done, Gerald. He's a tactician and great trainer and Winx was asked to pull out her best.'

Bowman seconds the motion. 'At the top of the straight I wasn't worried last start but today I really was.

'What she did today was incredible . . . everything she does is incredible, but I'm lost for words. I was concentrating on just keeping her balanced but when she hit the afterburners at the 150-metre mark today—I just can't explain the feeling.'

Josh Parr is left thinking how close he's come to bowling Bradman. 'I thought I had pulled it off,' he says of Red Excitement's run. 'Today he has just run into possibly the greatest ever.'

•

Randwick, 16 September 2017. George Main Stakes. #20

She jumps fairly, which is enough. Absence of bad luck is all she needs. Moves in front of two tail-enders to be sitting fifth of eight runners, four of them trained by Waller. Red Excitement and Parr have another shot at stealing the race from in front, stringing the field over a dozen lengths. Foxplay is in fourth spot. In the absence of Winx, she looks as if she's set to swoop if and when the mad leader folds up. Red Excitement hurtles around the turn like a stock car. At that point, Winx is third last and slow to take the initiative but there's nothing in her way when she does.

And now the champ gets going down the outside. Red Excitement being tackled by Happy Clapper but Winx is chiming in. Here we go again: Winx from right out the back powers away from Happy Clapper and Foxplay and the champ makes it twenty in a row.

Bowman stops riding Winx fifty metres from the line. This time Red Excitement melts and runs second last. Sprinting ahead of the mare is like trying to outrun a bushfire.

If there's a disappointment for Waller, it's that with four runners he can't nail the trifecta. The battler horse Happy Clapper splits Waller's team to run second. Life can be cruel like that.

It's a day of records. Winx passes the Zenyatta tally of nineteen wins and the straight win tallies of Desert Gold and Gloaming.

She sets a new race record of 1:33.65 and is the first mare to win successive George Main Stakes, which no horse has done since Kingston Town in 1982. It's also her thirteenth Group One, equalling Sunline's tally.

Still ahead are Black Caviar's fifteen Group One wins, Kingston Town's fourteen, and Makybe Diva's $14.52 million prize money. And she is sparkling in trackwork.

•

Flemington, 7 October 2017. Turnbull Stakes. #21

It is a perfect spring day at 'headquarters'. Winx might have looked this good in the past, surely never better. She is at the peak of maturity, just turned six, and her coat ripples and glows with the dapples that trainers love to see. She walks around the parade ring between the tie-up stalls, ominously calm, the dark earmuffs built into a full-face mask that adds to the impression of menace. Only six others are running, half the usual field size. The rest are scared off. Only three favourites have won the race in the previous eleven years but that's not worrying the Winx army. She will start at $1.20 and the prospectus says there are few sounder investments.

It is the first time she's raced at Flemington and you wonder why. It seems made for her. She works happily here, galloping the Melbourne way. It's spacious and downright peaceful and park-like compared with the ant hill at Rosehill. And the modern iteration of the Turnbull Stakes, over 2000 metres, is perfect: a dress rehearsal for the Cox Plate, three weeks later and forty metres longer.

Over this distance, the start is hardly vital but she does it well anyway. Bowman is happy to settle fifth of the seven runners, the cheetah behind the zebras. The field is soon strung out, with Magicool and Sir Isaac Newton opening a big break on the next bunch, in turn well ahead of Winx and the tail-enders. Winx is stalking the leaders and Humidor is attempting to stalk Winx.

Magicool and Sir Isaac Newton tear away to the front, opening a huge gap to Ventura Storm and Assign, which are three lengths ahead of Winx. But the call is calm:

Winx is in plenty of room, plenty of air at the 1200.

As the leaders wane, Winx waxes. Before the turn she's only four lengths from the leaders and cantering. Gravity is pulling Sir Isaac Newton and Magicool back to earth.

Five hundred metres to go. Assign moves up outside of Sir Isaac Newton. Winx—Bowman hasn't flinched, she's doing it easily . . . at the 300 Winx has ambled up on the outside . . . Racing royalty goes to the lead. Racing's wonder of the world puts up two lengths, three lengths . . . but it's all Winx, five or six lengths in front. Look at her go with a hundred metres to go—twenty-one today on the biggest dance floor of them all. Winx by eight lengths.

Humidor's trainer, the plain-speaking Darren Weir, is to bag Damian Lane for his forward ride on the horse in the Caulfield Cup two weeks later and sack him for the Cox Plate, but it's not Lane's fault today. He's latched Humidor onto Winx like a suckerfish on a shark but when the pressure hits, Humidor averts his gaze—hanging his head to the outside in a way that costs second place. He's never going to win the Turnbull and is ridden 'upside down' at Caulfield but Weir sees something he can change. Or, as it turns out, two things.

As for Waller, he ain't changing a thing. His report to the owners that night ends:

> There is no need to complicate things . . . we have a superstar on our hands and we will do everything to the best of our ability to keep it that way and we will have a lot of fun for a lot longer yet.

22

THE PRESENCE OF GREATNESS

It's 6.30 am at the Valley and the blue sky of the new day pushes pink dawn out of the way. The turf looks lush but they say the track is plenty firm enough underneath. The mare canters the reverse way down the straight like a lady's hack, as they used to say when ladies had hacks.

J.H. Bowman is standing in the stirrups, calm and business-like but radiating a sense of occasion that riders on lesser beasts don't have on a Tuesday morning at the track.

The pair get around the far side, where the course runs beside the freeway, out of sight of the crowd because temporary structures on the infield are already set up for the big day. The cameras pick her up soon after she starts her work.

Bowman keeps her steady, kind hands and iron knees trans-mitting exactly what they need to, so that she gradually increases pace up the straight. The tattoo of hoof beats doesn't just get louder as it gets closer; it gets faster.

As she nears the post, the crowd is so quiet you hear that distinctive breathing, loud but not 'roaring', in perfect synchronicity with her pace. It's something to see. Watchers stop chewing the free bacon and egg muffins as she daisy-cuts past and around the turn, easing to the steadiest of halts a long way off.

'She's just cruising, boys,' says Debbie Kepitis happily to no one in particular and everyone within range. 'Just showing off.' She is right. The mare just does what she has to do. For twenty-one consecutive starts she's done exactly that. Four days before her tilt at a third Cox Plate, the pressure of expectation is building on those around her.

Five minutes later, Bowman hacks back to the gate into the tunnel under the stand. It's time to get her back to her stall so she can be unsaddled, hosed and rubbed down then walked until she's completely cool. Her bell boots will be put on for the short trip south to Waller's Flemington stables. Back in her loosebox, she will have her feet iced and get her morning feed.

Stripped, she's just a horse again. As the wisest of racing writers Joe Palmer once noted about Man o' War, an American hero of mythic proportions between the wars, a horse doesn't know it is a champion or a celebrity. Its interests are in 'oats and clean hay and good grooming and a comfortable stall'.

Two nights before the Cox Plate, Waller appears on *That's Racing*, the racing.com show. He is guest of the week, maybe the season, and the co-hosts Ross Stevenson and Hamish McLachlan are delighted to have the man of the moment.

Waller knows the drill. He good-humouredly recounts how when Winx failed after winning her first three races as a light young filly, the stable thought she was 'handy' rather than good. Between the Queensland Oaks win and her first Cox Plate, 'the penny dropped' for him and Bowman and the owners. They realised almost how good she was. The penny turned into a grand piano after the revelation at Moonee Valley.

The panel hosts ask the compulsory question about taking her to Royal Ascot. Waller has mastered Bart's art of speaking without saying much. He does the tease. He mentions the Queen Anne Stakes at Ascot. He wonders if the six-furlong race at the same meeting might make an introduction to gradually longer races around Europe. But that's if they take her. Until the day they load her on a plane, it's hypothetical, right?

Waller is too astute to make promises about a horse, any horse, but it's hard not to entertain dreams, even for someone as focused and relentlessly practical as he is. If he didn't dream big dreams he wouldn't have got where he is. And if he didn't focus on practical detail, he wouldn't have got there, either.

Counting chickens is dangerous for a trainer. Forty-eight hours out from Cox Plate III, a million wishful thinkers see it as a foregone conclusion but he and Bowman never have. And the owners are more realistic than the public because they get it, and Waller and Bowman talk to them.

Still, at six years old, the mare is not the slip of a thing she was two years before. She's grown out slowly but well. Conventional wisdom, which is not necessarily science, says most mares are pretty well full-grown at four—but Winx has come back bigger and stronger from every lengthy spell. The combination of steady exercise, rest and ideal diet means she has developed with maximum efficiency.

She has started each preparation, except one, heavier than at the equivalent time of the previous one. Remarkably, says Waller, she holds her weight through each campaign. Whatever weight she is for her first start is within a kilogram of what she weighs for her fourth or fifth start. She is resilient. Aloof. A cool professional.

This race will test that professionalism. It's the one to silence critics, maybe, who mutter behind their hands about easy kills in Sydney against a couple of middleweights, puffed-up and puffed-out sprinters and slow stayers. To win a third Cox Plate, she has to equal Kingston Town's record set thirty-five years before.

'The King' was as good a horse as most have seen in their lifetime, and he had to produce a miracle to pull off that historic treble. Only a twenty-four carat champion could match it.

•

Moonee Valley, 28 October 2017. Cox Plate. #22

At midday the temperature is twenty degrees and rising. The turf looks as lush as it had at the trackwork breakfast four days earlier but Friday was close to hot and the jockeys say the track is on the hard side of firm.

The sky is blue with wisps of white cloud, promising to be perfect, but Melbourne in spring is notoriously fickle. A chopper hovers high above for filming, adding to the big occasion aura.

The first race, the Inglis Banner for babies, proves the point about the track. Setsuna wins in the relatively slick time of 58.99 for the 1000 metres, which shows the track is getting faster. And it becomes clear that the fastest lane is next to the rail.

This poses a problem for Bowman to ponder between races. If he hugs the rail, he's prey for those who are hunting him, and risks being held up behind horses or hemmed in, or even getting into a scrimmage. Two years earlier, no one was gunning for Winx, and he was at liberty to plot the shortest way home without any great recriminations if it went wrong. But this afternoon, he's on the world's best horse on turf, carrying the expectations of a vast public that now 'owns' Winx. It means there's a target painted on his back.

Signs of her popularity are everywhere. Blue is the colour of the day. There are blue suits and dresses, blue ties and hats. One jockey-size punter has blue suede shoes and he's not alone. Hundreds of fans have found a way to flaunt their allegiance. It's a touching echo of the past, when champions drew huge crowds in Australia and New Zealand, pastoral countries where the horse captured the public's imagination.

The old elms and giant pepper tree shading the parade ring are reminders of how old racing is in a young country. There's hardly a racetrack still operating in the United States that wasn't built in the twentieth century. Even the venerable Saratoga opened in 1863—two years after the first Melbourne Cup at Flemington, a track already well-established before that.

Winx is allocated the same corner stall as last year, facing east. It has her nameplate on it from the 2016 win. She was across the aisle the first time, the day she started to be famous.

Happy Clapper's trainer Pat Webster has been interviewed about his horse being bridesmaid to Winx twice and finishing behind her three more times. 'I was reading this week where six blokes in a marathon took a wrong turn and the seventh won!' he says. His horse is as big as a truck but not the main danger today.

At 1.40 pm the crowd, swelling steadily for a couple of hours, suddenly stirs. One veteran fan with a camera in his left hand and a phone to his right ear has taken block in front of the stall. The Melbourne weather strikes: the sun vanishes as if someone threw a switch. Grey clouds have blotted it out and threaten rain.

Winx's spotless white bridle hangs on one side of the stall, her leather head collar on the other. A purple towel and lead rope is neatly folded and draped over the offside rail, all laid out like a surgeon's utensils: neat and precise and predictable, right down to the white race-day buckets labelled RACEDAY.

Everything from Wallerland is exactly the same as it is every other race day. Horses are creatures of habit but so are humans. If everything is done perfectly and predictably ahead of time, there is less that can go wrong.

It's Waller's theory of doing things the right way, the same way, at the same time, every time.

There is a little superstition in this. Do what worked last time until it doesn't work anymore.

At 1.47 pm she comes in from stage left, quietly. Umut leads her, face as impassive and watchful as a secret serviceman minding the First Lady. Winx is in the building. He and Ben Cadden have already 'dressed' her and Winx's day-to-day minder Candice Persijn is there, pretty well-dressed herself.

For now, Winx is wearing the gunmetal-grey earmuffs that make her look ready for war. To add to the faint illusion of armour, her feet are heavily taped to stop her shoes coming loose in the truck. The extra padding also cuts the chance of her injuring herself if something went wrong in the short trip from Flemington.

Ben is wearing a sharp blue suit and grey waistcoat. A lot of Saturdays he's a starter's assistant or driving Waller's horse trucks but not today, when his all-time favourite is running in a Cox Plate. He's travelled the world with top horses but none like this one. Winx might not need three attendants and a trainer but the three attendants need *her* on this day of days. After the three years they have spent getting her to this point, the pull is irresistible.

It is Candice's first Cox Plate after nearly a decade in racing stables. She has been to plenty of Group races but never seen a race meeting with the intensity of the build-up here. It's like a stadium before a big rock concert or a title fight.

'All those people—it's mind blowing,' she is to recall. 'Everyone clapping and applauding. To think she has got this effect on so many people.'

The mare holds her feet up with patience born of practice while they strip the tape off. Then the strappers put on her bell boots, just in case.

The crowd is thickening, not quite pushing and shoving but ducking and diving. The bench seat fixed a few metres away is in high demand, especially for photographers both professional and amateur: anyone standing on it has a view across the crowd.

The dapples so obvious on Turnbull Stakes day three weeks ago still gleam under the dark coat. She can't possibly look better than the radiant picture she was then but seems to have held her condition. Under this suddenly overcast sky, her coat doesn't look as brilliant. Nothing does.

Later, that faint impression lingers as she's saddled and led around. It's no big thing, but a watcher might fancy she's a fraction more vulnerable today than she was earlier in the month: that the fourth run in a 'prep' is her peak. Who knows? Everybody will in a couple of hours.

She stands next to the wall, in the deepest shade, as still as a statue. People have to shuffle along, almost elbowing each other, and crane their necks to see her. She doesn't react. Exactly the way a trainer likes to see a horse before it runs, especially in a distance race.

There's a sprinkling of Winx caps and badges among the blue clothing but one fan takes the cake. He is a man in his sixties wearing a violently coloured blue and white 'tam o' shanter' with pompoms and a loud blue suit with a homemade Winx emblem sewn on for each race in her winning streak. His tie features horses and horseshoes. His two-tone shoes are blue and the shade of grey that interior designers might call taupe. He cuts such an alarmingly eccentric figure it is a relief to find him so disarmingly normal to talk to, friendly and not at all crazed.

His name is Lloyd Menz. He's come from Canberra. He is a modest man but one of rare judgement, it seems, because he has followed Winx since he saw her beaten in the Oaks in Sydney, which shows he is no fair-weather fan. The smart-looking young woman with him—also in blue, naturally—is his daughter Angela, who doesn't mind being a Winx camp follower.

Lloyd says he got the racing bug as a kid in Ballarat, going to the old 'Miners' gravel racecourse where the trotting track is now. He admits he mostly attends Winx's Sydney runs but made a special effort to bring Angela south today to see history made. Or not, depending what happens.

The signs are good or not, depending which ones you see.

Who Shot Thebarman wins the Moonee Valley Cup. Proof, not that it's needed, that Waller can train horses to give their best for years. The 'Barman' is nearly old enough to drink, drive and vote and he cost less than some of the wristwatches in the committee room. Then again, the win is one of Blake Shinn's four for the day. He is on fire and if that's an omen it's not a good one for the Winx camp.

Shinn is on Humidor, which Darren Weir has set for the big race. It means a new jockey, in career-best form, riding for the dominant hometown trainer who has put blinkers on his best galloper to stop it looking around the way it did at Flemington. Weir is on a hot streak and he's out to shoot Bambi.

Even while the Cup is being run, the worshippers are queuing to get a shot of Winx with their phone cameras. She is still tucked next to the wall in deep shadow, stock still, doing a Greta Garbo.

It's not as easy for Waller to stay out of the public eye. In the William Hill enclosure, Tom Waterhouse claims him, all white teeth and soft hands. There's been a lot of that. Waller shakes more hands than the Queen Mother.

Half an hour before the Cox Plate, he hurries down the tunnel towards the mounting yard, looking preoccupied. In moments when he's not meeting and greeting, the strain shows. His voice is hoarse from overuse, under the natural tan his skin a little pale from early mornings and late nights managing Waller Inc. and its booming subsidiary Winx Inc. across three states.

Before the horses file into the little yard tucked in a corner behind the stand, the Winx tribes gather. There are Tighes and the Kepitis clan and a heap of Richard Treweeke's family and friends from near and far. He can't be here himself due to age, heart trouble and vertigo but his extended family, including daughter Elizabeth and the New Zealand branch headed by his son Rick, has it covered in what they dub the 'Tre-winx' Marquee. Richard has a race-day ritual at home in Sydney, watching the races on television with his twin grandchildren Hugo and Pia, phone clutched in one hand to field and despatch calls to a small army of old mates.

Happy Clapper and Gailo Chop are first into the yard. You can tell Winx is coming by the whistles and cheers. She used to look like a netballer against track and field athletes. Now she's more a superhero, something like Catwoman in the sharp earmuffs worn over the bridle so the strappers can strip them off just before the race.

Royal Symphony is the slashing colt that Dwayne Dunn's equestrian wife Amanda picked out for $20,000. He's up on his toes and has a second strapper, just in case. Winx takes no notice. Like the seasoned traveller Gailo Chop, she's the complete pro, as cool as any world-class golfer ready to play at Augusta the umpteenth time.

So many good thoroughbreds are like this, especially at the top end: they are not nervous, let alone fearful or distressed. The ideal racehorse needs to be as fit as a title fighter but with the temperament of a snooker hustler when the money's on. Waller says the two strappers with Winx are just a precaution, almost for show. A child could lead her with one hand.

Humidor's new rider Blake Shinn, who's come a long way since he learned to ride at Kilmore, an hour north of Moonee Valley, has won half the card and wants more. 'How can he win five?' says Darren Weir to someone. It's hard to tell whether Humidor's trainer is acknowledging the hopelessness of the task or hinting an upset is possible. The softest thing about Weir is his teeth.

The Weir–Shinn combination must be stirring butterflies in Waller's stomach. He walks into the room where the jockeys are emerging to make their way to the yard. He shakes his head wryly at someone he knows, silently acknowledging the pressure he shares with Bowman. Each extra race in the streak has increased the burden. He craves the relief of winning to take the pressure off for a few weeks.

The countdown to race time is quick. The mechanics of this bit are no more complex than at a picnic meeting. The jockeys are tossed up, land lightly on the tiny saddles and slot toes into elfin stirrups.

They file through the tunnel onto the track where the crowd can see them. The club milks the moment, asking that Winx go out last. A drama-charged voiceover ratchets up the tension.

Ben whispers to Umut: 'You know you've got a rock star when the other strappers are taking photos on their phones.'

Bowman takes her up the straight to where the support acts are waiting at the 2040-metre start. But he knows once the barriers open, there will be no favours.

So far, Winx has kept her cool. There's a slight delay at the barrier and she gets toey and a barrier attendant calms her. She's drawn gate six but comes in to five because the English entry Kaspersky is scratched.

She jumps cleanly in line with the slickest of them before Bowman eases back to fourth of the eight runners, deliberately staying four wide.

The rail is fast but Bowman's having none of it. He backs Winx's superior ability to overcome the fact he's keeping her wide all the way. It is a trade-off: the horses close to the rail, especially Gailo Chop and Humidor, are going to finish closer to Winx than they otherwise would. But Bowman is almost guaranteed to stay out of trouble that way. Better a narrow win than to take any chances riding for luck on the rail.

According to conventional race tactics, he covers extra ground extravagantly. He camps behind and to one side of the scrum so he can launch around them when the time comes.

The French import Gailo Chop jumps well and leads most of the way. Winx sits outside Humidor, running far more truly than usual with the blinkers on him.

At the 800 metres, Bowman starts eating into the lead, sliding around the outside. Shinn stays as close as he can to the fence but keeps sight of Winx, waiting for the last possible moment to dart away from the fast lane and chase her.

As they pass the 600 metres, Bowman's clear move excites the crowd. Matt Hill, calling his first Cox Plate, has been waiting for this:

Here comes Winx!

The crowd murmur turns to a roar as she hits the outside and looms up behind the gallant Gailo Chop.

Winx peels to the outside now . . . so with 600 to go Gailo Chop in front but here comes Winx on the outside sliding up now.

We've waited thirty-five years for this—and Winx moves up to Gailo Chop . . .

Winx on the outside. Bowman hasn't moved yet.

The Valley's rocking and the world is knocking—Winx goes to the front!

The crowd roars, cheers and whistles. It is one of sport's better moments as a racing champion makes the run that turns her into a sports legend. As the field rounds the turn, it looks as if she will do it the way she did the previous year, and streak lengths ahead.

But Humidor and Shinn are under the influence of D.K. Weir, who doesn't believe in fairy stories. Shinn is in white-hot form. He has prudently saved every metre that Bowman prudently hasn't, and now he's riding with lethal intent, making desperation look easy.

Humidor, prepared on the straight uphill track at Ballarat that makes horses tough at the finish, is exactly that. Shinn scoots to the middle and past the rest, looking to draw a bead on Bambi. It gives everyone a scare—except Bowman, who doesn't look perturbed, let alone draw the whip. He rides harder with hands and heels but he's cool.

It's Winx in front by a length . . . Humidor is coming at her. Winx is holding on.

The mare responds exactly as much as she needs to. Bowman pumps his fist as he crosses the line half a length in front. He is more confident in the shadow of the post, maybe, than anyone else on the course. Humidor has given the crowd a fright, but it turns out Bambi is bulletproof.

The caller has his line ready.

The great mare completes the great trilogy of the turf.

She breaks her own race record, coming the long way home in the slow part of the track.

Interviewed on the way back to face the adulation, Bowman says he was born 'the year Kingston Town won his first Cox Plate'. Now his Queen has matched the King's three wins.

'We are in the presence of greatness,' he says. 'She'll be recognised as one of the greatest horses to grace the Australian turf.'

Before returning to scale, he rides alongside the roses lining the straight to salute Winx's subjects. Then he turns her around, takes off his goggles and then his helmet and tosses it into the crowd. Ayrton Senna couldn't do it better.

23

THE BOWMAN BRAND

Maybe two minutes after the Queen Elizabeth Stakes a television reporter grabs a bemused Jim Bowman, gushing about 'the boy from Dunedoo' being 'the toast of the country'.

The reporter is talking about Jim's son Hugh, who has just piloted the best horse Jim has seen in his life seal her reputation by matching Black Caviar's record of twenty-five straight.

Horse and rider have already broken the great sprinter's record of fifteen Group Ones by winning Winx's third Chipping Norton six weeks back, and a third George Ryder three weeks later.

Today is her eighteenth Group One and there is much excitement. Which is why the large man with the microphone is trying to stir an ecstatic reaction from a smaller man with face, suit and hat straight from the plains out Mudgee way. It's not quite going to plan.

Reporter, ingratiatingly: 'Do you remember the first time he jumped on a horse?'

Bowman senior, laconically: 'Didn't jump—he was lifted on.'

Translation: the boy could ride well before he could read and almost as soon as he could walk. The interview doesn't go too long. Jim's not much for big-noting, proud as he is right this minute. Not that sort of bloke.

His dark-brown Akubra hat has a brim just generous enough to shade his face, nothing like the ten-gallon rodeo specials on some of the young blokes down for the races.

The bigger the hat the smaller the farm, as they say where the Bowmans come from. Jim Bowman is a practical man and no slave to fashion: he has a handy pair of spectacles tethered around his neck so they can't wander.

Bowman senior has worn hats as long as he's ridden horses, which covers many decades. The hats haven't stopped him acquiring the weathered look and narrowed eyes farmers get from squinting into the sun. He looks a bit like the late, great jockey Jack Purtell and has the legs to prove it.

He looks exactly what he is—a lifetime farmer and grazier by occupation and birth; and a longtime amateur jockey, camp-drafter and polocrosse player by choice. One who's always kept good horses to ride around the stock. He believes if you're going to feed a horse or three, they ought to be well-bred. He most likely has similar views on cattle, sheep and dogs.

Jim Bowman is a livestock man and comes from a long line of them, like Chris Waller's forebears. Someone ought to paint his portrait for the Archibald before people like him are all gone, but no one will. He probably wouldn't sit still, anyway.

It's just as well for the Bowmans that blue is Winx's colour. Apart from an understated string of pearls, Hugh's mother Amanda has striking blue eyes that sparkle every bit as much as the big blue topaz stone her daughter-in-law Christine has on one overworked finger. That ring might weigh as much as the saddle that Hugh most likely used to earn it.

After he jumps off the mare and hands her to Umut and Candice, Hugh works politely through the scrum to the fence to see his parents who are waiting on the public side. He smiles at his beaming mother and pecks her on the cheek. Then he slowly winks at his father. Doesn't have to say much. They're not big on gush.

Hugh's wife, Christine, doesn't know whether to laugh or cry or kiss him so she does all those things at the same time. She doesn't need to say much, either, but it doesn't stop her having a red hot go. Irish eyes are smiling—and streaming tears of joy. She likes to call Hugh 'my little cucumber' because he's cool when it counts, notably in the last 400 metres of a Group One.

But don't imagine for a moment that father and son don't communicate. They do. It goes like this.

Bowman senior: 'She killed 'em in the end.'

Bowman junior: 'Yeah . . . she wasn't killing 'em at the thousand metres. But that's why she's so good.'

He leaves out the bits that go without saying. He means Winx can do what somebody once said of Kingston Town: a champion can win any race against any opposition from any position at any time.

Jim knows what he means. It's possible he nods but it would be easy to miss.

Bowman junior looks up at the excited crowd jamming the tiers of the new Randwick stand. It's a great moment for the new-look venue with its 'theatre of the horse'. Maybe the greatest it has had in its short life.

What he can't see from the track side of the stand is the brand new flag that has just been unfurled and run up the pole to flap in the hot wind gusts already fanning a bushfire just up the coast. The flag is in the blue Magic Bloodstock colours and reads **WINXXV**, marking the big milestone. Latin isn't dead, after all.

The scene around the winner's stall is a snapshot of the journey so far. It contains nearly all those brought together by the outrageous unlikelihood of being linked by the best race-horse in the world.

There's Hugh's sister, Kate, in black and pink, smiling shyly. Here's Stephanie Waller and her two children and relatives and friends, including Chris's sister Megan Waller. There's Debbie and Paul Kepitis and their daughters. Up in his corporate box is Winx's breeder, John Camilleri, with family members and business and breeding associates. In the Skyline Room on level three is Martin Wickins, the fly-in, fly-out tax accountant and thoroughbred aficionado from Toronto.

Craning over the fence is the not-so-oddball eccentric who wears homemade Winx memorabilia, backing up at Royal Randwick after the pilgrimage to the Cox Plate with his daughter. He doesn't have the right race tickets to be with the connections but an animated Patty Tighe rushes to greet them over the fence like old friends. In a sense, they are.

Patty knows Lloyd from Canberra is no johnny-come-lately. Like the Tighes, he has loyally followed Winx's campaigns from when she was a beaten favourite. Like Umut the Turkish actor turned horseman, he has always believed in this horse. Now, the world is in on it. Thousands on the course and a million more, from coast to coast, watching her race and praying the spell doesn't break.

All in thrall to an animal. None more so than the man who rides her.

•

Rewind ten minutes, to the start of the race. For Bowman, every carnival season has had its grand finals. But this second Queen Elizabeth Stakes is a milestone that once seemed as likely as climbing Everest in football shorts.

Imagine twenty straight wins, breaking the Zenyatta hoodoo. Imagine matching Kingston Town's three Cox Plates. Then imagine squaring off to equal Black Caviar's unbroken sequence. A fantasy come true.

He puts stray thoughts aside at the barrier, game face on and concentrating.

At least, he has no complicated tactics to rehearse. On the mare, he doesn't need to strategise any more than Bradman would going out to bat. Experience plus instinct plus reflex plus God-given talent should be enough to keep out of trouble.

That she can sustain a run longer and faster than maybe any horse racing will do the rest.

'The star of the show; the last to move in is Winx,' says Darren Flindell, the Sydney caller who has relished broadcasting most of her races.

She jumps cleanly from the outside alley, better than some but it hardly matters out that wide. Bowman drops her back to tail the field. Comfortably last at the mile crossing. Regular sparring partner Gailo Chop out in front ahead of the handsome Odeon, Winx eight lengths off them.

The pace is middling, which must annoy Bowman a bit. Like all jockeys, he has a counting exercise—'one apple, two apple, three apple'—to gauge the pace of each 200-metre furlong. The slower they go, the more juice Gailo Chop and Humidor and Happy Clapper will have at the sharp end. The best horse in a field needs a truly run race.

Gailo Chop still leads and Winx and Happy Clapper are still last at the 600 metres.

Craig Williams on the well-named Ambitious steals a move from the Winx playbook and strides around the field. Winx moves up, Humidor shadowing her. As Winx hooks around the field, Humidor follows and Happy Clapper heads inland, along the rails. Flindell calls them down the straight:

Gailo Chop tries to kick three lengths clear but Winx is getting into her work . . . and they've broken clear from the rest.

Gailo Chop in front but Winx moves up on the outside.

Winx takes the lead from Gailo Chop. And here's her second Queen Elizabeth!

This is a silver jubilee moment—on the throne for twenty-five consecutive wins to equal the record of the great Black Caviar. Wins it easily.

Bowman eases the mare before the line and raises his fist. His father hugs his mother, who might be blinking back tears. That's their boy.

To Jim and Amanda Bowman, it's doubly miraculous. Winx is a big miracle but that's a given. It's a minor miracle to them that Hugh got to ride her at all.

The miracle is that he fought his way back to race riding after a six-month suspension for a positive drug test in 2002. He was twenty-one and already getting heavy when the axe fell. Instead of skulking and sulking he went to work on cattle stations 'up north'. He came back a more seasoned all-round horseman and a more mature person . . . but also a bigger one.

When the prodigal son returned, his father took one look at him and said quietly he wouldn't be riding in races again. Jim pushes seventy kilograms and Hugh is his father's son.

That frank comment resurrected his son's career. It wasn't meant as a challenge but that's how young Bowman took it. As a spur.

In six months away, he'd grown up. Now he was determined to grow light and that meant big changes. The talented youngster who'd won best country apprentice then best Sydney apprentice had tired of starving off weight. At the same time, race riding had paid him well enough 'to live the dream', as he drily recalls it. Jockeys can't eat and can't drink and they get up far too early to sleep properly. Drugs that suppress appetite and make them feel artificially sharp are illegal but can be hard for hungry youngsters to resist.

But being forced out of racing into manual work gave him clarity. He saw the chances he was wasting. He took expert advice on diet and exercise and turned himself into one of the most dedicated professional sportsmen in the land. He won his first Group One in 2004 then kept going. He made himself into a specialist freelance jockey, mostly riding for smaller stables, trainers like Kris Lees, Joseph Pride and John O'Shea. He did it well and every season a little better.

That's what attracted an emerging small trainer to engage him. His name was Chris Waller and he didn't stay small.

Maybe the two farm boys saw something in each other.

•

Jockeys are tough because they have to be. There are few other occupations where an ambulance turns up to the job.

Take Avelino Gomez, a Cuban who became a Canadian hero. He rode more than 4000 winners at a strike rate of one in four before he died, still game, after a race smash at age fifty-two.

In 1960 a lunatic warned police and racing officials he was going to shoot Gomez on the home turn at Woodbine racecourse. This might have made most people take a day off but not Gomez: you understand, he told the Mounties, I'm riding the best colt in Canada in the Queen's Plate.

On race day, he put his head down lower than usual and tucked the colt into the middle of the pack until he got past the turn. Then he let rip and won, setting a track record.

This tells you something. Jockeys have nerve and the best have nerves of steel. If they didn't they wouldn't be doing it.

James Hugh Bowman is no powder puff. He has earned his share of suspensions for hard riding, doesn't baulk at buck-jumpers or green horses or rogues. He still alarms Waller and his manager and his old master Ron Quinton by jumping on young horses his father is breaking in when he goes home to Dunedoo.

Bowman might be the nearest thing to what old-timers called a 'gentleman rider' in Australian professional jockey ranks, a hangover from the day when owners and breeders had the right to ride their own horses. It's a safe bet he's the only flat rider in the world to have learned to play the bagpipes as a boarder at Scots College.

Jockeys have images. They dubbed the blond Kiwi jockey Shane Dye 'Billy Idol'. They called Mick Dittman 'the Enforcer'. Bowman is more Chips Rafferty: a lightweight horseman and heavyweight jockey who looks born to play the part of a Light Horse trooper with slouch hat, carbine and sabre.

Bowmans have gone to war. Hugh is named after James Hugh Bowman, his grandfather's brother, killed after drawing straws to see which brother would go to war and which would look after the property. Their cousin also went and didn't return.

Our Hugh Bowman lives in Coogee and jets around the horse-speaking world, but his country origins run deep. He often rides work in moleskin pants and Cuban heel boots.

There's another nod to family in his jockey gear. Jockeys have their names printed on their breeches. Bowman has the family stock brand on his gear as well. It's J joined by a horizontal bar to B: registered description 'J bar B'. The bar happens to form an H and makes the brand resemble his three initials run together: JHB.

The brand has been around a while, been on a lot of cattle and horses. The first Bowmans to Australia came on the convict ship *Barwell* in 1798 but not in chains. John and Honor (or Honora) Bowman and their children were the only free settlers aboard. Sir Joseph Banks had secured them free passage because of the Scotsman John Bowman's skill at building corn mills.

When not feuding with John Macarthur and siding with Governor Bligh in the Rum Rebellion, the colonial Bowmans ran up a family flag hand-painted on silk from Honor's wedding dress. It featured an emu and a kangaroo—an idea later borrowed for the national coat of arms, which is why the tattered original Bowman flag is in the Mitchell Library.

The first generation settled at Richmond, then at Jerrys Plains where Coolmore Stud now stands. Their descendants later moved further out. Wherever they went, they took horses. One forebear, James C. Bowman, dropped dead off his horse while riding from Jerrys Plains to Muswellbrook in 1898.

Family legend says that James's pioneer uncle, William Bowman, paid for the property named Merotherie at Dunedoo with a demijohn of rum. It was a good swap. The rum was no doubt drunk but the Bowmans still have Merotherie. They started building the first house in 1823 and bred shorthorn cattle there. Now it's where Jim and Amanda still live and where Hugh grew up, mostly on horseback.

Hugh and sister Kate had a pair of Welsh mountain ponies, Noddy and Scampy. Hugh moved up to a pony mare,

Thumbelina, one of a line of ponies the family has bred for generations. (One of Thumbelina's granddaughters, Tinkerbell, is now ready for Hugh and Christine's little girls.)

As Hugh grew more ambitious, he switched to an all-round performance horse, Simon, and his mother's polocrosse horse, Toinette. He campdrafted, played polocrosse, competed in novelty events such as flag, barrel and bending races, and rode in one-day events. Apart from that, he did stock work on the farm, which he credits with making him an 'instinctive' race rider rather than an overly analytical one. Working cattle and sheep and competing in horse sports sharpened instincts and reflexes that became second nature.

'Holding cattle in a corner while you cut some out, it's an art,' he says of the skill his father passed on through example and practice. 'He wasn't trying to teach me; we just did it. Things had to be done so I did them. It's important to have time to develop like that, just like with a young horse.'

Jim Bowman always bred a galloper or two. He still has one named Free Ticket that descends from a line of non-Stud Book horses bred on the property since the middle of last century, at least. Free Ticket's grandmother was a Bowman homebred, Scottish Emma: Hugh scored his first professional win on her at Gulgong in 1997. His first race ride was the year before, on Go Campese at Mungery Picnics. His first amateur win was on Slatts in the Wellington Picnic Cup soon after.

The boarding-school boy's ability stood out on the picnic circuit and in barrier trials, where he rode on weekends and holidays. Like the young Waller, he was keener on sport than schoolwork and most likely would not stay light enough to ride professionally if he didn't concentrate on it. His parents agreed to apprentice him to Leanne and Billy Aspros at Bathurst, initially combining it with attending a local school. School soon ran second.

Billy Aspros had been a gun country jockey. The first thing he did was hand the Bowman boy a stopwatch and ask him to learn to count to fifteen in exactly fifteen seconds, using the formula 'one red apple, two red apple'. His professional career had begun.

In two years Bowman outrode his 'claim' in the country and became the state's top country apprentice.

He switched to Ron Quinton's stable at Randwick. Quinton had learned his craft from the greatest teacher of apprentices, Theo Green. He'd ridden Kingston Town, Emancipation and four Golden Slipper winners and won six straight jockey premierships. Now he was passing on the knowledge. Bowman is one of five champion apprentices Quinton has moulded. Bowman has never forgotten it, and catches up with Quinton every other week.

Bowman reminds me of a sniper I once saw in Afghanistan, a quiet Digger from Central Queensland who shot a steel picket in half with a series of rifle shots to see if he had his eye in. He'd learned to shoot from the back of a ute as a kid, culling wild pigs, and the skill never deserted him. He was as lean as a rifle barrel with the steady gaze and slow heartbeat of a natural marksman.

Substitute saddles for rifles and there's Bowman. The things he absorbed on horseback as a child became part of him, like another language learned at a young age.

There are race riders as good as Bowman at the hair-trigger business of acrobatics at racing speed, but among his generation of city jockeys there might be no better horseman.

He has the hands and the seat of the rider he was before he got on a tiny racing pad, things he learned literally at his father's knee.

'When Hugh was tiny,' Jim tells a writer, 'I'd put him up on the front of the horse with me and he'd handle the reins, so when he started riding on his own he was quite natural. One time . . . we had him out at a local show and he won boy rider under-five or something. But one of the judges came up to me to say that that little boy had such lovely hands. He was only four.'

Bowman stands out because he still puts his feet most of the way home in the stirrups, the way almost everyone did when he started race riding. The jury is out on whether you make a horse go any faster that way but there are those who swear it is safer if a horse does anything unexpected.

Most modern jockeys insert just the toe of their boot with the stirrup iron turned almost in line with the horse, an overseas fashion brought back by Danny Brereton in the 1990s.

Bowman likes riding hands and heels, not relying on the whip. His younger peers find it old-fashioned, but it hasn't stopped him becoming one of the world's most acclaimed jockeys.

That became official in December 2017 when he was named the world's best jockey, ahead of global stars like Ryan Moore, Frankie Dettori and Joao Moreira. The Australian had in fact ridden nine different horses to win a total of sixteen international Group One races, including the Japan Cup. But there was no doubt which horse had the most to do with it.

The night Bowman stood on the podium in Hong Kong to accept the award, Winx was arriving back at Rosehill from her health farm holiday to prepare for a hat-trick of wins in autumn.

Bowman blinked under the bright lights the way he never does in a race, and deflected attention from himself as he nearly always does out of the saddle. Judging one top jockey from another was impossible, he said, because 'so many variables come into the equation'.

'This year, one of those variables is a horse called Winx.'

It takes another five months for officialdom to catch up with reality and formally anoint her the world's best racehorse, bar none.

24

THE WINX FACTOR

They are questions Hugh Bowman might spend the rest of his life answering. When did you realise she was so good? What's your favourite memory of her?

He thinks about it, the quiet man from Dunedoo who's ridden from Ascot to Japan. He sifts through extraordinary performances when she did what only the great ones can, conjuring a way to win even after giving very good horses a very big start. He thinks about the times when she's had to stop her run and start again, a recovery as unlikely as untangling a parachute in free fall then landing safely.

His head tells him there are other stellar performances; his heart can't ignore the memory of that first Cox Plate.

If they're honest, and a few are, jockeys will tell you there is nothing like the rush of adrenalin, the joy of battle when a horse quickens under you and hits the front with the post coming up fast, knowing you'll get there first. It's a drug.

The memory of that moment at Moonee Valley in 2015 sticks in Bowman's mind as vividly as the birth of a first-born. The first is not better or different or more special than the ones that follow, but the *event* sears itself into the mind.

It was the moment his world tilted a little. This otherwise ordinary-looking young mare was a champion and he was her rider. Every win afterwards just reinforced his belief in her.

The belief was shared by everyone around her. From Umut Odemislioglu and Candice Persijn and Ben Cadden to Chris Waller and his racing manager Charlie Duckworth and Analese Trollope and Jason Brettle the farrier and Olly Koolman at the spelling farm and Doug the float driver. And the others who played a part and quietly exited the stage with a story that will last for life.

Then there are the owners, of course. The ones who bought multiple tickets in an expensive lottery and landed first prize: a twenty-four carat, rolled-gold, once-in-a-lifetime champ.

But what is a champion? More to the point, what makes *this* champion?

Call it the Winx factor.

•

'She's not a show off, not a nervous horse. We just don't know how good she is. Every challenge we put in front of her she copes with.'
Chris Waller before Cox Plate III

•

Every family has secrets. The Winx family has theirs.

One morning in the autumn of 2017, Hugh Bowman arrives at Rosehill to gallop her. It is early enough that Bowman wishes he is still in bed, an understandable thing for a successful heavyweight jockey who can afford anything except to eat: breakfast is fresh air and the prospect of a salad before sundown.

It's the morning after the night before and the world's top jockey isn't feeling on top of the world. He heads onto the course proper, Winx's domain as Queen of Rosehill. He knows how far off the fence to work, because Chris Waller has plotted the course.

Most mornings after trackwork, before Waller starts the second half of his big day, he puts on a tracksuit and jogs around the course. It is the perfect Waller combination of exercise, recreation, work and mental arithmetic. This is not casual jogging: Waller scans the track and veers around to find the best going for Winx's next gallop. Other horses have to stick inside the witches' hats set out by the track manager; Winx goes where Waller thinks she should.

When Winx and Bowman hit the turf this particular morning, it's just dark enough that things are hard to see. The eyesight and reflexes of the world's best jockey aren't as acute as those of the world's best horse, so the mare sees the witch's hat in her way just before Bowman does. An ordinary racehorse might have blundered over the cone or shied to miss it, maybe even throwing the rider.

Winx doesn't deviate. She jumps it at full gallop, like a gazelle.

That fleeting moment, recalls Bowman, is proof of an opinion he already had: he has never ridden a horse with better balance. It's a big statement from someone who grew up riding agile performance horses around cattle, in novelty races and polocrosse tournaments and cross-country jumping. He says she could handle any of those things better than most. Jockeys don't often talk about racehorses in such terms, which tells you something about both horse and rider. They're different.

Winx's agility dazzles Olly Koolman, an unabashed fan who never tires of watching her pre-training and in the paddock. He says she could have been a champion dressage horse, a top show-jumper—or a buckjumper. When he lets her go in her paddock she can put on a rodeo display. But she's so tractable his little children have sat on her to have photographs taken. Another Winx family secret.

People who know a little of horses and take a close look at Winx after seeing her gallop are surprised how deceptively tall she is (16-2 hands as a six-year-old) because she moves so economically, as neat on her feet as a far more compact animal. The way she goes about everything, whether tied up or walking or trotting, has the no-nonsense, seen-it-all efficiency of a smart polo pony or stock horse. People who spend time on horseback dislike 'slugs', or 'doughy' horses, or ones that are fainthearted about tackling a hill or baulk at a jump or crossing water. Riders like horses with Winx's can-do attitude.

'She's all business,' says Bowman. 'I call her a businesswoman.' He seconds Waller's phrase that she 'does everything with purpose', even to the way she 'swims like bloody Dawn Fraser'.

A good temperament can't be learned, even if some tolerance can be instilled through repetition. Plenty of trainee guide dogs and police horses don't make the grade.

In Winx's last spell of pre-training before her spring campaign in 2018, staff at the Hermitage farm were saddling her and the flying filly Unforgotten in the tie-up shed when Olly Koolman fetched a gleaming racing trophy from his car nearby. It caught the light and the reflection flashed across the wall of the shed.

Unforgotten plunged in fright; Winx merely pricked her ears. That unflappable yearling a young girl led around the sales ring so easily five years before has seen plenty of shiny trophies since and doesn't startle much. She might be a star but she's also sensible, with attributes that transcend racing, attributes prized by people since Xenophon wrote about them in his treatise on horses in ancient Greece. Until the advent of the internal combustion motor relatively recently, the difference between a good horse and a bad one could be life and death.

A century ago a mount with Winx's attributes would have been a superb cavalry charger, eating her grain ration under artillery fire or jumping trenches with bullets whistling, the way another Australian thoroughbred mare, Midnight, did at Beersheba in 1917.

Before her Light Horseman owner took her to war, Midnight had proved herself the supreme all-rounder that Bowman says he sees in Winx. She could sprint and stay and play polo and shoulder a bullock. Before she died from a Turkish bullet as she raced ahead and leapt the trenches at Beersheba, Midnight and her rider Guy Haydon had won every competition in the 'Desert Olympics' against the best of the British cavalry in Egypt.

The Haydons, like the Bowmans and the Wallers, have always loved and valued the animal and they still do.

Like Winx, Midnight was bred in the Hunter Valley, nursery of the Australian bloodhorse. Like Winx, she was willing to do whatever she was asked and she excelled at it, and a horse can do no more. A pure heroine.

•

'She just has an attitude where she wants to win. She has the will to win—and the ability to match it.'

Jason Collett, winning rider in Winx's first two races

•

Chris Waller and his racing manager Charlie Duckworth have a secret, too. It involves the timing of gallops.

Because of the angle of sight from the Rosehill trainers' tower, they adjust stopwatch times to account for the optical illusion that a horse is passing a distance marker well before it actually does. To compensate, they add two seconds to every gallop, which reflects accurately how every horse is going in the final 400 metres of its pacework.

When Winx galloped on the Tuesday before the 2018 Queen Elizabeth Stakes, Waller walked over to the winning post so he could hear the mare breathing as she passed, while Duckworth watched from the tower with binoculars and electronic stopwatches.

As soon as Winx passed the post, Waller was curious about how fast she was going. He called Duckworth and asked him for the adjusted time for the 400 metres. When Duckworth replied,

Chris Waller and his maternal grandfather Don Johnston, who passed away when Chris was five. WALLER FAMILY

Trying the jockey crouch: young Chris on galloper Totara Park with his dad John Waller in the late 1970s. WALLER FAMILY

Chris at four with his paternal grandfather Colin Waller, 1978. WALLER FAMILY

Chris at ten years in 1984, coaching his latest entrant in the calf club competition. WALLER FAMILY

Chris at fifteen with Our Lillee, which he helped educate. WALLER FAMILY

RIGHT: Chris and his puppy, 1984. WALLER FAMILY

BELOW: Blue ribbon event: embryonic trainer with one of his first winners. WALLER FAMILY

ABOVE: Chris's mother Marilyn Waller holds the cherished picture of her late father and young Chris on the Fergie tractor. ROBERT McLAREN

LEFT: Signed boots and some Winx memorabilia. ROBERT McLAREN

Chris's father John Waller at home near Palmerston North, 2018. ROBERT McLAREN

LEFT: Hugh at four in his father Jim's jockey gear. BOWMAN FAMILY

BELOW: Hugh at rest with his favourite pony mare Thumbelina during a one-day event. BOWMAN FAMILY

Hugh Bowman's first day as a professional apprentice jockey, a long way from Royal Randwick. BOWMAN FAMILY

Renewing acquaintance with the family rocking horse. BOWMAN FAMILY

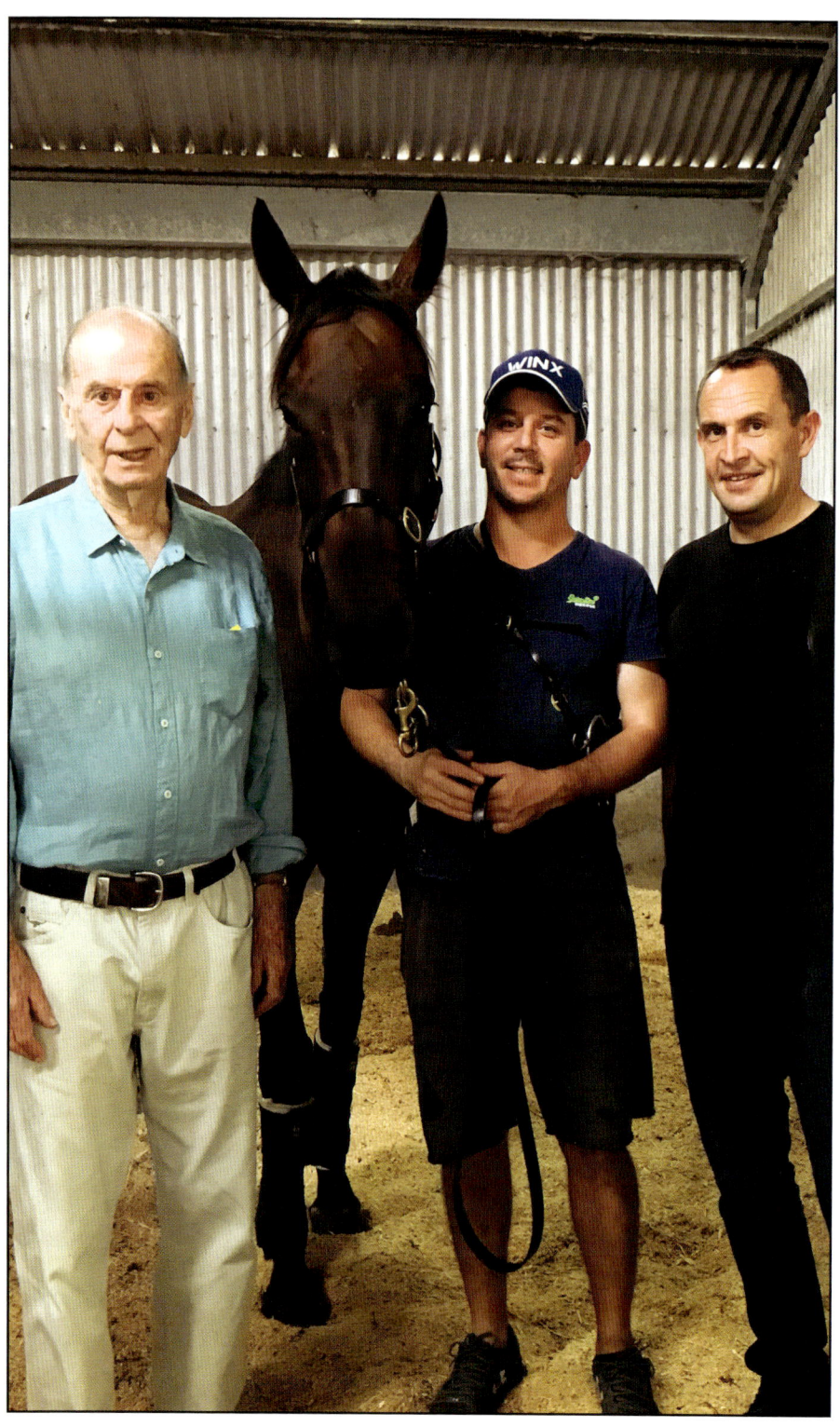

Winx with (from left) Richard Treweeke, strapper Umut Odemislioglu and Chris Waller at Chris Waller Racing, Rosehill. TREWEEKE FAMILY

Debbie Kepitis, Richard Treweeke and Peter Tighe with Juan-Carlos Capelli, Vice President of Longines, at the presentation for the 2017 Longines Queen Elizabeth Stakes. LISA GRIMM

Richard Treweeke leads Winx back to scale after the 2016 George Main Stakes. LISA GRIMM

Peter and Patty Tighe with Winx. PETER TIGHE

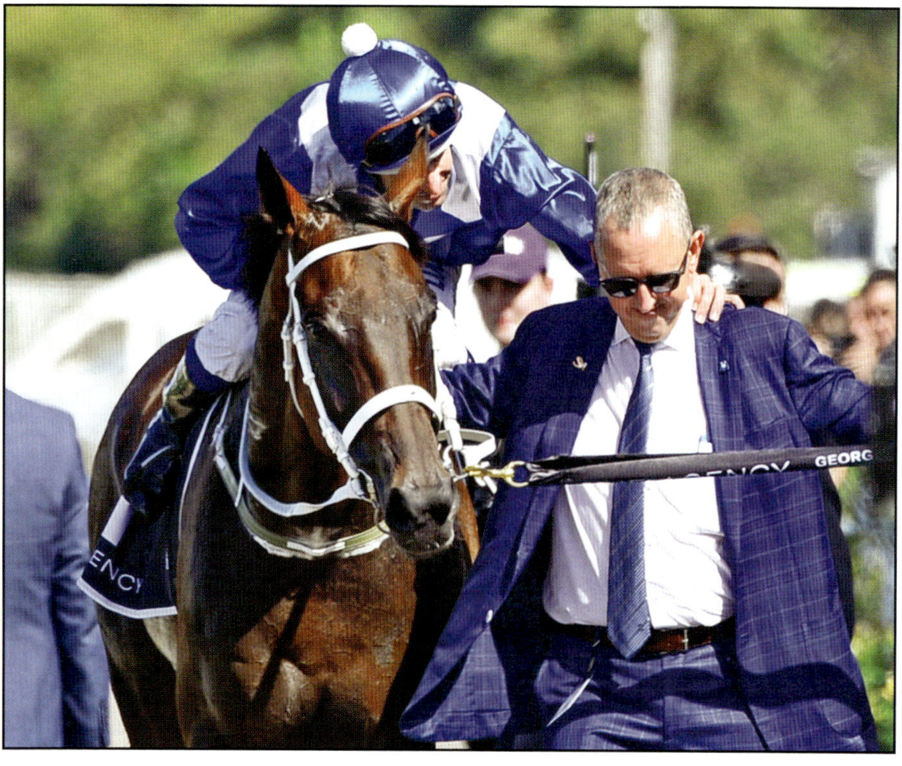

Peter Tighe leads Winx after the 2018 George Ryder, her twenty-fourth consecutive win.
LISA GRIMM

Another spring, another Cox Plate (left to right): Patty Tighe, Debbie Kepitis, Umut Odemislioglu and Paul Kepitis front a media conference the day after her third. BRONWEN HEALY PHOTOGRAPHY

Chris and Stephanie Waller and their children Tyler and Nikita, with Peter and Patty Tighe at the 2017 Chelmsford Stakes. LISA GRIMM

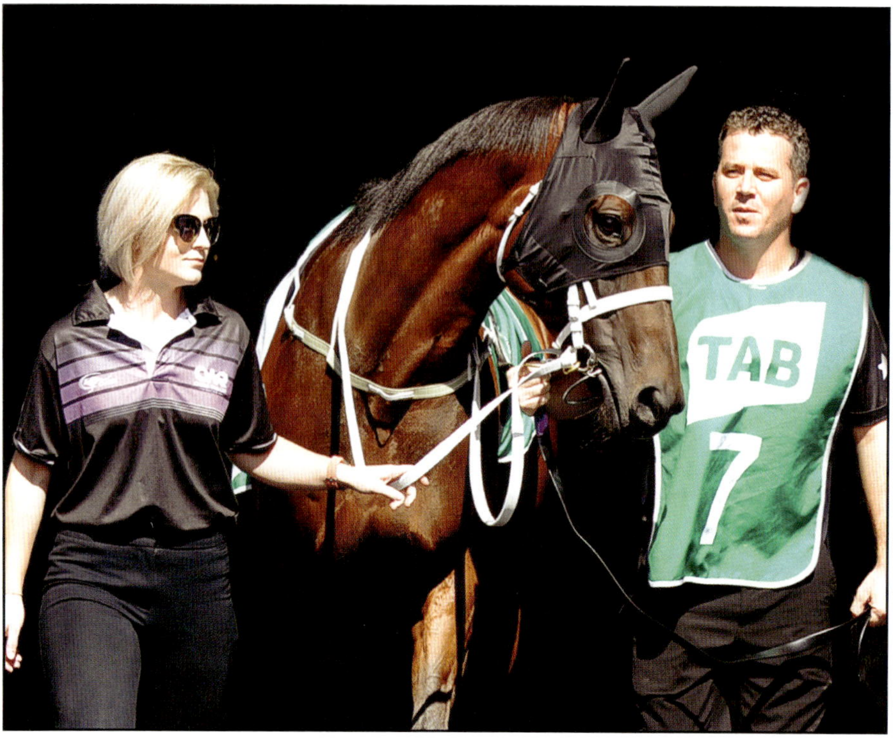

Umut and Winx's day-to-day minder Candice Persijn lead Winx at the 2018 Chipping Norton Stakes. LISA GRIMM

The one-off souvenir rug says it all: WINXXVI . . . 26 in a row. Winx Stakes, 18 August 2018. BRONWEN HEALY PHOTOGRAPHY

The lens captures the shared joy of owner, rider and the man who calls himself Winx's coach. BRONWEN HEALY PHOTOGRAPHY

Winx with the Rosehill staff the day before she went for a spell following her 2018 Queen Elizabeth Stakes victory. CHRIS WALLER RACING

The Winx team with Australia Post's commemorative stamp, celebrating her record-breaking twenty-sixth consecutive win at the 2018 Winx Stakes. DAVID SWIFT/AUSTRALIA POST

Champion horse and champion trainer: Bronwen Healy's flawless study of man and beast before the second Cox Plate in 2016. BRONWEN HEALY PHOTOGRAPHY

Waller was disbelieving. 'Haven't you added the two seconds?' he asked.

That's when Duckworth told him it wasn't a mistake: Winx had 'broken twenty-one' for 400 metres 'on the bit' in an unaccompanied workout.

There are specialist quarterhorse sprinters in America that run those times but they faint before they get to 600 metres. Black Caviar ran that fast to set a race record in the 2013 Lightning Stakes, but usually didn't have to because nothing could keep up with her.

A tricky Victorian sprinter named Lord Of The Sky could run sectionals that fast on the track, sustaining it in races just often enough to earn more than $1 million in stakes and a place on the stallion roster at Kingstar Farm in the Hunter Valley. He was no Black Caviar but a slashing type with eye-watering speed over short distances.

Those comparisons underline what Winx did on that Tuesday. No horse had worked that fast at Rosehill in living memory, let alone a middle-distance specialist lining up over 2000 metres that week, and undoubtedly capable of running farther.

So it was no wonder Bowman called Duckworth from his car afterwards and asked, 'How quick was I?' He whistled at the answer. He knew she had gone fast but, with Winx, it was hard to tell exactly how fast because she makes it feel normal.

When Duckworth went to the Queen Elizabeth barrier draw that day, he was asked how Winx had worked. He kept the answer general. He didn't want to mislead anyone but there were two problems with publishing the time she'd run.

The first was that some people would think he was mistaken or exaggerating. And if she happened to be beaten then or later, Waller and Bowman would be blamed for overworking her and 'leaving it on the track'. Just one more pressure when you're training a national treasure with a million 'owners', every one a critic.

Sports coaches say 'you can't put in what God left out'. Winx's inbuilt speed, agility and temperament make a rare athlete more extraordinary. Training doesn't really improve those attributes, although it can easily spoil them. But a trainer *does* try to enhance stamina and strength: conditioning a horse to extend racing pace a little longer is as good a definition of training as any.

With Winx, Waller started with a naturally strong animal, though she didn't look it until she was five. The jockey Kerrin McEvoy's observation that she feels as 'level as a billiard table' because of her core strength would chime with coaches of athletes of all sorts.

A wise senior football coach (and longtime schoolteacher) once told me he'd never coached a champion player, regardless of size or position played, who wasn't naturally strong for his weight. Not gym-swollen muscle but the lean strength of the born athlete, the sort a tomcat has and a guinea pig hasn't.

It's a given in professional sport that the best are hard to beat at anything they try: the Test batsman who plays golf off scratch and wins money at tennis or squash or poker is barely worth remarking on.

Innate coordination, strength, reflexes and competitiveness are as much part of the elite player's character as custom-made bats or racquets are part of his or her kit. Horses are a little the same. As the late George Hanlon once said, they are 'only human', and George won three Melbourne Cups.

There is one difference between horses and humans: the modern thoroughbred is so closely related to its tens of thousands of cousins that the potential for differing ability falls into a surprisingly narrow band. An average galloper running fifth at a bush race meeting is far closer to a Group One stablemate than the average fun runner is to an Olympian.

Any racehorse worthy of the name achieves what Americans call the 'twelve-clip', the yardstick racing pace on which race-winning performances are built, and which has hardly changed in a century.

The young horse is first accustomed to rating 'even-time' of fifteen seconds to the 'furlong' (200 metres) on the track until it can get down to twelve-second bursts over that distance. Then it has to graft stamina onto the speed until it can sustain that racing pace for 800 metres—preferably farther, if it is actually going to win races.

Each additional 200 metres at 'twelves' is exponentially harder: most racehorses can run 800 metres in forty-eight seconds but only good ones sustain that pace for 1600 metres and only the exceptional come anywhere near it at 2000 metres.

Northern Dancer, Napoleon of modern racehorses, set a record of two minutes flat for the Kentucky Derby in 1964, running with the help of the then banned drug, Lasix. This stood until the phenomenal Secretariat broke it in 1973—the landmark performance of an era that was later described by a few brave American breeders as the height of chemically enhanced Derby winners.

In Australia, middle-distance horses tend to 'sit and sprint', coasting slightly in the middle sections of races before quickening around 800 metres from home. Sectional times taken for the final 600 metres of races suggest that most horses produce their best at the business end of the race, though many fade in the last 100 metres.

The difference between the best horses and those finishing behind them is that the best run harder for longer—'hitting the line' while the others die in their run. Top horses are not necessarily *faster* over a short distance—but they have the 'heart', or lungs, or willpower, to gallop at peak speed a few seconds longer. Above this elite are the few freaks of nature whose peak is faster than the rest without losing stamina.

Winx is the rarest of combinations: she can sustain a high cruising speed then 'go through her gears' to produce a sustained run that climaxes with a finish as fast as a sprinter would in a shorter race. When called on to counter a poor start or to dodge a scrimmage, she can run world-beating times at the end of a middle-distance race.

Waller likens her to Usain Bolt winning at 800 metres instead of 100. He and Bowman and the owners think if she were trained specifically for either task, she could win the Newmarket Handicap, Australia's elite 1200-metre sprint, or the Melbourne Cup over 3200 metres. Not that they would exploit her bravery just to prove she could 'play out of position'.

The belief she could sprint or stay against the best doesn't faze people well placed to know. No one laughed when Lee Freedman said he could have prepared his triple Melbourne Cup winner Makybe Diva to 'win a Newmarket'. There is plenty of evidence, not all of it public, that Winx is faster than Makybe Diva ever was, although the jury is out on what would happen if they met over 3200 metres—surely the theoretical clash of the millennial era.

Speed is vital to the thoroughbred but without some stamina— enough to win at 1000 metres or more—it loses relevance because it has nowhere to go. Racing is littered with forgotten 'speedy squibs'. Bowman recalls riding a faster horse than Winx, a mare named Fantene. He says she would have won against Winx over 800 metres, 'but, even over 1000, Winx would have her covered'.

As for the hypothetical proposition of running Winx at either end of her specialty distances (world-class sprint or a Melbourne Cup), Bowman says neither will happen. But he's a sports fan and knows other sports fans can't resist speculating.

'I'd prefer to see her at two miles than at 1200 metres. You'd see a better horse at two miles. She'd switch off and win. But once you push a horse too much, they won't do it again. They'll only do it once.'

•

'Winx is just another good type to look at—you see a hundred like her—but she's a Lexus body with a V-12 motor.'

Trainer and commentator Richard Freedman

•

In the saddle, Bowman and day-to-day track rider Ben Cadden know Winx better than anyone. Their admiration is total but tempered by the experience of riding other good horses and plenty of lesser ones. Bowman points out, for instance, that Winx's busy action can be 'unattractive' on firm tracks, which make her 'choppy' compared with the smoother effect when 'there is a bit of cut out of the ground'.

As Waller puts it, when the ground has some give she 'just flows out onto the track'.

Most top horses lower their bodies and extend their stride when they are striving their hardest. But Winx is different: she cranks up the beat, like a drummer.

This is her trademark. She doesn't extend stride the way most of the great ones did—like Black Caviar and Saintly and Sunline and Phar Lap—she 'revs' faster, like a bike-track racer who pedals a fixed gear more quickly, whereas a road cyclist labours to push a higher gear with a slower pedal rate.

Some might say she's like an Olympic rower who maintains the same length of stroke in the water but lifts the rate without getting ragged. Bike riders call it 'cadence', and it underpins the Winx factor. This is not some airy assertion—a university professor has gone to the trouble of proving it.

Dr Graeme Putt was born the year after Bernborough was and recalls hearing the great champion's last race in the late 1940s. He grew up in country Victoria infected by the family weakness for racing. Riding around Benalla on his bike collecting bets for the local SP bookie didn't hurt his schoolwork. Young Putt won scholarships to university and combined his love of physics and racing.

After Secretariat won the 1973 Triple Crown, he was the Muhammad Ali of horseflesh. Putt was setting exam questions for university engineering students and used Secretariat's performances to create a physics question.

He would later write about the physics of performances by Phar Lap, Sunline and Black Caviar. In fact, he co-wrote a definitive account of Phar Lap's life that strips out myths in favour of facts, a strictly non-fiction approach that is a novelty in sports books.

Because Putt reduces a horse's performance to a physics exercise—using measurable elements like mass, velocity and stride length—he comes up with scientifically valid conclusions. He concludes, for example, that Black Caviar's supposedly 'worst' performance at Royal Ascot was actually outstanding because her large body mass works against her hugely in an uphill finish. It's all in the arithmetic.

A reporter who saw Putt's Black Caviar analysis pestered him to 'do the physics' on Winx. He studied slow-motion replays of the 2017 Ryder Stakes with a stopwatch and counted how many strides she took. He was surprised to find her galloping action differs from that of most champions, who tend to have a longer than average stride. Winx puts in fourteen strides where most horses put in twelve.

For the benefit of this book, Professor Putt measured step by step the actual distance travelled by each horse in the 2017 Cox Plate. It showed Winx was far better than suggested by her relatively slim winning margin over Humidor.

He calculates that Bowman's take-no-chances wide ride covered 2074 metres, 'while Shinn gave Humidor a comparatively dream run covering just 2066 metres'. The extra eight metres Winx covered adds up to a winning margin of nearly four metres over Humidor if they'd raced beside each other on a straight course over the same distance. As it was, Winx equalled her own track record. But if she'd run exactly the same distance as Humidor, she would have smashed the record by another half a second.

Putt concludes: 'Suffice to say it was another extraordinary performance and feather in the cap for Winx's record, rather than a close call (à la Black Caviar at Ascot). Humidor had everything going for him but still the luckless wonder-girl prevailed.'

He stresses his calculations are analytical, not predictive. But he believes Winx's true ability is often hidden by Bowman's cagey belt-and-braces tactics.

This must have been sobering news for those betting that the weight of history should beat Winx in a fourth Cox Plate. But it also places immense responsibility on Bowman's split-second reading of a race. So far, results suggest he is the man for the job.

•

'People are coming to the races not to see her race but to see her win. She defies the odds every time and that gets harder and harder for Chris and Hughie Bowman.'

Winx farrier Jason Brettle

•

Bowman rightly credits Winx as the 'variable' that has earned him the title of world's best jockey. Waller can't help but believe the reverse might have some truth, too: that Winx needs Bowman's head, hands and heels to steer her clear of the trouble that could torpedo her winning streak. This entered his calculations more and more as the streak lengthened and tension mounted.

The easy-going days of whistling up another good rider as a locum in 2015 became a 'variable' Waller wouldn't contemplate by 2018. Prolonged success had shaved the Winx training formula to its simplest components and Bowman was one of them, one leg of a three-legged stool.

Waller stuck religiously to what had worked before in the belief it would work in future. Replication of trips to and from the spelling paddock and the first trials of each preparation and first-up races had become a ritual: the Ground Hog Day principle. He was careful not to ask too much or to break the rhythm of the familiar.

At one level, a matchless racehorse and a nameless dairy cow are both creatures of habit, and the good livestock man never forgets that. Keep them content and they will keep producing.

Meanwhile, a wise jockey can't afford to rely on eggs in one basket any more than a trainer can. A champion is still a horse, and horses can go wrong any time and, in any case, they have a use-by date. Bowman has to ride other horses in other races because that's what he does, and with as much desperation as ever.

That's why, within weeks of being 'crowned', the world's best jockey was rubbed out for seven meetings for careless riding at Warwick Farm on Australia Day. An annoyance turned into a millstone when he collected another careless riding charge at the Karaka Million meeting in Auckland next day. Even racing royalty has to cop it sweet, a point Bowman stoically conceded after losing an appeal that might have made life much easier.

Instantly, Bowman's back-to-back suspension became Waller's problem. With both penalties appeal-proof, Bowman would not only miss fifteen meetings but he also wouldn't be able to ride Winx in her planned return, the Apollo Stakes on 17 February 2018.

Straight after the Karaka incident, there was much speculation about who would replace Bowman in the race, but Waller dodged the debate. He was already mulling over alternatives, and within a week had made up his mind. No Bowman, no race.

If Winx had been trained or owned by people understandably keen to win easy stakes money, then any one of several top-class jockeys could and would have been called in.

The reliable McEvoy, Cox Plate runner-up Blake Shinn or Bowman's friend Corey Brown were just three among many able riders a phone call away.

Waller killed the speculation and scratched Winx from the race. He and the owners could afford not to take the chance of breaking the streak.

Waller explained his reasoning to his office manager, Sophie Baker, in the form of a question.

'Would we race Winx if there was something wrong with her?'

'No.'

'Well, there *is* something wrong,' he said. 'Hughie always rides her but he can't this time. So she won't run.'

He already had the answer. The race club, aghast at the great drawcard's threatened absence, was delighted to approve a full-blooded 'trial' in prime time between races. It was as near to a race as it gets, without betting and stakes money, and overshadowed the rest of the card.

The gallop underlined Waller's dominance of Sydney racing. He was able to field five top-level horses to give Winx quality competition in a competitive gallop over 1200 metres.

She ran a faster time than the winner of the Group Three 1200-metre race run half an hour later. And, as it happened, Waller still won the Apollo Stakes that day with an imported horse, Endless Drama, who needed a good win to make it as a stallion. Clouds and silver linings.

•

'She's not a horse that behaves with any sort of presence—the aura has developed because of her success.'

Hugh Bowman

•

The wise warn against comparing the great. Les Carlyon, master writer about horses and people, quotes master trainer Bart Cummings: 'Celebrate champions, don't compare them.'

Comparisons are pointless but they are also inevitable. Racing runs on comparisons, the differences of opinion that lead optimists to pay fortunes for yearlings or huge service fees for fashionable new sires.

William Nack, Secretariat's best biographer, writes: 'Horse-men have always been loath to compare horses from different eras, seeing any attempt to do so as a diverting but futile exercise.'

He's right, it's diverting. As for futile, very little about racing isn't. At least Lord Derby and his fellow 'sports' could argue two centuries ago they were improving the breed of cavalry mounts and coach horses and hunters. That excuse has vanished: race-horses are now random changeable parts in an international casino, not a superior means of transport on which life might depend on the battlefield or in bandit country.

It might be pointless to compare this or that 'greatest' across the generations: Tyson with Ali with Louis, Spitz with Phelps. But people can't resist it. They want to know if a crocodile could whip a polar bear, too.

Champions of different eras are locked in their own time capsules but the impulse to sort them into a hierarchy is irresist-ible for armchair experts. Heroes vary but hero worship doesn't.

The thoroughbred horse has been around more than three centuries. If Winx isn't yet carved into the Mt Rushmore of all-time greats, she has earned the right to be mentioned with them.

Secretariat is the standard against which modern racehorses are judged. 'His only point of reference is himself,' decreed the venerable American racing writer Charles Hatton, whose memory ranged back to Seabiscuit's legendary grandsire Man o' War after World War I.

For half a century Hatton insisted Man o' War was the greatest American racehorse, then he saw Secretariat as a raw two-year-old and anointed him 'the greatest I have ever seen': a brilliant forecast of what the colt would become.

They called the big chestnut 'the horse God built'. When his trainer's son Roger Laurin watched him burst through the pack like a quarterback in an early race, he yelled: 'He's too much horse! They can't stop him!' And they couldn't.

Secretariat had shoulders like a buffalo bull and an extra layer of muscle down his hind legs. He dominated an era of American racing some might call the peak of performance-enhancement.

Drugs did not make Secretariat fast, or the best colt of his time—he was already both—but he didn't always win. When he did win, he was sometimes unbelievably dominant, coming out of the gate like Superman from his telephone box. Other times, he was just plenty better than the rest.

He was trained by a man who'd been branded a cheat as a jockey—banned for using a battery 'jigger' to shock horses—and who enjoyed electrifying success when he returned to training in the drug-soaked 1970s.

His name was Lucien Laurin and he was unusually lucky. In 1972 he won two legs of the Triple Crown with a lightly built horse named Riva Ridge, whose form crumbled after his three-year-old year. The next season Laurin trained Secretariat for the same owner, Penny Chenery, to win the 1973 Kentucky Derby in record time. He ran each 'quarter' (400 metres) faster than the one before it, an unheard-of feat never repeated since.

Secretariat's most jaw-dropping performance was winning the Belmont Stakes by thirty-one lengths. In retrospect, it was reminiscent of athletes (horse and human) now suspected of being drugged to the eyeballs. There was the shameful case of Rocket Racer, who 'did a Secretariat' by rocketing streets ahead of the field in the 1987 Perth Cup, only to collapse afterwards, almost certainly from the effects of the deadly stimulant etorphine, alias 'elephant juice'. Rocket Racer died after one more race, the same year a horse owned by the Aga Khan was disqualified from the Breeders Cup after testing positive to the same drug.

Like Riva Ridge, who died prematurely of a heart attack, Secretariat was a disappointment at stud despite getting superior mares. Some trainers seemed to produce winners that never quite recovered from the experience and did not pass on superior genes. And not just in America.

Fans get upset at such things, of course. Cycling fans didn't want to believe Lance Armstrong used a truckload of illegal chemicals to win seven straight Tours de France.

Whether Secretariat's more far-fetched performances were drug-enhanced or not, one thing is a $1.05 certainty: Winx's are not. A physics professor might one day calculate if her best times, adjusted and projected over the Kentucky Derby distance, could rival those of Secretariat and her ancestor Northern Dancer.

Regardless of a fourth Cox Plate, Winx has eclipsed every Australasian champion in history. No horse is ever going to be asked to do what Phar Lap and Tulloch were asked to, and so she won't repeat their unrepeatable feats. No trainer would now be allowed to run a horse four times in a week, as Phar Lap did when he won the 1930 Melbourne Cup and three other big races.

Phar Lap could beat the best local stayers then back up and do it again; it was like Bradman playing district cricket. He did not have to beat international horses the way he now would. It's safe to say Winx would toy with the fields Phar Lap, Tulloch and Bernborough beat.

Of modern Australian champions, Kingston Town is the obvious comparison, and she has overshadowed that wonderful animal. Overseas, Street Cry's other outstanding daughter Zenyatta doesn't rate, because most of her nineteen straight wins were against fillies or mares.

The English wonder, Frankel, was a stallion of speed and brute power comparable with Secretariat except that Frankel excelled over a mile on soft turf and Secretariat over ten furlongs or a mile and a half on fast dirt.

Unlike Secretariat, Frankel was never beaten and bore no suspicion of drug enhancement—although, ironically, he was named after an American trainer, the late Bobby Frankel, whose reputation is not exactly spotless. Frankel the horse's record stands alone not because of its length but because he beat the best of his generation in Europe with such arrogant ease.

It would take a wildly patriotic Anzac to argue Winx would have beaten Frankel at his best, especially over his pet distance of a mile. The stopwatch is a lousy means of comparison between different racecourses, let alone different hemispheres, but times suggest Winx might have tested the English champion over her pet Cox Plate distance more than any horse he met.

Meanwhile, she has 'outstayed' him. Frankel was retired after his fourteen straight wins, so Winx shades him on longevity, almost doubling his number of consecutive wins and greatly exceeding his stakes won and number of Group One horses beaten.

In this respect, she is more like a half-forgotten heroine of the horse world.

•

'We will look back on this as a golden age of horse racing. Sea The Stars, Frankel, Treve and Winx . . . these horses stack up against any in history.'

Martin Wickins, racing historian

•

Winx's one flaw, the one that could get her beaten by a lesser animal any time she races, is her barrier manners. Some horses leave the gate as if they are escaping a burning barn, Winx not so much.

In this she is like one of the greatest mares of history, perhaps overlooked in the English-speaking world because she was foaled in Hungary in 1874. Kincsem won fifty-four races straight (a handful by walkover) in five countries, including England. Like Winx, she was leggy and narrow and was prized for galloping ability, not looks. Lifelike paintings and drawings of her show a greyhound of a mare: a long, lean liver chestnut with no false muscles, much like Winx.

Kincsem's party trick was to mooch away from the start, sometimes chewing a mouthful of grass, giving the field a start before mowing it down at will. She won ten times as a two-year-old and raced for four seasons before going to stud. When she died of colic at thirteen, Hungarian newspapers edged their pages in black, flags flew at half-mast, and it was reported all over the world. There is a full-size statue of her in Kincsem Park near the Kincsem Museum in Budapest, and another in the United States.

Kinscem won from 900 metres to 3200 metres, although mostly the middle distances that Winx favours. Unlike almost all champion mares, she left behind stock that produced classic winners. But it was her versatility that suggests another comparison for Winx, with a horse remembered as Australia's greatest all-rounder.

Around the time Kincsem finished racing, a handsome bay colt was foaled in Tasmania in 1879. Like Winx, he won as a two-year-old. He was sold to the mainland for the big price of 500 guineas. He was worth it.

Re-named Malua, he won Australia's premier sprints, the Newmarket Handicap and the Oakleigh Plate of 1884, carrying big weights. After winning the Spring Stakes in Sydney the same year, he ran in the Caulfield Cup and showed enough form to run in the Melbourne Cup, which he won handily. Two days later he won a top-class sprint, the Flying Stakes.

Malua made a comeback in 1886 and won the Australian Cup. Two years later, as an aged horse, he won the Grand National Hurdle. He didn't try pole vaulting but did the next best thing—combining hurdling with standing at stud until he was ten years old.

No modern racehorse is ever going to be set so many tasks, but those who ride Winx have no doubt she is the sort that might handle it.

Anyone looking for patterns and similarities with other great ones will find them—in conformation and pedigree and any of the traits that distinguish one horse from another. Because thoroughbreds are so closely related, many share family resemblances that have little bearing on their galloping ability.

Nineteen of every twenty racehorses descend from probably the greatest progenitor of the breed after his ancestor the Darley Arabian. He was foaled in 1764, his name was Eclipse and he was racing's first and greatest superstar. Because Eclipse became a global hero, contemporary accounts are detailed. He was a leggy yearling who grew tall for the time—a now average size of around 16 hands—but was close to being gelded as a youngster because of his plain looks.

One observer noted: 'His hindquarters and croup appeared higher than his forehand; and in his gallop it was said no horse ever threw his haunches with greater effect, his agility and stride being on a par, from his fortunate conformation in every part and his uncommon strength.' Like Winx.

Portraits show him as long-necked, running with his head down. And he 'breathed loud and hard in his exercise'. Like Winx, whose low head carriage in a race can easily be picked at a distance and whose breathing can be heard at early trackwork before she can be seen.

As Eclipse galloped hard and low, someone wrote, his jockey sat motionless and never drew the whip. They could almost be describing Bowman on Winx.

When Waller's senior vet Tim Roberts inspected Winx as a yearling, he noted the way she was shaped 'like an arrow head'—her hindquarters being much broader than her front. Her heart and lung room came from her deep girth, not a wide chest. One description of Eclipse says you could 'wheel a barrow' between his hind legs when he moved.

Eclipse was as phenomenal in his day as Secretariat or Man o' War in theirs, and passed down his blend of speed and stamina to create the modern thoroughbred. He was, one historian noted, the Adam of his tribe. And he had many Eves.

When experts measured his skeleton, which is preserved in an English museum, they built a picture of a horse that by modern standards seems average in every way. Except, of course, for the bit no one could see. The will to win.

Eclipse is the first immortal racehorse and for that reason probably the greatest. In more than two centuries, only a handful of others have got near it.

As these words go to print, Winx's claim on immortality is a work in progress. She is being prepared for her fourth Cox Plate, sticking to the template that has worked before. History says she can't win. Sentiment says she can.

A spring preparation begins in winter. By August her coat is dappled, her eye is bright, those who know her best say she has never looked better or stronger.

Two days out from her return in the race they've re-named in her honour, she looks pin sharp after galloping at Rosehill. She stalks around the lawn easily, pausing here and there, ears pricked, to stare at something that catches her eye in the distance. Still, no one can be sure what will happen 'first up'. Caution says if she's ever going to be vulnerable, it will be when resuming over

1400 metres against a brilliant young horse like Kementari, the pride of Godolphin. After all, she's seven now . . .

Doubts linger right up until she rounds the turn at Randwick and straightens. Until then, it seems Kementari might make a fight of the Winx Stakes. But when she gets balanced and lifts the tempo, he melts. She wins her twenty-sixth straight, taking Black Caviar's record. She's back, as dominant as at any time since the streak began.

These things can change in a split-second, with accident or injury. Or, come spring, the invisible thing, the will to win, might trickle away. It happens. It's just a matter of when.

At some point a horse wants to be a horse more than to be a racehorse. She earned that right long ago. But while she is still up on the tightrope with the crowd cheering, it's hard to look away.

Afterword

William Nack of Secretariat fame runs a photo finish with my friend and mentor Les Carlyon in writing about horses and people.

Like Les, newspaperman turned author and historian, the young Nack broke into the sports pages after following more 'serious' pursuits, in his case after an editor saw him recite every winner of the Kentucky Derby from 1875. Nack was covering politics but his boss thought his talents were wasted. He made him racing writer, as an afterthought asking him for an 'application' letter.

Nack's reply included the line: 'After covering politicians for the last four years, I'd love the chance to cover the whole horse.' A year later Secretariat hit the track and Nack began the ride of his life. He never covered politics again.

Les Carlyon writes superbly about anything, but carried a torch for racing. On Winx, he gave me a little of the advice I have prized (and prised) from him all my working life:

> You've got two great themes: Winx in the foreground, and in the background the mad, capricious, addictive thing they call the racing 'industry'. As the publisher said to Tolstoy: 'Don't just do war, Leo. Do peace as well.'

That's Les. He wears his knowledge lightly, shares it generously, and I am one of many who owe him much. This work is dedicated to him.

A book is like a choir: it has many voices and each is needed to make the song. But without the drive and initiative of Winx's owners and trainer, Chris Waller, this one would not have happened. They backed it, did what they could to help and didn't put up roadblocks. They answered questions and pointed out the cast of characters who played a part in the story of the skinny foal that became the world's greatest galloper.

There is no hierarchy here but Chris Waller is first among equals. The story of his rise was remarkable before Winx came along but will now always be entwined with her. It says a lot for Waller that his parents, sister, aunts, and former employers and present employees speak so affectionately of him. So do the owners Peter and Patty Tighe, Debbie Kepitis and Richard Treweeke, who shared their own 'back stories' with warmth and frankness. There are also those who needn't have helped but cheerfully did, sharing stories never fully told before.

There's John Corcoran with his tale of breeding Winx's mother in New Zealand; the mercurial John Camilleri, who bought Vegas Showgirl and bred Winx; Camilleri's bloodstock adviser, the irrepressible 'wrong O'Brien', Peter, who was a joy to deal with. He shares that with Olly Koolman, who with his wife Karen and staff, looks after Winx at her 'country retreat' many months of the year.

There are citizens of 'Wallerland', starting with Stephanie Waller and Sophie Baker. Stephanie is a model partner in life and in business. Sophie set up key interviews with the efficiency of someone who could run the prime minister's office. The others are scattered through the story. Tim Boland, master breaker. Umut Odemislioglu, who delayed returning to Turkey as a trainer so he could stay with Winx. Ben Cadden, the track rider who has ridden the best here and overseas but never a better one. Candice Persijn, Winx's self-styled 'PA and dresser'. Jason Brettle, the friendly farrier. Analese Trollope, who has admired only one other horse as much: the one she rode 160 kilometres in the Quilty Cup endurance ride. Vets Tim Roberts and Ross Alexander, and the stable's business manager Liam Prior. Racing manager Charlie Duckworth, who timed Winx doing some low flying. Larry Cassidy, who started the streak. Jason Collett, in the saddle for Winx's first two wins.

Hugh Bowman, embarrassed to be called the world's best jockey, was happy to talk with absolute honesty about riding the world's best horse, a partnership that could yet prove the most enduring in racing history. Hugh's parents Amanda and Jim are proof that Hugh has pedigree on his side. There is the 'ring-in':

Martin Wickins, who flies from Toronto to watch Winx's every race. And Dr Graeme Putt, who graphs precisely how good she is.

Andrew 'Fast' Eddy and Matt 'Slow' Stewart read the draft for errors. Danny Power, Shelley Hancox and Tony Carter-Smith answered stupid questions. My oldest friend Rob McLaren drove me around New Zealand to find people and places like the champion he is. Bruce McAvaney stepped up with a foreword worthy of the greatest horse he has ever seen.

Andrew Rule
August 2018

Dear Andy,

A thought for the book:

Watching Winx last Saturday I was struck by something that may be a factor in her greatness, and something I should have noticed before. She never pulls, or even leans on the bit. She jumps and straight away relaxes on what is often close to a loose rein. She saves everything for one long run from the back of the field. Very few racehorses can relax like this. Most jump and immediately start fighting the bit. I think Winx could win at two miles, simply because she settles so easily and saves everything for the last three furlongs.

Best, Les

Appendix 1

VITAL STATISTICS

Horse	Head length (in.)	Girth (in.)	Below knee (in.)	Hip to hock (in.)	Hock to fetlock (in.)	Height (hands)
Ajax	32	73	9.5	42	18	16-1
Bernborough	27	72	9	40	18	17
Phar Lap	29	79	9	42	18.5	17-1
Secretariat	N/A	76	N/A	40	N/A	16-2
WINX	**27.5**	**76**	**8.5**	**40**	**19**	**16-2**

Appendix 2

RACE STATISTICS

Two-year-old season (August 2013 – July 2014)
2 starts for 2 wins

Wednesday, 4 June 2014
Ibis Milano Restaurant Handicap, Warwick Farm
Handicap for two-year-old fillies, no metropolitan wins
1100 metres, Good 4, rail normal
Winning time: 1 minute 3.79 seconds (track record: 1 minute 2.15 seconds)

	1st	Winx	Bay filly Street Cry (Ire) – Vegas Showgirl (NZ)	J. Collett (55 kg)	Gate 4; no. 10; SP $5	First start	C. Waller, Rosehill, NSW
0.8 L	2nd	Felines	Bay filly Conatus – Jellicles	B. Shinn (56.5 kg)	Gate 9; no. 3; SP $7	2 starts: 2 wins	K. Lees, Newcastle, NSW
5.1 L	3rd	Uratta Belle	Bay filly I Am Invincible – Littoral	N. Rawiller (57 kg)	Gate 1; no. 2; SP $4.50	4 starts: 1 second, 1 third	K. Gavenlock, Gosford, NSW

6.5 L	4th	Shama De Oro	Chestnut filly Sharmadal (USA) – Copa De Oro	K. McEvoy (55 kg)	Gate 7; no. 8; SP $11	First start	G. Waterhouse, Randwick, NSW
7.2 L	5th	Veselka	Bay filly Krupt – Riverview	J. Lloyd (56.5 kg)	Gate 10; no. 4; SP $8	1 start: 1 win	M. Smith, Warwick Farm, NSW
8.1 L		Aperture	Bay filly Shaft – Steamy	W. Costin (52 kg)	Gate 3; no. 6; SP $31	3 starts: 1 win	M. Dale, Canberra, ACT
9.3 L		Lucy's Look	Bay filly Lonhro – Anything But Love	J. Cassidy (55 kg)	Gate 6; no. 7; SP $4.50	First start	C. Waller, Rosehill, NSW
9.4 L		Vanishka	Bay or brown filly Written Tycoon – Shazee	P. Beggy (55 kg)	Gate 2; no. 9; SP $11	First start	S. Singleton, Hawkesbury, NSW
11.9 L		Ultimate Dancer	Bay filly Big Brown (USA) – Ultimate Rock	B. Avdulla (54 kg)	Gate 5; no. 11; SP $101	3 starts	A. Cummings, Randwick, NSW
12.7 L		Kokomo	Chestnut filly Choisir – Mia Cat Dancer (USA)	T. Angland (56 kg)	Gate 8; no. 5; SP $13	5 starts: 1 win, 1 second, 1 third	P. Perry, Newcastle, NSW

Scratchings: 1 Sheer Style   C. Nutman (59.5 kg)   G. Frazer

Saturday, 28 June 2014
TAB Early Quaddie Handicap, Rosehill
Handicap for two-year-olds
1400 metres, Good 3, rail normal
Winning time: 1 minute 23.72 seconds (track record: 1 minute 21.38 seconds)

	1st	Winx	Bay filly Street Cry (Ire) – Vegas Showgirl (NZ)	J. Collett (56 kg)	Gate 1; no. 3; SP $1.45	1 start: 1 win	C. Waller, Rosehill, NSW
1.5	2nd	Inz'n'out	Bay gelding Zariz – Bonne Bouche	B. Avdulla (59 kg)	Gate 5; no. 1; SP $5	2 starts: 2 wins	G. Ryan, Rosehill, NSW
2.3	3rd	Another Al	Brown gelding Al Maher – Crystal Clear	W. Costin (52.5 kg)	Gate 6; no. 6; SP $14	1 start	G. Waterhouse, Randwick, NSW
3.6	4th	Joadja	Bay filly Charge Forward – Okaylah	J. McDonald (55.5 kg)	Gate 4; no. 5; SP $11	3 starts: 1 win, 1 third	G. Begg, Randwick, NSW
6.3	5th	Win For Levi	Bay colt Onemore-nomore – Ocean Bridge	T. Angland (56 kg)	Gate 2; no. 4; SP $41	1 start: 1 second	J. Thompson, Randwick, NSW
8.7		Detach-ment	Chestnut gelding Show A Heart – Mille Miglia	B. Shinn (56.5 kg)	Gate 3; no. 2; SP $20	3 starts: 1 win, 1 third	P. and P. Snowden, Randwick, NSW

Scratchings: 7 Aesop   K. McEvoy (54.5 kg)   G. Ryan

RACE STATISTICS

Three-year-old season (August 2014 – July 2015)
10 starts (all at Group level, four at Group One) for 4 wins (one Group One), 3 seconds; commences winning streak (2 successive wins)

Saturday, 6 September 2014
Coolmore Furious Stakes, Randwick
Group Two for three-year-old fillies, set weights
1200 metres, Heavy 9, rail out 4 metres
Winning time: 1 minute 11.99 seconds (track record: 1 minute 8.03 seconds)

	1st	Winx	Bay filly Street Cry (Ire) – Vegas Showgirl (NZ)	H. Bowman (56 kg)	Gate 6; no. 5; SP $6.50	2 starts: 2 wins	C. Waller, Rosehill, NSW
2.8	2nd	Alpha Miss	Bay filly Lucky Owners (NZ) – Soiree Girl	J. Collett (56 kg)	Gate 4; no. 4; SP $26	7 starts: 3 wins, 1 third	G. Nickson, Warwick Farm, NSW
2.9	3rd	Earthquake	Bay filly Exceed And Excel – Cataclysm	K. McEvoy (56 kg)	Gate 2; no. 1; SP $2.05	5 starts: 4 wins, 1 second	J. O'Shea, Warwick Farm, NSW
3.1	4th	Sultry Feeling	Bay filly Encosta De Lago – Visual Emotion (USA)	T. Angland (56 kg)	Gate 5; no. 6; SP $6	5 starts: 2 wins, 1 third	J.B. and J. Cummings, Randwick, NSW
4.1	5th	Peggy Jean	Brown filly Myboycharlie (Ire) – Lady Of Love	B. Shinn (56 kg)	Gate 3; no. 2; SP $7.50	6 starts: 2 wins, 2 seconds, 1 third	G. Ryan, Rosehill, NSW
6.6		Memorial	Chestnut filly Street Cry (Ire) – Mnemosyne	J. McDonald (56 kg)	Gate 1; no. 3; SP $8	7 starts: 2 wins, 2 seconds	J. O'Shea, Warwick Farm, NSW

Scratchings: 7 Sailing Past (NZ)   B. Avdulla (56 kg)   J. Sargent

Saturday, 20 September 2014
Coolmore Tea Rose Stakes, Randwick
Group Two for three-year-old fillies, set weights
1400 metres, Good 3, rail out 8 metres
Winning time: 1 minute 22.83 seconds (track record 1 minute 20.33 seconds)

	1st	First Seal	Bay filly Fastnet Rock – Episode	B. Shinn (56 kg)	Gate 1; no. 7; SP $19	3 starts: 1 win, 1 second	J. Thompson, Randwick, NSW
0.8	2nd	**Winx**	**Bay filly Street Cry (Ire) – Vegas Showgirl (NZ)**	**J. Collett (56 kg)**	**Gate 2; no. 4; SP $1.80**	**3 starts: 3 wins**	**C. Waller, Rosehill, NSW**
1	3rd	Earth-quake	Bay filly Exceed And Excel – Cataclysm	K. McEvoy (56 kg)	Gate 3; no. 1; SP $3.60	6 starts: 4 wins, 1 second, 1 third	J. O'Shea, Warwick Farm, NSW
2.8	4th	Alpha Miss	Bay filly Lucky Owners (NZ) – Soiree Girl	B. Avdulla (56 kg)	Gate 6; no. 3; SP $20	8 starts: 3 wins, 1 second, 1 third	G. Nickson, Warwick Farm, NSW
4.2	5th	Sultry Feeling	Bay filly Encosta De Lago – Visual Emotion (USA)	T. Angland (56 kg)	Gate 5; no. 5; SP $18	6 starts: 2 wins, 1 third	J.B. and J. Cummings, Randwick, NSW
4.5		Lady Sharapova	Bay filly Fastnet Rock – Perfect Persuasion	J. McDon-ald (56 kg)	Gate 4; no. 6; SP $11	4 starts: 1 win, 2 thirds	M., W. and J. Hawkes, Rosehill, NSW
4.9		Peggy Jean	Brown filly Myboy-charlie (Ire) – Lady Of Love	J. Cassidy (56 kg)	Gate 7; no. 2; SP $21	7 starts: 2 wins, 2 seconds, 1 third	G. Ryan, Rosehill, NSW

Scratchings: 8 Melanya   S. Clipperton (56 kg)   B. Dais

RACE STATISTICS

Saturday, 4 October 2014

Coolmore Flight Stakes, Randwick

Group One for three-year-old fillies, set weights

1600 metres, Good 3, rail normal

Winning time: 1 minute 34.71 seconds (track record: 1 minute 33.13 seconds)

	1st	First Seal	Bay filly Fastnet Rock – Episode	B. Shinn (56 kg)	Gate 4; no. 2; SP $2.30	4 starts: 2 wins, 1 second	J. Thompson, Randwick, NSW
3	2nd	Winx	**Bay filly Street Cry (Ire) – Vegas Showgirl (NZ)**	H. Bowman (56 kg)	Gate 7; no. 1; SP $2.70	4 starts: 3 wins, 1 second	C. Waller, Rosehill, NSW
4.3	3rd	Thinking Of You (NZ)	Chestnut filly Thorn Park – Sympathy	J. Parr (56 kg)	Gate 2; no. 6; SP $6	2 starts: 2 wins	P. Moody, Caulfield, Vic
4.5	4th	Press Report	Chestunt filly Written Tycoon – Grenada	W. Costin (56 kg)	Gate 6; no. 3; SP $51	8 starts: 1 win, 2 seconds	L. Curtis, Rosehill, NSW
6.1	5th	Echo Gal	Bay filly Stratum – Pink Siris	T. Angland (56 kg)	Gate 3; no. 4; SP $18	8 starts: 3 wins, 1 second	G. Waterhouse, Randwick, NSW
6.3		Lady Sharapova	Bay filly Fastnet Rock – Perfect Persuasion	J. McDonald (56 kg)	Gate 5; no. 7; SP $19	5 starts: 1 win, 2 thirds	M., W. and J. Hawkes, Rosehill, NSW
7.7		Dynamic Rock	Bay filly Fastnet Rock – Dynamic Love	T. Clark (56 kg)	Gate 1; no. 9; SP $81	4 starts: 1 win, 1 third	C. Waller, Rosehill, NSW

Scratchings: 5 Twirl   G. Schofield (56 kg)   G. Waterhouse

             8 Muscovado   T. Huet (56 kg)   G. Waterhouse

Saturday, 14 February 2015
Liberty International Underwriters Light Fingers Stakes, Randwick
Group Two for three-year-old fillies, set weights
1200 metres, Good 4, rail normal
Winning time: 1 minute 9.48 seconds (track record: 1 minute 8.03 seconds)

	1st	Adrift (NZ)	Bay filly Zabeel (NZ) – Stray (NZ)	T. Angland (56 kg)	Gate 11; no. 10; SP $41	3 starts: 2 wins	G. Waterhouse, Randwick, NSW
0.8	2nd	First Seal	Bay filly Fastnet Rock – Episode	B. Shinn (56 kg)	Gate 1; no. 3; SP $3.70	6 starts: 3 wins, 2 seconds	J. Thompson, Randwick, NSW
1	3rd	Slightly Sweet	Bay filly Charge Forward – Semitone	K. O'Hara (56 kg)	Gate 10; no. 9; SP $31	3 starts: 2 wins	J. Coyle, Warwick Farm, NSW
1.4	4th	Peggy Jean	Brown filly Myboy-charlie (Ire) – Lady Of Love	K. McEvoy (56 kg)	Gate 8; no. 2; SP $26	8 starts: 2 wins, 2 seconds, 1 third	G. Ryan, Rosehill, NSW
2.2	5th	One-morezeta	Bay filly Onemore-nomore – Little Zeta	C. Reith (56 kg)	Gate 6; no. 8; SP $10	4 starts: 3 wins	K. Lees, Newcastle, NSW
3		Mossfun	Bay filly Mossman – Eye For Fun	T. Berry (56 kg)	Gate 7; no. 1; SP $3.60	5 starts: 4 wins, 1 second	M., W. and J. Hawkes, Rosehill, NSW
3.1	7th	**Winx**	**Bay filly Street Cry (Ire) – Vegas Showgirl (NZ)**	**J. Collett (56 kg)**	**Gate 3; no. 6; SP $5**	**5 starts: 3 wins, 2 seconds**	**C. Waller, Rosehill, NSW**
3.2		Memorial	Chestnut filly Street Cry (Ire) – Mnemo-syne	J. McDonald (56 kg)	Gate 4; no. 5; SP $9	8 starts: 2 wins, 2 seconds	J. O'Shea, Warwick Farm, NSW

3.6		Amicus	Bay filly Fastnet Rock – Gold Chant	H. Bowman (56 kg)	Gate 5; no. 4; SP $10	7 starts: 2 wins, 2 seconds, 2 thirds	C. Waller, Rosehill, NSW
3.7		Supara	Grey filly Domesday – Unabated	G. Schofield (56 kg)	Gate 2; no. 11; SP $31	3 starts: 1 win, 2 seconds	G. Waterhouse, Randwick, NSW
3.8		Press Report	Chestnut filly Written Tycoon – Grenada	W. Costin (56 kg)	Gate 9; no. 8; SP $26	10 starts: 1 win, 2 seconds	L. Curtis, Rosehill, NSW

Scratchings: —

Saturday, 28 February 2015
Surround Stakes, Warwick Farm
Group Two for three-year-old fillies, set weights
1400 metres, Soft 5, rail true
Winning time: 1 minute 22.93 seconds (track record: 1 minute 21.06 seconds)

	1st	First Seal	Bay filly Fastnet Rock – Episode	B. Shinn (56 kg)	Gate 7; no. 2; SP $1.50	7 starts: 3 wins, 3 seconds	J. Thompson, Randwick, NSW
2.8	2nd	Supara	Grey filly Domesday – Unabated	T. Berry (56 kg)	Gate 2; no. 11; SP $26	4 starts: 1 win, 2 seconds	G. Waterhouse, Randwick, NSW
4.1	3rd	Slightly Sweet	Bay filly Charge Forward – Semitone	K. O'Hara (56 kg)	Gate 3; no. 9; SP $21	4 starts: 2 wins, 1 third	J. Coyle, Warwick Farm, NSW
4.3	4th	Amicus	Bay filly Fastnet Rock – Gold Chant	H. Bowman (56 kg)	Gate 8; no. 3; SP $26	8 starts: 2 wins, 2 seconds, 2 thirds	C. Waller, Rosehill, NSW
4.8	5th	**Winx**	**Bay filly Street Cry (Ire) – Vegas Show-girl (NZ)**	**J. Collett (56 kg)**	**Gate 9; no. 4; SP $9**	**6 starts: 3 wins, 2 seconds**	**C. Waller, Rosehill, NSW**
4.9		Wine Tales	Bay filly Tale Of The Cat – Vinavion	J. Cassidy (56 kg)	Gate 1; no. 8; SP $21	6 starts: 2 wins, 3 seconds	C. Waller, Rosehill, NSW

5.3		Adrift (NZ)	Bay filly Zabeel (NZ) – Stray (NZ)	T. Angland (56 kg)	Gate 6; no. 7; SP $8.50	4 starts: 3 wins	G. Waterhouse, Randwick, NSW
6.1		Candelara	Chestnut filly Real Saga – Jadana	G. Schofield (56 kg)	Gate 10; no. 10; SP $151	11 starts: 1 win, 2 seconds, 2 thirds	B. Baker, Warwick Farm, NSW
6.5		High Above	Bay filly High Chaparral (Ire) – World Event	C. Reith (56 kg)	Gate 12; no. 12; SP $51	3 starts: 1 win, 1 third	A. Cummings, Randwick, NSW
7.2		Peggy Jean	Brown filly Myboycharlie (Ire) – Lady Of Love	K. McEvoy (56 kg)	Gate 5; no. 1; SP $18	9 starts: 2 wins, 2 seconds, 1 third	G. Ryan, Rosehill, NSW
7.8		Abduction	Bay filly Street Cry (Ire) – Hold To Ransom (USA)	J. McDonald (56 kg)	Gate 11; no. 6; SP $21	7 starts: 2 wins, 2 seconds	J. O'Shea, Warwick Farm, NSW
8		Lucky Raquie	Bay filly Encosta De Lago – Monsoon Wedding	B. Avdulla (56 kg)	Gate 4; no. 5; SP $81	8 starts: 1 win, 1 third	G. Ryan, Rosehill, NSW

Scratchings: —

Saturday, 14 March 2015
Cellarbrations Phar Lap Stakes, Rosehill
Group Two for three-year-olds, set weights
1500 metres, Good 4, rail normal
Winning time: 1 minute 30.26 seconds (track record: 1 minute 27.21 seconds)

	1st	Winx	Bay filly Street Cry (Ire) – Vegas Showgirl (NZ)	T. Berry (54.5 kg)	Gate 6; no. 6; SP $2.45	7 starts: 3 wins, 2 seconds	C. Waller, Rosehill, NSW

1.8	2nd	Hauraki	Bay colt Reset – Youthful Presence	J. McDonald (56.5 kg)	Gate 8; no. 4; SP $7.50	4 starts: 2 wins	J. O'Shea, Warwick Farm, NSW
1.9	3rd	Supara	Grey filly Domesday – Unabated	C. Reith (54.5 kg)	Gate 1; no. 8; SP $4.60	5 starts: 1 win, 3 seconds	G. Waterhouse, Randwick, NSW
2	4th	Diamond Valores (NZ)	Bay gelding Tavistock (NZ) – Special Diamond (NZ)	B. Shinn (56.5 kg)	Gate 4; no. 3; SP $8	6 starts: 2 wins, 2 seconds	P. and P. Snowden, Randwick, NSW
3.5	5th	Testa-shadow	Bay gelding Testa Rossa – Moonlight Shadow	B. Avdulla (56.5 kg)	Gate 2; no. 2; SP $6.50	11 starts: 2 wins, 4 seconds, 1 third	G. Portelli, Warwick Farm, NSW
5.4		Hampton Court	Bay colt Redoute's Choice – Roses 'N' Wine (Can)	J. Parr (56.5 kg)	Gate 3; no. 1; SP $11	11 starts: 3 wins, 1 second, 1 third	G. Waterhouse, Randwick, NSW
6.7		Pounamu	Grey gelding Authorized (Ire) – Tangiwai	G. Scho-field (56.5 kg)	Gate 5; no. 5; SP $71	8 starts: 2 seconds, 1 third	A. Denham, Wyong, NSW
8.5		High Above	Bay filly High Chaparral (Ire) – World Event	J. Collett (54.5 kg)	Gate 7; no. 9; SP $26	4 starts: 1 win, 1 third	A. Cummings, Randwick, NSW

Scratchings: 7 Wine Tales   J. Cassidy (54.5 kg)   C. Waller
               10 Heavens Above   K. McEvoy (54.5 kg)   T. Martin

Saturday, 28 March 2015
Vinery Stud Stakes, Rosehill
Group One for three-year-old fillies, set weights
2000 metres, Good 3, rail out 4 metres
Winning time: 2 minutes 3.27 seconds (track record: 1 minute 59.99 seconds)

	1st	Fenway	Bay filly High Chaparral (Ire) – Deedra	B. Shinn (56 kg)	Gate 11; no. 10; SP $21	5 starts: 1 win, 1 third	L. and S. Hope, Seymour, Vic
0.2	2nd	First Seal	Bay filly Fastnet Rock – Episode	J. McDonald (56 kg)	Gate 7; no. 1; SP $1.80	9 starts: 4 wins, 4 seconds	J. Thompson, Randwick, NSW
1.2	3rd	Thunder Lady (NZ)	Bay filly Master-craftsman (Ire) – Thunder-chine	T. Angland (56 kg)	Gate 9; no. 5; SP $51	10 starts: 1 win, 2 seconds, 2 thirds	J. Sargent, Randwick, NSW
1.4	4th	Ballet Suite	Bay filly High Chaparral (Ire) – Suitely	K. McEvoy (56 kg)	Gate 13; no. 9; SP $41	5 starts: 3 wins, 1 second	C. Waller, Rosehill, NSW
2	5th	**Winx**	**Bay filly Street Cry (Ire) – Vegas Showgirl (NZ)**	**T. Berry (56 kg)**	**Gate 6; no. 4; SP $5.50**	**8 starts: 4 wins, 2 seconds**	**C. Waller, Rosehill, NSW**
2.2		Amicus	Bay filly Fastnet Rock – Gold Chant	T. Clark (56 kg)	Gate 8; no. 3; SP $21	10 starts: 2 wins, 2 seconds, 2 thirds	C. Waller, Rosehill, NSW
2.7		Slightly Sweet	Bay filly Charge Forward – Semitone	K. O'Hara (56 kg)	Gate 3; no. 6; SP $31	6 starts: 3 wins, 2 thirds	J. Coyle, Warwick Farm, NSW
2.9		Sweet and Speedy	Bay filly Street Cry (Ire) – Speedy Natalie	B. Avdulla (56 kg)	Gate 10; no. 7; SP $71	6 starts: 3 wins, 1 second, 1 third	P. Moody, Caulfield, Vic

3.5		Adrift	Bay filly Zabeel (NZ) – Stray (NZ)	D. Oliver (56 kg)	Gate 5; no. 8; SP $9	5 starts: 3 wins	G. Waterhouse, Randwick, NSW
3.7		Heavens Above	Bay filly Street Cry (Ire) – Reggie (NZ)	J. Collett (56 kg)	Gate 4; no. 13; SP $101	3 starts: 1 second, 2 thirds	T. Martin, Rosehill, NSW
4.8		Set Square	Bay filly Reset – Dynastar	C. Williams (56 kg)	Gate 12; no. 2; SP $11	6 starts: 3 wins, 1 second, 2 thirds	C. Maher, Caulfield, Vic
6.7		Wilden-stein	Bay filly Redoute's Choice – Allez France	M. Walker (56 kg)	Gate 1; no. 12; SP $201	9 starts: 2 wins, 2 thirds	P. Perry, Newcastle, NSW
8		Lady Macan	Bay filly Where's That Tiger (USA) – Lady Jakeo	G. Schofield (56 kg)	Gate 14; no. 11; SP $201	10 starts: 1 win, 1 second	D. Payne, Randwick, NSW
9.7		Miss Interiors	Bay filly Flying Spur – Ballet D'Amour (USA)	N. Hall (56 kg)	Gate 2; no. 14; SP $201	10 starts: 1 win, 1 second, 1 third	A. Cummings, Randwick, NSW

Scratchings: —

WINX

Saturday, 11 April 2015
Seven News ATC Australian Oaks, Randwick
Group One for three-year-old fillies, set weights
2400 metres, Soft 7, rail out 6 metres
Winning time: 2 minutes 32.40 seconds (track record: 2 minutes 26.36 seconds)

	1st	Gust Of Wind (NZ)	Bay filly Darci Brahma (NZ) – Starry-starrynight (Ire)	T. Angland (56 kg)	Gate 5; no. 12; SP $17	4 starts: 2 wins	J. Sargent, Randwick, NSW
2.5	2nd	Winx	**Bay filly Street Cry (Ire) – Vegas Showgirl (NZ)**	J. Moreira (56 kg)	Gate 1; no. 2; SP $2.80	9 starts: 4 wins, 2 seconds	C. Waller, Rosehill, NSW
4.8	3rd	Candelara	Chestnut filly Real Saga – Jadana	H. Bowman (56 kg)	Gate 2; no. 5; SP $7	14 starts: 2 wins, 2 seconds, 2 thirds	B. Baker, Warwick Farm, NSW
6	4th	Rustic Melody	Bay filly Snitzel – Laurinel Argie	B. Avdulla (56 kg)	Gate 7; no. 9; SP $17	9 starts: 2 wins, 4 seconds, 1 third	K. Lees, Newcastle, NSW
8.6	5th	Thunder Lady (NZ)	Bay filly Master-craftsman (Ire) – Thunder-chine	Z. Purton (56 kg)	Gate 8; no. 1; SP $8.50	11 starts: 1 win, 2 seconds, 3 thirds	J. Sargent, Randwick, NSW
9.3		Savaria (NZ)	Bay filly Savabeel – Amathea (NZ)	J. McDon-ald (56 kg)	Gate 9; no. 4; SP $5	6 starts: 3 wins, 1 second, 1 third	R. Bergerson, Awapuni, New Zealand
9.5		Zarzali	Bay filly Hussonet – Zarakiysha (Ire)	C. Williams (56 kg)	Gate 6; no. 13; SP $26	5 starts: 2 wins, 1 third	J.B. and J. Cummings, Randwick, NSW
15.7		Ballet Suite	Bay filly High Chaparral (Ire) – Suitely	R. Moore (56 kg)	Gate 10; no. 10; SP $6.50	6 starts: 3 wins, 1 second	C. Waller, Rosehill, NSW

16.4	Sweet And Speedy	Bay filly Street Cry (Ire) – Speedy Natalie	C. Schofield (56 kg)	Gate 4; no. 6; SP $21	7 starts: 3 wins, 1 second, 1 third	P. Moody, Caulfield, Vic
32.2	Wilden-stein	Bay filly Redoute's Choice – Allez France	B. Loy (56 kg)	Gate 3; no. 11; SP $101	10 starts: 2 wins, 2 thirds	P. Perry, Newcastle, NSW

Scratchings: 3 Fenway   B. Shinn (56 kg)   L. and S. Hope
            7 Wine Tales   T. Berry (56 kg)   C. Waller
            8 Adrift   D. Oliver (56 kg)   G. Waterhouse

Saturday, 16 May 2015
XXXX Sunshine Coast Guineas, Sunshine Coast
Group Three for three-year-olds, set weights
1600 metres, Good 3, rail true
Winning time: 1 minute 36.19 seconds (track record: 1 minute 34.74 seconds)

	1st	**Winx**	**Bay filly Street Cry (Ire) – Vegas Showgirl (NZ)**	**L. Cassidy (55 kg)**	**Gate 14; no. 11; SP $2.60**	**10 starts: 4 wins, 3 seconds**	**C. Waller, Rosehill, NSW**
1.8	2nd	Ulmann	Brown gelding Sebring – Darsini	L. Nolen (57 kg)	Gate 7; no. 4; SP $26	8 starts: 2 wins, 2 seconds	P. Moody, Caulfield, Vic
3.3	3rd	Worthy Cause	Bay or brown colt Choisir – Tahnee Tango	J. Stanley (57 kg)	Gate 1; no. 2; SP $5.50	9 starts: 3 wins, 3 seconds, 1 third	J. Zielke, Sunshine Coast, Qld
4.8	4th	Right Or Wrong	Bay gelding Manhattan Rain – Impulsive Lass	R. Wiggins (57 kg)	Gate 2; no. 10; SP $31	4 starts: 2 wins, 1 third	L. Gough, Eagle Farm, Qld
4.9	5th	Whata-lovelyday	Bay filly Domesday – Krysia	M. Cahill (55 kg)	Gate 8; no. 13; SP $71	18 starts: 3 wins, 3 seconds, 3 thirds	J. Walk, Eagle Farm, Qld

5.1		Rhodin Drive	Bay gelding Reset – Love Buggy	L. Tarrant (57 kg)	Gate 10; no. 3; SP $41	9 starts: 3 wins, 2 thirds	H. Page, Gold Coast, Qld
6.4		Merion (NZ)	Bay gelding O'Reilly (NZ) – Sapphire Belle (NZ)	D. Browne (57 kg)	Gate 11; no. 1; SP $4.40	11 starts: 3 wins, 3 thirds	M. Moroney, Flemington, Vic
6.5		Rising Luck	Bay gelding Bradbury's Luck – Riseupsinging	J. Taylor (57 kg)	Gate 17; no. 9; SP $61	10 starts: 1 win, 2 second, 2 thirds	T. Thomas, Sunshine Coast
6.6		Swift Lady (NZ)	Grey filly O'Reilly (NZ) – Sweet Lady	R. McMahon (55 kg)	Gate 16; no. 14; SP $12	9 starts: 3 wins, 1 second	J. Sargent, Randwick, NSW
6.7		Abduction	Bay gelding Street Cry (Ire) – Hold To Ransom (USA)	T. Bell (55 kg)	Gate 4; no. 12; SP $13	10 starts: 2 wins, 2 seconds	J. O'Shea, Warwick Farm, NSW
6.8		Eljetem	Bay gelding Jet Spur – El Manto	J. Lloyd (57 kg)	Gate 12; no. 5; SP $41	12 starts: 1 win, 2 seconds, 1 third	B. Hill, Gold Coast, Qld
8.1		Skylimit	Bay colt Flying Spur – Bahia	T. Harrison (57 kg)	Gate 6; no. 6; SP $11	3 starts: 1 win, 1 second, 1 third	G. Waterhouse, Randwick, NSW
11.4		Game Of Fame	Bay filly Stratum – Search For Fame	D. Griffin (55 kg)	Gate 9; no. 16; SP $101	12 starts: 1 win, 2 seconds, 2 thirds	J. McLachlan, Sunshine Coast, Qld
12.7		Elusive Catch (NZ)	Brown filly Elusive City (USA) – Milord A Lady (NZ)	P. Hammersley (55 kg)	Gate 13; no. 15; SP $31	10 starts: 3 wins, 2 seconds, 1 third	L. Birchley, Eagle Farm, Qld
15		Redeem Code (NZ)	Bay gelding Nedeem – Market Leader (UK)	M. Cameron (57 kg)	Gate 3; no. 7; SP $31	5 starts: 2 wins	S. Ritchie, Cambridge, New Zealand
17.5		Hawaydah	Bay filly Hotel Grand – Samsara	J. Orman (55 kg)	Gate 15; no. 17; SP $201	6 starts: 1 win, 1 second, 1 third	R. Wilson, Sunshine Coast, Qld

18.8		Buckin The Blues	Chestnut gelding Husson (Arg) – Blushing Rahy (USA)	J. Byrne (57 kg)	Gate 5; no. 8; SP $61	7 starts: 2 wins, 1 second	M. Dunn, Murwillumbah, NSW
22.8		Silver Heels	Grey filly Ferocity – All Legs	A. Taylor (55 kg)	Gate 18; no. 18; SP $201	7 starts: 1 win, 1 second	R. Wilson, Sunshine Coast, Qld

Scratchings: 19 Sam de Hero   R. Fradd (57 kg)   C. Anderson

Saturday, 30 May 2015

Treasury Casino & Hotel Queensland Oaks, Doomben

Group One for three-year-old fillies, set weights

2200 metres, Good 3, rail out 5 metres

Winning time: 2 minutes 14.09 seconds (track record: 2 minutes 11.67 seconds)

	1st	Winx	Bay filly Street Cry (Ire) – Vegas Show-girl (NZ)	H. Bowman (56.5 kg)	Gate 10; no. 2; SP $1.95	11 starts: 5 wins, 3 seconds	C. Waller, Rosehill, NSW
3.5	2nd	Ungrate-ful Ellen	Bay filly Grey Swallow (Ire) – Degeneres	C. Williams (56.5 kg)	Gate 9; no. 13; SP $12	11 starts: 2 wins, 1 second, 3 thirds	R. Smerdon, Caulfield, Vic
4	3rd	Imperial Lass (NZ)	Bay filly Tavistock (NZ) – Tricia Ann (NZ)	B. Shinn (56.5 kg)	Gate 1; no. 17; SP $51	10 starts: 1 win, 2 thirds	P. Moody, Caulfield, Vic
5.3	4th	Zarzali	Bay filly Hussonet – Zarakiysha (Ire)	T. Berry (56.5 kg)	Gate 6; no. 15; SP $15	7 starts: 2 wins, 2 thirds	J.B. and J. Cummings, Randwick, NSW
5.7	5th	Rustic Melody	Bay filly Snitzel – Laurinel Argie	J. McDonald (56.5 kg)	Gate 13; no. 5; SP $18	11 starts: 2 wins, 5 seconds, 1 third	K. Lees, Newcastle, NSW
7		No Tricks	Brown filly Savabeel – Mezaire (NZ)	M. Cahill (56.5 kg)	Gate 2; no. 14; SP $151	11 starts: 2 wins, 3 seconds, 1 third	W. Walters, Mount Gambier, SA
7.2		Ballet Suite	Bay filly High Cha-parral (Ire) – Suitely	K. McEvoy (56.5 kg)	Gate 16; no. 4; SP $9.50	8 starts: 4 wins, 1 second	C. Waller, Rosehill, NSW

7.5		Yulong Baby	Bay filly Commands – Paris Tryst	C. Newitt (56.5 kg)	Gate 15; no. 16; SP $51	9 starts: 2 wins, 2 seconds, 1 third	M. Price, Caulfield, Vic
9.3		Sebrina	Chestnut filly Sebring – Crown Princess	G. Boss (56.5 kg)	Gate 5; no. 11; SP $8.50	7 starts: 2 wins, 1 second, 1 third	B. Baker, Warwick Farm, NSW
9.5		Whata-lovelyday	Bay filly Domesday – Krysia	T. Harri-son (56.5 kg)	Gate 8; no. 7; SP $91	19 starts: 3 wins, 3 seconds, 3 thirds	J. Walk, Eagle Farm, Qld
11		Col 'N' Lil	Grey filly Bradbury's Luck – Jyler	L. Tarrant (56.5 kg)	Gate 4; no. 6; SP $31	12 starts: 3 wins, 3 seconds, 3 thirds	B. Currie, Toowoomba, Qld
11.8		Platinum Witness	Bay filly California Dane – Chartreuse (NZ)	D. Browne (56.5 kg)	Gate 11; no. 3; SP $15	16 starts: 4 wins, 6 seconds, 1 third	L. Latta, Awapuni, New Zealand
12		Exquisite Jewel (NZ)	Bay filly Lucky Uni-corn (NZ) – Game Duchess (NZ)	J. Byrne (56.5 kg)	Gate 3; no. 8; SP $19	15 starts: 4 wins, 1 second, 1 third	S. Walsh, Foxton, New Zealand
16		Anaphora	Chestnut filly Dylan Thomas (Ire) – Power Of Love (NZ)	T. Bell (56.5 kg)	Gate 14; no. 12; SP $71	10 starts: 2 wins, 2 seconds, 2 thirds	T. Noonan, Mornington, Vic
16.8		Swift Lady (NZ)	Grey filly O'Reilly (NZ) – Sweet Lady	T. Angland (56.5 kg)	Gate 12; no. 10; SP $26	10 starts: 3 wins, 1 second	J. Sargent, Randwick, NSW
18.8		Heavens Above	Bay filly Street Cry (Ire) – Reggie (NZ)	G. Scho-field (56.5 kg)	Gate 7; no. 9; SP $31	6 starts: 1 win, 1 second, 3 thirds	T. Martin, Rosehill, NSW

Scratchings:
1 Bohemian Lily (NZ) B. Shinn (56.5 kg) G. Waterhouse
18 Champion Stage (NZ) — (56.5 kg) J. Sargent
19 Shandaara (NZ) — (56.5 kg) R. Laing
20 Mine With Lime — (56.5 kg) M. Kropp
21 Stewball K. Wharton (56.5 kg) P. Kalinowski

RACE STATISTICS

Four-year-old season (August 2015 – July 2016)

7 starts (all at Group level, five at Group One) for 7 wins (five Group Ones); winning streak extends to 9 successive wins

Saturday, 12 September 2015

Theo Marks Stakes, Rosehill

Group Two for three-year-olds and upwards, Quality (handicap)

1300 metres, Good 3, rail out 2 metres

Winning time: 1 minute 15.77 seconds (track record: 1 minute 14.92 seconds)

	1st	Winx	4yo bay mare Street Cry (Ire) – Vegas Showgirl (NZ)	J. McDonald (54.5 kg)	Gate 11; no. 8; SP $3.50	12 starts: 6 wins, 3 seconds	C. Waller, Rosehill, NSW
0.2	2nd	Sons Of John	5yo brown gelding Oratorio (Ire) – Mountain Echo	J. Penza (53 kg)	Gate 7; no. 13; SP $31	15 starts: 6 wins, 2 seconds, 2 thirds	J. Attard, Hawkesbury, NSW
0.4	3rd	Ninth Legion	6yo bay gelding Fastnet Rock – Xaar's Jewel	T. Angland (57 kg)	Gate 1; no. 5; SP $13	31 starts: 6 wins, 6 seconds, 3 thirds	M., W. and J. Hawkes, Rosehill, NSW
0.6	4th	Strawber-ry Boy	7yo brown gelding Redoute's Choice – Strawberry Girl (USA)	J. Cassidy (58 kg)	Gate 5; no. 3; SP $15	24 starts: 9 wins, 3 seconds, 5 thirds	C. Waller, Rosehill, NSW
1.6	5th	Famous Seamus (NZ)	7yo bay gelding Elusive City (USA) – Clinique (NZ)	K. O'Hara (59 kg)	Gate 13; no. 1; SP $31	39 starts: 10 wins, 2 seconds, 7 thirds	N. Mayfield-Smith, Hawkesbury, NSW
2.8		Turbulent Jet	6yo bay gelding Jet Spur – Touched In Flight	W. Costin (53 kg)	Gate 14; no. 15; SP $26	19 starts: 4 wins, 3 seconds, 1 third	L. Curtis, Rosehill, NSW

3.6		Vashka	5yo bay gelding Exceed And Excel – Zaroyale (NZ)	J. Moreira (53 kg)	Gate 6; no. 12; SP $5	13 starts: 6 wins, 3 seconds, 1 third	J. O'Shea, Warwick Farm, NSW
2.7		Messene	7yo bay gelding Lonhro – Belle Giselle	T. Berry (58.5 kg)	Gate 2; no. 2; SP $7.50	18 starts: 9 wins, 3 seconds, 1 third	M., W. and J. Hawkes, Rosehill, NSW
4.3		Decision Time	8yo chestnut gelding Foreplay – Daunting Thought	C. Reith (53.5 kg)	Gate 10; no. 9; SP $61	33 starts: 10 wins, 3 seconds, 3 thirds	C. Conners, Warwick Farm, NSW
6		Heart Testa	6yo bay gelding Testa Rossa – Graciela	J. Collett (55.5 kg)	Gate 9; no. 6; SP $13	26 starts: 8 wins, 4 seconds, 3 thirds	C. Waller, Rosehill, NSW
8.6		Amanpour	5yo chestnut mare Northern Meteor – Newscaster	B. Prebble (57.5 kg)	Gate 8; no. 4; SP $21	18 starts: 4 wins, 6 seconds, 2 thirds	G. Waterhouse, Randwick, NSW
8.8		Boss Lane	5yo chestnut gelding Dubawi (Ire) –Lyricalworks	S. Clipperton (53 kg)	Gate 12; no.10 ; SP $15	22 starts: 6 wins, 1 second, 1 third	R. Quinton, Randwick, NSW
9		Nostradamus	4yo bay Medaglia D'Oro (USA) – Leone Chiara	T. Clark (53.5 kg)	Gate 4; no. 11; SP $13	14 starts: 3 wins, 2 seconds	M., W. and J. Hawkes, Rosehill, NSW
12.5		Aomen (Ire)	8yo bay gelding Shamardal (USA) – Kathy Caerleon (Ire)	B. Avdulla (55 kg)	Gate 3; no. 7; SP $21	30 starts: 7 wins, 3 seconds, 1 third	A. Cummings, Randwick, NSW

Scratchings: Vezalay – (53 kg)   L. and T. Corstens

RACE STATISTICS

Saturday, 3 October 2015

The Star 150th Epsom, Randwick

Group One for three-year-olds and upwards, Handicap

1600 metres, Good 3

Winning time: 1 minute 34.58 seconds (track record: 1 minute 33.18 seconds)

	1st	Winx	4yo bay mare Street Cry (Ire) – Vegas Showgirl (NZ)	H. Bowman (57 kg)	Gate 12; no. 4; SP $3	13 starts: 7 wins, 3 seconds	C. Waller, Rosehill, NSW
2.3	2nd	Ecuador	6yo bay gelding High Chaparral (Ire) – Bak Da Princess (NZ)	G. Boss (56 kg)	Gate 6; no. 8; SP $26	18 starts: 6 wins, 7 seconds	G. Waterhouse, Randwick, NSW
2.4	3rd	Sons Of John	5yo brown gelding Oratorio (Ire) – Mountain Echo	J. Penza (56 kg)	Gate 14; no. 12; SP $17	16 starts: 6 wins, 3 seconds, 2 thirds	J. Attard, Hawkesbury, NSW
2.5	4th	Messene	7yo bay gelding Lonhro – Belle Giselle	J. Ford (57 kg)	Gate 7; no. 5; SP $17	20 starts: 9 wins, 3 seconds, 2 thirds	M., W. and J. Hawkes, Rosehill, NSW
3.5	5th	Entirely Platinum	6yo chest-nut gelding Pentire (UK) – Platinum Blond (NZ)	T. Berry (57.5 kg)	Gate 13; no. 3; SP $8.50	22 starts: 6 wins, 6 seconds, 2 thirds	M., W. and J. Hawkes, Rosehill, NSW
3.6		Teronado	5yo brown gelding Testa Rossa – Nassi Doll	J. Collett (56 kg)	Gate 5; no. 14; SP $67	19 starts: 4 wins, 3 seconds, 3 thirds	B. Hill, Gold Coast, Qld
3.7		Malice	5yo bay gelding Teofilo (Ire) – Afore-thought	J. Moreira (56 kg)	Gate 1; no. 13; SP $41	20 starts: 5 wins, 5 seconds, 2 thirds	J. O'Shea, Warwick Farm, NSW

417

3.8		Lucia Valentina (NZ)	5yo brown mare Savabeel – Staryn Glenn (NZ)	Z. Purton (57.5 kg)	Gate 4; no. 2; SP $9	21 starts: 5 wins, 1 second, 4 thirds	K. Lees, Newcastle, NSW
3.9		Sadler's Lake	4yo bay gelding High Chaparral (Ire) – Mingshan	J. Cassidy (56 kg)	Gate 3; no. 11; SP $8	10 starts: 5 wins, 1 second	C. Waller, Rosehill, NSW
4.4		Kirramosa (NZ)	5yo bay mare Alamosa (NZ) – Freyja (NZ)	B. Shinn (56 kg)	Gate 9; no. 9; SP $10	15 starts: 4 wins, 1 second	J. Sargent Randwick, NSW
4.5		Hooked	5yo bay horse Casino Prince – Absolute Lure	T. Angland (58 kg)	Gate 2; no. 1; SP $21	27 starts: 5 wins, 2 thirds	J. Thompson, Randwick, NSW
4.9		Sweynesse	4yo bay or brown horse Lonhro – Swansea (Ire)	J. McDonald (56 kg)	Gate 10; no. 10; SP $15	12 starts: 4 wins, 2 seconds, 1 third	J. O'Shea, Warwick Farm, NSW
5.7		Rudy	5yo bay gelding Red Dazzler – Go On Now Go	L. Tarrant (56 kg)	Gate 8; no. 6; SP $12	26 starts: 7 wins, 4 seconds, 4 thirds	H. Page, Gold Coast, Qld
5.9		Pressing	4yo brown horse Sebring – Lamiraqui	G. Schofield (56 kg)	Gate 11; no. 15; SP $61	8 starts: 2 wins, 1 third	M. Price, Caulfield, Vic

Scratchings: 7 Silverball (Fr)   B. Avdulla (56 kg)   C. Waller

RACE STATISTICS

Saturday, 24 October 2015
William Hill Cox Plate, Moonee Valley
Group One for three-year-olds and upwards, standard weight-for-age
2040 metres, Good 3, rail out 3 metres
Winning time: 2 minutes 2.98 seconds (new track record: previous record 2 minutes 3.54 seconds)

	1st	Winx	4yo bay mare Street Cry (Ire) – Vegas Showgirl (NZ)	H. Bowman (55.5 kg)	Gate 1; no. 14; SP $4.50	14 starts: 8 wins, 3 seconds	C. Waller, Rosehill, NSW
4.75	2nd	Criterion (NZ)	5yo chestnut horse Sebring – Mica's Pride	M. Walker (59 kg)	Gate 7; no. 1; SP $6	30 starts: 7 wins, 6 seconds, 5 thirds	D. Hayes and T. Dabernig, Flemington, Vic
5.5	3rd	Highland Reel (Ire)	4yo bay horse Galileo (Ire) – Hveger	R. Moore (56 kg)	Gate 4; no. 13; SP $8	9 starts: 4 wins, 2 seconds,	A. O'Brien, County Tipperary, Ireland
9	4th	Pornichet (Fr)	5yo bay horse Vespone (Ire) – Porza (Fr)	K. McEvoy (59 kg)	Gate 11; no. 7; SP $61	20 starts: 7 wins, 2 seconds, 3 thirds	G. Waterhouse, Randwick, NSW
10.25	5th	Hartnell (UK)	5yo bay gelding Authorized (Ire) – Debonnaire (UK)	J. McDonald (59 kg)	Gate 3; no. 4; SP $16	19 starts: 7 wins, 4 seconds, 1 third	J. O'Shea, Warwick Farm, NSW
10.45		Fawkner	8yo grey gelding Reset – Dane Beltar	D. Oliver (59 kg)	Gate 14; no. 2; SP $21	29 starts: 11 wins, 6 seconds, 3 thirds	R. Hickmott, Macedon, Victoria
10.55		The Cleaner	8yo bay gelding Savoire Vivre (UK) – Dash of Scotch	N. Callow (59 kg)	Gate 2; no. 6; SP $17	52 starts: 19 wins, 12 seconds, 4 thirds	M. Burles, Longford, Tas

12.55		Gailo Chop (Fr)	5yo chestnut gelding Deportivo (UK) – Grenoble (Fr)	B. Rawiller (59 kg)	Gate 8; no. 10; SP $21	12 starts: 7 wins, 2 seconds, 1 third	A. de Watrigant, Chantilly, France
12.65		Preferment (NZ)	4yo bay horse Zabeel (NZ) – Better Alternative	N. Rawiller (57.5 kg)	Gate 9; no. 12; SP $13	14 starts: 3 wins, 4 seconds, 1 third	C. Waller, Rosehill, NSW
13.05		Happy Trails	8yo chestnut gelding Good Journey (USA) – Madame Flurry	M. Zahra (59 kg)	Gate 13; no. 3; SP $21	55 starts: 7 wins, 10 seconds, 7 thirds	P. Beshara, Morphetville, SA
13.8		Arod (Ire)	5yo bay horse Teofilo (Ire) – My Personal Space (USA)	C. Williams (59 kg)	Gate 5; no. 8; SP $8.50	11 starts: 4 wins, 3 seconds, 2 thirds	P. Chapple-Hyam, Marlborough, UK
16.05		Mourinho	8yo bay gelding Oratorio (Ire) – Benevolent (NZ)	V. Duric (59 kg)	Gate 12; no. 5; SP $41	38 starts: 11 wins, 4 seconds, 5 thirds	P. Gelagotis, Moe, Vic
20.3		Kermadec (NZ)	4yo bay horse Teofilo (Ire) – Hy Fuji	G. Boss (57.5 kg)	Gate 10; no. 11; SP $9	12 starts: 4 wins, 2 seconds, 2 thirds	C. Waller, Rosehill, NSW
35.3		Complacent	5yo bay horse Authorized (Ire) – Insouciance	J. Doyle (59 kg)	Gate 6; no. 9; SP $21	10 starts: 5 wins, 3 seconds, 1 third	J. O'Shea, Warwick Farm, NSW

Scratchings: —

RACE STATISTICS

Saturday, 13 February 2016

Optus Business Apollo Stakes, Randwick

Group Two for three-year-olds and upwards, standard weight-for-age

1400 metres, Good 3, rail out 3 metres

Winning time: 1 minute 22.03 seconds (track record: 1 minute 20.33 seconds)

	1st	Winx	4yo bay mare Street Cry (Ire) – Vegas Showgirl (NZ)	H. Bowman (57 kg)	Gate 1; no. 8; SP $1.57	15 starts: 9 wins, 3 seconds	C. Waller, Rosehill, NSW
1	2nd	Solicit	5yo bay or brown mare Street Cry (Ire) – Princesa	K. McEvoy (57 kg)	Gate 4; no. 10; SP $5.50	27 starts: 6 wins, 6 seconds, 3 thirds	G. Ryan, Rosehill, NSW
3.8	3rd	Hauraki	4yo bay gelding Reset – Youthful Presence	S. Clipperton (59 kg)	Gate 2; no. 5; SP $41	11 starts: 3 wins, 3 seconds	J. O'Shea, Warwick Farm, NSW
3.9	4th	Dibayani (Ire)	6yo bay gelding Sharmardal (USA) – Dibiya (Ire)	T. Angland (59 kg)	Gate 11; no. 4; SP $21	17 starts: 2 wins, 3 seconds, 6 thirds	D. Hayes and T. Dabernig, Flemington, Vic
4.1	5th	Leebaz	6yo bay gelding Zabeel (NZ) – Polish Princess (UK)	T. Berry (59 kg)	Gate 8; no. 6; SP $13	23 starts: 7 wins, 4 seconds, 2 thirds	M., W. and J. Hawkes, Rosehill, NSW
5		Bohemian Lily (NZ)	4yo bay mare O'Reilly (NZ) – Bohemian Blues (NZ)	T. Clark (57 kg)	Gate 9; no. 11; SP $31	16 starts: 3 wins, 3 seconds, 3 thirds	G. Waterhouse, Randwick, NSW

6.8		Magic Hurricane (Ire)	6yo bay gelding Hurricane Run (Ire) – Close Regards (Ire)	J. McDonald (59 kg)	Gate 5; no. 2; SP $17	16 starts: 5 wins, 2 seconds, 3 thirds	J. O'Shea, Warwick Farm, NSW
7.1		Centre Pivot	5yo bay or brown gelding More Than Ready (USA) – Waterwise (NZ)	W. Costin (59 kg)	Gate 3; no. 7; SP $21	19 starts: 8 wins, 4 seconds, 2 thirds	P. Robl, Randwick, NSW
8.1		Who Shot Thebar-man (NZ)	7yo bay gelding Yamanin Vital (NZ) – Ears Carol (NZ)	C. Reith (59 kg)	Gate 7; no. 1; SP $81	26 starts: 9 wins, 3 seconds, 1 third	C. Waller, Rosehill, NSW
12		Gust Of Wind (NZ)	4yo bay mare Darci Brahma (NZ) – Starry-starrynight (Ire)	B. Avdulla (57 kg)	Gate 10; no. 9; SP $81	10 starts: 3 wins	J. Sargent, Randwick, NSW
13.4		Grand Marshal (UK)	6yo brown gelding Dansili (UK) – Margarula (Ire)	J. Collett (59 kg)	Gate 6; no. 3; SP $151	27 starts: 7 wins, 5 seconds, 3 thirds	C. Waller, Rosehill, NSW

Scratchings: —

RACE STATISTICS

Saturday, 27 February 2016

Precise Air Chipping Norton Stakes, Randwick

Group One for three-year-olds and upwards, standard weight for age

1600 metres, Good 3, rail out 6 metres

Winning time: 1 minute 33.92 seconds (track record: 1 minute 33.13 seconds)

	1st	Winx	4yo bay mare Street Cry (Ire) – Vegas Showgirl (NZ)	H. Bowman (57 kg)	Gate 8; no. 11; SP $1.36	16 starts: 10 wins, 3 seconds	C. Waller, Rosehill, NSW
1.5	2nd	Dibayani (Ire)	6yo bay gelding Sharmardal (USA) – Dibiya (Ire)	B. Shinn (59 kg)	Gate 1; no. 7; SP $15	18 starts: 2 wins, 3 seconds, 6 thirds	D. Hayes and T. Dabernig, Flemington, Vic
2.5	3rd	Hauraki	4yo bay gelding Reset – Youthful Presence	S. Clipperton (59 kg)	Gate 10; no. 8; SP $26	12 starts: 3 wins, 3 seconds, 1 third	J. O'Shea, Warwick Farm, NSW
4.1	4th	Prefer-ment (NZ)	4yo bay horse Zabeel (NZ) – Better Alternative	T. Berry (59 kg)	Gate 5; no. 2; SP $67	17 starts: 3 wins, 4 seconds, 1 third	C. Waller, Rosehill, NSW
4.7	5th	Hartnell (UK)	5yo bay gelding Authorized (Ire) – Debonnaire (UK)	J. McDonald (59 kg)	Gate 7; no. 3; SP $9	21 starts: 7 wins, 4 seconds, 1 third	J. O'Shea, Warwick Farm, NSW
5		Centre Pivot	5yo bay or brown gelding More Than Ready (USA) – Waterwise (NZ)	D. Browne (59 kg)	Gate 9; no. 9; SP $61	20 starts: 8 wins, 4 seconds, 2 thirds	P. Robl, Randwick, NSW

5.1		Storm The Stars (USA)	4yo bay horse Sea The Stars (Ire) – Love Me Only (Ire)	T. Angland (58.5 kg)	Gate 6; no. 10; SP $26	11 starts: 3 wins, 4 seconds, 2 thirds	C. Waller, Rosehill, NSW
6.1		Grand Marshal (UK)	6yo brown gelding Dansili (UK) – Margarula (Ire)	J. Collett (59 kg)	Gate 3; no. 6; SP $101	28 starts: 7 wins, 5 seconds, 3 thirds	C. Waller, Rosehill, NSW
6.7		Magic Hurricane (Ire)	6yo bay gelding Hurricane Run (Ire) – Close Regards (Ire)	W. Buick (59 kg)	Gate 11; no. 5; SP $51	17 starts: 5 wins, 2 seconds, 3 thirds	J. O'Shea, Warwick Farm, NSW
6.9		Who Shot Thebar- man (NZ)	7yo bay gelding Yamanin Vital (NZ) – Ears Carol (NZ)	C. Reith (59 kg)	Gate 12; no. 4; SP $101	27 starts: 9 wins, 3 seconds, 1 third	C. Waller, Rosehill, NSW
7.1		Mongo- lian Khan	4yo bay horse Holy Roman Emperor (Ire) – Centafit (NZ)	K. McEvoy (59 kg)	Gate 4; no. 1; SP $12	13 starts: 8 wins, 1 third	M. Baker and A. Forsman, Cambridge, New Zealand
12		Gust Of Wind (NZ)	4yo bay mare Darci Brahma (NZ) – Starry- starrynight (Ire)	B. Avdulla (57 kg)	Gate 2; no. 12; SP $81	11 starts: 3 wins	J. Sargent, Randwick, NSW

Scratchings: —

RACE STATISTICS

Saturday, 19 March 2016

China Horse Club George Ryder Stakes, Rosehill

Group One for three-year-olds and upwards, standard weight for age

1500 metres, Good 4, rail out 2 metres

Winning time: 1 minute 28.70 seconds (track record: 1 minute 27.21 seconds)

	1st	Winx	4yo bay mare Street Cry (Ire) – Vegas Show-girl (NZ)	H. Bowman (57 kg)	Gate 7; no. 5; SP $1.90	17 starts: 11 wins, 3 seconds	C. Waller, Rosehill, NSW
1.5	2nd	Kermadec (NZ)	4yo bay horse Teofilo (Ire) – Hy Fuji	Z. Purton (59 kg)	Gate 6; no. 2; SP $13	14 starts: 4 wins, 2 seconds, 3 thirds	C. Waller, Rosehill, NSW
3.3	3rd	Press Statement	3yo bay colt Hinchin-brook – Kaaptive Empress	J. McDonald (56 kg)	Gate 1; no. 8; SP $4.50	9 starts: 6 wins, 2 seconds	C. Waller, Rosehill, NSW
4.7	4th	First Seal	4yo bay mare Fastnet Rock – Episode	B. Shinn (57 kg)	Gate 5; no. 6; SP $11	13 starts: 5 wins, 6 seconds	J. Thompson, Randwick, NSW
5.2	5th	Happy Clapper	5yo bay gelding Teofilo (Ire) – Busking	B. Avdulla (59 kg)	Gate 2; no. 4; SP $51	13 starts: 6 wins, 2 seconds, 2 thirds	P. Webster, Randwick, NSW
6.5		Turn Me Loose (NZ)	5yo bay horse Iffraaj (UK) – Indomita-ble (NZ)	O. Bosson (59 kg)	Gate 8; no. 1; SP $7	13 starts: 7 wins, 3 seconds, 1 third	M. Baker and A. Forsman, Cambridge, New Zealand
6.6		Tinto	5yo brown mare Red Dazzler – Truly Brave	C. Williams (57 kg)	Gate 4; no. 7; SP $101	25 starts: 7 wins, 4 seconds, 1 third	R. Lipp, Toowoomba, Qld
7.5		Huckle-buck	5yo bay or brown gelding Elvstroem – Kondari (NZ)	D. Tourneur (59 kg)	Gate 3; no. 3; SP $41	17 starts: 8 wins, 1 second, 2 thirds	P. Stokes, Morphetville, SA

Scratchings: —

Saturday, 2 April 2016
The Star Doncaster Mile, Randwick
Group One for three-year-olds and upwards, Handicap
1600 metres, Soft 6, rail true
Winning time: 1 minute 35.27 seconds (track record: 1 minute 33.13 seconds)

	1st	Winx	4yo bay mare Street Cry (Ire) – Vegas Showgirl (NZ)	H. Bowman (56.5 kg)	Gate 11; no. 3; SP $1.80	18 starts: 12 wins, 3 seconds	C. Waller, Rosehill, NSW
2	2nd	Happy Clapper	5yo bay gelding Teofilo (Ire) – Busking	B. Avdulla (50.5 kg)	Gate 8; no. 10; SP $13	14 starts: 6 wins, 2 seconds, 2 thirds	P. Webster, Randwick, NSW
2.2	3rd	Azkadellia (NZ)	4yo bay or brown mare Shinko King (Ire) – Raving (NZ)	G, Boss (50 kg)	Gate 12; no. 11; SP $9	12 starts: 5 wins, 5 seconds, 1 third	C. Maher, Caulfield, Vic
6.3	4th	Vergara	5yo bay mare Snippetson – Graces Spirit	K. O'Hara (50 kg)	Gate 6; no. 15; SP $151	31 starts: 8 wins, 4 seconds, 2 thirds	A. Cummings, Randwick, NSW
7.5	5th	Bow Creek (Ire)	5yo bay or brown horse Shamardal (USA) – Beneventa (UK)	J. McDonald (54.5 kg)	Gate 4; no. 5; SP $21	22 starts: 6 wins, 3 seconds, 2 thirds	J. O'Shea, Warwick Farm, NSW
8.2		Stratum Star	4yo chest-nut horse Stratum – Purely Spectacular (NZ)	M. Zahra (55 kg)	Gate 2; no. 4; SP $41	24 starts: 5 wins, 6 seconds, 6 thirds	D. Weir, Ballarat, Vic
8.3		Good Project	4yo bay horse Not A Single Doubt – Euchre	C. Newitt (52 kg)	Gate 7; no. 8; SP $61	23 starts: 5 wins, 8 seconds, 4 thirds	C. Waller, Rosehill, NSW

8.6		He Or She	5yo chest-nut gelding Kendel Star – Danessa	P. Moloney (50 kg)	Gate 13; no. 12; SP $21	18 starts: 9 wins, 2 seconds, 1 third	D. Hayes and T. Dabernig, Flemington, Vic
8.8		Rudy	5yo bay gelding Red Dazzler – Go On Now Go	T. Harrison (50 kg)	Gate 15; no. 13; SP $67	32 starts: 7 wins, 4 seconds, 5 thirds	H. Page, Gold Coast, Qld
9.4		Volk-stok'n' barrell (NZ)	4yo bay gelding Tavistock (NZ) – Volkster (NZ)	C. Brown (52.5 kg)	Gate 10; no. 7; SP $21	18 starts: 8 wins, 1 second, 3 thirds	D. Logan and C. Gibbs, Ruakaka, New Zealand
10.2		Ecuador	6yo bay gelding High Chaparral (Ire) – Bak Da Princess (NZ)	T. Clark (52 kg)	Gate 14; no. 9; SP $101	23 starts: 6 wins, 8 seconds	G. Waterhouse, Randwick, NSW
13.5		First Seal	4yo bay mare Fastnet Rock – Episode	T. Berry (53 kg)	Gate 1; no. 6; SP $26	14 starts: 5 wins, 6 seconds	J. Thompson, Randwick, NSW
14.1		Aomen	8yo bay gelding Shamardal (USA) – Kathy Caerleon (Ire)	W. Costin (50 kg)	Gate 5; no. 14; SP $201	32 starts: 7 wins, 3 seconds, 1 third	A. Cummings, Randwick, NSW
14.8		Turn Me Loose (NZ)	4yo bay horse Iffraaj (UK) – Indomita-ble (NZ)	O. Bosson (57 kg)	Gate 9; no. 2; SP $21	14 starts: 7 wins, 3 seconds, 1 third	M. Baker and A. Forsman, Cambridge, New Zealand
17		Kermadec (NZ)	4yo bay horse Teofilo (Ire) – Hy Fuji	Z. Purton (57 kg)	Gate 3; no. 1; SP $11	15 starts: 4 wins, 3 seconds, 3 thirds	C. Waller, Rosehill, NSW

Scratchings: —

Five-year-old season (August 2016 – July 2017)
Eight starts (all at Group level, six at Group One) for 8 wins (six Group Ones);
winning streak extends to 17 successive wins

Saturday, 20 August 2016
Warwick Stakes, Randwick
Group Two for three-year-olds and upwards, standard weight for age
1400 metres, Good 4, rail out 3 metres
Winning time: 1 minute 23.83 seconds (track record: 1 minute 20.33 seconds)

	1st	Winx	5yo bay mare Street Cry (Ire) – Vegas Showgirl (NZ)	H. Bowman (57 kg)	Gate 4; no. 6; SP $1.25	19 starts: 13 wins, 3 seconds	C. Waller, Rosehill, NSW
3.5	2nd	Hartnell (UK)	6yo bay gelding Authorized (Ire) – Debonnaire (UK)	J. McDonald (59 kg)	Gate 3; no. 2; SP $21	22 starts: 7 wins, 4 seconds, 1 third:	J. O'Shea, Warwick Farm, NSW
4.3	3rd	Rebel Dane	7yo bay or brown horse California Dane – Texarcana	T. Berry (59 kg)	Gate 2; no. 4; SP $11	32 starts: 7 wins, 4 seconds, 4 thirds	G. Portelli, Warwick Farm, NSW
4.4	4th	Lucia Valentina (NZ)	6yo brown mare Savabeel – Staryn Glenn (NZ)	K. McEvoy (57 kg)	Gate 1; no. 7; SP $11	27 starts: 7 wins, 1 second, 4 thirds	K. Lees, Newcastle, NSW
8.9	5th	Vanbrugh	4yo bay horse Encosta De Lago – Soho Secret	G. Schofield (58.5 kg)	Gate 6; no. 5; SP $31	13 starts: 4 wins, 2 seconds	C. Waller, Rosehill, NSW
10.1		Who Shot Thebarman (NZ)	8yo bay gelding Yamanin Vital (NZ) – Ears Carol (NZ)	B. Avdulla (59 kg)	Gate 7; no. 1; SP $81	31 starts: 9 wins, 4 seconds, 2 thirds	C. Waller, Rosehill, NSW

11.1		Grand Marshal (UK)	7yo brown gelding Dansili (UK) – Margarula (Ire)	J. Collett (59 kg)	Gate 5; no. 3; SP $201	32 starts: 7 wins, 5 seconds, 5 thirds	C. Waller, Rosehill, NSW

Scratchings: —

Saturday, 17 September 2016
Colgate Optic White George Main Stakes, Randwick
Group One for three-year-olds and upwards, standard weight for age
1600 metres, Good 4
Winning time: 1 minute 36.18 seconds (track record: 1 minute 33.13 seconds)

	1st	**Winx**	**5yo bay mare Street Cry (Ire) – Vegas Showgirl (NZ)**	**H. Bowman (57 kg)**	**Gate 5; no. 8; SP $1.09**	**20 starts: 14 wins, 3 seconds**	**C. Waller, Rosehill, NSW**
1.3	2nd	Hauraki	5yo bay gelding Reset – Youthful Presence	J. McDonald (59 kg)	Gate 4; no. 2; SP $13	18 starts: 4 wins, 6 seconds, 2 thirds	J. O'Shea, Warwick Farm, NSW
4.6	3rd	It's Somewhat (USA)	6yo bay gelding Dynaformer (USA) – Sometime (Ire)	T. Clark (59 kg)	Gate 3; no. 3; SP $31	26 starts: 5 wins, 3 seconds, 5 thirds	J. O'Shea, Warwick Farm, NSW
4.8	4th	Vanbrugh	4yo bay horse Encosta De Lago – Soho Secret	G. Schofield (58.5 kg)	Gate 2; no. 7; SP $101	14 starts: 4 wins, 2 seconds	C. Waller, Rosehill, NSW
4.7	5th	Spiritjim (Fr)	7yo bay horse Galileo (Ire) – Hidden Silver (UK)	B. Avdulla (59 kg)	Gate 6; no. 4; SP $101	20 starts: 6 wins, 1 second, 1 third	C. Waller, Rosehill, NSW

6.5		Great Esteem	6yo bay gelding Redoute's Choice – Park Esteem (Ire)	K. McEvoy (59 kg)	Gate 1; no. 5; SP $51	35 starts: 8 wins, 4 seconds, 3 thirds	S. Webb, Caulfield, Vic

Scratchings: 1 Tosen Stardom (Jpn)   C. Williams (59 kg)   D. Weir
           6 Le Romain   C. Reith (58.5 kg)   K. Lees

Saturday, 8 October 2016
Ladbrokes Caulfield Stakes, Caulfield
Group One for three-year-olds and upwards, standard weight for age
2000 metres, Good 3, rail true
Winning time: 2 minutes 3.42 seconds (track record 2 minutes 0.38 seconds)

	1st	Winx	5yo bay mare Street Cry (Ire) – Vegas Showgirl (NZ)	H. Bowman (57 kg)	Gate 3; no. 3; SP $1.25	21 starts: 15 wins, 3 seconds	C. Waller, Rosehill, NSW
2	2nd	Black Heart Bart	6yo bay gelding Blackfriars – Sister Theresa	B. Rawiller (59 kg)	Gate 1; no. 1; SP $4.75	34 starts: 14 wins, 10 seconds, 2 thirds	D. Weir, Ballarat, Vic
6	3rd	He Or She	6yo chestnut gelding Kendel Star – Danessa	C. Williams (59 kg)	Gate 2; no. 2; SP $21	22 starts: 9 wins, 3 seconds, 2 thirds	D. Hayes and T. Dabernig, Flemington, Vic

Scratchings: —

RACE STATISTICS

Saturday, 22 October 2016

William Hill Cox Plate, Moonee Valley

Group One for three-year-olds and upwards, standard weight for age

2040 metres, Soft 5, rail true

Winning time: 2 minutes 6.35 seconds (track record: 2 minutes 2.98 seconds)

	1st	Winx	5yo bay mare Street Cry (Ire) – Vegas Showgirl (NZ)	H. Bowman (57 kg)	Gate 3; no. 8; SP $1.80	22 starts: 16 wins, 3 seconds	C. Waller, Rosehill, NSW
8	2nd	Hartnell (UK)	6yo bay gelding Authorized (Ire) – Debonnaire (UK)	J. McDonald (59 kg)	Gate 7; no. 3; SP $5	26 starts: 10 wins, 5 seconds, 1 third	J. O'Shea, Warwick Farm, NSW
8.8	3rd	Yankee Rose	3yo bay or brown filly All American – Condesaar	D. Yendall (47.5 kg)	Gate 1; no. 10; SP $13	7 starts: 4 wins, 1 second	D. Vandyke, Sunshine Coast, Qld
9.8	4th	Vadamos (Fr)	6yo bay horse Monsun (Ger) – Celebre Vadala (Fr)	M. Zahra (59 kg)	Gate 2; no. 6; SP $21	18 starts: 8 wins, 5 seconds	A. Fabre, Chantilly, France
10.5	5th	Awesome Rock	5yo bay horse Fastnet Rock – Awesome Planet	S. Baster (59 kg)	Gate 5; no. 7; SP $101	23 starts: 3 wins, 3 seconds, 4 thirds	L. and T. Corstens, Flemington, Vic
11		Happy Clapper	6yo bay gelding Teofilo (Ire) – Busking	B. Avdulla (59 kg)	Gate 4; no. 5; SP $51	19 starts: 6 wins, 3 seconds, 3 thirds	P. Webster, Randwick, NSW
12.3		Lucia Valentina (NZ)	6yo brown mare Savabeel – Staryn Glenn (NZ)	K. McEvoy (57 kg)	Gate 9; no. 9; SP $16	29 starts: 7 wins, 1 second, 5 thirds	K. Lees, Newcastle, NSW

12.5		Hauraki	5yo bay gelding Reset – Youthful Presence	D. Dunn (59 kg)	Gate 8; no. 4; SP $31	20 starts: 5 wins, 7 seconds, 2 thirds	J. O'Shea, Warwick Farm, NSW
13.2		Black Heart Bart	6yo bay gelding Blackfriars – Sister Theresa	B. Rawiller (59 kg)	Gate 6; no. 2; SP $15	35 starts: 14 wins, 11 seconds, 2 thirds	D. Weir, Ballarat, Vic
14.5		Happy Trails	9yo chestnut gelding Good Journey (USA) – Madame Flurry	B. Melham (59 kg)	Gate 10; no. 1; SP $101	63 starts: 7 wins, 10 seconds, 7 thirds	P. Beshara, Morphetville, SA

Scratchings: —

Monday, 13 February 2017
The Star Apollo Stakes, Randwick
Group Two for three-year-olds and upwards, standard weight for age
1400 metres, Good 4, rail out 8 metres
Winning time: 1 minute 22.57 seconds (track record: 1 minute 20.33 seconds)

	1st	Winx	5yo bay mare **Street Cry (Ire) – Vegas Showgirl (NZ)**	H. Bowman (57 kg)	Gate 2; no. 11; SP $1.14	23 starts: 17 wins, 3 seconds	C. Waller, Rosehill, NSW
2.8	2nd	Hartnell (UK)	6yo bay gelding Authorized (Ire) – Debonnaire (UK)	J. Doyle (59 kg)	Gate 5; no. 1; SP $12	28 starts: 10 wins, 6 seconds, 2 thirds	J. O'Shea, Warwick Farm, NSW
6.8	3rd	Endless Drama (Ire)	5yo horse Lope De Vega – Desert Drama (Ire)	T. Angland (59 kg)	Gate 12; no. 7; SP $26	9 starts: 2 wins, 3 seconds, 1 third	C. Waller, Rosehill, NSW

9	4th	Dibayani (Ire)	7yo bay gelding Sharmardal (USA) – Dibiya (Ire)	C. Brown (59 kg)	Gate 4; no. 5; SP $16	26 starts: 2 wins, 7 seconds, 7 thirds	D. Hayes and T. Dabernig, Flemington, Vic
9.4	5th	Magic Hurricane (Ire)	7yo bay gelding Hurricane Run (Ire) – Close Regards (Ire)	C. Reith (59 kg)	Gate 10; no. 6; SP $201	24 starts: 5 wins, 2 seconds, 4 thirds	J. O'Shea, Warwick Farm, NSW
9.7		Prefer-ment (NZ)	5yo bay horse Zabeel (NZ) – Better Alternative	J. Collett (59 kg)	Gate 6; no. 2; SP $201	25 starts: 5 wins, 4 seconds, 1 third	C. Waller, Rosehill, NSW
10		Leebaz	7yo bay gelding Zabeel (NZ) – Polish Princess (UK)	T. Berry (59 kg)	Gate 9; no. 3; SP $151	29 starts: 9 wins, 4 seconds, 2 thirds	M., W. and J. Hawkes, Rosehill, NSW
10.1		Libran (Ire)	6yo bay or brown gelding Lawman (Fr) – True Crystal (Ire)	B. Avdulla (59 kg)	Gate 11; no. 4; SP $151	19 starts: 8 wins, 2 seconds, 1 third	C. Waller, Rosehill, NSW
10.2		Shiraz	7yo brown gelding Zariz – Moville Slipper	J. Parr (59 kg)	Gate 7; no. 9; SP $26	26 starts: 10 wins, 4 seconds, 1 third	K. Waugh, Wyong, NSW
10.6		Lasqueti Spirit	3yo bay filly Beneteau – Supriym Story	J. Ford (53.5 kg)	Gate 8; no. 14; SP $201	10 starts: 1 win, 1 second, 3 thirds	L. Curtis, Rosehill, NSW

11.8		Ambience	4yo bay mare Street Cry (Ire) – Miss Right Note (Ire)	K. O'Hara (57 kg)	Gate 1; no. 12; SP $201	13 starts: 3 wins, 3 seconds, 3 thirds	J. O'Shea, Warwick Farm, NSW
19.7		Sacred Master (NZ)	5yo bay gelding Mastercraftsman (Ire) – Trickle (NZ)	G. Schofield (59 kg)	Gate 3; no. 8; SP $101	19 starts: 7 wins, 2 seconds, 2 thirds	C. Waller, Rosehill, NSW

Scratchings: 10 Savvy Nature (NZ) T. Clark (59 kg)   G. Waterhouse and A. Bott
              13 Global Glamour   T. Clark (53.5 kg)   G. Waterhouse and A. Bott

Saturday, 25 February 2017
TAB Chipping Norton Stakes, Randwick
Group One for three-year-olds and upwards, standard weight for age
1600 metres, Heavy 9, rail true
Winning time: 1 minute 40.37 seconds (track record: 1 minute 33.13 seconds)

	1st	Winx	5yo bay mare Street Cry (Ire) – Vegas Showgirl (NZ)	H. Bowman (57 kg)	Gate 4; no. 9; SP $1.22	24 starts: 18 wins, 3 seconds	C. Waller, Rosehill, NSW
2	2nd	Lasqueti Spirit	3yo bay filly Beneteau – Supriym Story	J. Ford (53 kg)	Gate 9; no. 10; SP $151	11 starts: 1 win, 1 second, 3 thirds	L. Curtis, Rosehill, NSW
3	3rd	Who Shot Thebarman (NZ)	8yo bay gelding Yamanin Vital (NZ) – Ears Carol (NZ)	T. Clark (59 kg)	Gate 1; no. 4; SP $151	38 starts: 9 wins, 6 seconds, 2 thirds	C. Waller, Rosehill, NSW
3.1	4th	Magic Hurricane (Ire)	7yo bay gelding Hurricane Run (Ire) – Close Regards (Ire)	C. Reith (59 kg)	Gate 2; no. 6; SP $101	25 starts: 5 wins, 2 seconds, 4 thirds	J. O'Shea, Warwick Farm, NSW

6.3	5th	Tavago (NZ)	4yo bay gelding Tavistock (NZ) – Sara Ann (NZ)	T. Berry (59 kg)	Gate 6; no. 7; SP $41	9 starts: 3 wins, 1 second, 1 third	T. Busuttin and N. Young, Cranbourne, Vic
7.2		Endless Drama (Ire)	5yo horse Lope De Vega – Desert Drama (Ire)	T. Angland (59 kg)	Gate 7; no. 8; SP $26	10 starts: 2 wins, 3 seconds, 2 thirds	C. Waller, Rosehill, NSW
7.8		Libran (Ire)	6yo bay or brown gelding Lawman (Fr) – True Crystal (Ire)	G. Scho-field (59 kg)	Gate 3; no. 5; SP $101	20 starts: 8 wins, 2 seconds, 1 third	C. Waller, Rosehill, NSW
9		Hartnell (UK)	6yo bay gelding Authorized (Ire) – Debonnaire (UK)	B. Avdulla (59 kg)	Gate 10; no. 1; SP $6.50	29 starts: 10 wins, 7 seconds, 2 thirds	J. O'Shea, Warwick Farm, NSW
10.3		Grand Marshal (UK)	7yo brown gelding Dansili (UK) – Margarula (Ire)	J. Collett (59 kg)	Gate 5; no. 3; SP $101	38 starts: 8 wins, 6 seconds, 5 thirds	C. Waller, Rosehill, NSW
25.3		Prefer-ment (NZ)	5yo bay horse Zabeel (NZ) – Better Alternative	J. Parr (59 kg)	Gate 8; no. 2; SP $101	26 starts: 5 wins, 4 seconds, 1 third	C. Waller, Rosehill, NSW

Scratchings: —

435

Saturday, 18 March 2017

China Horse Club George Ryder, Rosehill

Group One for three-year-olds and upwards, standard weight for age

1500 metres, Heavy 10, rail out 3 metres

Winning time: 1 minute 34.87 seconds (track record 1 minute 27.21 seconds)

	1st	Winx	5yo bay mare Street Cry (Ire) – Vegas Showgirl (NZ)	H. Bowman (57 kg)	Gate 7; no. 8; SP $1.27	25 starts: 19 wins, 3 seconds	C. Waller, Rosehill, NSW
7.3	2nd	Le Romain	4yo bay gelding Hard Spun (USA) – Mignard	G. Schofield (59 kg)	Gate 6; no. 2; SP $10	15 starts: 6 wins, 6 seconds, 1 third	K. Lees, Newcastle, NSW
8.6	3rd	Chautauqua	6yo grey gelding Encosta De Lago – Lovely Jubly	T. Berry (59 kg)	Gate 1; no. 1; SP $9	26 starts: 12 wins, 7 seconds, 3 thirds	M., W. and J. Hawkes, Rosehill, NSW
10.5	4th	Hauraki	5yo bay gelding Reset – Youthful Presence	W. Buick (59 kg)	Gate 2; no. 3; SP $26	23 starts: 5 wins, 8 seconds, 3 thirds	J. O'Shea, Warwick Farm, NSW
12.1	5th	McCreery (UK)	5yo brown gelding Big Bad Bob (Ire) – Dolma (Fr)	K. McEvoy (59 kg)	Gate 5; no. 6; SP $31	14 starts: 6 wins, 4 seconds, 1 third	C. Waller, Rosehill, NSW
13		Sylpheed	3yo chestnut filly Real Saga – Domitilla	K. Fujii (54 kg)	Gate 4; no. 9; SP $201	7 starts: 2 wins, 1 second, 1 third	T. Edmonds, Gold Coast, Qld
15.2		Leebaz	7yo bay gelding Zabeel (NZ) – Polish Princess (UK	C. Reith (59 kg)	Gate 3; no. 5; SP $201	31 starts: 9 wins, 4 seconds, 2 thirds	M., W. and J. Hawkes, Rosehill, NSW

Scratchings: 4 Tosen Stardom   C. Williams (59 kg)   D. Weir

7 Endless Drama   T. Angland (59 kg)   C. Waller

RACE STATISTICS

Saturday, 8 April 2017

Longines Queen Elizabeth Stakes, Randwick

Group One for three-year-olds and upwards, standard weight for age

2000 metres, Soft 7, rail out 4 metres

Winning time: 2 minutes 7.22 seconds (track record: 2 minutes 0.19 seconds)

	1st	Winx	5yo bay mare Street Cry (Ire) – Vegas Showgirl (NZ)	H. Bowman (57 kg)	Gate 3; no. 9; SP $1.13	26 starts: 20 wins, 3 seconds	C. Waller, Rosehill, NSW
5.3	2nd	Hartnell (UK)	6yo bay gelding Authorized (Ire) – Debonnaire (UK)	J. Doyle (59 kg)	Gate 1; no. 1; SP $17	31 starts: 10 wins, 8 seconds, 2 thirds	J. O'Shea, Warwick Farm, NSW
5.7	3rd	Sense Of Occasion	6yo bay gelding Street Sense (USA) – Saywaan	C. Brown (59 kg)	Gate 4; no. 5; SP $151	31 starts: 7 wins, 6 seconds, 1 third	K. Lees, Newcastle, NSW
6.5	4th	The United States (Ire)	7yo horse Galileo (Ire) – Beauty Is Truth (Ire)	D. Oliver (59 kg)	Gate 7; no. 4; SP $41	24 starts: 7 wins, 4 seconds, 3 thirds	R. Hickmott, Macedon, Vic
7.7	5th	Happy Clapper	6yo bay gelding Teofilo (Ire) – Busking	B. Shinn (59 kg)	Gate 5; no. 3; SP $21	24 starts: 7 wins, 5 seconds, 4 thirds	P. Webster, Randwick, NSW
19.2		No Doubt	4yo horse Not A Single Doubt – Alalunga (USA)	T. Berry (59 kg)	Gate 6; no. 8; SP $201	8 starts: 2 wins, 2 seconds, 1 third	A. and E. Cummings, Randwick, NSW
19.5		Exospheric (UK)	5yo horse Beat Hollow (UK) – Bright And Clear (UK)	K. McEvoy (59 kg)	Gate 2; no. 2; SP $61	16 starts: 4 wins, 5 thirds	L. and A. Freedman, Flemington, Vic

19.9		Harlem (UK)	5yo bay or brown gelding Champs Elysees (UK) – Casual (UK)	C. Williams (59 kg)	Gate 8; no. 6; SP $151	9 starts: 2 wins, 1 second, 2 thirds	D. Hayes and T. Dabernig, Flemington, Vic
20		Singing (Fr)	7yo bay horse Singspiel (Ire) – Ring Beaune (USA)	S. Clipperton (59 kg)	Gate 9; no. 7; SP $301	19 starts: 4 wins, 4 seconds, 2 thirds	K. Lees, Newcastle, NSW

Scratchings: —

Six-year-old season (August 2017 – July 2018)

Eight starts (all at Group level, six at Group One) for 8 wins (six Group Ones); winning streak extends to 25 successive wins

Saturday, 19 August 2017
Bob Ingham Warwick Stakes, Randwick
Group Two for three-year-olds and upwards, standard weight for age
1400 metres, Good 3, rail out 3 metres
Winning time: 1 minute 21.87 seconds (track record: 1 minute 20.33 seconds)

	1st	Winx	6yo bay mare **Street Cry (Ire) – Vegas Showgirl (NZ)**	H. Bowman (57 kg)	Gate 2; no. 7; SP $1.10	27 starts: 21 wins, 3 seconds	C. Waller, Rosehill, NSW
0.2	2nd	Foxplay	4yo grey mare Foxwedge – Butters (USA)	K. McEvoy (56.5 kg)	Gate 3; no. 8; SP $20	13 starts: 5 wins, 3 seconds	C. Waller, Rosehill, NSW
0.6	3rd	Ecuador	8yo bay gelding High Chaparral (Ire) – Bak Da Princess (NZ)	A. Hyeronimus (59 kg)	Gate 6; no. 1; SP $26	34 starts: 10 wins, 8 seconds, 2 thirds	G. Waterhouse and A. Bott, Randwick, NSW

1.7	4th	Red Excitement	8yo bay gelding Excites – Obsession	J. Parr (59 kg)	Gate 4; no. 2; SP $101	43 starts: 13 wins, 4 seconds, 6 thirds	G. Ryan, Rosehill, NSW
3	5th	Antonio Giuseppe (NZ)	5yo brown gelding Shocking – Crystal-thecowgirl (NZ)	T. Angland (59 kg)	Gate 5; no. 4; SP $51	13 starts: 6 wins, 2 seconds	C. Waller, Rosehill, NSW
4.5		Inference	4yo horse So You Think (NZ) – Pontiana	T. Berry (58.5 kg)	Gate 8; no. 5; SP $26	11 starts: 4 wins, 2 seconds, 2 thirds	M., W. and J. Hawkes, Rosehill, NSW
4.6		Harper's Choice	4yo brown or black gelding Street Cry (Ire) – Oxigenada (Arg)	G. Schofield (58.5 kg)	Gate 7; no. 6; SP $31	12 starts: 2 wins, 5 seconds, 1 third	G. Ryan, Rosehill, NSW
5.4		Allergic	6yo bay gelding Street Cry (Ire) – Cajou	T. Clark (59 kg)	Gate 1; no. 3; SP $151	32 starts: 8 wins, 5 seconds, 7 thirds	J. Cummings, Randwick, NSW

Scratchings: —

Saturday, 2 September 2017
Tattersalls Club Chelmsford Stakes, Randwick
Group Two for three-year-olds and upwards, standard weight for age
1600 metres, Good 3, rail out 6 metres
Winning time: 1 minute 34.11 seconds (track record: 1 minute 33.13 seconds)

	1st	Winx	6yo bay mare Street Cry (Ire) – Vegas Showgirl (NZ)	H. Bowman (57 kg)	Gate 3; no. 11; SP $1.09	28 starts: 22 wins, 3 seconds	C. Waller, Rosehill, NSW
1	2nd	Red Excitement	8yo bay gelding Excites – Obsession	J. Parr (59 kg)	Gate 5; no. 2; SP $26	44 starts: 13 wins, 4 seconds, 6 thirds	G. Ryan, Rosehill, NSW

4.8	3rd	Chocante (NZ)	5yo bay gelding Shocking – Strictly Maternal (NZ)	R. Hutchings (59 kg)	Gate 9; no. 7; SP $81	15 starts: 5 wins, 2 seconds, 4 thirds	S. Marsh, Cambridge, New Zealand
6.2	4th	Antonio Giuseppe (NZ)	5yo brown gelding Shocking – Crystal-thecowgirl (NZ)	T. Angland (59 kg)	Gate 10; no. 6; SP $41	14 starts: 6 wins, 2 seconds	C. Waller, Rosehill, NSW
8	5th	Life Less Ordinary (Ire)	6yo bay gelding The-wayyouare (USA) – Dont Cross Tina (Ire)	K. McEvoy (59 kg)	Gate 11; no. 9; SP $26	20 starts: 5 wins, 8 seconds	C. Waller, Rosehill, NSW
8.8		Libran (Ire)	7yo bay or brown gelding Lawman (Fr) – True Crystal (Ire)	G. Schofield (59 kg)	Gate 8; no. 4; SP $201	24 starts: 8 wins, 2 seconds, 1 third	C. Waller, Rosehill, NSW
8.9		Harper's Choice	4yo brown or black gelding Street Cry (Ire) – Oxigenada (Arg)	B. Avdulla (58.5 kg)	Gate 6; no. 10; SP $81	13 starts: 2 wins, 5 seconds, 1 third	G. Ryan, Rosehill, NSW
10.4		Sense Of Occasion	6yo bay gelding Street Sense (USA) – Saywaan	C. Brown (59 kg)	Gate 2; no. 1; SP $31	34 starts: 8 wins, 6 seconds, 3 thirds	K. Lees, Newcastle, NSW
10.5		Who Shot The-barman (NZ)	9yo bay gelding Yamanin Vital (NZ) – Ears Carol (NZ)	C. Reith (59 kg)	Gate 1; no. 3; SP $101	42 starts: 9 wins, 7 seconds, 3 thirds	C. Waller, Rosehill, NSW
10.6		Allergic	6yo bay gelding Street Cry (Ire) – Cajou	T. Clark (59 kg)	Gate 12; no. 5; SP $201	33 starts: 8 wins, 5 seconds, 7 thirds	J. Cummings, Randwick, NSW

11.3		Sarrasin	6yo brown horse Monsun (Ger) – Sand River (Ire)	M. Walker (59 kg)	Gate 4; no. 8; SP $51	7 starts: 2 wins, 1 second, 2 thirds	C. Waller, Rosehill, NSW
14		Lasqueti Spirit	4yo bay mare Beneteau – Supriym Story	J. Ford (56.5 kg)	Gate 7; no. 12; SP $101	17 starts: 1 win, 2 seconds, 4 thirds	L. Curtis, Rosehill, NSW

Scratchings: —

Saturday, 16 September 2017
Colgate Optic White George Main Stakes, Randwick
Group One for three-year-olds and upwards, standard weight for age
1600 metres, Good 3, rail out 7 metres
Winning time: 1 minute 33.65 seconds (track record: 1 minute 33.13 seconds)

	1st	Winx	6yo bay mare Street Cry (Ire) – Vegas Showgirl (NZ)	H. Bowman (57 kg)	Gate 1; no. 7; SP $1.12	29 starts: 23 wins, 3 seconds	C. Waller, Rosehill, NSW
1.3	2nd	Happy Clapper	7yo bay gelding Teofilo (Ire) – Busking	B. Shinn (59 kg)	Gate 7; no. 1; SP $15	26 starts: 9 wins, 5 seconds, 3 thirds	P. Webster, Randwick, NSW
5.8	3rd	Foxplay	4yo grey mare Foxwedge – Butters (USA)	B. Avdulla (56.5 kg)	Gate 3; no. 9; SP $21	14 starts: 5 wins, 4 seconds	C. Waller, Rosehill, NSW
7.6	4th	McCreery (UK)	6yo brown gelding Big Bad Bob (Ire) – Dolma (Fr)	M. Walker (59 kg)	Gate 8; no. 4; SP $151	20 starts: 6 wins, 4 seconds, 1 third	C. Waller, Rosehill, NSW
7.7	5th	Mack-intosh (NZ)	5yo bay gelding Pins – Lolly Scramble (NZ)	G. Scho-field (59 kg)	Gate 2; no. 5; SP $101	15 starts: 6 wins, 1 third	C. Waller, Rosehill, NSW

8.1		Heavens Above	6yo bay mare Street Cry (Ire) – Reggie (NZ)	T. Angland (57 kg)	Gate 6; no. 8; SP $91	23 starts: 5 wins, 5 seconds, 4 thirds	T. Martin, Rosehill, NSW
9.3		Red Excitement	8yo bay gelding Excites – Obsession	J. Parr (59 kg)	Gate 4; no. 3; SP $26	45 starts: 13 wins, 5 seconds, 6 thirds	G. Ryan, Rosehill, NSW
9.5		Ecuador	8yo bay gelding High Chaparral (Ire) – Bak Da Princess (NZ)	A. Hyeronimus (59 kg)	Gate 5; no. 2; SP $81	36 starts: 10 wins, 8 seconds, 3 thirds	G. Waterhouse and A. Bott, Randwick, NSW

Scratchings: 6 Tom Melbourne (Ire)   M. Walker (59 kg)   C. Waller

Saturday, 7 October 2017
Seppelt Turnbull Stakes, Flemington
Group One for four-year-olds and upwards, set weights plus penalties
2000 metres, Good 4, rail out 9 metres
Winning time: 2 minutes 2.07 seconds (track record: 1 minute 58.73 seconds)

	1st	Winx	6yo bay mare Street Cry (Ire) – Vegas Showgirl (NZ)	H. Bowman (57 kg)	Gate 2; no. 2; SP $1.20	30 starts: 24 wins, 3 seconds	C. Waller, Rosehill, NSW
6.5	2nd	Ventura Storm (Ire)	5yo bay gelding Zoffany (Ire) – Sarawati (Ire)	R. Bayliss (56.5 kg)	Gate 5; no. 3; SP $17	15 starts: 6 wins, 1 second, 1 third	D. Hayes and T. Dabernig, Flemington, Vic
7.3	3rd	Humidor (NZ)	5yo bay gelding Teofilo (Ire) – Zalika (NZ)	D. Lane (59 kg)	Gate 4; no. 1; SP $7.50	18 starts: 6 wins, 6 seconds, 1 third	D. Weir, Ballarat, Vic

9	4th	Assign (Ire)	7yo bay or brown gelding Montjeu (Ire) – Belesta (UK)	K. Mallyon (56.5 kg)	Gate 6; no. 4; SP $51	18 starts: 6 wins, 2 seconds, 2 thirds	R. Hickmott, Macedon, Vic
11.3	5th	Sir Isaac Newton (UK)	6yo bay gelding Galileo (Ire) – Shastye (Ire)	D. Oliver (54.5 kg)	Gate 7; no. 6; SP $31	16 starts: 3 wins, 3 seconds, 1 third	R. Hickmott, Macedon, Vic
26.3		Magicool	6yo bay gelding Fastnet Rock – Perfect Truth (Ire)	C. Brown (54.5 kg)	Gate 1; no. 5; SP $201	25 starts: 4 wins, 1 second	T. Romeo, Diggers Rest, Vic
26.5		Skyfire	6yo bay gelding Testa Rossa – Skye Gold	D. Dunn (54.5 kg)	Gate 3; no. 7; SP $201	28 starts: 3 wins, 2 seconds, 3 thirds	A. Johnston, Mornington, Vic

Scratchings: —

Saturday, 28 October 2017
Ladbrokes Cox Plate, Moonee Valley
Group One for three-year-olds and upwards, standard weight for age
2040 metres, Good 3
Winning time: 2 minutes 2.94 seconds (new track record: previous record
2 minutes 2.98 seconds)

	1st	Winx	6yo bay mare Street Cry (Ire) – Vegas Showgirl (NZ)	H. Bowman (57 kg)	Gate 5; no. 8; SP $1.18	31 starts: 25 wins, 3 seconds	C. Waller, Rosehill, NSW
0.4	2nd	Humidor (NZ)	5yo bay gelding Teofilo (Ire) – Zalika (NZ)	B. Shinn (59 kg)	Gate 7; no. 3; SP $31	20 starts: 6 wins, 6 seconds, 2 thirds	D. Weir, Ballarat, Vic

4.7	3rd	Folkswood	5yo bay gelding Exceed and Excel – Magic Nymph (Ire)	K. McEvoy (59 kg)	Gate 4; no. 5; SP $26	13 starts: 4 wins, 4 seconds, 3 thirds	C. Appleby, Newmarket, UK
6.2	4th	Royal Symphony	3yo bay or brown colt Domesday – Naturalist	D. Yendall (49.5 kg)	Gate 6; no. 9; SP $19	6 starts: 4 wins	T. McEvoy, Angaston, SA
6.3	5th	Gailo Chop (Fr)	7yo chestnut gelding Deportivo (UK) – Grenoble (Fr)	M. Zahra (59 kg)	Gate 3; no. 2; SP $21	21 starts: 10 wins, 2 seconds, 3 thirds	D. Weir, Ballarat, Vic
6.6		Happy Clapper	7yo bay gelding Teofilo (Ire) – Busking	D. Oliver (59 kg)	Gate 8; no. 1; SP $31	29 starts: 10 wins, 7 seconds, 3 thirds	P. Webster, Randwick, NSW
13.6		Seaburge	4yo chestnut horse Sebring – Polska	R. Bayliss (57.5 kg)	Gate 1; no. 6; SP $101	16 starts: 2 wins, 3 seconds	D. Hayes and T. Dabernig, Flemington, Vic
14.8		Hardham	4yo bay horse Redoute's Choice – Nureyev's Girl	L. Nolen (57.5 kg)	Gate 2; no. 7; SP $101	13 starts: 3 wins, 1 second, 2 thirds	D. Brideoake, Mornington, Vic

Scratchings: Kaspersky (Ire) M. Payne (59 kg) J. Chapple-Hyam

Saturday, 17 February 2018

Trial, Randwick

Open

1200 metres, Good 4

Winning time: 1 minute 10.30 seconds

	1st	Winx	6yo bay mare Street Cry (Ire) – Vegas Showgirl (NZ)	H. Bowman	Gate 4; no. 1	C. Waller, Rosehill, NSW
3.8	2nd	Mackin-tosh (NZ)	4yo bay gelding Pins – Lolly Scramble (NZ)	J. Ford	Gate 3; no. 5	C. Waller, Rosehill, NSW
7.6	3rd	Unforgot-ten	3yo bay or brown filly Fastnet Rock – Memories Of You (Ire)	B. Avdulla	Gate 5; no. 6	C. Waller, Rosehill, NSW
8.5	4th	Libran (Ire)	7yo bay or brown gelding Lawman (Fr) – True Crystal (Ire)	G. Schofield	Gate 2; no. 2	C. Waller, Rosehill, NSW
9.1	5th	McCreery (UK)	6yo brown gelding Big Bad Bob (Ire) – Dolma (Fr)	J. Collett	Gate 6; no. 4	C. Waller, Rosehill, NSW
12.8		Who Shot Thebar-man (NZ)	9yo bay gelding Yamanin Vital (NZ) – Ears Carol (NZ)	C. Reith	Gate 1; no. 3	C. Waller, Rosehill, NSW

Saturday, 3 March 2018
TAB Chipping Norton Stakes, Randwick
Group One for three-year-olds and upwards, standard weight for age
1600 metres, Soft 5, rail out 3 metres
Winning time: 1 minute 34.92 seconds (track record 1 minute 33.13 seconds)

	1st	Winx	6yo bay mare **Street Cry (Ire) – Vegas Showgirl (NZ)**	H. Bowman (57 kg)	Gate 6; no. 7; SP $1.09	32 starts: 26 wins, 3 seconds	C. Waller, Rosehill, NSW
7	2nd	Prized Icon	4yo brown horse More Than Ready (USA) – Tropical Affair	G. Schofield (59 kg)	Gate 4; no. 4; SP $16	22 starts: 3 wins, 6 seconds, 5 thirds	K. Lees, Newcastle, NSW
7.5	3rd	Classic Uniform	5yo bay gelding Al Maher – Pyrotechnics	A. Adkins (59 kg)	Gate 2; no. 1; SP $51	37 starts: 7 wins, 8 seconds, 8 thirds	G. Moore, Rosehill, NSW
8.5	4th	Libran (Ire)	7yo bay or brown gelding Lawman (Fr) – True Crystal (Ire)	B. Avdulla (59 kg)	Gate 1; no. 3; SP $71	30 starts: 9 wins, 3 seconds, 1 third	C. Waller, Rosehill, NSW
10.9	5th	Stampede	5yo bay horse High Chaparral (Ire) – Nothin' Leica Cat (NZ)	T. Clark (59 kg)	Gate 5; no. 5; SP $21	12 starts: 6 wins, 3 seconds, 1 third	G. Waterhouse and A. Bott, Randwick, NSW
11.1		Who Shot Thebarman (NZ)	9yo bay gelding Yamanin Vital (NZ) – Ears Carol (NZ)	T. Angland (59 kg)	Gate 3; no. 2; SP $91	47 starts: 10 wins, 7 seconds, 3 thirds	C. Waller, Rosehill, NSW

14.2		Lasqueti Spirit	4yo bay mare Beneteau – Supriym Story	J. Ford (57 kg)	Gate 7; no. 8; SP $101	18 starts: 1 win, 2 seconds, 4 thirds	L. Curtis, Rosehill, NSW
23.1		Vinland	3yo bay colt Sebring – Viking Turf Belle	K. McEvoy (56 kg)	Gate 8; no. 9; SP $71	7 starts: 2 wins	T. McEvoy, Angaston, SA
32.8		Jemadar	4yo bay gelding Sepoy – Daanet Al Dunya (USA)	A. Hyeronimus (59 kg)	Gate 9; no. 6; SP $101	16 starts: 4 wins, 4 seconds, 1 third	D. Pfieffer, Warwick Farm, NSW

Scratchings: —

Saturday, 24 March 2018
The Agency George Ryder Stakes, Rosehill
Group One for three-year-olds and upwards, standard weight for age
1500 metres, Soft 7, rail out 2 metres
Winning time: 1 minute 31.48 seconds (track record: 1 minute 27.21 seconds)

	1st	Winx	6yo bay mare Street Cry (Ire) – Vegas Showgirl (NZ)	H. Bowman (57 kg)	Gate 6; no. 4; SP $1.16	33 starts: 27 wins, 3 seconds	C. Waller, Rosehill, NSW
0.8	2nd	Happy Clapper	7yo bay gelding Teofilo (Ire) – Busking	B. Shinn (59 kg)	Gate 4; no. 1; SP $21	32 starts: 10 wins, 8 seconds, 3 thirds	P. Webster, Randwick, NSW
1.6	3rd	Kemen- tari	3yo colt Lonhro – Yavanna	B. Avdulla (56 kg)	Gate 5; no. 6; SP $8.50	9 starts: 4 wins, 2 seconds, 1 third	J. Cummings, Warwick Farm, NSW
4.5	4th	Crack Me Up	4yo bay gelding Mossman – Chuckle	J. Collett (59 kg)	Gate 2; no. 3; SP $71	23 starts: 6 wins, 5 seconds	B. Baker, Warwick Farm, NSW

4.6	5th	Invincible Gem	4yo bay mare I Am Invincible – Diamond Day	Z. Purton (57 kg)	Gate 1; no. 5; SP $41	12 starts: 5 wins, 3 seconds, 2 thirds	K. Lees, Newcastle, NSW
5.4		Clearly Innocent	6yo bay gelding Not A Single Doubt – No Penalty (NZ)	T. Berry (59 kg)	Gate 3; no. 2; SP $81	21 starts: 9 wins, 1 second, 2 thirds	K. Lees, Newcastle, NSW

Scratchings: —

Saturday, 14 April 2018
Longines Queen Elizabeth Stakes, Randwick
Group One for three-year-olds and upwards, standard weight for age
2000 metres, Good 4, rail out 3 metres
Winning time: 2 minutes 1.65 seconds (track record 2 minutes 0.19 seconds)

	1st	**Winx**	**6yo bay mare Street Cry (Ire) – Vegas Showgirl (NZ)**	**H. Bowman (57 kg)**	**Gate 10; no. 9; SP $1.24**	**34 starts: 28 wins, 3 seconds**	**C. Waller, Rosehill, NSW**
3.8	2nd	Gailo Chop (Fr)	7yo chestnut gelding Deportivo (UK) – Grenoble (Fr)	M. Zahra (59 kg)	Gate 5; no. 2; SP $26	28 starts: 13 wins, 3 seconds, 3 thirds	D. Weir, Ballarat, Vic
4.1	3rd	Happy Clapper	7yo bay gelding Teofilo (Ire) – Busking	K. McEvoy (59 kg)	Gate 9; no. 1; SP $11	34 starts: 11 wins, 9 seconds, 3 thirds	P. Webster, Randwick, NSW
4.9	4th	Humidor (NZ)	5yo bay gelding Teofilo (Ire) – Zalika (NZ)	B. Shinn (59 kg)	Gate 1; no. 3; SP $14	25 starts: 7 wins, 7 seconds, 2 thirds	D. Weir, Ballarat, Vic

5.4	5th	Comin' Through	4yo bay horse Fastnet Rock – Mica's Pride	M. Walker (59 kg)	Gate 2; no. 7; SP $51	14 starts: 5 wins, 2 seconds, 3 thirds	C. Waller, Rosehill, NSW
8		Consensus (NZ)	6yo bay mare Postponed (USA) – Kate Cross (NZ)	J. Collett (57 kg)	Gate 3; no. 10; SP $201	44 starts: 8 wins, 8 seconds, 4 thirds	S. McKee, Takanini, New Zealand
10.4		Odeon (NZ)	4yo bay gelding Zacinto (UK) – Theatre Buff (USA)	D. Lane (59 kg)	Gate 6; no. 8; SP $101	20 starts: 6 wins, 3 seconds, 1 third	M. Ellerton and S. Zahra, Flemington, Vic
12.2		Ambitious (Jpn)	6yo brown or black horse Deep Impact (Jpn) – Carnival Song (Jpn)	C. Williams (59 kg)	Gate 7; no. 6; SP $31	18 starts: 5 wins, 3 seconds, 2 thirds	L. and A. Freedman, Flemington, Vic
16.1		Classic Uniform	5yo bay gelding Al Maher – Pyrotech-nics	A. Adkins (59 kg)	Gate 4; no. 4; SP $151	39 starts: 7 wins, 8 seconds, 9 thirds	G. Moore, Rosehill, NSW
18.1		Success Days (Ire)	6yo grey horse Jeremy (USA) – Malaica (Fr)	J. Moreira (59 kg)	Gate 8; no. 5; SP $61	19 starts: 6 wins, 4 seconds, 1 third	K. Condon, The Curragh, County Kildare, Ireland

Scratchings: —

Seven-year-old season (August 2018)

One start (a Group One) for 1 win; winning streak extends to 26 successive wins, breaking Black Caviar's record of 25.

Saturday, 18 August 2018

Winx Stakes (formerly Warwick Stakes), Randwick

Group One for three-year-olds and upwards, standard weight for age

1400 metres, Good 4, rail out 7 metres

Winning time: 1 minute 22.5 seconds (track record 1 minute 20.33 seconds)

	1st	Winx	7-year-old bay mare Street Cry (Ire) – Vegas Showgirl (NZ)	H. Bowman (57 kg)	Gate 5; no. 10; SP $1.20	35 starts: 29 wins, 3 seconds	C. Waller, Rosehill, NSW
2	2nd	Invictus Prince (UK)	6-year-old bay gelding Dansili (UK) – Golden Stream (Ire)	J. Collett (59 kg)	Gate 4; no. 5; SP $151	15 starts: 2 wins, 4 seconds, 2 thirds	M. Smith, Warwick Farm, NSW
3	3rd	D'Argento	4-year-old grey horse So You Think (NZ) – Fullazz	J. McDonald (58.5 kg)	Gate 9; no. 9; SP $17	7 starts: 4 wins, 1 third	C. Waller, Rosehill, NSW
3.2	4th	Kementari	4-year-old bay horse Lonhro – Yavanna	G. Schofield (58.5 kg)	Gate 7; no. 7; SP $6	12 starts: 4 wins, 3 seconds, 2 thirds	J. Cummings, Warwick Farm, NSW
3.4	5th	Cabeza De Vaca	7-year-old bay gelding Northern Meteor – Dirty	T. Clark (59 kg)	Gate 2; no. 4; SP $71	17 starts: 7 wins, 4 seconds, 3 thirds	G. Water-house and A. Bott, Randwick, NSW
3.8		Unforgot-ten	4-year-old bay or brown mare Fastnet Rock – Memories Of You (Ire)	K. McEvoy (56.5 kg)	Gate 6; no. 11; SP $51	9 starts: 5 wins, 2 seconds	C. Waller, Rosehill, NSW

4.1		Religify	8-year-old chestnut gelding Choisir – Sacred Witness	J. Ford (59 kg)	Gate 1; no. 2; SP $101	34 starts: 13 wins, 7 seconds, 2 thirds	C. Waller, Rosehill, NSW
4.9		Libran (Ire)	8-year-old bay or brown gelding Lawman (Fr) – True Crystal (Ire)	T. Berry (59 kg)	Gate 11; no. 3; SP $151	33 starts: 9 wins, 4 seconds, 1 third	C. Waller, Rosehill, NSW
5.4		Oriental Runner	5-year-old chestnut gelding Hussonet (USA) – Loose Caboose	B. El-Issa (59 kg)	Gate 3; no. 6; SP $101	12 starts: 3 wins, 3 seconds, 1 third	G. Neale, Warwick Farm, NSW
6.7		Classic Uniform	6-year-old bay gelding Al Maher – Pyrotechnics	A. Adkins (59 kg)	Gate 8; no. 1; SP $201	40 starts: 7 wins, 8 seconds, 9 thirds	G. Moore, Rosehill, NSW
8		Ace High	4-year-old brown or black horse High Chaparral (Ire) – Come Sunday	T. Angland (58.5 kg)	Gate 10; no. 8; SP $51	17 starts: 4 wins, 2 seconds	D. Payne, Randwick, NSW

Scratchings: —

Index

B

Baiada, Celestino (Charlie) 55–9, 65, 121
Baiada, Giovanna 56–7
Baiada Group 55–9
Bailey, Alan 143–4
Baker, Bjorn 209, 273–5
Baker, Murray 273, 274, 275
Baker, Sophie 380
balance 367–8
Ballet Suite 209
Banks, Sir Joseph 360
Barley Sugar 134–5, 138
barrier manners 329–31, 386
barrier trial 202
Batavian 79, 83–4
Beadman, Darren 21, 241
Beadman, Kim 145
Begg, Neville 50
Bentham 62–3
Bernborough 204, 205, 272, 376,
    385, 397
Berry, Tommy 208, 324
Best Bets 278
Better Alternative 145, 146
Big Dreams 22
birth 102–6
Black Caviar 13, 34, 67, 94, 244–6, 272,
    276, 284, 303, 315, 334, 351, 355,
    357, 371, 376, 377
Black Heart Bart 304–7
Bletchingly 62
bloodstock agent 154–6, 159
Bluebird 51
Bob Ingham Warwick Stakes 329–31,
    438–9
Boland, Sarah 173
Boland, Tim 173–85, 250–1
bone-chip operation 292–9
Boss, Glen 2, 131
Bowman, Amanda 353, 357, 360
Bowman, Christine 259, 308, 353, 361
Bowman, George 52, 62, 148
Bowman, Honor (Honora) 360

Bowman, Hugh (James Hugh) 1–18,
    21–2, 27, 52, 62, 207, 209, 246,
    248, 251, 256–63, 269–72, 276–7,
    279–81, 288–9, 291, 302–3, 305–8,
    316, 320–2, 324–5, 327, 330–3, 335,
    337–8, 341, 347–50, 353–66, 375–6,
    378–81
Bowman, James C. 360
Bowman, Jim 351–4, 357, 360, 361, 363
Bowman, John 360
Bowman, Kate 354, 360
Bowman, William 360
Boynton Park 191
Bragger 240
Braithwaite, Daryl 5
branding 107–8
breaking in 177–85
Breasley, Scobie 148
Brendanstown Riding Stables 50
Brereton, Danny 363
Brettle, Jason 197, 366, 378
Bright, Alan 220
broodmare bands 66–71
Broodwar 128
Brown, Corey 380
build 16–17, 162, 196–7, 388–9
'bum-high yearling' 177
Burles, Mick 7
Burns, Grant 168
Bush, Jane 225
Busuttin, Paddy 216, 221, 234–5
By Boon 126
Byrne, Martin 49

C

Cadden, Ben 37, 252, 260–1, 284, 298,
    299, 305, 342–3, 347, 366, 376
'cadence' 376–8
California Chrome 316
Callow, Noel (King) 7–8
Caloundra, 16 May 2015 246–8,
    411–13
Camilleri, Deborah 64

INDEX

INDEX

INDEX

INDEX

INDEX